FIRE *on the* PRAIRIE

FIRE *on the* PRAIRIE

◆

CHICAGO'S

HAROLD WASHINGTON

AND THE

POLITICS OF RACE

◆

Gary Rivlin

Henry Holt and Company   New York

Library of Congress Cataloging-in-Publication Data
Rivlin, Gary.
Fire on the prairie : Chicago's Harold Washington and the politics
of race / Gary Rivlin.
p.   cm.
Includes bibliographical references and index.
1. Washington, Harold, 1922–1987.   2. Chicago (Ill.)—Politics and
government—1951–   .   3. Chicago (Ill.)—Race relations.   I. Title.
F548.54.W36R58   1992
977.3′11043′092—dc20   91–38748
                                                            CIP

ISBN 0-8050-1468-3

Henry Holt books are available at special discounts
for bulk purchases for sales promotions, premiums,
fund-raising, or educational use. Special editions
or book excerpts can also be created to specification.
For details contact: Special Sales Director, Henry Holt and Company, Inc.,
115 West 18th Street, New York, New York 10011.

First Edition—1992

Book design by Claire Naylon Vaccaro

Printed in the United States of America
Recognizing the importance of preserving
the written word, Henry Holt and Company, Inc.,
by policy, prints all of its first editions
on acid-free paper. ∞

1 3 5 7 9 10 8 6 4 2

To Denny

Acknowledgments

There were many who contributed to this book, but none more than Denny Martin, whose constant love and support sustained me through the most trying moments of this project. To Denny, my eternal gratitude for your patience and your wise counsel, and also a vow never to allow a book to separate us again.

I'm indebted to my siblings—Rich, Laurie and Jay—and to my parents for their support during the long writing process; Tiffany Martin has been my most loyal cheerleader. I'm also grateful to Kevin Morison and Ellen Leander, who shared their home and put up with my chaotic schedule during those months I lived in Oakland, California, and needed a base in Chicago. Mike Kelly's wizardry inside a computer program proved invaluable, as did his friendship. Thanks also to Joe Feinglass, Susan Matteucci, Mike Loftin, Nick Wechsler, Laurie Tannenbaum, Judy Hatcher, and Paul Igasaki, all of whom taught me a great deal about Chicago politics. I was lucky to have met Lee Anderson and Robert Lineberry, both political science professors, at Northwestern; I'll be forever

ACKNOWLEDGMENTS

indebted to Pat Clinton, Mike Miner, and Charlie White for all they taught me about writing. Pat especially helped me believe that I can write a book when I was inclined to think otherwise. Thank you, too, to Joel Mollner, Bob Shelby, and Richard Bray for their sage advice, and to Mark Ketelsen for his contribution.

Thanks to Larry Bennett, Salim Muwakkil, Matt Piers, Paul Kleppner, Jeff Cohen, and Ted Cox, all of whom read my manuscript in one form or another. My appreciation also to Ted, Catherine Cox, Michael Warr, Mike Buchman, David Cohen, Jim Paul, and Naomi Rivlin, all of whom helped me with my book proposal.

A first-time book author couldn't have been more fortunate in his choice of agents. Elizabeth Kaplan was not only a savvy negotiator but a great confidence booster throughout. I was lucky, too, in my choice of editors. From the start Bill Strachan at Holt had a strong sense of what this book needed, and, more important, what it did not.

Contents

CONTENTS

Prologue

Long before sunrise, people jammed the sprawling grounds of the Christ Universal Church. A pair of black women, both well past sixty, had been the first to arrive, there since five o'clock the previous evening. Others soon joined them as twilight gave way to a raw November night. Word had spread that some seats for Harold Washington's funeral were to be had on a first-come basis and, with sleeping bags and wool blankets and other armaments against the cold, each took his or her place, partaking in a ritual more commonly reserved for the World Series and concerts featuring big-name musical acts. Thousands more arrived after sunrise—ten thousand people in all, according to the newspapers.

A soft steady rain fell the day Chicago buried Harold Washington. Along the route mapped out for the cortege, people leaned out second-story windows peering into the distance. Tens of thousands stood on the street, waiting, two solid lines running the entire seventy blocks from chapel to cemetery. Three hundred cars crept by in endless procession, snaking their way through the streets of the city's south side, flowing like a creek between twin banks of people.

As the procession approached the cemetery, five or six or ten deep, the crowd was thicker still, as at a downtown parade. Another three thousand stood at the edge of the cemetery waiting for the hearse to appear. The crowds occasionally broke into a spontaneous rhythmic chant of the dead man's name: "Ha-rold. Ha-rold." It was startling, a sound more familiar to a baseball stadium, to fans pumping their favorite for a do-or-die base hit. "Ha-rold. Ha-rold." A politician.

The national news stories reporting Washington's death stressed his color and his thirty-six days in the county jail on a misdemeanor charge. These accounts also highlighted the ugly 1983 election that first brought Harold Washington to national attention, casting him as a symbol of the racial conflict that was besetting the nation's great urban centers and of the political battle for control against white political rivals. Chicago's deep racial divisions dominated Washington's obituaries.

Yet Washington was far rarer than another trailblazing black, and his tenure was notable for much more than the racial backlash his rule inspired. His victory was heralded for reviving a national black empowerment movement mired by splits and apathy in the early 1980s. "His oratory, the use of words like a weapon—his style was very attractive to the black imagination," one eulogizer said. "It was similar to the way Malcolm X captured the black community. He would face down white people in their own realm, in their own intellectual realm, and look good, yet still kept his so-called black credentials."

Most of those standing in the long lines to view Washington's open casket were black, yet many whites, Latinos, and Asians joined those waiting for as long as three hours to view his body. His was a black-led coalition, to be sure, based not on nationalism but on issues that crossed racial lines: affordable housing, affirmative action, and other progressive totems. "He put people together who really were enemies of each other," said another eulogizer; "that was Harold's gift." Around the country they could only dream of a Jesse Jackson–like Rainbow Coalition growing into a dominant political force; in Chicago, the country's third largest city and also the country's most political metropolis, the Washington coalition ruled for five years. In a decidedly conservative era, Chicago was an intriguing anachronism, a beacon from the country's heartland that projected into the future more encouraging possibilities. To have lived in Chicago and shared a certain political bent was to glow with pride when Washington was mayor.

Jesse Jackson was there when Chicago buried Harold Washington. Jackson had been in the Persian Gulf when Washington died, and although the 1988 presidential race was upon him, Jackson returned home. He had been all but banished during the Washington campaign of 1983, asked by Washington emissaries to leave town until after the election, but Chicago was where Jackson came of age politically. He was there when King and Daley went toe-to-toe in the mid-1960s; in Chicago, Jackson made his first run for political office when he ran for mayor in 1971. From Chicago, Jackson learned the ways of the Rainbow, for it was on the heels of Washington's success at building his coalition that Jackson set out to re-create it on a national scale. The newspapers showed pictures of Jackson standing by Washington's casket, hand in hand with a Latino alderman on one side and a black alderman on the other. "God got a lot of mileage out of Harold Washington," Jackson said at the funeral.

The media estimated that two hundred thousand to half a million mourners passed by Washington's open casket; only twenty-five thousand amassed in Memphis to view Elvis Presley's. It may be crass to compare two famous men by counting heads at their funerals, but how else to make the point that the reaction to Washington's death resembled the death of a celebrity more than that of a local politician? His mourners were not sobbing women throwing themselves at the foot of the king's sepulcher but people of all races and ages who abandoned themselves to spontaneous and unrestrained grief. In interview after interview reporters heard the same words from the men and women who attended the funeral. They spoke of Washington as a favorite uncle or a father figure. Love was on people's lips, and it was also written in thick letters on cut-up cardboard boxes. GONE BUT NOT FORGOTTEN, WE LOVE YOU HAROLD, one homemade sign read. A bearded white man wearing round wire-frame glasses held on his shoulders a child who held a pennant that read THANK YOU MR. MAYOR. WE ALL LOVE YOU.

Wariness, cynicism, resignation to the lesser of two evils—around the country voters rarely feel something as mild as affection for a politician. What's love got to do with politics?

A
Racial
Thing
1983

If the misery of our poor be caused

not by the laws of nature, but by our

institutions, great is our sin.

—Charles Darwin, *Voyage of the Beagle*

1

A

CRY

IN THE

WIND

From off the prairie the man arrived, settling at the bend of the great lake. There along its swampy shores he built himself a cabin; there among the Indians he made his home.

His name was Jean Baptist Point du Sable. It was only years later— the land no longer a field of wild flowers but a seething metropolis of three million—that historians salvaged his name and declared him Chicago's first permanent settler. Their discovery was heavy in irony. Du Sable was not an expatriate of European descent but a dark-skinned trapper from Haiti in search of a haven. In spite of all the firebombs, the bricks, and the harsh words and the pain because whites looked on blacks as intruders encroaching on their land, the fact was that the city's first homesteader was a black man. Of all the ethnic groups laying claim to Chicago, none could trace its local lineage further back than the city's black population.

Much had passed since Al Capone was the city's most famous citizen, the Saint Valentine's Day Massacre its most celebrated event, yet the mob still had its reputed front man in City Hall, and judges were still chosen primarily based on the clout of their sponsors. The city was like a universe unto itself, a reminder of a time long past, as if preserved for study. Chicago politics has long been the stuff of national legend, the benchmark by which the national media measures fixed elections in this country or in the third world. In Chicago old-timers boast of the city's political machine fixing the 1960 presidential election for John F. Kennedy, its ward bosses waiting until the downstate precincts reported in before producing the required votes to swing Illinois and therefore the election.

Patronage, endemic to politics, was practiced to its extreme in Chicago. Bridge tenders worked year-round even during those months the Chicago River was frozen, and wizened machine functionaries ran elevators that had been automated years earlier. Local folklore held that Richard J. Daley had no less than one hundred relatives on the city payroll.

In Chicago the politicians were bolder, their dealings crass and transparent. The city's diary was a tale of tainted deals, politicians on the take, and scoundrels made rich by playing it the machine's way. Since 1970 Chicago aldermen have been hauled into court on criminal indictments at a pace of one per year. "I wish to defend my city from people who keep saying it is crooked," the writer Nelson Algren stated in his book, *Chicago: City on the Make*. "In what other city can you be so sure a judge will keep his word for five hundred bucks?" Only in Chicago was a major-league baseball team caught throwing a World Series.

The Cook County Democratic machine thrived long after machines were no longer supposed to function. When famous urban cousins like New York's Tammany Hall had gone the way of the icebox, the Chicago organization hadn't even reached its peak. It seemed invincible, immune to scandal. In Daley's last full term as mayor, seven machine aldermen, including Daley's floor leader, were convicted of crimes committed while in office, as was Daley's press secretary of nineteen years (a conviction that would later be overturned). Yet Daley won the 1975 general election with three-quarters of the vote.

When Daley died, his political heirs no longer enjoyed an iron grip on city government, but still there was no doubting the machine's power. Even machine defeats, such as Jane Byrne's stunning upset in 1979, ended up victories: the same "cabal of evil men" Byrne had campaigned against as a candidate for mayor were, within six months, counted among her top aides.

Yet in 1983, when a challenger finally toppled the machine, no one seemed to notice. His victory made headlines across the country, but the machine was scarcely mentioned. The last great bastion of nineteenth-century urban politics had fallen, but what people reported on was the color of the man who kicked it over and the hatred on the faces of those opposing him. Such was the power of race in Chicago and everywhere.

Skirmishes along the uneasy border between black and white neighborhoods on the city's south side were frequent, often bloody, in the early part of the century. The worst incident occurred on a steamy summer day in 1919. A black boy named Eugene Williams went swimming in Lake Michigan and made the fatal mistake of drifting over the invisible barrier separating the black water from white. Williams tired, the story went, but white bathers with stones prevented him from coming ashore, and he drowned. Over the next few days a riot raged. Black gangs stormed white neighborhoods; white gangs retaliated. Thirty-eight were killed, more than five hundred injured, and one thousand homes were damaged by fire. It wasn't the country's only race riot that summer, but it was by far the worst.

The riot capped the first great wave of black immigration from the South. Between 1915 and 1920, 50,000 blacks moved to Chicago. In one sense it was a drop in the bucket; Chicago was in the midst of a growth spurt that saw its population swell by half a million each decade. In 1920 the city was home to 109,000 black citizens; by 1930 nearly a quarter of a million blacks lived in Chicago, accounting for seven percent of the population. World War II and the invention in 1944 of a mechanical cotton picker brought about a still greater migration, but the city never accommodated its Negro residents as it did immigrants from foreign lands.

The Airport Homes were built as temporary housing just after World War II for returning veterans. The site was an all-white community on the city's southwest side where the idea of black neighbors, even war veterans, did not sit well with the locals. Thousands came to protest. A white minister who helped a black family unload its belongings was pelted with rocks; later he found his car tipped over. Only one black family actually moved in, and it was never permitted to forget how the neighbors felt. A four-foot-high wooden cross was set afire in a vacant lot across the street from the unwanted blacks. Bullets were fired into their apartment in the middle of the night; one shattered a window and a lamp, sending shards of glass into the baby's crib. With that, two months after they had arrived, the only black occupants of Airport Homes packed their belongings and were gone.

From 1945 on, the city's black population rose dramatically—by an average of thirty-three thousand a year through the 1950s—and by 1970 over one-third of the city's population was black. At the same time the city was losing an average of twenty thousand jobs per year from World War II on. The postwar loss of jobs, coupled with the dramatic increase in their numbers, made life difficult for the city's blacks—not least because a great many whites blamed them for all the city's ills.

The burgeoning black belt was soon bursting at the seams. In the 1940s an estimated 375,000 blacks lived in an area that could house 110,000 adequately. Landlords charged exorbitant rents for hovels that lacked plumbing and sufficient heating. Rats thrived on garbage that was not hauled away quickly enough. Rates of disease were routinely twice those of the white community. The cramped and infested apartments that slept five to a room were the inspiration for the character Bigger Thomas, the protagonist of Richard Wright's novel *Native Son,* which is set in Chicago. Blacks needed room, and white neighborhoods were the logical place to look for it.

And so the story repeated itself. In one community it was a black judge whose purchase of a home was seen as the beginning of the end; in another it was a teacher and a postal worker. Residents protested and picketed; when that did not work, bricks crashed through windows and garages burned in the night. Gunshots were not a given, but they weren't the exception, either. Panic spread through white communities, fueled by real estate agents who understood that panic was good for business. Working-class whites who had scrimped for their modest homes sold low, lost thousands, and found themselves in alien neighborhoods, far from friends and their parish. The old neighborhood, meanwhile, went all black, no longer the small patch of Chicago the former residents could call their own. Resentment seethed.

Other northern cities had their own versions of panic peddling and white flight, but Chicago seemed a special case for the virulence of its racial hatred. In a 1952 *New Yorker* article, A. J. Liebling described a Chicago street scene that even a hardened New Yorker could not quite believe: a white couple, loaded down with packages, allowed cab after cab to pass, shivering in the cold rather than let a black man drive them. Told by a black driver that this was common, Liebling noted in his piece that although New Yorkers were uneasy around blacks, they weren't willing to freeze over it. In the 1940s the Congress of Racial Equality (CORE) moved its headquarters from Chicago to New York in search of a climate more favorable to its cause.

In the mid-1960s the black comedian Dick Gregory, then living in Chicago, led a small group of about seventy-five protesters past Mayor Daley's home in Bridgeport. Nearly a thousand whites greeted them, chanting, "Two, four, six, eight, we don't want to integrate." Then, to the tune of the Oscar Meyer wiener jingle they sang, "I wish I was an Alabama trooper . . . Cuz if I was an Alabama trooper, I could kill the niggers le-gal-ly." It was not long afterward that the Reverend Martin Luther King, Jr., his skull still smarting from the crack of a brick tossed at his head on the city's southwest side, said, "The people of Mississippi ought to come to Chicago to learn to hate."

The simplicity of the city's racial geography underscores the extent of Chicago's segregation. The northwest side is white, as is the southwest side. The west side is black. The Latino communities stretch westward to the north and south of the black west side, serving as an unofficial buffer between black and white. Along the lakefront, the largely white north side does contain all races, but the south is almost entirely black. The Loop serves as a buffer between north side and south, but there is no buffer between the south side and the white southwest side. It is there that race relations are the worst.

Over the years countless studies pointed to Chicago as the country's single most segregated city.* A 1973 Johns Hopkins study found that the Chicago school system was the most segregated among the eighty-one northern cities examined. Yet it wasn't until the bitter battle of 1983, when the city was on the verge of electing its first black mayor, that Chicago's noteworthy racial problems revealed themselves so forcefully to the world.

---

*Chicago's "segregation index" in 1980 was 91.9, where an index of 100 means that every city block is either 100 percent black or zero percent black, and where a zero indicates that each block is perfectly integrated according to the proportion of blacks to whites in a city.

In a sense the political battle that seemed fresh and raw when the city was dubbed "Beirut on the Lake" in the 1980s was actually an old story that dated back to the time when blacks, no longer curiosities, came to be seen as intruders. It was only a matter of time before the battle between race and community took center stage in the city's political theater.

Richard J. Daley was already chairman of the Cook County Democratic party when he first ran for mayor in 1955. The party held the real power in Chicago; its central committee ran city government just as the Communist party's politburo ran the Soviet Union. As chairman, Daley was more powerful than the mayor.

The same held true on the ward level. Each of the city's fifty wards was represented in the City Council by an alderman, but it was the Democratic party official from each ward—a committeeman—who rationed out patronage jobs, delivered favors, and turned out the vote. If some committeemen doubled as aldermen, it was mainly to rid themselves of the threat of an ambitious number-two man. Daley pulled off that same trick but on a grand scale; as mayor, he controlled forty thousand city jobs; as party chairman, he decided who got what share of them. It was the same with the tens of millions in contracts the city parceled out each year and the other spoils of victory. Dick Daley, even in 1955, was not a force to be underestimated.

And yet underestimated he was—by men who should have known better. Daley was a squat man with shoulders rounded from years of weightlifting in his basement. He lacked magnetism and charisma; he was a wooden speaker who often got lost in his own words. He was smart, though not brilliant or quick on his feet; he was tough and determined. Other machine politicians thought he was plodding until they watched him move to unprecedented power.

Born at the turn of the century to Irish parents of modest means, Daley grew up at a time when the Irish were dismissed as inferior. He worked in the stockyards (his handlers created the impression that he was a "cowboy" who herded cattle through the stockyards, but the truth was that he worked as a secretary) while putting himself through college and night law school. After graduating he made the right connections and understood what was expected of him. He was patient and had a talent for numbers and ledger sheets that put him in good stead within the machine ranks. The incumbent state legislator died, and the party slated Daley in his place. More people died, and Daley stepped up the machine hierarchy: ward committeeman, county clerk, party chairman, and two years later, mayor.

Daley did not invent the Chicago political machine; he perfected it. His enormous drive fueled his power. No one outworked Richard J. Daley. He was at mass praying while his enemies were still in bed, one biographer wrote, and at his desk while they caroused the night away. No detail seemed unworthy of his attention. To Daley, a city job meant a potential party worker out knocking on doors in the precincts. He reviewed job applicants even for entry-level positions—political connections were everything. Committeemen who racked up votes were rewarded; those who failed at the polls were punished. A trusted aide maintained a file box that spelled out the perks each committeeman received, but Daley had an incredible memory and often startled ward bosses by rattling off the positions their people held. "For God's sake," one said after meeting with Daley, "you wonder how he can run the city, keeping all that shit about how many jobs you've got in his head."

There were labor bosses and well-connected developers, but mostly Daley saw city politics in terms of the city's fifty Democratic ward organizations. Each was its own fiefdom. Each ward committeeman had his own supplicants, each his own means for raising funds. Just as the ward committeeman was beholden to Daley, the precinct worker was beholden to the ward committeeman. A strong showing on election day could mean a promotion or a raise, a poor showing cause for dismissal. The more ambitious among them competed for the honor of the top vote-getter, for that could mean a plum job down at the Hall. Ultimate supervision for city employees rested with the ward committeeman, not with city department heads. Promoting people based on their success at campaigning rather than their job performance might not have been a rational management system, but it made for an impressive election force.

The city election board reinforced the machine's power. The board was long Vito Marzullo's turf. Marzullo was a powerful west side boss who ruled a ward predominantly black and Latino. When an upstart Latino dared challenge the Marzullo organization for state representative, the challenger's change of address card was mysteriously lost after he moved within the district. The board magistrate assigned to hear his case was a Marzullo protégé. Marzullo walked in during the hearing, made eye contact with his appointee, and then walked out. Witnesses confirmed that the man had filled out his form, but the magistrate kicked him off the ballot anyway.

By state law at least two of the five election judges who handle the voting in each precinct must be Republicans. Yet for years few wards had Republican committeemen, so the Democrats chose for them. The same crew of loyal Democrats who campaigned on the party's behalf typically served as that precinct's election day judges. The police officer assigned to each precinct also worked for the city and looked the other way when the election judges broke the rules.

It was understood that a city contract meant repaying the favor in the form of a campaign contribution. You do for me, I do for you—that was a machine motto. A powerful Democratic committeeman died with more than $100,000 in cash in a safe deposit box. Years later an old-time ward boss named Paudy Bauler explained how his colleague might have come into all that cash on an alderman's modest salary: "They got to have somethin' done—raise the cab fare or get a city parkin' lot lease or somethin' like that—holy Cry, you don't think they expect to get it for nothin', do ya? What's fair is fair, you know." Just as almost every city job was a means of strengthening the machine, most city functions were means of leveraging money. "Personally honest," it was said of Daley: he did not enrich himself through politics but looked the other way. Frank Sullivan, who took over as Daley's press secretary when his predecessor landed in jail, confessed long after Daley's death that he at times felt himself "a front man for thieves."

Daley controlled the perks, and therefore he controlled both the committeemen and the aldermen who served at a committeeman's pleasure. When Daley wanted a measure passed, the City Council voted it in by a margin of forty-five to five or so; when Daley wanted a measure killed, it lost by that same margin.

He had enormous influence over the courts as well. Officially, judges were elected, not selected by the party, but the Democratic slate invariably swept every citywide election, including those lawyers Daley chose to sit on the local bench. Because of the party's prowess, it could be said he chose virtually every elected official in Chicago, from congressmen to metropolitan sanitary district commissioner.

The country's founding fathers would have found this political system a horrifying breach of the separation of powers among the branches of government, but the result was a city government that acted as one. Once a group of doctors at the south side's Michael Reese Hospital called a press conference to complain that the city building inspectors were not enforcing a ban on lead paint, which was potentially fatal to children and a problem endemic in the city's ghettos. Building inspectors then cited the hospital for obscure violations totaling over $100,000 in remodeling costs. The shopkeeper who dared place a poster of a machine adversary in his window would receive a similar fate.

It was no wonder that people outside the city's borders looked on Chicago with awe and horror. It was home to not only the last of the great big-city machines but also the most awesome of them all.

To Daley "machine" implied something cold and inhuman; he preferred to call his creation "the organization." The regular Democratic organization, Daley might lecture, stands for God and family and the hardworking precinct captain who maintained a watchful eye over his small plot of the city.

In Chicago, government wasn't a nameless bureaucrat downtown; the government had a face and a name and lived on the next block in the shape of a precinct captain. Each of the city's three thousand precincts was assigned a captain, if not an entire team, to serve its 300 or 400 voters. The captain sent a city crew to uproot dead trees in people's yards or called for a truck to cart away old discarded refrigerators. The captain provided garbage cans free of charge, courtesy of the local Democratic organization. (Daley once said to New York's John Lindsay, whom he pitied as hopelessly naïve about urban politics, "John, you forget why you were elected—to collect the garbage.") The precinct captain helped frantic mothers find their errant sons picked up for stealing. Around election time he walked door-to-door asking about the family, reminding people of past favors, and asking what they might need done.

There was a cost attached to the precinct captain's favors. His petitions had to be signed and his posters put up in the window. The party slate had to be supported, no questions asked. Let the pointy-headed do-gooders criticize—things were expected of people, but they received in return. What was a vote worth on the open market in other big cities? Was it worth even a dime?

Daley's omnipotence was never plainer than when he protected his Bridgeport neighbors from blockbusters. Once, to prove a point, two black college students moved into an apartment a block from Daley's home. Protesters gathered to express their horror, but they needn't have bothered. While the two students were at school, policemen broke into the apartment, confiscated their belongings, and by that evening the apartment was leased to two white men from the neighborhood. When the two students returned that night, they were escorted to the police station, given their belongings, and told they no longer lived in Bridgeport.

During Daley's tenure the Dan Ryan Expressway was built along Bridgeport's eastern border, and the Stevenson Expressway along its northern boundary. Perhaps it was only coincidence that the highways reinforced the borders Bridgeport shared with neighboring black communities, but in the 1960s an iron gate was erected across 42nd Street, cutting Bridgeport off from the predominantly black Fuller Park neighborhood. Long after Daley was dead, an official with the U.S. Commission on Civil Rights challenged the city to tear down this "iron curtain," and it was finally removed. The symbolism wasn't lost on Bridgeporters, who saw Daley as a personal bulwark against change. "It got into your thinking, from hearing your parents," one neighbor explained to a reporter after the mayor's death, that "if Daley were not mayor, the blacks would take over."

Daley fought integration with resolve. A professor examined the public housing proposals of the Chicago Housing Authority (CHA) from 1955 through 1966 and discovered that of the forty-one to-be-constructed sites in white areas, the City Council approved only two. By contrast, the council approved forty-nine of the sixty-two projects slated for the already dense slums of the south and west sides. The CHA advocated modest-sized walk-up apartments, yet only by building bunched-together towering high rises could the city confine public housing to areas of the city that were already unalterably black. Not surprisingly, Chicago became home to the country's largest housing project and several others ranking among the ten largest.* Even public housing complexes for the aged were seen as unfit by most

---

*Housing expert Oscar Newman would study high-rise projects in New York City and conclude that crime rates increased with the height of the building and the size of the project. Newman found that the lack of streets within most of these developments isolates the projects and makes routine police patrol difficult.

white aldermen, who feared that some federal judge would require the place to accept elderly blacks.

Yet no part of the electorate was under Daley's spell like the black community. The city's poorest, least educated voters could be bought for a modest price: a pint of drink, a canned ham, or a five-dollar bill wrapped around a punch card. The machine's captains were not above threats, either: vote against the machine's candidate, a public housing resident might be told, and you'll lose your apartment or your welfare check.

The black church was another source of Daley's power. Preachers loyal to Daley were blessed with large donations around election time. Columnist Vernon Jarrett wrote about an acquaintance of his, a black minister on the city payroll. The preacher once confided that his job was simple: he endorsed whomever Daley asked him to, visited City Hall as a prop for endorsement sessions, and opened his church to Daley and any of the party's slate of candidates. In 1963, Daley lost the white vote but was reelected to a third term because of his overwhelming majority among black voters.

Daley boasted of all that the machine did for the city's blacks, and there was evidence to back up his claims. Congressman William Dawson dominated the city's black wards from the early 1950s until his death in 1970 as surely as Daley dominated all of Chicago. Dawson's Harlem contemporary, Congressman Adam Clayton Powell, Jr., was certainly better known but did not play nearly the role in New York politics that Dawson did in Daley's Chicago. "Where else," Dawson liked to ask, "but in the Democratic organization could a black man, whose ancestors were slaves, rise so high?"

Daley slated blacks for office in the same way that he balanced a ticket with a Jew and an Italian. Blacks sat on the CHA and on school boards. To his mind, he fared well in comparison to big-city mayors. In New York City, Daley said, no black policemen served above the rank of lieutenant. Chicago could boast three black police commanders and no less than seven black police captains. "We have more Negro judges than New York," he said.

Yet even by the machine's own standards blacks were shortchanged—of basic city services, such as garbage pickup and road repairs, and of jobs.

Blacks accounted for nearly one-third of the city's population in the mid-1960s but only one-sixth of the city's work force; fewer than one in every thirty city managers was black. Daley's meeting in 1965 with a talented young black man interested in a job with the machine seems as instructive as it is ironic. The twenty-four-year-old came with credentials: a letter of introduction from the Democratic governor of North Carolina, where he had gone to college, and an impressive résumé. He was a star at college, an athlete, and an honor student; he was married with children and politically connected to a Democrat—the perfect machine protégé. Yet all Daley offered the young Jesse Jackson was a job collecting coins at a tollway booth.

The Democratic machine's list of abuses is astonishing in its length and breadth. The three battlegrounds between black and white in Chicago have been housing, education, and police. In each area the Daley record is telling. There were the infamous Willis Wagons of the early 1960s: to alleviate overcrowding in the black community, mobile homes were carted into black communities to serve as classrooms while schools in bordering white neighborhoods sat half empty. Despite the Willis Wagons, some black schools were forced to adopt a double shift; lower grades met in the morning, senior grades in the afternoon. There were not enough desks, so students sat on windowsills or took turns leaning against a wall. It wasn't a question of busing, for many black schoolchildren actually lived closer to a school in a white community than to their own school. Benjamin Willis, the school superintendent then, said he was afraid whites would flee the school system rather than tolerate integration.

Blacks may have been represented in greater numbers in Chicago than in other cities, but the quality of that representation was something else entirely. In the 1960s the half-dozen black aldermen loyal to the machine were derisively called the "Silent Six." One, Claude Holman, was renowned for standing up at each council meeting and exhorting, "Thank God for Mayor Daley!" Another was Ralph Metcalfe, who could boast that he was the council's first black president pro tem, but that seemed to say it all. The pro tem position was an honorary post long on symbolism but short on genuine power. Holman held it after Metcalfe, and Wilson Frost, another black machine regular, would follow Holman. It was a perfect metaphor for the machine's treatment of black Chicago.

After Dawson died, Metcalfe took his place in Congress and also assumed the mantle of the machine's top power broker in the black community. Yet Metcalfe's turn at the top came to an abrupt end in 1972, when he spoke out publicly about police brutality. For years black activists, including his son, Ralph, Jr., lobbied Metcalfe to use his clout to fight police brutality; the 1972 beating of a friend of his, a black south side dentist, during a routine traffic incident finally turned his head. He tried going through proper channels—he spoke to Daley but got nowhere, so he went public with his criticism. "It's never too late to be black," he declared before a cheering crowd of two thousand.

For criticizing the city's finest, Daley came down hard on Metcalfe. He stripped him of his patronage and plucked someone from the ranks to oppose him for reelection. City inspectors descended on Metcalfe's Third Ward headquarters shortly after the speech, writing him up for a myriad of building code violations.

In the mid-1960s a nun who worked in the black belt pleaded with Daley to come and see the conditions of those living there. Daley barely allowed her a word: "Look, Sister, you and I come from the same background . . . parents and grandparents came here with nothing . . . took care of their houses. . . . Look at Bridgeport . . . houses as old as on the west side, but the people took care of them, worked hard, kept the neighborhood clean. . . . Let me tell you something about those people. . . . They should lift themselves up by their bootstraps like our grandparents did . . . work hard . . . take care of their homes."

Bridgeport never suffered the overcrowding of the black belt, of course. The Irish didn't face the same prejudices that walled in the blacks. Bridgeport was a union neighborhood, whereas the trade unions were off-limits to the blacks. An Italian walking into a Bridgeport bar might get the cold shoulder, but a black would be chased out. If a bartender was feeling generous, he would charge a black extra, serve him the drink, and then throw away the glass. Two communities side by side: in Englewood, the median educational level was the eleventh grade; in Gage Park, the ninth grade. But the average income level in Gage Park was more than double the median income of Englewood, for it was a white community and Englewood was black.

Richard Daley refused to acknowledge problems in his city. "There are no ghettos in Chicago," Daley declared in a speech before the National Association for the Advancement of Colored People (NAACP) in 1963. Much later, when a fiery riot broke out on the west side, Daley surveyed the smoldering scene from a helicopter. "I never believed it could happen here," he muttered, then he took to speculation. He did not wonder why the rioters had taken to burning and looting their own neighborhood, nor did he ask why they did this to their fellow neighbors. He asked instead, "Why did they do this to me?" In the ensuing weeks Daley spoke of his programs and the sizable share of patronage jobs enjoyed by black ward organizations. After all I've done for them, he seemed to say, this is the gratitude I'm shown. It was with this same sense of incredulity that Daley contemplated Martin Luther King, Jr.'s declaring Chicago in 1965 the new frontier of his civil rights movement.

Chicago's fledgling black empowerment movement could claim some success, albeit symbolic. When Daley tried speaking before a giant rally downtown three days after denying there were slums in Chicago, the crowd booed him loudly. There *are* slums in Chicago, hecklers yelled out. Daley stepped from the microphone to let NAACP leaders quiet the crowd, but the outburst only grew louder. Daley left the stage, his face bright red with anger.

In 1963 an estimated 225,000 black children stayed home from school one day to protest the Willis Wagons and the miserable conditions of the ghetto schools. An estimated 20,000 circled City Hall calling for Benjamin Willis's resignation. The protests continued through the school year, yet Daley proved more resolute than the protesters. ("By that summer we had a dozen bodies if you included the dog one protester brought with him," said Al Raby, who was a young black schoolteacher at the time he helped organize the demonstrations.) A telegram was sent to King, and in the summer of 1964 he was the featured speaker at a rally held at Soldier Field and then the grand marshal of a march through the Loop three days later. King drew more than 75,000 to Soldier Field and more than 30,000 for the march downtown. Yet Daley did not budge, and the problems of overcrowding were as acute as ever.

In 1965 King's organization, the Southern Christian Leadership Conference (SCLC), planned a full-scale assault on Chicago and its political machine. The SCLC had never organized in a city outside the South, but the problems King saw firsthand in Chicago and other northern cities convinced him that blacks there were hardly better off than their southern brethren. It was to cities like Chicago that millions of poorly educated and otherwise traumatized black expatriates fled. King needed to broaden his movement and turn his attention north.

King was acutely aware that his northern campaign would be viewed as a test of the movement's potential there; he chose Chicago as his target only after careful consideration. The tension in Chicago between the races would work to his advantage. The city's extreme conditions made for symbols he could exploit. Daley seemed another advantage. The mayor's one-man rule over Chicago meant there would be no need to negotiate his way around factional politics. Before stepping foot in town he knew precisely whom he needed to see.

An SCLC advance team of around fifteen set up an outpost in Chicago. They arrived as winter was descending on the city, bringing with them the clothes they wore in the deep South; several lacked gloves and winter coats. The oversight was easy enough to correct, but it was symbolic of the bigger problems King would face when taking on this strange new beast. One member of the advance team wondered aloud about the towering brick edifices on either side of the expressway: what were these warehouselike buildings? The projects, she was told; people live there. That was another bad sign, for the SCLC had chosen housing as the issue around which to organize. On January 15, 1966, King's thirty-seventh birthday, he and his wife Coretta took up temporary residence in a tenement on the city's west side.

King was by then a potent force, able to alter the nation's laws. In the ten years since he had catapulted into the national news with the Montgomery bus boycott, King had won a Nobel Prize and graced the cover of *Time* magazine. In the middle of his third term as mayor, Daley, too, had been on *Time*'s cover. He was not yet the legend he would become, but no one doubted his ability to rule for as long as he desired. The King-Daley confrontation was thus promoted by the press as a clash of titans.

Daley was no Bull Connor; he wouldn't give King an easy target. A Daley representative greeted King at the airport. "All right-thinking people," Daley declared, should support King's stances against poverty and discrimination. Building inspectors combed the west side community that King chose for his temporary home, citing countless slum landlords for code violations. Daley would not have to speak out against King because there was no lack of blacks willing to perform that task on his behalf. Congressman Dawson denounced King as an "outside agent" who had no business in Chicago, and other black politicians dismissed him as a trouble-maker. In the South the church was the birthplace of King's movement; in Chicago preachers vied to denounce him loudly.*

In Chicago King learned defeat. After months of moves and counter-moves, the titans convened, and King, Daley, and their lieutenants hammered out an agreement. The city would promote integration, Daley agreed. He admitted, probably for the first time, that discrimination existed in Chicago and that he wasn't doing everything in his power to end it.

Daley made all sorts of additional promises, all of them soon forgotten. (Reminded of the summit agreement a few months later, Daley's number-two man, Alderman Thomas Keane, said, "There is no summit agreement.") Three years later the federal courts ordered the city to build the majority of any new federally subsidized housing *outside* the black belt, so Daley instead did without federal subsidies. Better no new housing than a few six-flat apartment buildings in a white community.

The scattered-site housing promise represented but one betrayal, yet Daley still reigned over Chicago in no small part because of his support among black Chicagoans. No less a figure than Martin Luther King, Jr., showed up in Chicago to weigh in on the black community's behalf, but even the mighty King left Chicago empty-handed, defeated.

Daley was inflexible by nature, resistant to change. An old-time politician who had cut his political teeth in the thirties and forties, he already seemed an atavism by the late 1960s, yet he ruled Chicago until his death in 1976. The turbulence of the sixties seemed to make him only more rigid and intolerant in the face of black demands. After King's assassination in 1968 prompted rioting on the west side, Daley said in a press conference, "I was most disappointed to know that every policeman out on his beat was

---

*So fervid was the anti-King sentiment among black preachers in Chicago that one renowned King nemesis, the Reverend J. H. Jackson, changed his church's mailing address to a side street off South Parkway after it was renamed Dr. Martin Luther King Jr. Drive. South Parkway was the perfect choice for Daley's purposes—it ran the length of the black south side but conveniently ended on the edge of the south Loop.

supposed to use his own discretion. . . . In my opinion, policemen should have instructions to shoot arsonists and looters—arsonists to kill and looters to maim and detain." A reporter mentioned that eight- and ten-year-old kids were among those rummaging for stolen items. Okay, Daley conceded, Mace the kids.

In December 1969, Edward Hanrahan, state's attorney for Cook County and a Daley protégé, oversaw an early-morning raid on an apartment building that housed several Black Panthers. Two Panther leaders, Fred Hampton and Mark Clark, were shot dead. Hanrahan claimed it was a miracle that none of his men were hurt, so ferocious was the hail of bullets and shotgun blasts from inside the safe house, but ballistic evidence, confirmed by a grand jury, proved otherwise. FBI ballistic experts were able to trace only a single spent bullet to a Panther gun; the other ninety or so expended bullets were fired from police shotguns, pistols, and machine guns. The killing of Fred Hampton, the leader of the Illinois Panthers, revealed the state's attorney's true intentions. The schema the FBI provided police in preparation for their raid included a special notation that indicated Hampton's room. A mattress soaked with blood and littered with bits of his flesh proved that Hampton was still in bed when he was killed. Three Panthers were in Hampton's bedroom when the police burst in. They were escorted out and claimed to have heard two shots fired. "He's good and dead now," one cop was quoted as saying. The grand jury did not charge the police with murder, but the evidence makes it hard to call the incident anything less.

The black vote turned Hanrahan out of office in 1972 in the first city-wide antimachine insurrection, black or white, yet Daley himself still won a majority of the black vote in 1971. (The black vote no longer provided his margin of victory, but that was because Daley carried the white vote by large margins as well.) Thereafter, the courts stepped in to regulate the Chicago Housing Authority, the park district, the police department, and other agencies, all because of judgments that Chicago discriminated against blacks. In 1975 when Daley faced a black independent state senator and a white liberal from the lakefront in the Democratic primary, most blacks didn't bother to vote, but Daley took first among those who did.

When Daley died, the man he handpicked to represent his ward, Michael Bilandic, was chosen as his replacement. A special election was held in 1977 to complete the rest of Daley's term, and a black state legislator named Harold Washington was among those challenging Bilandic. A maverick Democrat, Washington got his start with the machine, but he was a fiercely proud man who never really fit in. When Daley made it clear he wanted none of his people taking part in any King demonstrations, Washington, then a state representative, made it a point to march. "He had no intention of going," one longtime friend from the 1960s said, "until he was told not to go."

Bilandic was a bland machine soldier who was the butt of jokes by reporters and politicians alike. The boys in the press room dubbed him Daley's coat holder, and an ally, Ed Vrdolyak, joked that Bilandic's idea of a good time was a three-ounce glass of wine and the City Council proceedings. Yet Bilandic won handily, beating Washington throughout the city except in a few south side wards. Washington was bright and able, a state senator whose bold antimachine pronouncements should seemingly have stirred black Chicago, yet only twenty-seven percent of the registered black voters participated in that election. No black bothered running for mayor in 1979. It was as if Chicago had not changed since King delivered a sermon from a west side pulpit entitled "The Strange Negroes in Chicago."

In 1965 Hosea Williams, a member of King's advance team, arrived in Chicago boasting that the SCLC would register a hundred thousand new black voters. When they came nowhere near that goal, when they fell more than ninety thousand voters short, Williams left muttering aloud whether blacks in Chicago wanted to be "freed." Only in Chicago had the local black leadership called a press conference telling King and the SCLC to go back to the South where they belonged. King, too, questioned black Chicago's hunger for freedom.

But where Hosea Williams left disgusted, King cast Chicago as a great challenge, a bellwether of wider possibilities. "If we crack Chicago," King said, "then we crack the world." Black empowerment in Chicago, he proclaimed, "would take off like a prairie fire across the land."

2

THE

CONSPIRATORS

The day's featured speaker, Harold Washington, was shivering. He jumped from foot to foot, and small puffs of steam escaped from his mouth. The wind chill was near eighty below zero, yet inside on this frigid Sunday in January 1982 the radiators weren't working. Inside, people sat wrapped in every bit of clothing they brought with them. Washington, the sort who barely made time for things as mundane as adequate clothing, arrived with no hat, no scarf, and no gloves, though forecasters were saying it might be the coldest day in Chicago history. Washington shivered on stage as he cursed himself for bothering to show.

The event was a commencement exercise honoring the first graduates of Lu Palmer's political training classes. Washington blamed Palmer for his discomfort. A familiar figure within Chicago's black community, Palmer had initiated the classes the previous year with an eye toward the 1983 mayor's race; they were as much for Washington's benefit as anyone else's. The broken heater was no one's fault unless one could blame Palmer for having no money, yet he was the sort of disagreeable personality who inspired irrational thoughts. He was a stone-faced man on whose countenance a smile seemed out of place. "Uncompromising," friend and foe alike said, ideologically rigid and personally abrasive. The relationship between Palmer and Washington was especially stormy. Those who knew them both understood they couldn't get along because they were both so hardheaded.

Palmer was heartened by the size of the crowd assembled, yet an outsider—had any reporter working out of the City Hall press room taken the group seriously enough to attend the graduation—would have seen the event as confirmation of all his doubts about talk in political circles of a black mayor. Held in an unheated room in a rundown part of town, the commencement seemed prima facie evidence that those pushing Washington for mayor were taking themselves too seriously. Two hundred graduates was nothing but a minor battalion against a machine that was thirty-five thousand political workers strong. Palmer, a radio personality and a former newspaper columnist, seemed the least likely organizer to pull off the political miracle of electing a black mayor.

Had the City Hall press corps shown up, they would have gone home thinking less of Washington. Why was this seemingly seasoned politician, a U.S. congressman, bothering with a band of ragtag militants instead of going about the real work of raising funds and lining up the endorsements of politicians downtown?

Nearly two years earlier Palmer had picked up the phone and invited about a dozen or so other people to his home to talk politics. Some recall Palmer calling to talk about Jane Byrne's proposed appointments to the school board; other participants say it was the new ward map drawn by Byrne and ratified by the City Council. Palmer himself remembers only that he was enraged by some transgression or another of Byrne's. Whatever the impetus, none of those invited to Lu and Jorja Palmer's place had to be told what else Lu may have on his mind. They, too, were pondering the 1983 mayor's race.

They would become known as the "basement meetings" among those in Chicago who spoke of politics using terms like "the movement" and "the struggle." For the next couple of years a group of ten to twenty black intellectuals and activists met periodically in the Palmers' basement to talk about their chances of defeating Byrne. They discussed voter registration strategies and tactics for rallying the resigned, but always they came back to the topic of unity—or, in the words of the writer Salim Muwakkil, the "petty squabbling and rigid intolerance of ideological disagreement that hindered black progress."

Those attending the basement meetings could lay claim to his or her own constituency, yet in their more candid moments they knew their turf battles to be part of the problem. Often they worked against one another, not necessarily out of spite but out of a lack of coordination and because of widely diverse agendas. Black Chicago was not unique in this regard, but that was no consolation. There would be no black mayor without first a triumph of coalition within the black community. Palmer had always seemed adept at causing disunity within the black community; perhaps if he set his mind to it, he could now prove invaluable in bringing everyone together.

Electoral politics, Lu Palmer liked to tell his radio listeners, was white politics. Liberal or conservative, it didn't make a difference: white politicians suffocated black interests. He and other black nationalist leaders preached a different kind of participation.

Until the early 1980s, Palmer's political interests lay more in embracing what was lost between the motherland of Africa and the plantation— "cultural nationalism," it was sometimes called. Self-esteem was foremost on his agenda, not voter registration. The spiritual search for their own rich heritage, Palmer believed, would do more to free African Americans of the internalized debris of racism than participation in electoral politics. So, too, would economic self-reliance.

Yet by 1980 Palmer came to see the connections between electoral politics and the black psyche. Black dignity began to seem an elusive concept when black Chicago was perpetually slighted and demeaned in the political realm. A black mayor reigned in Atlanta, Los Angeles, Washington, D.C., Detroit, and even Birmingham, Alabama—but not in Chicago.

Harold Washington could be alternately amused and frustrated by the nationalist's polemics about black liberation and the masses. He was a career politician who cared neither for lost causes nor for the nationalist's esoterica. Washington thought more in terms of hard numbers and building winning coalitions across racial lines; he prided himself on his abilities as a legislative horse trader, where Palmer boasted of an unwillingness to compromise, especially with whites. An avid radio listener, Washington recognized that Palmer tapped a deep vein within the black community. Yet at the same time he dismissed many of Palmer's views as crude and defeatist. Mistrusting all white people struck him as an ill-fated strategy in a country dominated by whites.

Still, he recognized Palmer's potential as an ally. Within movement circles Chicago was reputed to be the country's most nationalistic city; it was the hub of nationalist thought, and because of the city's severe segregation, a de facto nationalism seemed to reign, more so than in other cities. Washington knew intimately the city's nationalist community; he understood Palmer's influence over large segments of black Chicago. If harnessed, the nationalists could be the engine he needed to reach black youth and the poor, two critical groups, should he run.

Who knew? Palmer and his associates might just awaken the disaffected black masses on whose behalf they claimed to speak. If nothing else, by drawing the nationalists into electoral politics, they would at least stop muddling the message by preaching against the vote.

Lutrelle (Lu) Fleming Palmer, Jr., was born in 1922 in Newport News, Virginia. His father founded a black high school in Newport News and was also a strong advocate for equal pay for black teachers, who were paid much less than their white counterparts. The senior Palmer, president of Virginia's black teachers' association, fought a twenty-year fight for equal pay. When he finally won that battle, when he finally convinced local officials to pay black and white teachers the same, he was dismissed as principal of the school he had founded twenty-three years earlier. The way Palmer remembers it, that battle broke his father, a soft-spoken but proud and independent man. It would be years before Palmer came to terms with the political meaning of his father's death.

Crosses were burned on the junior Palmer's front lawn when he worked for a black newspaper in Memphis. When Palmer was at work as a newspaper reporter in Chicago, sneering doormen would say to him, "Deliveries in the rear, boy." Cops excluded him from crime scenes he was assigned to cover. Palmer suffered all sorts of racial bruises, small, large, and imagined, but the main reason he was who he was, he said, was his father.

"As far as I'm concerned they killed him," he said. No mob tied a rope around his father's neck, but to Palmer he was lynched by a racist system just the same.

Palmer tried making it in the white world. He bounced around among newspapers until he landed a once-a-week column at the *Chicago Daily News.* There his columns were routed through special channels, straight to the paper's chief editor, Roy Fisher. Diplomacy seemed Fisher's watchword for Palmer's writing. This lead needs to be softened, Fisher might say; "You don't use a sledgehammer, you have to persuade." Fisher saw himself as something of a translator—"translating Lu's black rhetoric into an impartial white language," he said.

Fisher was a powerful and infamous figure within Chicago journalism, stubborn and strong-willed. Another columnist may have brooded for a time, then capitulated or quit, but Lutrelle Fleming Palmer, Jr., was not the sort to back down from a fight with a middle-aged honkie telling him how to write about black folks. Both recall their regular Friday afternoon meetings as bombastic sessions that could last as long as two hours.

In the late 1960s Palmer scored the sort of newspaper coup that brightens the day of a dyed-in-the-wool newspaperman like Roy Fisher, but that also exemplified their relationship. The number-two man in the infamous Black P. Stone Nation gang, Charles Bey, was on the lam after allegedly shooting a cop. Palmer persuaded Stone leaders to let Bey surrender to him at the *News,* to guard against any trigger-happy policeman out for revenge. Fisher wrote the page-one story himself. It was past midnight but he felt terrific—a major outlaw had surrendered to the *News.*

Palmer was incensed. To his mind Bey did not surrender to the *Chicago Daily News* but to a black reporter. That is how the lead should read, Palmer argued: Charles Bey surrendered to a black reporter working for the *News.* A black man on the run does not surrender to a white institution, he explained to Fisher. At one point Palmer was up on a desk calling Fisher a motherfucker this and a motherfucker that. Fisher was not in the mood for debate: the lead would stand.

Thirty minutes later an entourage of Stones walked into the *News,* led by Jeff Fort. Fort is an imposing and hulking figure, a notorious Chicago character. Years later Fisher couldn't recall exactly what happened next but said that Palmer's recollections were probably accurate. Palmer recalled explaining to Fisher that he had asked Fort and the others down to the *News* to help clear up this journalistic point. Who knows what Fisher might have been thinking when he said to Palmer, "Okay, Lu, you can write that lead."

Lu Palmer was still with the *News* in 1972 when Cook County State's Attorney Edward Hanrahan, the man overseeing the raid on Fred Hampton's apartment, lost his bid for reelection. The election was a red-letter date: it was the regular Democratic organization's first citywide defeat under Daley's control and also a spur to black political empowerment. "The black community came together in a way," Palmer said, "that I've never seen before."

On the surface Fred Hampton seemed an unlikely candidate for launching an electoral movement. He voiced slogans such as "Off the pig" and described all black convicts as "political prisoners." He preached the need for blacks to arm themselves against the police. Yet to dismiss Hampton as nothing but a fringe revolutionary is to make the same sort of political blunder committed by Hanrahan. Hampton was a suburban kid from Maywood and the president of the local NAACP youth council. He won honors in high school and dreamed of a career as a lawyer. He also spoke out against the injustices he saw around him, and for that he was branded a troublemaker. The more he spoke out, the more Maywood's city fathers turned the screws, fueling Hampton's militancy. At the age of nineteen he helped found the Illinois Black Panthers.

Hampton was a charismatic figure whose two-year tenure as chief of the Panthers won him the admiration of a great many blacks, poor and wealthy alike. He was well read; at twenty-one he could quote not only Malcolm X and Stokely Carmichael but also Gandhi, Mao, and Che Guevara—a range of radical thinkers. On a podium he was spellbinding. The Panthers set up free food clinics and breakfast programs for black school kids. They ran several health care clinics and organized teams to test black children for sickle-cell anemia.

Hampton sought out like-minded allies in the white and Latino communities. Other chapters scorned the Chicago Panthers for their talk of a vanguard of black, white, and Latino revolutionaries, but Hampton was making inroads. A "rainbow coalition," he called it.

26

The *Chicago Defender*, the country's oldest black-owned daily, is no radical organ; those invited to talk politics in Lu Palmer's basement in the early 1980s tended to dismiss the *Defender* as the *Pretender*, the *Offender*, or a similar taunt. Yet in the days after Hampton's and Mark Clark's deaths, the lines between the militants and moderates were all but erased. An "ugly, dark, ominous mood" had descended on Chicago, the *Defender* reported. "The people seem ready for a showdown with the police or any other symbol of white power." The legal system had dispensed with the reading of Hampton's and Clark's rights, a trial, and all the other provisions that distinguish the United States from other countries. The double killing, said black independent Alderman Sammy Rayner, "made middle-class people think black for the first time."

Ed Hanrahan's defeat three years later was a stunning upset. State's attorney was a key political post—the office that Daley's son Richard would choose as a stepping-stone to the mayor's office—and Hanrahan was no common Daley loyalist. Hanrahan was being groomed as a possible successor to Daley. A Harvard Law School graduate, Hanrahan was a Daley favorite; in both temperament and belief he was not unlike the mayor he so faithfully served. A "vile-tempered intense man . . . [whose] answer to most social problems boiled down to locking people up for the maximum sentence," Mike Royko wrote of Hanrahan in his book, *Boss*.

On the night of Hanrahan's defeat, Palmer wrote a news analysis piece slated for page one. The article's tone was triumphant, casting the defeat as nothing short of black Chicago's political awakening. Black voters had defeated Hanrahan, he wrote.

Palmer's editors saw it differently. Hanrahan's foe received a large share of his votes in the suburbs, they pointed out. Republicans always win votes in the suburbs, Palmer countered; the reason this qualified as a page-one story was that a majority of black voters rejected the Democratic machine and voted for a Republican. Palmer's piece was pulled before the final edition.

By then Palmer's column was rarely appearing in the paper. No one came right out and said the obvious—that Palmer's perspective was too black—but Palmer believed it just the same. "It was my *assignment* to write a once-a-week column from the black perspective," Palmer told a fellow black reporter. "But, see, them honkies didn't understand what the black perspective was." When the *News* ran a point-by-point refutation beside one of Palmer's columns, he had had enough. At a press conference announcing his resignation, he said, "The concerns of black people have no priority in the system of white-controlled media." He vowed never again to allow a white man to edit his work. Anticipating trouble removing his files from the building, he called on a few friends to help. A half-dozen Black Panthers, dressed in full regalia—black berets, dark sunglasses, black leather gloves—carried Palmer's boxes out of the *News*.

Four months after his resignation Palmer unveiled his own newspaper, the *Black X-Press*. Palmer envisioned for the *X-Press* a "black communication system through which black people can communicate with each other without the repressive control of The Man." He boasted that he would permit nothing white to intrude on the *X-Press:* he would neither accept white advertising nor hire any white employees. Palmer took to wearing around his neck a green, black, and red map of Africa medallion.

The first issue of the *X-Press* was dated May 9—Malcolm X's birthday. Palmer had chosen Martin Luther King's birthday for his last day at the *News*. No longer would he work for black liberation within the white system, as King had; black salvation would come only by living a life separate from and hostile to the white world. For Palmer it was the end of a twenty-year struggle to come to terms with the rage born while watching his proud father broken by a racist system. He had found his way.   .

In the mid-1950s Richard Barnett was just a guy who saw baseball as a means for keeping kids out of trouble and teaching them a few things about life. His interests lay more in building a middle-class mecca for his young family than in battling politicians. In 1953 the Barnetts bought a home in Lawndale, on the city's west side, then a desirable community although it was in the throes of racial change. Several years earlier the block to which the Barnetts moved was almost entirely white; by the time Barnett took title on his house most of the whites had already moved away.

A few months later Barnett approached some kids on the street about forming a baseball team. Within a few years Barnett's idea blossomed into a local Little League that had grown to thirty-two teams, and by 1959 he was waging a small war against the city.

Barnett's political involvement began when a local company offered his Little Leaguers a vacant field behind its factory. A group of kids and their fathers were able to clear out the junk that had piled there, but they needed something called a grader—a contraption that could smooth over the bumps and ruts that marred the field. Barnett approached the local alderman, Ben Lewis, a black man, but was told that the city couldn't afford the $300 grading the field would cost. The next day's newspapers reported that the city had spent $18,000 fixing several hundred feet of curbs along Michigan Avenue downtown in preparation for Queen Elizabeth's visit. Barnett was so incensed that he joined a small band organizing to oust Lewis—"a chap who always smiled and called every white he ever met mister," Barnett said.

Lewis was reelected by a twelve-to-one margin. Of the fifty or so zealots working hardest to defeat Lewis, nearly every one ended up abandoning the cause. Most joined the machine ranks, Barnett said, seduced by well-paying city jobs and fooled by their own rhetoric that working within the system was the best avenue for change. Barnett was one of the stalwart few who did not.

Blacks from the South tended to settle on the west side; for many, moving up in the world meant leaving the west side for the city's south side. It was on the city's west side that unemployment was the most severe, the people the least educated, and the crime rate the highest. For a time Barnett's Lawndale community seemed an exception to the rule, but Barnett watched his community disintegrate into a ghetto in barely a decade's time. Slumlords allowed their property to deteriorate, and a federal housing program granted mortgages to black families that could not afford the upkeep on their new homes. A decline in city services accompanied the white flight. What riled Barnett was that no one in power seemed to care.

On the south side there were genuine machine power brokers who were black; on the west side there were only black puppets. The true power in the Twenty-fourth Ward wasn't Ben Lewis but a white man named Irwin "Izzy" Horowitz, a real estate mogul who lived miles away in a Gold Coast condominium. Horowitz rarely visited the ward, a grim reminder of his old neighborhood's decline. The other black west side wards were similarly cursed. "Plantation politics," it was called.

The city's most notorious gangsters operated on the west side. The next candidate Barnett endorsed over Lewis withdrew from the race after a couple of local hoods threatened to break his kneecaps. Shortly after his reelection, Lewis was killed, an apparent victim of the mob. He had tried to use his connections to horn in on the local insurance business of a recently deceased west side politician. Shortly thereafter he was discovered dead in his office, three bullets in his head, his arms handcuffed to a chair.

There may have been others as committed as Barnett but none more so. After a candidate he backed was tossed off the ballot on a technicality, Barnett became a self-taught expert in election law. He mastered the mechanics of politics and came to serve as manager of nearly every antimachine challenge in his part of the city. The machine had at its disposal an army of workers, thirty-five thousand in all, so Barnett stressed the need for a precinct operation—workers going door-to-door asking for votes—in every election he managed. To him there was no other way.

A postal worker, Barnett had a family and a mortgage, yet he paid rent on a nearby office that served as a hub for his political activities. For years Barnett worked the graveyard shift so that he could do his political work during the day. In the full swing of a campaign the phone rang all day in the Barnett home when most of those working the graveyard shift were sleeping.

Time brought more defeats. In 1964 a black woman running for Congress from a west side district lost to a white machine loyalist who died on the morning of the election. The district was more than half black, yet she lost by nearly a ten-to-one margin. Even as the west side's fledgling antimachine movement picked up new recruits, they lost old ones. Barnett called them "quislings"—traitors who collaborated with the people invading his land. That, to him, was the Democratic machine—like a colonial force occupying a third world nation.

The 1960s brought a new set of frustrations for Barnett—increasing black militancy. A devout coalitionist in the tradition of a Martin Luther King, Jr., Barnett had little tolerance for those who first divided the world into black and white and then lumped in with promachine blacks all of white Chicago. He worked with anyone—lakefront liberals, suburban Republicans—as long as they aligned with him against the machine. He recalled with irritation the time he brought to a meeting a white lawyer long involved in movement causes, and several young blacks challenged the white man's presence. Barnett looked on their militancy as ignorant and also as bad strategy. How were blacks ever going to defeat Daley when they accounted for less than fifty percent of the population?

The ideological gulf between the nationalist and the coalitionist stretched back at least to the early twentieth century when Marcus Garvey preached black separatism, and the "New Negroes" called for a working-class unity that crossed racial lines. The nationalist saw the enormous energies of the coalitionist wasted on reforms that were little more than symbolic. What was the use of liberal tinkering with a system they viewed as hopelessly imbued with deep-seated cultural, economic, and political biases— a society brutal to the black psyche? The more militant nationalist dismissed the coalitionist as a collaborator with their white oppressors. "The Northern Fox," Malcolm X said of the white liberal, "is more vicious than the Southern Wolf because he poses as your friend." Malcolm X (the nationalist) had no use for the desegregation that was advocated by Martin Luther King, Jr. (the coalitionist).

Yet King and Malcolm X made strides toward unity in their short lives. Near the end of his life Malcolm abandoned his belief that all whites were the devil, and encouraged blacks to work with sympathetic whites; King drifted left and was anxious to find a common ground with the young black militants. Their respective disciples took up the unity effort, culminating in an assembly of over eight thousand black activists and politicians in Gary, Indiana, in 1972. Amiri Baraka (formerly LeRoi Jones), the convention's driving force, was largely motivated by the 1970 election of Newark's first black mayor, Kenneth Gibson. "Unity without uniformity," the delegates at Gary repeated among themselves. One participant, Jesse Jackson, described the meeting as a "lightweight miracle."

In Chicago the various strands of the black community united during the 1972 state's attorney race, yet there was hardly time to celebrate before it began unraveling. (Chicago was not the only place where this "unity without uniformity" was short-lived: Gibson was still in his first term when Baraka dismissed him as "a neocolonialist.") No great epiphany had dawned on the city's nationalists or the disaffected voters who registered to vote for the first time in their lives. Ed Hanrahan's defeat only confirmed for them that they weren't voting *for* anyone or anything, only against the worst excesses of the machine. The lesson Lu Palmer said he learned was that his political participation meant the dumping of one white in favor of another whose political views were barely distinguishable from his predecessor's. Palmer stopped voting altogether.

Barnett dreamed that Hanrahan's defeat would prove to black Chicago its potential as a political force. But he was not the type to dwell on disappointments with upcoming important local races in 1974. That year a black man named Jesse Madison, whom Washington would later put in charge of the city's park district, was elected state representative, becoming the first west side independent to defeat the machine. But there would be more disappointments. Barnett would endure insults for backing a white mayoral candidate over a black one, and he listened to activists who were organizing against school overcrowding but who failed to make the connection between the problem and the machine's control of the school board. He was disappointed that there wouldn't be a concerted effort to defeat Daley in 1975, but unity would come, Barnett believed. It would just take a little longer than he hoped.

"Lu was really on the fringes for a while," said one black activist who himself resided well to the left of the mainstream through much of the 1970s. "Many people really thought that Lu had snapped, that he had lost it." Still, people paid their respects to Palmer. "It was like with the Black Muslims. No one wants to get involved with them, people crossed to the other side of the street when they saw them coming, but to have their respect was some amorphous seal of black authenticity."

Palmer's *Black X-Press* lasted all of fourteen months. After its demise, he converted the coach house behind his home into a grocery store, heralding "Palmer's Place" as a vehicle for black self-reliance. Black folks, he said, should support black-owned businesses rather than patronize those owned by whites or recent Asian or Arabic émigrés. Palmer also began a career as a radio personality. Four black-owned stations carried his daily commentaries, and once a week he hosted his own two-hour talk show.

Over the radio Palmer scoffed at the supposed advances of the civil rights movement. He questioned whether black America was any better off after the changes of the 1960s. Just posing the question then was heresy in some black quarters, but the black woman who worked on her knees all day scrubbing floors only to return home to a crime- and rat-infested tenement on the west side might be considering the same question. Where other voices rejoiced that there were more blacks in the middle class than even imaginable a generation earlier, Palmer was more inclined to note that the unemployment rate was higher than ever in the black ghettos. More blacks were entering medical school, but homicide emerged as the leading cause of death for young black men, and the cancer rate for blacks far surpassed that for whites. Palmer's words were heard by a great number still living—many civil rights victories later—in squalor. "It's enough to make a Negro think Black," Palmer would say, signing his commentary with his trademark tag line.

People who didn't like Palmer nonetheless tuned in to hear his "On Target" and "Talking Drums" shows just to see whom he was assaulting that day. Palmer always named names: black clergy he believed to be Daley toadies, black politicians for their "spineless acquiescence" to downtown political interests, fellow grass roots activists who he believed had compromised the cause. Palmer was most outspoken when it came to white Chicagoans, of course, but white politicians didn't listen to black radio stations. Those whose feathers Lu Palmer ruffled were blacks who understood the power of the radio in the black community. To be lambasted by Palmer might well ruin one's reputation.

Controversy followed Palmer—or perhaps it was Palmer who sought controversy. One black leader or another always seemed to be after him, pulling any string he could to get him fired. Once Palmer incurred black displeasure when he scolded a prominent black businessman named George Johnson for raising $10,000 to help the white victim of a crime committed by two black men. (Can you recall, he asked his listeners, a single time—a single time!—a white businessman passed the hat to aid a black victim of a hate crime?) The black machine aldermen even introduced legislation that would have banned Palmer from the airwaves.

Palmer's followers always rallied to their man's cause. A "People for Palmer Movement" formed: "A vital link to our culture and well-being," the group wrote during one controversy; "an institution" in black Chicago.

Palmer had regular targets. He had little use for James Compton and Edwin (Bill) Berry of the Urban League, hailed by liberals as twin rulers of

33

the city's civil rights movement. Both fell into the same coalitionist category that housed Richard Barnett, but whereas Palmer respected Barnett as a grass roots organizer, he dismissed Berry and Compton as wealthy black businessmen who were part of the local civil rights elite. He thought neither could see beyond his own economic station in life. Palmer joked on the radio about people never seeing Bill Berry anywhere except at a nice restaurant downtown eating with someone white. The Urban League, Palmer would say, is an organization that allows itself to be used by white politicians seeking to blunt the impact of black activists, the true voices of black Chicago.

Jesse Jackson was another regular target. Palmer judged Jackson to be guilty the time he allowed himself to be photographed by both the *Tribune* and the *Sun-Times* clasping hands with Mayor Daley in the "soul" handshake popular at the time. "More committed to raising himself than raising the quality of life for black people," Palmer said of Jackson on the radio. There were those who said Palmer was very much the same way except that he was not nearly so adept as Jackson at promoting himself. But most kept those kinds of views to themselves for fear of provoking Palmer's ire.

Palmer even rebuked himself on the air when in 1977 he allowed himself to be drawn into electoral politics after Harold Washington launched his first campaign for mayor. Though Palmer was forever telling people that voting was nothing but a distraction in the quest for black liberation, Washington presented him with a dilemma. Palmer believed in Washington. His wife Jorja worked with Washington on and off for years, helping to mobilize constituents for demonstrations when Washington needed a show of support for some bill he was carrying in the state legislature. Thus Palmer devised a strange solution to his predicament. He worked exhausting hours for the campaign, distinguishing himself as one of the more dedicated members of Washington's team, but he never registered to vote. He spent countless hours trying to convince people to vote for Washington, yet he was not able to convince himself to do the same.

The nationalist denounces the process. It is the nationalist, then, who must take the first leap in pushing for a unity of purpose. Not just any peacemaker would do. He or she must be militant to the point that no one would think of questioning his or her legitimacy—or perhaps psychologically secure to the point that he or she does not worry when his or her so-called black credentials are questioned. He or she must also carry the necessary clout to sway opinions. The Newark (New Jersey) and Gary (Indiana) efforts had the perfect figure in Amiri Baraka—poet, playwright, and well-known revolutionary, tainted only by a first marriage to a white woman. About the only black leader who could boast similar credentials in Chicago's sizable nationalist community was Lu Palmer.

Palmer was no diplomat. His manner was as strident as his beliefs. Yet in 1980 when the state legislature tentatively approved a redistricting plan that would probably reduce black representation, Palmer sought James Compton and the Urban League. The previous year Palmer had denounced Compton and his organization as "traitors" to the black cause, yet the two worked together on that issue and future projects as well. Palmer registered that same year in order to vote for Harold Washington who was running for Congress.

Not long after extending his olive branch to Compton and others, Palmer began talking on the radio about the 1983 election, still two years off. Soon he spoke of little else. He ceaselessly promoted Washington as the kind of man whose election would really mean something to black Chicago. He criticized Jane Byrne for betrayals, and he closed his commentary with, "We shall see in '83." He repeated the slogan so often that for many blacks it became their rallying cry. He organized a political conference ("Toward a Black Mayor") in 1981 that was held at the west side's Malcolm X College and attended by thousands. When Palmer was summing up the importance of electing a black mayor, he began to cry; he did not finish his talk.

Palmer initiated the basement meetings to enlist the support of others, and he formed a group he called CBUC—Chicago Black United Communities. He came up with the idea of training volunteers to do battle with the machine's patronage army; they would attend voter education classes held in the coach house behind his home. Richard Barnett was among those whose help Palmer sought. Barnett said he was delighted to participate—just as Compton and others welcomed Palmer's extended hand. Supposedly, CBUC's voter education classes turned out two thousand volunteers by the primary.

The basement meetings were never self-consciously about unity. The conversations did not revolve around building on Baraka's 1972 convention in Gary, still that's what the basement meetings represented: a bridging of the wide ideological gap that divided the coalitionist and the nationalist. While no convention followed, as the 1972 Gary convention followed Kenneth Gibson's win in Newark, Chicago was nonetheless viewed as having profound implications for blacks in other locales. At least a few black intellectuals credited Chicago with rekindling the unity inspiration that died shortly after the Gary convention.

Amiri Baraka was roundly criticized by some when he first made a call for unity. Nearly ten years later Lu Palmer was also confronted by admirers who did not embrace his actions. Palmer admitted in an interview with a black journalist back in 1981, "A lot of folks are asking what the hell is going on."

Most controversial was Palmer's alliance with Jesse Jackson. Jackson had called Palmer shortly after he began holding his basement meetings, and not long afterward the news spread through the nationalist community that Palmer would appear at Operation PUSH. "A lot of people told me [that] was one of the biggest mistakes I ever made," Palmer said.

It was a moment for the initiated only—a pair of quick smiles, the brief clasping of hands. Only those clued in to the codes of black politics understood the significance of the picture: Lu Palmer and Jesse Jackson up on stage, standing before two thousand on a Saturday morning in 1982, a picture of unity.

Saturday mornings at PUSH were an occasion. Two distinct groups attended PUSH meetings. There were the faithful who would no sooner miss a Saturday at PUSH than skip church on Sunday. Jackson was their minister; they were his congregation. On a routine Saturday morning the crowd tended toward matronly black women and well-dressed black men who greeted one another formally: "And how are you this morning, Mr. Johnson?" "Oh, fine, Miss Thompson, I'm fine." To these folks Jackson was always "the Reverend Jackson."

Jackson was simply "Jesse" to a group who wore the garb and demeanor of community organizers. This second group showed up at PUSH whenever things were heated on the local political scene. If some pronouncement from City Hall had those in the black community steaming, there was no need for anyone to make turnout calls. People knew that PUSH was the place to be at 10 A.M. on Saturday morning. If the audience was made up of as many people who disliked Jackson as people who believed him a wonderful man, that only underscored the importance of his role in black Chicago.

Jackson had what no one else had—a weekly forum that drew people week after week. A community organization that turns out fifty people for a monthly meeting has cause for celebration. The Saturday crowd at PUSH ranged from the hundreds to a thousand; when there was a big event a capacity crowd of two thousand would attend. Jackson, one black activist said, "was our minister of information. He was channels 2, 5, 7, and 9 for the movement." His analysis was often brilliant. "I'd be in meetings all week long where people were cussing out Jesse," said Walter "Slim" Coleman, a white community activist, "and then come Saturday, we'd all be standing up cheering, 'Right on, Jesse.'" One rite of passage into the upper echelons of movement politics was to sit on the stage at PUSH while Jackson performed. Of course there were those who chose not to be so honored because they simply couldn't stand him—people such as Lu Palmer.

The Jackson-Palmer rift was as much personal as ideological. Jackson teased the nationalists, Palmer believed. He called for a Black Liberation Party in Gary in 1972, but Palmer remembered Jackson doing more to block a third-party effort than push for one. "Jesse talks in a way that you can interpret what he says in more than one way," Palmer said. In the 1970s, Jackson took to closing his syndicated "Country Preacher" column with the nationalist slogan, "It's Nation-Time." Yet there were more than a few nationalists who believed he borrowed the phrase only for show. It was as if he sought to cover every conceivable base, seeking to please the nationalists at the same time that he offered them nothing at all. He assumed a nationalist's posture when convenient and disposed of it just as quickly.

Palmer couldn't say he was suddenly won over by Jesse Jackson—it would be years before he could say he genuinely respected the man—but Palmer came to see the infighting as a luxury blacks could not afford. Ronald Reagan was president. A Republican, James Thompson, served as Illinois's governor. And there was Jane Byrne, the only large-city mayor who refused to criticize Ronald Reagan despite the devastating cuts he sought in funds on which cities like Chicago relied. For the time being there were more important tasks than fighting the likes of Jackson.

The unity would not last, but those at Operation PUSH on the morning that Palmer appeared on stage considered themselves among the lucky.
Historic, some described it; critical, said others. A third group, including
Richard Barnett, was just glad the nonsense was out of the way so they
could get down to the business of electing a mayor who was at once black
and antimachine.

3

THE

CHOSEN

In the summer of 1982 two thousand committed movement soldiers showed up at a south side church for a day-long event that Lu Palmer had billed as a "black plebiscite." The idea was to invite everyone who was anyone in black movement politics, and there, at this gathering of the clan, crown Harold Washington their man for mayor. The plebiscite went as planned through most of the day. Speaker after speaker cited informal polls that showed Washington far ahead of Palmer, Jesse Jackson, and other well-known black political figures. Near the day's end a vote was taken: Washington outdistanced the second-place finisher by something like five to one. All that remained was the formality of Washington's humble acceptance of their mantle as the movement's preferred choice and declaration of his candidacy. That, at least, was the way Palmer's script read.

The crowd treated Washington to a standing ovation as he made his way to the microphone to deliver the plebiscite's keynote address. But he didn't declare his candidacy; he didn't drop even a hint that he was considering a run for mayor. Instead he started talking about "the plan, not the man," urging the crowd not to get too hung up on any one candidate yet. Washington's words confused almost everyone in the room except Palmer, who was feeling overcome with rage.

Palmer didn't even try to mask his feelings. He was bone tired from weeks of work that culminated in a long day of last-minute hassles and worries. He and countless others had already poured an enormous amount of energy into Washington. From the start most of those conspiring to elect a black mayor assumed Washington was their man; their challenge, as they saw it, was manufacturing a consensus behind him. When in 1980 Byrne named a controversial appointee to the school board, Washington was not the moving force behind the ensuing protest, yet the flyers passed around the black community pretended that he was. Every week Palmer seemed to invent a new pretext for mentioning Washington's name on the air. Other journalists in the black media were doing the same. Press releases and pictures flooded the black media as if Washington were already a declared candidate in a current race. Washington always seemed more than willing to accommodate plans to promote him at every turn. To Palmer, it was simply too late for cold feet.

Palmer confronted Washington after the latter's speech. "I'm not planning on running," Washington told him, and Palmer lost his cool. He cursed, hollered, and threatened to grab a microphone and tell the assembled crowd that the man they had just chosen overwhelmingly as their candidate for mayor was as full of it as the next politician. "I'm going to kill that man," Palmer said to anyone within earshot.

Renault Robinson, a close ally of Washington's, witnessed Palmer's tirade and decided to intervene. Blasting Washington in front of all these people would probably not help matters, he explained. It wasn't easy, but Robinson talked Palmer into meeting with Washington again to work things out.

For a couple of years Robinson had been among those gathering with Washington at his local congressional office to toss around the idea of a black challenge to Jane Byrne. Everyone there had assumed Washington was exploring the possibilities of his own candidacy, though he was always careful to refer to this candidate as an unnamed third person. The strange world of electoral politics tickled Robinson, and one thing struck him as one of its more peculiar oddities: a strained modesty in an immodest world. It was, he figured, akin to a buddy beginning a conversation with "Let's say this friend has a problem." Robinson was just as surprised by Washington's "it's the plan" speech as Palmer.

Robinson and Washington showed up at Palmer's for a meeting a few weeks later. Palmer started things off by asking Washington to tell the group of about a dozen people what he had said to him after the plebiscite. Washington didn't mince words: "I told Lu that I'm not going to run and never intended to run."

The room exploded with noise. Everyone fought to speak except Washington, who remained quietly defiant. He sat and listened as people accused him of betraying the cause and playing with people's lives. When someone mentioned a rumor that Washington had cut a deal with the machine, Washington only said, "You can hear anything on the street." The way Palmer remembered it, Washington and several people almost came to blows. Others there that night dismissed the claim as Palmer's usual hyperbole: there were harsh words, nerves were frayed from one of those unrelenting Chicago summer days that drain the body of all moisture, but no one was about to trade punches with Washington just because he was acting as if the idea of running for mayor never crossed his mind.

Washington grew tired of the assault. "You can't tell me what to do," he said and stalked out. After he had gone they called him a coward, untrustworthy, and also a fool. In their minds they were casting him as savior opposite Byrne's antebellum master. What more enviable circumstance could a politician want? For the life of them they couldn't understand Washington.

He was born on the city's south side three years after the 1919 race riot that left thirty-eight dead and over five hundred injured. The south side smelled of dead flesh then, its skies burned orange at night. The stockyards and slaughtering houses, two of the few places where blacks could find a job, dominated the part of the city that the Washington family called home. "Hog butcher to the world," wrote Carl Sandburg—and the Washingtons lived breathing distance from the entrails and gore.

Chicago was a Republican city when Harold Washington was born. The man regarded as father of the Chicago Democratic machine, Anton

Cermak, would not be elected until 1931, and blacks, too, were still firmly Republican, loyal to the party of Lincoln. Among the exceptions was Roy Washington, Sr. Long before black America swung to the Democrats, Roy Washington worked a precinct for the party. Not even Harold Washington's mother voted Democratic then.

The senior Washington, a burly man who weighed upward of 275 pounds, was born in a small Kentucky town called Lovelaceville, the son of a Methodist minister. By twenty-one he was on Chicago's south side working the slaughtering floor of a meat-packing house. He attended law school at night and graduated the year after his son Harold was born. Roy was only twenty-five, and his wife Bertha twenty-four, but Washington was their fourth child.

Roy Washington worked another two years at the stockyards before quitting to become a solo law practitioner. He struggled for years until he was offered a job as an assistant city prosecutor, working out of a south side police station. He jumped at the chance. It meant working a precinct, but a decent-paying job with the city was what he had dreamed about since joining the party more than ten years earlier.

Bertha Washington had ambitions of her own. Where Roy Washington was rough and crude, she was genteel and refined. She read poetry to her children and encouraged them to express themselves artistically. She worked as a domestic for a time but dreamed of a career on stage. Independent and strong-willed, Bertha Washington walked out on the family when Harold was only four, leaving Roy with custody of their four children.

Roy Washington shipped Harold and his brother off to a Benedictine boarding school in Milwaukee, Wisconsin, that catered to the children of black professionals. It was a progressive school that taught black history and introduced students to black writers, unusual for the time, but it was also renowned for its regimentation. Church attendance three times a day was mandatory; discipline was severe.

The school was well over an hour away by car, but within the week the Washington boys escaped, showing up on their father's doorstep. Harold was not yet five, his brother all of six, but somehow the two had managed to hitchhike home. Washington claimed to have run away thirteen more times during the next three years. His father finally gave up and enrolled the boys in Chicago public schools.

Washington grew up surrounded by the black political elite. The legendary south side boss William Dawson was an occasional guest at the Washington home; so, too, was Arthur Mitchell, the country's first black Democratic congressman. Washington was aware of mayors and aldermen and knew the names of countless party functionaries before he reached his teens. Old-timers remember Washington tagging along with his father at one political rally or another; by fourteen he was helping his father in the precinct.

Washington's mother remarried and lived close enough so that her son could stop by to visit, but Roy Washington raised him. "A very affectionate man who tried to play the role of mother and father," Washington said. He said he idolized his father; the old man would raise an eyebrow, he said, and young Washington jumped.

Washington was not outgoing. Childhood friends years later would not describe him as a born leader destined for greatness. What people tended to remember of Washington in his teens was that he was always reading. High school friends recall him seated in the corner of the school cafeteria reading a book. When playing baseball he read on the bench between at bats; legend has it that he read while walking to his position out in the field. Supposedly he would set the book down beside him when play resumed. He lived only a few blocks from a public library with the most comprehensive collection of Afro-American works in the library system, and after school he took up residence there. Washington's brothers teased him about eating the dictionary for lunch. How else to explain the highfalutin words that came out of his mouth?

Washington was given the middle name Lee at birth, as was each of his brothers. Through his reading he learned that Lee was the surname of the commander in chief of the Confederate army, and what that meant; from then on he stopped using his middle name. Never in his career would Washington even use his middle initial.

Washington attended Du Sable High, a school designed for twenty-five hundred but crammed with more than thirty-five hundred students when Washington was there. He was an intense young man, introverted and determined, but a skinny kid others bullied around. In his early teens he came across a Charles Atlas ad in a detective magazine and practiced Atlas's magic cure for the ninety-eight-pound weakling. After several playground victories he had solved the problem of other kids picking on him.

In a citywide track meet held in 1939, Washington placed first in the 110-yard high hurdles and second in the 220-yard low hurdles. He dropped out of high school between his junior and senior years, claiming he was no longer challenged by the classwork.

For a time Washington worked for one of the city's packing plants, hauling meat in and out of a freezer, before his father used connections to secure him a desk job at the local U.S. Treasury office. While he was working at the treasury he married a girl who lived in his building, Dorothy—"Peaches," he affectionately called her, because of her peach fuzz. He was only nineteen when they married, his new wife seventeen. Seven months later Pearl Harbor was bombed, and Washington was drafted.

The rigors of the army ate at Washington. It brought back bad memories of the Catholic boarding school and its regimentation. Several racial incidents while in boot camp also soured him. He was sent overseas to the South Pacific but saw little action. He took an array of courses while in basic training, including one that taught him to test whether a given field could support an airfield, which is how a skinny black kid from Chicago ended up a soil technician in the Guam theater. Mainly Washington spent his time studying for each of the thirty army correspondence courses he took while stationed overseas. He eventually made first sergeant, but so deep was his hatred for his three-year stint that he didn't bother lugging back his duffel bag of belongings. He returned to Chicago with nothing but the clothes on his back and a toiletry kit. About the only good that came of his time in the army, Washington said, was that between missions he had earned his high school equivalency diploma.

His wife had written to him near the end of the war about the unique new college that was opening up in downtown Chicago; back home it seemed everyone he knew was talking about Roosevelt University. Shortly after returning stateside he enrolled. Dedicated in 1945, Roosevelt was a bold experiment in higher education. It was integrated, one of the few such institutions anywhere in the country. Black students could not eat with their classmates at nearby lunch counters in the Loop, nor could their parents sleep at a downtown hotel, but that only made Roosevelt more special. The school developed a reputation as a sanctuary for leftists and idealists—"the little red schoolhouse" it was called among those in the know.

Roosevelt provided Washington his first sustained contact with whites. Growing up he could ride his bicycle for blocks through the segregated streets of the south side without ever seeing a single white. Whites were people in positions of authority or members of some world to which he was not invited. Washington recalled spending hours at his bedroom window staring out at the Grand Terrace Club, across the street from his building. The Grand Terrace was in the heart of the black belt, a mecca for black music but a club for whites only. His army years were hardly different, for the army was still segregated through World War II. At Roosevelt he related with whites as equals and thrived.

He was a serious student, hardworking and focused. He was never the sort for demonstrating. When his friend Gus Savage was organizing lunch counter sit-ins at nearby restaurants, Washington was not someone upon whom he could rely—although his closest friends were the campus radicals. No longer the shy recluse, Washington was elected school president, the first black to fill that post. In school one of his political heroes was Henry Wallace, a Democratic hopeful in the 1948 presidential campaign whose aim it was to drag the Democratic party left. With time his support for Wallace would take on increased significance among those who knew him then. It was as if he were modeling himself on Wallace, a man who mastered the process yet stood for principles held by those on the outside.* At Roosevelt he was one of those rare individuals who was an insider yet respected by those on the outside.

After Roosevelt, Washington attended Northwestern University's law school. Northwestern was no Roosevelt. It didn't crackle with the same energy and spirit, nor was he embraced with open arms. He was the only black in his class, and mostly he stayed to himself. Still, at the age of thirty, he had earned a law degree from a prestigious law school.

Washington went into practice with his father. Across the hall was the office of the new ward committeeman, Ralph Metcalfe. Roy Washington was always prodding his son to tie his future to Metcalfe. Mark my words, Roy Washington would say, he's a young man going places.

Metcalfe was an immensely popular south side figure. He placed second in the 100-meter dash at the 1936 Olympic Games, missing by a fraction of a second the glories bestowed on Jesse Owens, and won a gold

---

*"Radicals don't win," Washington said when he was mayor. "They may shake up the goddamn ground, but they don't win, and the ones who win are those who make the quantum changes and shifts and move. . . . I'd rather be one of those who work within the vineyards . . . than be the revolutionist who was pushing them to do so."

medal as a member of the U.S. relay team. Metcalfe was working as a hotel manager when the machine set him up as alderman and committeeman of the Third Ward. Metcalfe knew nothing of politics, but as Roy Washington saw it, that only boded well for an experienced hand like his son.

Washington's father died a year after the two went into business together. Within the week Metcalfe offered Washington a job with the city on the condition that he take over his father's old precinct.

Running a precinct would be no problem; he had been gradually taking over as precinct captain, trying to give his father a break. Economics was another consideration. In the early 1950s a black lawyer's options were limited: either he scraped by as a solo practitioner or worked for the government. The lucky ones landed a government job that had something to do with the law, but it wasn't at all unusual to find black lawyers working at the post office while practicing law on the side.

It didn't take Washington long to make up his mind; he told Metcalfe he would be free as soon as he cleared up his father's estate. In 1954, Washington went on the city payroll as a lawyer in the corporation counsel's office.

The next year Washington found himself on a dais beside Richard J. Daley at a dinner celebrating Roosevelt University's tenth anniversary. Washington attended as Roosevelt's alumni representative. Also on the dais that night were Eleanor Roosevelt and Chief Justice Earl Warren. Before his speech Washington and Daley shared small talk; afterward the two discussed meatier topics.

Daley had just been elected mayor that year; among his preoccupations then was Congressman William Dawson, the undisputed boss of the black south side. Dawson was an ally—supposedly he cast the deciding vote that gave the machine's endorsement to Daley—but he was also a man to keep in check. Daley did not seek to destroy Dawson, only to dilute his power. He needed blacks who were loyal both to the machine and to him personally.

Washington seemed Daley's type of man. He was a member of the machine family, the son of a precinct captain who had made the organization proud. At the Roosevelt dinner Daley learned that Washington had a gift for words and a fancy law degree, yet he seemed willing to pay his dues in the organization. Working his father's precinct was another plus in Daley's book. Daley liked a young man who understood the importance of family.

A few days after the Roosevelt dinner, the city's top lawyer called his young charge into his office. You're being groomed for city prosecutor, he told Washington. That would rank Washington among the few top blacks in government. One year into his tenure with the city, he was already a rising star.

Maybe Washington should have been better prepared for the trouble ahead; maybe he should have anticipated co-workers nasty with envy. The word around the office was that Washington was granted his break only because he was black. Matters quickly escalated. I was young and unsophisticated then, Washington confided to Dempsey Travis, a friend since childhood. One day he engaged in a screaming match with one of the white lawyers. Washington laughed as he told Travis about it; he laughed about threatening to throw the man out a window.

A noisy scene between two political lawyers is the sort of story that spreads fast through City Hall, and Daley was a hands-on mayor who monitored such things. The mayor dispatched an emissary, a black woman attorney, to speak with Washington. It is similar to Jackie Robinson, she told him; the spiking and ugly insults are just a part of the job. But Washington was more like Robinson's teammate Don Newcombe, a black pitcher who threw at any white ball player who gave him lip. Washington complained, "I can't get along with these racist mothers." Only later did he understand how he should have played it. He should have employed the clout of his powerful patron on the fifth floor. "Instead of getting rough," he told Travis, "I should have jumped cool and bypassed them."

Daley called Washington at home to express his disappointment and confirm for him that he had blown his chance at the prosecutor's post. He wasn't quite the perfect machine man Daley had measured him to be. Washington stayed with the city, but his attitude changed.

Friends recall Washington no longer caring about the job. Associates remember that he was frequently absent from work. There were weeks when he showed up only on pay day and then stayed long enough only to pick up his check. Yet Washington did not worry about losing his job because he had Metcalfe shielding him. Washington was spending all his time in the Third Ward working for Metcalfe, whose stock was rising in the organization. He, too, was being groomed by Daley as a power independent of Dawson, and if Metcalfe needed Washington for political work, then the city could always hire another lawyer to take up the slack. Similar accommodations were made all the time.

Washington was proving himself an able captain, effectively turning out the vote each election. For a time Washington served as Metcalfe's ward secretary, a position beneath a Northwestern law graduate, perhaps, but a perfect one for learning the ward organization from top to bottom. Metcalfe also asked Washington to take charge of the ward's Young Democrats outpost. The Young Democrats (YDs) became Washington's preoccupation.

A sort of junior varsity for developing young political prospects, the Young Democrats fought and jockeyed among themselves in the style of backroom wheeler-dealers. Under Washington the Third Ward YDs had several hundred members, and Richard Elrod, chairman of the YDs around that time, described Washington's branch as the organization's largest and best organized.

Washington treated the YDs as a training ground for those he brought into the organization. He would choose certain young blacks and take them under his wing, teaching them what he knew about politics. Back at the ward office Washington was forever offering late-night sessions on parliamentary procedure, political strategy, and the like. Ostensibly Washington was only trying to recruit new blood for Metcalfe, but his true aim was apparent once he emerged as the ringleader behind the campaign to elect a black man named Bill Harris as the next chairman of the YDs.

Sam Patch was among those Washington recruited into the group. Patch vividly recalled a Washington speech after Harris was defeated (he would win the next year). Never before had he seen a black man stand up to a roomful of whites and call them racist. "Here was a black man in a white hotel pointing his finger and shaking his fist at white folk during a period when they were calling blacks 'colored' to their faces," Patch said. What's Harold up to anyway? Patch remembers asking himself back then.

Ralph Metcalfe, who didn't need the controversy, asked himself the same question. He was a comer in the organization, in line to take Dawson's place as the black community's top power broker. The trouble that Washington stirred could hurt him.

Metcalfe was forever losing his temper with Washington. Other captains and lawyers in the organization showed up at headquarters a few nights a week just in case they were needed. With Washington it was different. "It was like, 'You want me, come find me,'" said Charles Freeman, the first black Supreme Court justice in Illinois history but at that time just another lawyer who was part of Metcalfe's organization. "Go find that goddamn Washington," Metcalfe would yell, sometimes for days on end. "Harold just checked out for days at a time," Freeman said. "You would have no idea where he was." Sometimes Washington would be at home but not answer his phone; he would make himself scarce just to make himself scarce.

Yet Metcalfe endured Washington because he needed him. Metcalfe derived his power from the Third Ward's eminence as a strong machine ward. In the 1963 mayor's race, the toughest election of his career, Daley won more votes in the Third Ward than any other except his own. Metcalfe was a plugger, but his true gift was that he had run the 100-yard dash faster than almost any human alive. Washington was bright and able and a font of political wisdom; by all accounts Washington, though he was twelve years Metcalfe's junior, served as his mentor.

When the local state representative retired, Metcalfe saw a perfect opportunity: he would reward Washington by sending him downstate to Springfield. He would keep him in the organization but promote him out of his hair. Metcalfe understood that he was gambling, but he also sensed that Washington was growing impatient—he had to give him something. In 1964, with the regular organization's backing, south side voters elected Washington their new state representative.

Renault Robinson admits that as a young cop shopping around for a state legislator bold enough to stand up to the machine he never gave Harold Washington a thought. To him, being part of the machine automatically meant you were just a ward heeler. In the late 1960s, Robinson was quickly making a name for himself as an antimachine crusader—a "wild-eyed dreamer," the press dubbed the twenty-six-year-old Robinson. Robinson may have been green, but he knew enough to know wild-eyed dreamers didn't get anywhere with machine pols. To him, Washington was a middle-aged black man with middle-class sensibilities who didn't much care about police brutality against the poor.

Robinson had graduated from the police academy a few years earlier. He saw firsthand cops beating blacks for the sport of it—what Mike Royko once described as "the natural instinct of Chicago policemen to knock around the poor, the black, and the politically impotent." Assignment to a black precinct was, Robinson said, "almost like a rite of passage for some of these guys . . . They'd get their yah-yahs out in a black district and then be transferred to a white district once they had gotten it out of their system."

Robinson and others founded a small group called the Afro-American Patrolmen's League (AAPL). Its symbol was a raised black fist against a police star; its aim was to fight the racism they felt as minority officers within a white-dominated department. Two months after the league's birth, Robinson was written up by his superiors, besmirching his otherwise exemplary record. He was written up a second time a few weeks later and cited dozens more times for minor infractions routinely broken by the entire force. The AAPL further angered the top police brass by asking after the Panther raid that left Fred Hampton and Mark Clark dead why the officers did not first use tear gas if their aim was merely to seize weapons. The AAPL grew in stature, and Robinson was suspended from the force. After a court order reinstated him, he was banished to the graveyard shift, his assigned beat a single block behind central police headquarters.

His fight against police brutality prompted Robinson to go shopping for a legislator. In other locales, civilian review boards were established to monitor police brutality. The AAPL had in mind a similar proposal, though more modest by comparison—they proposed a board mixing police and civilians—but even the black independents and the white liberals shied away from the bill.

Robinson understood why. His own experience taught him what it meant to accuse the Chicago police of racism. Robinson said each of the independents had the same answer: I'll go along with you but not as the chief sponsor. They were independent of the machine, but none were keen on giving Daley cause to go after them with a vengeance. The police department was Daley's; his own interest was all the civilian input the department ever needed. No one told Daley how to run his police department.

Thus it was with a sense of resignation that Robinson approached Harold Washington. Washington said sure, he would sponsor the bill.

By the late 1960s, Metcalfe must have been questioning his sanity in slating Washington for the state legislature. It was more than his sponsorship of Robinson's measure—from the start Washington was trouble.

In Springfield it was called the "idiot card"—a sheet the machine printed up showing state representatives how they should vote, bill by bill. The loyal machine soldier was expected to follow it as gospel, yet Washington was forever voting the wrong way. Adlai Stevenson III, Washington's seatmate, noticed how seriously Washington contemplated the idiot card. Washington didn't vote willy-nilly. He carefully chose those issues on which he would buck the machine.

In Chicago, Washington got himself into a different kind of trouble. Bennett Johnson, a good friend from his Roosevelt days, was a leading force in antimachine politics and an unrepentant leftist, as was his friend Gus Savage. All Washington's good friends, it seemed, were radicals of one kind or another. The women he saw were more often than not part of some movement; one friend credited Washington with first making her aware of Frantz Fanon* and other radical thinkers. Both the Chicago police and the FBI kept files on Washington's political activities.

In the late 1950s Bennett Johnson and Gus Savage helped start a group called the League of Negro Voters; in 1963 both were involved in the creation of another group, Protest at the Polls, which was meant to extend beyond the black community. Washington regularly attended their meetings, though both were expressly antimachine organizations. "Our unofficial adviser," Johnson described Washington. When Johnson ran for alderman, Washington tried to convince Metcalfe that he would be wise to support him. Expand your powers, Washington cajoled; add a satellite to your orbit. Metcalfe refused, but a core of Third Ward Young Democrats worked for Johnson. "Harold's irregulars" they were called—young Washington acolytes who showed up at Protest at the Polls meetings.

More than once Daley instructed Metcalfe to dump Washington and find someone who would toe the line, but Metcalfe stood by Washington. Perhaps Metcalfe was displaying a flash of boldness and loyalty, but it was more likely he feared a mutiny. The backbone of his organization was the

---

*Frantz Fanon, a psychiatrist, was a hero of the black power advocates, and his book *The Wretched of the Earth* was a guiding light. Fanon's thesis, that violence by an oppressed people is not only tactically sound but psychologically healthy, made him required reading among the Panthers. *The Wretched of the Earth* was among the books found beside the murdered Fred Hampton's bed, splattered with blood.

51

Young Democrats, who were more committed to Washington than to him; the young blood that coursed through his organization was the secret of its success. "Washington was indispensable to Metcalfe," said one former captain, "so he got away with a whole lot."

But aligning himself with the Afro-American Patrolmen's League, jamming Daley with federal discrimination suits and bad press, was too much. Metcalfe informed Washington that he was on his own. He would no longer stand up to Daley on his behalf.

Washington called Metcalfe every nasty thing he could think of and then told him he didn't need him anyway. "You have your white man and I've got mine," he yelled at Metcalfe. Metcalfe had Daley, but Washington had the support of a man named John Touhy, the Speaker of the Illinois House and a former state party chair.

Touhy chewed Washington out—"What the hell do you think Daley would do?"—and then smoothed things with Daley, who exacted a price. The organization would slate him for reelection, but in turn Washington would agree to serve on the Chicago Crime Commission, the group Daley formed to investigate the AAPL's charges of racial discrimination inside the force.

Washington would later recall these days with anger and humiliation. He had to trot out a powerful white patron to save his hide because he dared to speak out against cops beating on blacks without provocation. As he had expected, Daley's Crime Commission was nothing more than a means for quieting down the protest; the commission declared the AAPL's allegations unwarranted. Washington admitted he felt like Daley's "showcase nigger."

Legislators Washington was friendly with had warned him: don't confront Daley, a national symbol of law and order, on the police. Yet who understood what made this Washington fellow from the south side tick?

There were two kinds of Chicago politicians, and Washington fit neither profile. He was certainly a cut above most of the others the machine sent to Springfield; he was bright, talented, and had a way with words. But he did not resemble the prototype of an antimachine independent. He was a savvy parliamentarian who understood how to leverage his vote to attain support for his own pet bills. He did not possess the Chicago independent's aversion to legislative horse trading nor her penchant for hopeless causes. Washington defied the idiot card but, characteristically, only when he thought he could win.

Yet Robinson's civilian review board, an anathema to Chicago Democrats and Republicans alike, stood no chance of passage. It was as if Washington the canny politician was suddenly playing Washington the activist. He pushed the bill hard as its chief sponsor, mostly, it seemed, to draw some attention to the issue. No, they could never figure out this guy Washington.

Washington divorced his wife while he was still in his twenties, before taking a job with the city. By all accounts theirs was never much of a marriage. They lived thousands of miles apart in their first years as man and wife; by the time Washington returned stateside, he said, it was plain to both of them that they had grown apart. Others saw the relationship as doomed from the start. They were young and both were headstrong. "Not the marrying kind," Bennett Johnson said of his friend.

He was a man set in his routines, unforgiving of intrusions. "A rigorous S.O.B. in that regard," said an ex-girlfriend who remained a lifelong Washington intimate. Each day he woke up to WBBM, the city's all-news radio station; in the car he listened only to the news. There were always meetings to attend and never time for a vacation. He was always too busy to perform basic tasks like washing his clothes yet always made time for carousing. One was as likely to catch up with Washington at a bar called the Black Hole in the basement of the building housing the Third Ward offices as reach him by phone at home.

Bennett Johnson was a frequent drinking buddy. Through the 1960s "we drank scotch and chased women, spending a lot of time being boys," Johnson said. "Kind of an asshole" to women, Johnson described his friend. He advocated on behalf of women in Springfield, often placing himself at odds with the machine (on abortion, for instance), but back in Chicago he was always dumping on one woman or another. Washington's longtime secretary, Delores Woods, lived in the same building as Washington when he and Bennett Johnson were at their wildest. Woods declined to talk about the man with whom she worked for twenty years, but colleagues quote her as saying, "If every woman Harold slept with stood at one end of City Hall, the building would sink five inches into LaSalle Street."

Visitors to Washington's apartment were always struck by its appearance. The refrigerator was usually empty, and there were only a few personal touches; one frequent visitor said it looked more like a motel room than an apartment. Little hung on the walls. Newspapers, magazines, and clothes were invariably strewn about. Several books lay open facedown, partially read. As often as not he woke up and realized he didn't have a matching pair of clean socks, a former girlfriend said.

Friends saw a lot of the little boy in Washington—his stubbornness, playfulness, and sense of fairness not unlike a five-year-old's. He bruised easily and was known to pout. He was also forgetful, always missing appointments or promising to call someone and then failing to do so. More than once Dempsey Travis and his wife delayed a dinner party, waiting for Washington. Lost in what I was reading, he would say and then smile, hoping his charm would set everything straight.

One girlfriend knew from the start he was a different kind of man. On their first date he gave her a book by Harold Cruse called *The Crises of the Negro Intellectual;* published in 1967, it was then the rage among black militants and intellectuals. On their second date they ate on 63rd Street and talked about Roy Washington, Jr.'s involvement in the numbers with a cop who Washington told her was on the take. Washington called her around 6 P.M. on New Year's Eve. He seemed hurt, she said, when she told him she already had plans.

On her way home she passed Washington's car wrapped around a telephone pole at 33rd Street. He had gotten drunk at his mother's place and then gone to a bar. Later he said he was driving the streets looking for her when he lost control of the car. "I'm in the hospital and it's all your fault," he lisped through his jaw, which was wired shut. He showed he could forgive her for a circumstance that was his fault by forever referring to the scar on his face by her name.

Washington's distracted air was troubling to more than just friends. He failed to file his income tax forms in 1964 and 1965—his first two years in Springfield—and then again in 1967 and 1969. When the IRS caught up with him in 1971, he was sentenced to forty days in jail and fined $1,000. Washington was the rare individual sentenced to jail for a misdemeanor tax violation.*

*Old associates figured his punishment was due to his wars with Daley, though Washington believed it was Metcalfe who blew the whistle on him. Another theory was that he was one of countless victims of the Nixon White House: he was prosecuted after he led a walkout of fellow legislators when then–Vice President Spiro Agnew spoke before the Illinois General Assembly.

Years later those contemplating Washington as a potential candidate for mayor did not fail to take his tax troubles into account—they just didn't see it as a big liability. The $508 he ended up owing the government was minor, so it obviously wasn't the money; he simply never bothered to settle up yearly with the government to see who owed how much to whom.

In a 1974 endorsement of Washington, the *Sun-Times* said "his contributions to the legislature and to his constituents far outweigh personal problems he had in the past." The *Tribune* declared that Washington had "redeemed himself" through hard work and service. The media didn't see Washington's past sin as an impediment to their support. Why should it make a difference a decade later?

Washington did not begin his political career thinking the machine would be a progressive force on the issue of race and then, with time, mend its racist ways, those who knew him best said. He would leave when the regular Democratic organization became unnecessary, when he was finally strong enough to get elected without it. For him it had never been anything more than a means to an end.

Yet in the meantime dignity was something Washington found increasingly difficult to maintain. Washington's friend Charles Freeman remembers picking him up at a local tavern in 1966 on the night a new black organization was born, devised for the sole purpose of informing Martin Luther King, Jr., that he was not welcome in Chicago. Freeman understood why he was hooking up with Washington at a bar and understood instinctively why his friend was bracing himself with alcohol. This was the evening the bill came due; attendance was mandatory. "We just sat there in the car for a while, maybe fifteen or twenty minutes," Freeman said. "Just sat. I don't remember if Harold said a single word." Washington sat in the back of the room and then blew off subsequent meetings, but by showing up that one time he had taken part.

King's visit to Chicago was one clarifying event for Washington, the Panther killings another. Washington was initially troubled by the murders of Hampton and Clark but he remained distanced. Then at a friend's insistence he toured the bullet-ravaged apartment, a scene she said that shook

Washington to the bone. He was outraged, yet what was he but a machine loyalist?

If anything, Washington had grown more cautious after butting heads with Daley over the police brutality issue. In 1967 the Independent Voters of Illinois ranked Washington third among the assembly's 177 legislators; by 1973 he had dropped to thirty-third. Every so often he ducked a vote when his conscience wouldn't allow him to support a machine proposal, yet opposing it was futile. One vote he avoided was a bill outlawing state-funded abortions.

Richard Barnett for one was not impressed with the fine line that Washington walked. As late as the mid-1970s, Washington was still pro-patronage, an anathema to the independents, and had a mixed record on election reform ("the machine's means for maintaining its grip on our community," Barnett said). Barnett appreciated that Washington was not some fool foisted on the black community (the machine, the black activist was always saying, gave us a Negro or a Colored thinking they're giving us a Black). But that made it worse in his eyes; a man of Washington's caliber lent it credibility. In 1974 when Washington moved up to the state Senate, he still had not fully broken with the machine.

Washington's violations of the idiot card were numerous. He voted for the Equal Rights Amendment, against state aid for those parents sending their kids to private and parochial schools, and in favor of an annual cost-of-living review of public aid. He successfully pushed a range of consumer protection measures, a fair housing code, and a bill strengthening the state's Fair Employment Practice Act. He helped organize the legislature's first ever black caucus and introduced a bill to establish a statewide holiday on Martin Luther King, Jr.'s birthday. In 1973 Illinois was alone among the fifty states in giving schoolchildren and state workers a day off in commemoration of King. Still, this was little solace. No matter what he accomplished in Springfield, back in Chicago he helped turn out the vote for Metcalfe and the machine he was coming to despise. After a time he told Dempsey Travis, "I looked at myself as one of the Toms."

In 1977 Washington ran for mayor, winning only eleven percent of the vote. He lost the black vote and got beat in one west side ward by more than three to one. But unlike Roman Pucinski, another challenger to Michael Bilandic's race for mayor, Washington did not return to the fold apologetic and contrite. "I'm going to do what maybe I should have done ten or twelve years ago," he told a group of black journalists. "I'm going to stay outside of that damn Democratic organization and give them hell."

In his first election free of the machine, in 1978, when Chicagoans chose their representatives in county and state governments, the organization slated several candidates against Washington, including Sabrina Washington and Denise Washington—both unknowns, both presumably nothing more than a machine tactic for diluting Washington's vote total. The machine's endorsed candidate was an obscure precinct captain of whom few people had ever heard, but they had the soldiers and their voters were registered. Washington won by only 219 votes.

Not long afterward Ralph Metcalfe died, and the party named a machine loyalist named Bennett Stewart to serve the rest of Metcalfe's term as congressman. Washington challenged Stewart in the next election, in 1980, beating Stewart and two other opponents. Though Jane Byrne, who had been elected mayor in 1979, offered several prominent black politicians a formidable campaign chest and unlimited manpower if they challenged Washington in 1982, none accepted the offer.

Washington's election to Congress was like an invigorating trip to the countryside after years in the city. For half his life he operated within the milieu of Chicago politics, a confining world of wheeling and dealing and turf battles that left little time for much else. Washington was no prima donna, but to him the fight was a means to some end. In Chicago there was never much end beyond survival.

Congress was long a dream of Washington's. During college he, Dempsey Travis, and Gus Savage would gather at Savage's apartment for evenings of study that turned into late-night bull sessions. The three created glorious futures for themselves: Travis was going to be a self-made millionaire, Savage an important publisher, and Washington a congressman representing the city's south side. By the end of the 1950s, Savage was publishing a chain of community papers, and Travis had cleared his first million. The slowest of these overachievers was stuck in downstate Illinois.

If Congress was not quite as he had envisioned it in his college days, Washington, D.C. was still a far cry from Springfield, where they turned off microphones in mid-speech and legislative aides cast votes on behalf of absent legislators, not per instruction but as a way of screwing a rival. In Springfield obsequious functionaries completely reliant on party honchos swaggered with power they did not possess.

Congress had its share of lightweights and fools, of course, but in Congress, Washington liked to say, he discovered his peers. He believed that he had finally reached his station in life.

Ronald Reagan and Harold Washington arrived in the capital at the same time. Reagan's victory was a disaster for Washington's constituents but a boon to his career. Democratic congressmen with far more seniority were ticklish about taking on the popular new president. The fight fell to braver, more resolute souls.

On Washington's congressional agenda was a full complement of causes crucial to the same people pushing him to run for mayor. In his first term Washington served as a floor leader in the House fight to extend the Voting Rights Act, the most significant civil rights victory of Ronald Reagan's first term. Mike Robinson, a reporter with the Associated Press, covered the Illinois congressional delegation, and Washington's handling of the voter rights fight impressed Robinson. Washington, Robinson told one Washington biographer, participated as an equal with congressional leaders with far more seniority. In a world where the typical freshman legislator "sits around and listens and occasionally comes up with some off-the-wall idea," he said, Washington's performance was "unheard of. . . . Washington is as astute in the cloakroom as any politician I've seen, and I've been in this business seventeen years."

Washington's politics were about as contrary to Reagan's as any elected official's. He supported a nuclear freeze and advocated a twenty percent cut in the defense budget (money spent on weapons systems, he argued, was money diverted from the cities) and opposed intervention in Central America. The *Congressional Quarterly* ranked him fifth in anti-Reagan votes among the House's 435 representatives.

Bold and articulate in his critique of Reagan, Washington appeared as a regular guest on the "MacNeil-Lehrer Newshour" and emerged as a leading figure in the congressional black caucus. Several colleagues were pushing Washington as the next caucus leader. Washington felt as if he was sitting on top of the world. He told people he could live out the rest of his days in Congress and die a happy man.

Those committed to electing a black mayor could have chosen any of a half-dozen others anxious to make the run. After the big blowup between Washington and Lu Palmer, Jesse Jackson told a *Sun-Times* columnist: "I am eligible. I am qualified. I could gain a significant following, which I deserve." Yet no one seemed to consider Jackson's trial balloon seriously. Jackson had placed fourth in the poll Lu Palmer based on the thirty-five thousand surveys he mailed out; in a survey of seventy-seven black leaders by a small monthly called the *Chicago Reporter,* Jackson tied for tenth place. Years later several of those most active in the push for a black mayor couldn't even recall that Jackson had expressed an interest.

Palmer dogged Washington throughout the fall, as did others. It seemed every week another half-dozen delegations dropped in on Washington, urging him to run. He put them off, telling them he was considering it but he also liked Congress. Meanwhile, those pushing for a black mayor acted as if he had already declared he would run. Around Labor Day, Renault Robinson was named manager of a phantom candidate's campaign.

Several weeks later Robinson phoned David Canter, a white independent with whom Washington spoke regularly. "Harold won't return my calls," Robinson complained. He asked Canter if he could let Washington know it was important that he call him, yet Canter couldn't reach Washington either. His D.C. staff told callers that he was traveling the country aiding fellow congressmen who were facing tough reelection battles. It seemed no one in Chicago could get through to Washington. (A headline in the *Metro News* in early October read, HAROLD WASHINGTON!—WHERE ARE YOU?) He wasn't acting like a man intent on changing jobs.

"I feel like a fool," Anna Langford, a black woman who had expressed an interest in running for mayor, cried out at one meeting in mid-October, with the election only four months off. They were challenging the Chicago machine, a formidable foe in any circumstance, yet they didn't even have a candidate. "I said I would run, and nobody paid me any attention,"

Langford said. "I went and printed up all kinds of stuff and spent money. And now here you are begging Harold and he won't run."

What Langford found frustrating, reporters saw as baffling. Why Washington, they wondered. Why did it have to be Washington, a candidate whom they saw as terribly flawed.

Most beat reporters knew as little about him as they knew about the rest of the black community: a stay in the county jail over taxes; machine most of his career; a protégé of Ralph Metcalfe; a run for mayor back in 1977. What they did know didn't jibe with the commitment to Washington by well-known figures like Renault Robinson and Lu Palmer.

The machine politicians who regularly dropped by the City Hall press room assured reporters there wasn't much of a story there. Washington was just a canny politician, they said, who understood that reform was a possible ticket to the mayor's seat, a man who was machine until it became unpopular in black Chicago. No less an authority than Mike Royko, Chicago's reigning columnist, dismissed Washington as a phony. "It wasn't until Metcalfe developed a late-life social conscience and independent streak that Washington decided he, too, should try it," Royko wrote.

Reporters like Royko never stopped long enough to ask what the black independents might know that they did not. Instead they assumed the likes of Robinson and Palmer were again being taken for fools.

For a Chicago politician nothing supersedes local politics. Chicago's Dan Rostenkowski is a powerhouse in Washington politics as chairman of the House Ways and Means Committee, but every four years he runs for reelection as the Democratic committeeman of the city's Thirty-second Ward. Conventional political wisdom holds that becoming a big-city mayor is a sure way to dash any hopes of higher office. Yet to the typical Chicago pol, there is no post higher than mayor.

When he was elected to Congress, Washington resisted stepping down as state senator, knowing that the machine would name his rival, State Representative James Taylor, to take his place. A hefty former prizefighter from Arkansas, Taylor was more loyal than he was bright, and he emerged as one of the south side's top political forces in the mid-1970s. Among the blacks beholden to the Daley machine, it was Taylor for whom Washington held a special contempt. (Taylor, south side activist Dorothy Tillman once said, was a powerhouse only because he was always "grinning and skinning" for the party honchos—"laughing when it's not funny," Tillman explained, "and scratching where it's not itching.") Washington couldn't hold both positions at once, of course, but his short-lived stance demonstrated that his promotion to Congress did not mean he was relieving himself of local grudges.

While he was campaigning for Congress, Washington's speeches were as much an occasion for blasting the machine as blasting Reaganomics. "They tell us no black person has the qualifications to be mayor," he said. "They tell us business wouldn't go along. . . . No black can run this town? He couldn't do any worse than Jane Byrne." He spoke of the need for a "black political revolt" to defeat a political organization that he described as "a hardy and resilient beast." He made countless appearances outside his congressional district, traveling to the city's north side for a peace rally or to a west side church for a Sunday morning service. He spoke of his 1977 run for mayor and the mistakes he made back then, though he always added that he did not intend to play the sacrificial lamb again.

There were signs that the time was now ripe for a black challenge. Early in Byrne's term, Washington's pollster reported that more than nine out of every ten blacks said they would vote for a "qualified black candidate" for mayor. (So high was the number that Washington insisted a second poll be taken.) Yet a willingness to vote for someone black didn't mean that people would. Black registration lagged an average of ten percentage points behind white registration. Give me fifty thousand new voters, Washington said at one meeting, and then we'll talk. Prove to me, Washington seemed to be telling them, that there's a vigor in the black community that will make this work. Fifty thousand voters, Washington told one intimate, is "the minimum number of chips I need to get into the game."

Some thought Washington just tossed out a number high enough to stop people from talking. What chance did they have at registering fifty thousand voters within a few months' time? Others, however, picked up the number as a challenge. Washington had finally given them something concrete.

The key, of course, would be to whip up enthusiasm. A declared candidate would have helped, but as any civil rights movement veteran knew, a far more important ingredient was a bogeyman against which to run.

4

THE
CATALYST

Early on in her tenure as mayor, Jane Byrne regularly invited Renault Robinson to her office to talk about the black community. Byrne had named Robinson to the board overseeing the Chicago Housing Authority (CHA), a selection so controversial and notable that, though Byrne appointed her brother's brother-in-law to another post that same day, it was Robinson who made headlines. The machine regulars were nearly apoplectic: the thought of lending support to this rapscallion, whose racial discrimination suit against the city established hiring and promoting quotas in the police department, sickened them.

Robinson's place as a trusted Byrne adviser lasted perhaps a year, but during their time together he laid out for Byrne how she might remain popular among blacks. Respect the black community, he advised; don't think you're fooling anyone by empowering a black lackey more loyal to you than to them. Robinson's assessment of Byrne was clouded by later events, but even then he said he was not impressed with Byrne. Given the machine's past abuses, securing the black community's support should have been as easy as choosing respected figures for top positions. Robinson could have offered no better example than his own appointment.

Long after the two had broken their alliance, Robinson stood in City Hall before an assembly of reporters to criticize Byrne. Just days after Lu Palmer's black plebiscite in July 1982, Byrne had appointed three people to the CHA board; all three were white. When she named Robinson and another well-respected black figure to the CHA board, she was hailed inside the black community for tipping the board's racial balance from white to black. Now, just seven months before election day, she was reinstalling a white majority on a board that oversaw a public housing system that was eighty-five percent black.

Publicly, Robinson voiced his indignation. The mayor had again shown a callous disregard for black Chicago, he said. To himself, though, he chuckled. Ain't that just like Janie, he thought. The woman inadvertently provided the kindling just when they were trying to start a fire.

Jane Byrne was elected mayor in 1979 in a stunning political upset. She had next to no money and little field organization. Still, Byrne's election was no more improbable than the rest of her political career.

She grew up comfortably, the second of six children born to a well-off Irish couple living on the city's northwest side in Sauganash. Years later she would admit that she was "a very spoiled girl," one who "never had to worry about anything." She dreamed of becoming a doctor, but while studying at Barat College of the Sacred Heart, a small woman's school north of Chicago, she met a Notre Dame man named William Byrne. Like a great many bright young women of that era, Byrne chose marriage over a career. After graduation she took a job teaching fourth graders in a parochial school but she stayed in the job less than a year. The two were married soon after, just before William Byrne entered the Marine Corps.

Tragedy hit in 1959. Byrne was twenty-seven-years old, at home with a five-month-old baby, when she learned her husband was killed in a plane crash. She moved back into her family's Sauganash home, and although money wasn't the problem, the question was, what would she do with her life?

To shake her out of her grief, Byrne's family cajoled her into joining the presidential campaign of a young Irish Catholic politician named John

F. Kennedy. She had no political experience, but family connections won her a good spot in the campaign. After that she dabbled in politics, treating it more as a social thing than anything else. She attended fancy receptions in and around Sauganash, a community of judges, city commissioners, and other Irish Americans with heavy clout at City Hall, which is how she met Richard J. Daley, then in his third term as mayor.

Daley was at a party honoring a Sauganash pastor who had known Byrne since she was a girl. The way Byrne tells it, the pastor introduced her to Daley, and Daley asked her why her face looked so familiar. They chatted briefly, and then Daley said the magic words: "Come see me."

Daley took an immediate liking to Byrne, not yet thirty, dressed in ruffles and short skirts, with ribbons in her hair and thickly applied eye shadow. In their first meeting, according to Byrne, Daley lectured her about the company she kept—the swells who pooh-poohed the machine as something crude and beneath them. If you worked with us during the Kennedy campaign, Daley told her, you might have gotten something out of it—a job, maybe.

The average person finding herself in a one-on-one with Richard Daley simply nodded her head a lot. But Byrne—at least in her telling—shot right back that she got out of the election just what she wanted: Kennedy won. Daley supposedly smiled and told her she would have to pay her dues before he could consider her for a job. Yet only six months later Byrne was working as a mid-level bureaucrat with special access to the mayor.

It was always Daley's way to pick people throughout the bureaucracy he could trust to serve as his eyes and ears. Byrne also may have served as a window on the Sauganash crowd whose support Daley coveted. Winning over the "lace-curtain" Irish was a Daley priority; until the racial upheaval of the mid-1960s, Daley was far more popular among black voters than white.

Daley could hardly contain himself when he called Byrne into his office four years after she started with the city to talk to her about problems in the city's Department of Consumer Sales, Weights, and Measures. What the department needed, he told her, was a new commissioner. When he asked what she thought that new commissioner would need to do to improve things, Byrne confessed that she had never heard of the department. Daley giggled. He was a burly man, looked upon as a tyrant by many, yet he emitted a high-pitched, girlish laugh whenever excited. Byrne never forgot his next words: "If I'm not mistaken, you will be the first woman commissioner in any major city in the United States."

Consumer Sales was a small department rife with corruption. Those charged with inspecting the meat and produce scales under the department's charge were the main problem. In a city notorious for employees on the take, legend held that the city's inspectors were the most corrupt of them all.* Plenty of store owners found it cheaper to slip cash to an inspector than meet the codes; many inspectors were happy to oblige them. Off on their own all day, some inspectors double-dipped, meaning they worked a second job on city time. The less ambitious spent their time in a bar or at home.

Byrne did a good job at Consumer Sales. She had no management experience or experience as a consumer advocate, but she tapped another source—ambition or perhaps naïveté—that served her well. She cleaned up the more blatant corruption; she rotated routes, and in the black community she replaced many of the white inspectors with black inspectors. At least several of the double-dippers were fired or, if protected by enough clout, transferred to another department to become someone else's headache.

Where most department heads shied away from reporters, Byrne actually pursued media attention. She pushed for a ban on phosphates and favored legislation that limited the permissible lead levels in house paint, battles she fought as much by leaking stories to reporters as twisting arms within the bureaucracy. Years later Ralph Nader publicly commended Byrne for the job she did as commissioner.

By the early 1970s, Byrne was proving herself an invaluable asset to Daley, someone with some media savvy whom he could trust. She was also one of the few women inside the machine family at a time when feminists were pressing him to open up the party to women. Of the eighty Democratic committeemen (fifty from the city, thirty from suburban townships) who constituted the Cook County Democratic organization, only one was a

---

*In 1979 nearly half the inspectors in a single bureau were indicted by a grand jury for accepting bribes. The majority of them were convicted.

woman. The numbers inside City Hall were no better. Byrne was still the only woman among the fifty-plus city commissioners, and hers was a small and obscure department.

At Daley's behest Byrne headed up a project aimed at starting a ladies auxiliary in each ward. The stated goal was to give women a greater role in party politics, yet the ward-based women's groups were little more than social clubs offering courses on the proper way to apply makeup and so on. Daley bolstered Byrne's prestige when in 1975 he announced that the two of them would serve as co-chairs of the Cook County Democratic organization. It was a safe assumption that Daley was not relinquishing half of his powers to Byrne after spending twenty-two years consolidating his control over the party.

Women's groups pushed Byrne to use her new position as co-chair to champion the pro-ERA bill languishing in the Illinois legislature. Advocates of the ERA had identified Illinois as a key swing state, but Byrne would not even endorse the proposed amendment let alone push for its passage. "There are a lot of women on the southwest side who aren't for it," one pro-ERA lobbyist quoted Byrne as saying. Daley, who saw no reason for the Equal Rights Amendment, also opposed the measure.

Byrne's influence ended abruptly with Daley's death in 1976. She was not fired, but suddenly she was merely the head of a small city department located several blocks from City Hall. Mayor Bilandic did not call her in for political talks, and no one seemed even to consider her to take Daley's place as the new chairwoman of the party. Where once hers was a charmed existence inside City Hall, she now had to contend with sexism and the bad feelings of other committeemen. Wayward inspectors and others who resented her high-profile ambitions won retribution by simply freezing her out.

Byrne retaliated by going public with an allegation she would never have made in the past: she accused the new mayor and several of his allies of pushing through an illegal taxi fare hike. Federal prosecutors assigned to the case found no evidence on which to indict, but her accusations won her positive media attention. People recognizing her on the street called out words of encouragement. Her firing soon afterward fueled suspicions that she was telling the truth and won her more headlines. In less than a year she had gone from Daley protégée to antimachine hero.

Byrne announced her candidacy for mayor five months after she was fired. City Hall could not have changed much in the sixteen months since Bilandic took over as caretaker, yet she charged that the city was now run by a "cabal of evil men." If elected, she promised to expel the "devious and dishonorable" from City Hall. Fighting Jane declared war on the mighty machine.

The snow fell with a vengeance during the 1979 campaign—eighty-seven inches that winter, more than twice the thirty-seven-inch average. Bilandic assured people that the streets were already plowed, though a peek out the window showed they had not been. After one bad storm he ordered people to move their cars to designated city lots to allow the plows to pass, yet many of the lots had not been plowed. The newspapers carried headlines about the machine crony who received $90,000 the previous year to draw up a new snow-removal plan—a report he had left unfinished.

Conventional wisdom held that Byrne won because of the snow, but the furor over the snow was only a symptom. The black vote elected Byrne mayor; even the success of Byrne's snow campaign was largely a black phenomenon. During one storm the city closed ten stops on the elevated train line during the morning and evening commute hours. All ten were located in black communities. On one line the train made its regular suburban stops, whizzed by six inner-city stations, then resumed its regular stops once it reached downtown. A Bilandic spokesman pointed out that the closings affected only one in every five riders, but that was hardly consolation for those waiting on street corners for jam-packed buses that were as likely to pass as stop because they were already too crowded.

Candidate Byrne said all the right things in the black community. She lambasted Bilandic for the el closings and promised to take full advantage of any available federal housing dollars—off-limits since the city refused to build scattered-site housing in nonblack areas of the city. A strong-willed woman, she was generally well received by black audiences.

Byrne won the Democratic nomination by only seventeen thousand votes. She lost the white vote but more than made up the difference by beating Bilandic by a three-to-two margin among black voters. She beat her Republican foe with eighty-seven percent of the vote.

Jane Byrne's election night celebration was a bittersweet affair for many of her supporters. Elena Martinez had joined the Byrne campaign the previous summer when it was little more than a family affair. Martinez became the campaign's office manager and proved a valuable political asset as well. Politically active, Martinez served as a liaison to a community in which Byrne did not have many contacts. A certified therapist, Martinez cut her client pool to free her time and borrowed money to meet her monthly bills. On several occasions, Martinez told one Byrne biographer, Byrne told her that, if elected, she wanted to find a place for her in city government.

After Byrne won the primary, Martinez wrote a memo laying out her ideas for initiating Byrne's promises to the Latino community, yet not until after she had already given notice at her job did Martinez begin noticing the changes. Where formerly Byrne would chat with her and other staff members by the coffeepot, she was suddenly available by appointment only. Martinez sought a meeting with Byrne to discuss her memo, but her requests were ignored. The two ran into each other once, but Byrne told her that she would respond to the memo when she was good and ready.

Byrne also began meeting with Vito Marzullo. Byrne did not specifically single out Marzullo as one of the evil caballeros, but she might as well have. A ward boss from the near west side who ruled over an area of the city that was predominantly Latino, Marzullo didn't even bother slating a Latino front man to serve as alderman. Instead he chose to keep both the alderman and committeeman posts for himself. Martinez had joined the Byrne campaign to rid her community of the Marzullos, yet he now seemed to have more access to Byrne than she did.

Perhaps it was desperation that drove Byrne to turn to those like Marzullo who were part of her past. A relatively anonymous department head who parlayed a few headlines into a serious run for mayor, she was ill-prepared to govern. "Get rid of all those crackpots," Marzullo said he told Byrne—get rid of the pointy-headed liberals and loud-talking minorities who had always been the bane of his life. Before election day the campaign staff was abuzz with talk that Byrne had already cut a deal with Marzullo and the other party regulars. In her acceptance speech Byrne assured her supporters that she would not sell out "the chairman of the party and the people in the neighborhoods"—those she credited with placing her in office. Elena Martinez was not surprised when, after Byrne took office, there was no job waiting for her.

THE CATALYST

After the election Don Rose, the campaign manager, suggested to Byrne that they splurge on a big party for all the volunteers. Not interested, Byrne told him. "One day it was a camaraderie in the struggle," Rose said, "the next day it was ice." It was, Rose said, as if they had carried her to the newly vacated castle by torchlight, set her in power, and then returned in the morning only to be chased from the grounds.

An experienced hand in independent politics, Rose did not doubt that the candidate-elect had already sold out "to the party bosses and wanted none of these antiparty people visible and close to her." Rose recalls giving her a spontaneous hug the night of her victory. Byrne recoiled.

As a writer familiar with the dark catacombs of Chicago history, Mike Royko is a man difficult to impress. In his book *Boss,* Royko wrote about the City Hall–Cook County Building: though a single building divided equally into two nearly identical parts, the city's half cost substantially more to build. "Chicago history is full of such oddities," Royko wrote. "Flip open any page and somebody is making a buck." For years Royko said the city should change its motto to *Ubi Est Mea*—Where's Mine?

Byrne managed to impress Royko. Comparing her government to the Daley administration struck him as inadequate; instead he traveled further back into history, comparing her to a pair of Chicago legends who ruled the city through the 1930s and into the 1940s. "Chicago," he wrote, "is being run by the most dubious set of characters since the days of the Kelly-Nash machine."

Daley was an iron-fisted despot, but the Daleys of this country cut the deals that gave national liberal figures access to real power. Under Daley, Chicago was dubbed "the city that works." That may have been like heralding Mussolini for making the trains run on time, but at least a citizen got *something* in the deal. Byrne's government reflected none of the stability of the Daley era. In her first two years in office Byrne employed three chiefs of staff, three press secretaries, and three police superintendents. She acted decisively and swiftly, and then would undo her own actions six months later.

The same evil caballeros she denounced during her campaign dominated her administration. While still a city commissioner, Byrne had fingered Alderman Ed Vrdolyak as the "middle man" in the taxicab scheme she railed against. "A fast-buck artist," she said of Vrdolyak during the campaign. Yet where Vrdolyak was powerful in the past, under Byrne he consolidated his clout. He took over as her council floor leader and with Byrne's assistance seized control of the party.

Byrne denied that she took part in Vrdolyak's coronation, but there were many who said otherwise, such as the committeeman who said on the record that Byrne's patronage chief offered him extra jobs to cast his ballot for Vrdolyak as Cook County Democratic party chairman. Through most of the Byrne years the pundits and editorialists referred to Vrdolyak as the "co-mayor."

Byrne's betrayal of the antimachine independents was thorough and complete. She promised to cut the city work force by at least ten percent, yet there were about six hundred more people on the payroll when she left office than in 1979. As a mayoral candidate she vowed to champion an ethics ordinance and a freedom of information act, yet she never moved on either promise despite her council majority. Her pledge to place a $1,000 limit on campaign contributions from city contractors was similarly empty. The neighborhood groups that supported Byrne because she promised to see beyond downtown interests were disappointed as well; under Byrne nearly three-fourths of the city's economic development money was spent fixing up downtown, an area that provided less than one-fifth of the city's jobs. Incredibly, women held few positions of power in the administration of the first woman to be elected mayor of a major American city.

Byrne's betrayal of black Chicago came more gradually. At first she amply rewarded black Chicago for its support. Four in every five Chicago public school students were black or Latino, yet the school board was always ruled by a white majority. Byrne named five blacks and three Latinos to the school board, shifting the balance of power on the eleven-member board. She chose a black man to head the Chicago Transit Authority (CTA) and named a black cop to serve as the acting chief of police. Both were not only significant firsts but important offerings to the black community, given past discrimination in both of these departments. Renault Robinson was another break with the past. Byrne chose Robinson knowing that he was not someone whose vote she could be certain of controlling.

Yet suddenly it was as if a new mayor more hostile to black Chicago took over at midterm. Claiming she wanted to recruit a new police chief from outside the department, she eased out the acting chief and then promoted a white insider to take his place. She fired the CTA director and replaced him with someone white. In 1981 when the school board was working out a court-ordered desegregation plan, she replaced two blacks on the board with two whites, reshifting the majority to the white board members. The two white women Byrne chose were neighborhood leaders in the fight against further desegregation of the Chicago public schools.

Even Byrne's gifts to black Chicago fueled mistrust. She appointed the school system's first black school superintendent but simultaneously created a finance authority that took the budget out of the superintendent's hands. The first black superintendent had the dubious distinction of serving as the first one who didn't control the money.

The *Chicago Reporter*, which specialized in race issues, discovered a peculiar drop in the hiring of blacks during Byrne's tenure. The city's population was forty percent black when Byrne took over as mayor, and in 1980 and 1981, forty-seven percent of the new city employees hired by Byrne were black. Yet in 1982 only twenty-eight percent of the city's new jobs went to blacks, while sixty-four percent went to whites.*

The highest-ranking black in Byrne's administration was Harold Washington's rival, James "Bull-Jive" Taylor. The origin of his nickname was instructive. In 1978 two women approached Taylor about a liquor license for a bar they had in mind. Taylor, in turn, told them that they would have to sleep with him first. He confessed this to Mike Royko, adding, "It was some jive talk because I didn't want to get into the lounge thing with them." Two years later Byrne named Taylor her deputy chief of staff. Still, Taylor's promotion seemed minor compared to Byrne's overseeing the final triumphant years of the black community's bête noire, Charles Swibel.

Swibel seemed the perfect symbol of the city's indifference to blacks in Chicago. He made his money operating fleabag apartment buildings along the city's Madison Street skid row ("Flophouse Charlie," the editorialists

---

*The *Reporter* also found that Byrne was hardly better than her predecessors in her appointments to the major boards and commissions in Chicago government. Where twenty-one percent of Daley's and twenty-one percent of Bilandic's appointments had been black, Byrne accelerated that pace only to twenty-three percent.

and columnists dubbed him). Yet in 1956, Daley named him to the CHA board and then, in the early 1960s, elevated him to board chairman.

Swibel wouldn't remain a slumlord for long. Somehow the owner of skid-row hotels scraped together around $50 million in loans to invest in Marina City, a pair of imposing self-contained apartment buildings built downtown along the Chicago River. Much of the money he borrowed from the Continental Bank which held the CHA's deposits of millions of dollars at a time. At least twice Swibel blocked attempts to transfer the CHA's money to another bank, thwarting other CHA board members who believed the agency could get better interest rates.

Swibel never fully paid Continental all the money he owed. In just one of its many astute business deals of that era, the bank absolved Swibel's corporation of the remaining $3.4 million it still owed on Marina City. Continental deemed the money uncollectible though an IRS official told the *Sun-Times,* which broke the story, that Continental didn't try very hard to collect. Of course Continental might want to avoid muscling someone like Swibel, for at the time Continental was negotiating a $50 million redevelopment deal with the city. Swibel was the city's chief negotiator on the project.

Renault Robinson said he accepted a spot on the CHA board only because Byrne encouraged him to fight Swibel at every turn. Yet, like Mayors Daley and Bilandic before her, Byrne found Swibel indispensable.

Robinson hadn't been on the CHA board a year when Byrne asked him to resign. How about a spot on the school board? Robinson said Byrne asked him. Or if not the school board, then another board or a handsome salary on the city payroll—anything if he would step down from the CHA board. Robinson was dumbfounded but clear-headed enough to read between the lines: the fool had cut herself a deal with old Charlie, he told himself.*

"I can't govern this city unless I cut a deal with them," Robinson quoted Byrne. "I have no constituency in the council. I don't have anything

*One of Robinson's fellow CHA board members was a black man named Leon Finney. Finney, the head of a community organization in a poor black neighborhood called Woodlawn, would also prove an appointment that Byrne regretted. Yet Byrne had something over Finney—a $30 to $50 million city commitment to finance the construction of about four hundred town houses in Woodlawn—and was able to swing Finney's vote to Swibel on several key matters.

in the bureaucracy. I bark orders from the fifth floor and nobody listens. If I don't have these people along with me, government won't operate."

Swibel was an adviser to Daley and Bilandic, but it was under Byrne that he found new roles and power. Byrne made no secret of her reliance on Swibel. He was there on the tarmac standing beside her when Ronald Reagan flew into town, and he served as her chief negotiator in a firefighters' strike, a state-financed CTA bailout, and other high-profile crises. In 1982 the City Club, a local civic group, released a report criticizing "political meddling" in the Chicago public library, from the hiring of clerks to the granting of big-money contracts. "Virtually every controversy, every example of political manipulation of the library board staff and finances is traced to Swibel," the report concluded. A Royko column appearing during the 1983 election ran under the headline, ELIMINATE MIDDLEMAN: ELECT CHARLIE!

Swibel was most invaluable to Byrne as a fund-raiser. A federal investigation into the CHA revealed that "some $50 million in CHA modernization funds have been sitting in local banks earning comparatively low interest rates"—banks, not coincidentally, that contributed handsomely to Byrne's 1983 campaign. When he ran as the Democratic candidate for governor in 1982, Adlai Stevenson III accused Swibel of shaking him down for a $5,000 contribution in exchange for Byrne's endorsement. The Stevenson allegation made the papers, but this bit of political extortion was treated as a relatively minor story. It was like the old newspaper adage about a dog biting a man: where was the news?

Those gathering in Lu Palmer's basement or at Washington's 79th Street office or in countless similar meetings around town were fed up with the Swibels and the Hanrahans, fed up with politicians who relied on the black vote and gave little in return. The black grass roots had taken a critical step toward crafting a unity between ideological factions; they endured long meetings with people they could barely tolerate. Black Chicago was equally disgusted, they told themselves. Yet these committed souls were hardly a barometer of black Chicago's mood.

Byrne aligned herself with Swibel, but so had Bilandic and so had Daley. Why would black Chicago react any differently this time? At the south side's Robert Taylor Homes, the nation's largest housing project, anger at the government's indifference should have been high. Taylor's residents suffered crime rates that were tragically greater than the rest of the city's. The murder rate among Taylor's fifteen thousand residents was more than twenty-five times greater than the city average; a woman living in Taylor was twenty times as likely to be raped. Yet the registration rate in the projects lagged well below the average for the rest of the black community.

At around the same time that Washington was giving the commencement address to the graduates of Palmer's first voter education classes, the federal government released a dryly worded report critical of the CHA. Released in early 1982, it seemed nothing more than a rehashing of the already well documented: a "profound confusion and disarray" besets the CHA; "no one seems to really care"; top managers are less interested in good-quality housing than acquiring federal dollars for patronage; political connections serve as the main criteria for promotion, not competence or experience. This latest Housing and Urban Development (HUD) report would have gathered dust on a shelf somewhere if HUD's regional director hadn't made headlines tying future funding to Charles Swibel's dismissal.

Rather than accepting HUD's ultimatum, Byrne spent $35,000 in city funds on advertisements defending Swibel. But several months later Byrne capitulated. The same week that Lu Palmer held his plebiscite Byrne picked a new white CHA chairman. She also unveiled a CHA reorganization plan that expanded the board by two people, naming two whites to fill the posts. The two new board members were older women. One had no housing experience, and the other was the wife of a politically connected judge, an insurance saleswoman who had won top sales awards at Prudential Life Insurance Company but whose housing experience amounted to participation in her condominium association and a place on the board of a local nursing home.

Worse still was the man Byrne chose to take Swibel's place, a thirty-year-old named Andrew Mooney. Swibel had hired Mooney the previous year to serve as executive director, and the same HUD report that scored Swibel criticized Mooney as ill-prepared to contend with the serious fiscal, administrative, and physical problems confronting the CHA. Mooney had no managerial experience or any management training, and he acknowledged as much when he confessed to a HUD investigator that he had been appointed primarily because of loyalty to the mayor.

The furor that followed was as intense as it was predictable. Hundreds amassed at City Hall on the day the three appointees were scheduled to appear before the City Council. Some arrived as early as 7 A.M., but few were granted a seat inside. The doors were not opened to the public until the council chambers were already packed with city employees slipped in through a side door. Byrne ducked out a back door after the vote, eluding both the public and the press. When demonstrators gathered outside Byrne's apartment, she had them arrested. Lu Palmer was among those taken into custody. Byrne couldn't have done more to cast Palmer and others as both heroes and victims if she tried.

The midterm turnabout in Byrne's treatment of blacks was dramatic and transparent, as if it was a purposeful attempt to alienate this large and seemingly vital segment of her coalition. One theory making its way around City Hall in the summer of 1982 was that Byrne, down in the polls, took a calculated risk by attempting to appease white voters. One black Byrne adviser explained in a not-for-attribution interview that Byrne antagonized the black community to increase her support among whites. With the black ward bosses on her side in 1983, conventional wisdom held that she could count on a bedrock forty percent of the black vote, as had Bilandic in 1979 despite closing the el stations in the black community during the big snow.

Byrne denied the charge. It was not her policy, she said, to appoint people on the basis of their race. Yet desperation appears to have been a factor. The party's polls showed that Daley's eldest son, Richard M. (Rich), should he run, would beat Byrne handily. One conducted shortly before Byrne made her CHA appointments showed Daley, the county's state's attorney, a full thirty points ahead of her. Byrne held her own among black voters but was well behind among whites. These same polls showed that whites widely regarded Byrne as too pro-black.

If Byrne did not deliberately turn the black community on herself, then she was less a politician than people believed. Byrne learned politics at the knee of the mighty Buddha himself, yet she violated a cardinal rule of machine politics when she upset the CHA board's fragile balance. Think long and hard before swinging control over the Board of Elections to the Poles if it was defined long ago as an Italian enclave. Byrne compounded her error by violating that rule as the outlines of a black political movement were taking shape.

Shifting the CHA board's racial balance was not unlike Bilandic's CTA blunder—an easily exploited symbol that allowed organizers to state things in simple and unmistakable terms. Three whites named to a board that oversees housing projects nearly all black revealed a much simpler message than a carefully reasoned critique of Byrne's flip-flop on scattered-site housing or other issues important to the black community.

Don Rose is certain Byrne deliberately turned her back on the black community as a strategy for winning white support. "It wasn't like it was a well-kept secret at City Hall," Rose said. Yet Paul McGrath, a former Byrne chief of staff, dismissed the charge as absurd. People at City Hall aren't smart enough to carry off conspiracies, McGrath said. Besides, to his mind, Byrne cared deeply about the black community. "She had these feelings and this sort of commitment, this bond with those people," he said. Byrne gave tens of thousands of dollars in campaign funds to black causes. "Show me any politician in this country at any level who has ever done anything like that, who has even given a penny," McGrath said. Others pointed out that Byrne revealed her concern for the plight of indigent blacks when she and her second husband, Jay McMullen, moved into the Cabrini-Green projects for two weeks after a particularly violent crime spree there.

If there was any conspiracy in the months leading up to the 1983 election, McGrath said, it was constructed by those pushing Washington for mayor. Byrne was not unpopular among blacks, McGrath said—not until Palmer and his co-conspirators exploited race to galvanize the black community against Byrne. "They exploited a couple of stupid political blunders," McGrath said, casting Byrne as a northern Bull Conner despite her concerns for the black community.

Had he known about it, McGrath might have seized on one particular moment from that time—the CHA board's first meeting that summer. Palmer was there, as were two black women, Dorothy Tillman and Marion Stamps. Stamps, squat and powerfully built, headed up the Chicago Housing Tenants Organization; Tillman, tall and imposing, was known citywide for her quest to oust a white high school principal she believed was a racist. Also on hand was the CHA's chief of security, a heavyset black man named Winston Moore.

Tillman and Stamps showed Moore little mercy. Tillman sidled up next to him and whispered in his ear, "You fat faggot." Stamps was on his other side, telling him he was "nothing but a bald-headed faggot." Both kept goading Moore, a former Cook County Jail warden renowned for his temper, until he exploded.

The ensuing fracas made all three television stations that night. Moore ordered the demonstrators to leave the room. They refused. He then ordered the CHA security force to remove them. There was no mention on television of the comments that enraged Moore, only a quick shot of a heavyset guard pushing around protesters as if possessed.

SEVEN SEIZED IN MELEE AT CHA MEETING, read a headline in the next day's *Sun-Times*. The picture that accompanied the article showed a pair of security guards dragging a middle-aged black woman across the floor by her legs. The *Metro News,* a paper that proclaims itself the "largest BLACK oriented weekly" in Chicago, asked on its front page that week if Moore was "a sick NIGGER attacking black women for whites."

The Sunday after the big blowup at CHA headquarters, Jesse Jackson appeared as a guest on a radio call-in show. Why not a black boycott of ChicagoFest in retaliation? asked a caller from Gary, Indiana. ChicagoFest, the city's annual summer music and food festival, was Byrne's party. The joke around town was that her name took up more space on the bumper stickers and posters promoting the festival than the name of the event itself. Jackson listened but was noncommittal. Later he called around to hear what other people thought.

Jackson later admitted that his first instincts told him a boycott was impractical. Stevie Wonder, Kool and the Gang, and other big-name acts that appealed to a black audience had already committed to playing the festival. But then Wonder agreed to forfeit the $160,000 he was to have been paid for an evening's work, and other entertainers canceled as well. The ChicagoFest boycott was born.

Byrne tried thwarting the boycott. The black ward bosses were told to tell their captains that attendance was mandatory, and the city sent mailbags of free tickets to CHA residents. That only prompted symbolic ticket-burning parties in the projects. After Stevie Wonder canceled, the festival organizers said they were talking with Aretha Franklin about taking his place. They also threatened reprisals against musicians who broke their contracts. Fearful of a lawsuit, Kool and the Gang announced that they would play, but the band endorsed the boycott nonetheless. They wore black arm bands the night they played.

Promoters claimed that one in every five ChicagoFest-goers was black, but that was wishful thinking. "About the only black faces you saw inside were those working there," said Clarence Page, a black reporter who covered the boycott for Channel 2. Even the chance to see Kool and the Gang at an outdoor show for just $6 was not enough to draw blacks inside. From the band's vantage point it must have looked as if they were playing in an Iowa town rather than a city with as many black residents as white.

As always, the ChicagoFest story was a fixture on the news for its two-week run except that now reporters talked about more than the good time everyone seemed to be having. The story wasn't presented with much sympathy (what does ChicagoFest have to do with the CHA anyway?), but that made little difference when organizers—Jesse Jackson in particular—repeated their stinging thirty-second anti-Byrne news bites night after night. Jackson was all over the news in August 1982, a time when black Chicago was boasting about how they spoiled the mayor's annual summer party.

The timing was perfect. The crusade to register the fifty thousand new voters that Washington had set as a precondition of his candidacy was launched just as the festival was scheduled to start. The festival was a confidence booster, proof that organizers behind Washington were not fooling themselves. With time the perceived significance of the boycott only grew. It became, for the Washington faithful, a way of marking time. There was the period before the festival and the period after.

Jackson viewed the boycott as a turning point in his career. That summer in Chicago, he said, he saw with clarity the potential of electoral politics to tap black anger and frustration. While the boycott story was still hot, Jackson declared himself an eligible candidate, even as everyone was trying to convince Washington to run.

Not all of the black organizers active in the fight to oust Byrne were appreciative of the role Jackson played. While they recognized something remarkable in this man who could take a simple suggestion and transform it into a potent demonstration of power and unity, they felt more used than grateful. Jackson was traveling the country when they were doing the tedious work of organizing against Byrne. To their minds Jackson was again riding herd on a stampede of someone else's making.

Others were more practical. Jackson hogged the spotlight and could be terribly vain and self-centered, yet even in 1982, he attracted the attention of the television cameras like no other local political figure, black or white. The simple fact was, if Jackson had not been the boycott's central figure, the festival would have made no one's list of red-letter dates.

Harold Washington had an entirely different perspective on the boycott. He was genuinely pleased by Jackson's role but more because it relieved him of the task of inventing a role for Jackson to play. Washington and his circle of advisers shared a good laugh over that one. If they spoke of him as if he was a mischievous child whom they needed to keep occupied and out of trouble, that only reflected the general low regard with which many Chicago activists viewed him.

5

THE
JESSE
JACKSON
FACTOR

Two emissaries representing Harold Washington were ushered into Jesse Jackson's living room on Chicago's south side where Jackson's icy reception confirmed what they already knew. Years later Renault Robinson spoke with pride of his intimate sessions with Washington during those months when electing a black mayor was only a far-fetched dream. Yet tarnishing his memories were assignments like this one, an interminable visit that lasted well past midnight on a hot summer night in August 1982.

Even under the best of circumstances it is not easy to deal with Jesse Louis Jackson, a man alternately capable of nobility and of peevishness. And the circumstances were not ideal. I am qualified, he had said after Washington voiced reservations about running for mayor; I am deserving. Yet no one paid him any attention. On top of that, Jackson's comrades were plotting an election strategy without him. He, the city's best-known black leader, a seasoned veteran in The Struggle, was being ignored.

Jackson was indignant. Around the country he was preaching involvement in the system: channel the rage of our community, he told audiences near and far; redirect those feelings into a positive movement for political change. Yet in Chicago—in his own backyard—his cohorts were attempting just that without him. Compounding his righteousness was the prominent role he had just played in the summer's big political happening, the protest concerning Byrne's CHA appointments. Despite his seminal role in the ChicagoFest boycott, the black community was talking voter registration without him.

Countless disagreements frustrated those meeting through the early 1980s to discuss the prospects of electing a black mayor, yet one matter they easily agreed on was that *something* had to be done to harness Jesse. No one doubted Jackson's strengths. They had all witnessed firsthand Jackson's bringing critical media attention to a given cause. As if by magic an issue would vault from the lowly status of incidental news buried deep in the paper to a page-one barn burner. And Jackson had the ability to rouse an audience.

Whether Jackson was more irritant than asset was a matter of debate among the city's activists. He didn't nurture a project through infancy and adolescence; instead he intruded on other people's plans once they had matured. Vernon Jarrett, a regular at Lu Palmer's basement meetings, wrote in his *Tribune* column that Jackson lent himself to a cause only after the hard work had already been completed. He then invariably stole the show, Jarrett wrote, leaving little behind "but a fifteen-second piece of rhetoric for the evening news." That wasn't quite right—Jackson also left behind bad feelings and resentment.

By 1982 a great many activists of all races had sworn they would have no part of a coalition that Jackson was allowed to dominate. Allow the campaign for mayor to become the Jesse Jackson show, Washington understood, and the enthusiasm within the city's activist community would be blunted before the campaign even began. "We felt after the thing got going, after it got rolling, that Jesse could be a part of it because then he wouldn't be able to derail by trying to take it over," Robinson said. "The last thing we needed was people fighting over who sits in the front seat and who sits in the third seat."

One didn't simply ignore Jackson, for Jackson was not someone who allowed himself to be ignored. The ChicagoFest seemed a godsend, a role that was at once meaningful and limited. Yet to Jackson his starring role seemed proof that he deserved an even greater role in the black community's next big challenge: voter registration.

Washington dispatched Robinson and another aide to meet with Jackson, but that only made things worse. They offered nothing. They had no invitation from Washington for Jackson to take a prominent seat at one of the big tables. Instead they dropped hints and skirted around the core issue: he was being kept at bay because he stood in the way of their unity efforts. "What Harold wanted," Robinson said, "was an equitable situation where everybody was as important as the next guy so that we wouldn't chill the thing before it got going. But we couldn't come right out and say that."

The next day Jackson worked the phones. He called established grass roots leaders, asking them to attend an emergency summit meeting he was calling. Jackson didn't come right out and say he felt snubbed. He had a politician's gift for making it sound as if he were talking about something far nobler, a higher cause. Instead he spoke of a cliquishness that threatened efforts to elect a black mayor. Only some have been asked to participate; others have been excluded, he said. Voter registration was only one example.

The registration strategy sessions were held in a boardroom at Soft Sheen Products, Inc., a black-owned company on the south side. Soft Sheen had been selected because it was neutral turf that didn't favor one faction over another. At his summit meeting Jackson pushed for a new locale. What better place than Operation PUSH, where he, as the meeting's chairman, would make sure everyone was invited to take part?

In the late 1960s, Jesse Jackson's cause became the black manufacturers who felt locked out of local stores because of their skin color. Jackson organized boycotts of supermarket chains on their behalf, focusing on stores with outlets in the black community that did not sell a single product produced by someone black. The same scenario occurred in chain after chain: the boycott took a toll on profits, Jackson and his negotiating team were invited in for discussions, and gradually that store's shelves were integrated with products created by black-owned companies.

Nate Clay, a former PUSH staffer, was still in school then, dreaming of a job in journalism, but twenty years later he could still tick off some of the products Jackson promoted every Saturday on the radio: Joe Louis Milk, Parker House Sausage, Baldwin Ice Cream. "Maybe Jesse's finest moment," Clay said. The boycotts were still on Clay's mind when he became Jackson's director of communications in the 1970s.

By that time Clay was no longer a naïve student taken by this daring young black man who gave the white store owners what for. After several years as a *Chicago Defender* reporter, Clay looked on Jackson as a flawed leader, but one who usually did more good than bad. But several years as a top Jackson aide taught him that his boss's vision was at once broader and narrower than he had suspected. The grocery store boycotts and all the other well-publicized actions, Clay came to believe, were of a single purpose: to promote Jackson as the preeminent black figure in Chicago. From the mid-1960s, shortly after he arrived in Chicago, through the early 1980s, Jackson's primary goal, Clay said, was to serve as black Chicago's great liberator.

"To Jesse that was his divinely ordained status in life," Clay said. "As far as I'm concerned, that's not a point even open for discussion. It was too bad for anyone in Jesse's way."

Jackson was a twenty-four-year-old student at the Chicago Theological Seminary when he persuaded a group of his fellow seminarians to join him for a trip south. Ostensibly Jackson, a South Carolina native, was responding to King's call in 1965 for a mass march from Selma to Montgomery, Alabama. Jackson, however, seemed more interested in rumors that King was looking to establish a movement beachhead in Chicago.

Years later Ralph Abernathy, King's second in command, remembered Jackson from that weekend. He remembered an intense and eager young man who offered to help run errands or pitch in in any way he could. Andrew Young, another member of the King inner circle, recalled Jackson complimenting him on an essay that he had recently published. Jackson is best remembered for the speech he gave that weekend. He just walked up during a dead moment and gave it, with no one's authority. Some were dumbfounded by Jackson's audacity; others, including Abernathy, were impressed by his oratory.

King opposed a major role for Jackson in Chicago. James Bevel, who would play a central role in King's Chicago campaign, claimed King saw something potentially dangerous in this young man who seemed to have no appreciation of boundaries. Where Bevel saw Jackson's weakness as nothing more serious than immaturity, King feared that Jackson, as Bevel told one interviewer, was a man out to "build an empire at the expense of his people." But Abernathy and others lobbied on Jackson's behalf. Already at twenty-four he was a powerful speaker. His energy seemed boundless. He was at least acquainted with the alien world of Chicago, which put him one up on everyone else in King's inner circle. Besides, what harm could he do?

Al Raby wasn't pleased when Jesse Jackson was assigned to help him prepare for King's visit. As one of King's point men in Chicago, Raby spent most of his time negotiating among factions and among difficult egos. He had enough trouble keeping together a coalition that included black organizers impressed with their past accomplishments and downtown business leaders who fancied themselves liberal on matters of race. He didn't need a nettlesome young staffer with a demanding ego.

Jackson and Raby couldn't have been more different. Where Jackson was brazen and brash, Raby was deliberate, respectful, and wise beyond his years. Jackson burned with one idea after another; Raby was the sort who, in meetings, offered the sobering perspective that only so much could be accomplished, so priorities had to be set. If Raby had one skill above all others that won him the task of organizing on King's behalf, it was his ability to keep peace among large and unwieldy groups.

Jackson handled with skill the job he had been assigned—lining up support among Chicago's black clergy. It wasn't an easy task in Chicago, where joining with King could mean a lot of trouble for a church, but Jackson worked exhausting hours and proved himself a creative organizer. He was smart and had good instincts. The problem was he had a propensity to intrude on other people's work.

Jackson was forever freelancing his own tasks. Shortly after King arrived in Chicago, Jackson was granted the honor of introducing him at a major rally downtown. He was to say a few words in praise of King and then sit down. Instead Jackson gave a speech of his own, delivering a stemwinder, legend holds, that lasted as long as King's. Jackson defenders say their man just got a little carried away by the moment, yet Raby remembered Jackson pulling notes from his pocket before delivering this supposedly impromptu speech. "Let's just say that Jesse was not content to be one of those merely associated with King," Raby said.

Jackson's ambitions could be more than a harmless annoyance. During King's Chicago campaign there was talk in strategy sessions of a march through the all-white town of Cicero. King had led marches through various Chicago neighborhoods, but a demonstration in Cicero was different—

"the Selma of the North," King had said of this rough working-class town just west of Chicago. Talk of a demonstration in Cicero was nothing more than an idea batted around as a potential threat—leverage in negotiations. Yet Jackson decided on his own to designate Cicero as the movement's next target. "The march announcement came one night when the cameras were on him," said Don Rose, the King campaign's publicist. "It was as if Jesse couldn't resist saying something sensational that would get his name in the paper. . . . Jesse was often making major policy statements without clearing them with anyone."

King and his disciples bid good riddance to Chicago in 1966, leaving the fight against Daley to those hearty souls who chose the city as their hometown. Jackson was among those anxious to pick up where King had left off, so King put him in charge of Operation Breadbasket.

Breadbasket used economic boycotts to pressure white-owned businesses that profited from the black community to hire black workers and subcontract with black-owned businesses. One of countless successful Breadbasket campaigns was the boycott of the dairy industry that resulted in hundreds of thousands of dollars in spoiled milk and other dairy by-products. After a meeting with Jackson, the dairies began hiring black drivers.

Still, Jackson was not impressing King's staff in Atlanta. Whenever a photo opportunity presented itself, Jackson positioned himself so that he was standing beside King as the cameras snapped. When Jackson was in charge of an event, he was sure to include a picture of himself on the flyer. Supposedly he was the only King staffer to do so. Perhaps what annoyed top staffers more than anything else was Jackson's disrespect in King's presence. In strategy sessions he habitually told King what he would do if he were running the show.

King, for his part, ran hot and cold on Jackson. At times he laughed off his ambitious young aide. The poster Jackson conceived to advertise one King rally featured a modest-sized King beneath a towering shot of Jackson, with a crucifix looming above them both. "At least he put the good Lord over him," King reportedly joked.

Yet King was forever losing his patience with Jackson. The most publicized of these confrontations was in the spring of 1968. Jackson was pressing a point, and King snapped, "Jesse, don't bother me. It may be that you want to carve your own niche in society. Go ahead and carve it. But for God's sake don't bother me." This story has been told again and again because five days later, in Memphis, King made his peace with Jackson. "Join us for dinner," King called down to him. Minutes later a rifle shot rang out and King was dead.

The day after King's assassination Jackson made a quick stop in New York to appear on NBC's "Today Show" and then went straight to Chicago. Jackson's colleagues were surprised to see him in a New York television studio—he had told people he was returning to Chicago for some medication—but they were awestruck by a gesture he made later in a speech before the Chicago City Council. He gestured to his brown turtle-neck and claimed it was stained by King's blood the day before. The shirt, a *Playboy* writer gushed, "demonstrated both the militant indignation and the dramatic flair that mark Jackson's charismatic style." Others who had been with King in Memphis were less impressed. Jackson was standing in the courtyard, not on the balcony where King was shot. If his shirt was soiled with King's blood, then it was only because Jackson smeared it on himself. Jackson also claimed he cradled the dying King as he breathed his last breath; that was not true, either.

Back in Chicago, Jackson asked Don Rose to set up some television interviews for him that week, and Rose rode with Jackson as he traveled from one interview to another. Between stops the two of them, at Jackson's behest, spoke of ways of packaging Jackson as the "next King." Among other things it was decided that Jackson should play up the coincidence that King was twenty-seven when he led the Montgomery bus boycott, just as Jackson was twenty-seven now. His young age would work to his advantage, Rose quoted Jackson as saying: he alone among the possible successors could appeal to the young militants. The way Rose remembers it, Jackson didn't dance around the subject but spoke frankly of pursuing the appellation, like a presidential hopeful might speak with a trusted aide about securing his party's nomination.

Shortly after King's assassination a painting was hung at Breadbasket's headquarters showing a pair of matching silhouettes, King and Jackson side by side. Another painting portrayed Jackson in the foreground beneath a faded drawing of King. While around the country black intellectuals were assailing any new black messiahs, Jackson was doing everything in his power to create the impression that he was the Second Coming.

The media proved no match for Jackson. Over the next year he was featured in *Harper's* (JESSE JACKSON HEIR TO DR. KING?), the *Wall Street Journal* ("Many observers feel that Mr. Jackson is the most important black leader to emerge since the Reverend Martin Luther King"), and *Playboy* (the "fiery heir apparent to Martin Luther King"), among other national periodicals. AT 27 HE'S REGARDED AS MARTIN LUTHER KING'S HEIR, said the headline over a story in the *Chicago Daily News.*

According to *Harper's,* Jackson was "born in poverty"; in the *Journal* he had "come a long way from the dilapidated shack in Greenville, S.C., where he grew up"; yet the truth was his stepfather was a white-collar worker at the local post office and his mother was a beautician. In one interview Jackson claimed he stole to survive when younger, but this seemed the fabrication of a man understanding the preferred pedigree for the leader of a poor people's movement. The *New York Times,* in its Jackson profile, placed Jackson at King's side in Memphis ("cradled Martin's head when King was shot . . ."), as did *Harper's* and at least a hundred other media outlets, according to Jackson biographer Barbara Reynolds, who bothered to count. More than shoddy journalism, race seemed at the root of these misinformed feature stories. In editorial rooms across the country, white reporters covering black politics wrote authoritatively about a subject they seemed to know little about.

Jackson hobnobbed with publishers and television executives in Chicago and periodically made the rounds of the local editorial boards. "Jackson," a black reporter wrote in the *Chicago Journalism Review,* "has closer personal relationships with more white media executives than any other black leader in modern times." A journalist's shorthand description of Jackson in the *New York Times* provided a clue to Jackson's media appeal: "Militant but nonviolent, good copy but safe copy; radical in style, not in action." He wore his Afro long but knew to wear a suit when appropriate; an African pendant hung around his neck and he flirted with the nationalists, but with reporters he came across as perfectly reasonable.

Nate Clay would stop by Jackson's home for some business and find white reporters "sitting around Jesse's house like it was a hangout." Jackson's "media angels," they were dubbed, for it was his access to the press that served as the source of his power. ("People who would otherwise tell you how much they hated Jackson," Clay said, "would come over bowing to Jesse, dropping money in the plate at PUSH.") It didn't take a reporter long to learn she could save herself time and hassles by simply phoning Jackson when she wanted the black point of view in a story. Her editors respected Jackson, and he was always happy to weigh in on any issue involving black Chicago.

Occasionally a black reporter wrote a piece aimed at deflating Jackson's mythical media persona. Jackson, in turn, would dismiss the article as the by-product of an insecure reporter. "Black journalists see themselves as leaders," he said in one interview, "and they are threatened by a real leader." Jackson went a step further after a black woman named Angela Parker wrote an unflattering piece about him in the *Chicago Tribune*. Jackson attacked Parker at his weekly Breadbasket meeting, which was broadcast over the radio. Referring to Parker as "your enemy," he compared her to the crazed black woman who in the early 1960s stabbed King while he was shopping in a New York City department store. Protesters picketed Parker's apartment building; inside, she was harassed by threatening phone calls.

Another black reporter, Barbara Reynolds, was treated in a similar fashion. Reynolds, however, had been forewarned. "She can't hold her head up in her own community," Jackson said of Parker. "Now, I wouldn't want that to happen to you. . ."

After King's assassination Ralph Abernathy took over the Southern Christian Leadership Conference (SCLC) as King had instructed in case of his death. Jackson, though, looked on Abernathy as a rival rather than his ostensible boss.

Jackson snubbed Abernathy at every turn. When Abernathy arrived in Chicago for a scheduled trip, Jackson was away on business. Jo Ella Stevenson, a former PUSH staffer, claimed she was fired because she made the mistake of helping Breadbasket's women's auxiliary plan a program in Abernathy's honor. That same year Breadbasket hosted its annual Black Expo (a convention for black entrepreneurs). Portraits of various black leaders, past and present, hung on the walls. A Jackson poster graced one wall, but there was no Abernathy poster. "Ralph says all the right things," Jackson told *Life* magazine. "So what if he doesn't say them well."

From Abernathy's perspective, Breadbasket was Chicago-based, not Chicago-*only*. Yet Breadbasket staffers seemed to spend more time developing policies on issues such as the Chicago Transit Authority's proposed bus fare hike than a new Breadbasket chapter in Saint Louis. At times it seemed Jackson had no time to administer the organization under his direction. Breadbasket never had the national punch originally hoped for, but at least under the previous director the SCLC could boast of active chapters in several cities.*

Late in 1971, Abernathy announced he was moving Breadbasket to Atlanta. As expected, Jackson resigned. Despite his maneuverings to best Abernathy, Jackson blamed their squabble on the media. "When education and welfare should have made headlines these last few weeks," Jackson said at a press conference, "differences between myself and Dr. Abernathy have hidden the real problems, and the papers have dealt with a personality called Jesse." Jackson formed a new organization he ambitiously—extravagantly— called People United to Save Humanity.** Operation PUSH's prime mission—the economic empowerment of blacks—did not change. Every Saturday morning one could still hear Jackson preach to the faithful at the former south side synagogue that served as PUSH headquarters. The same wealthy black executives who served as the financial backbone of Breadbasket served as the lifeblood for PUSH. PUSH was like Breadbasket in every way except that Jackson now called all his own shots.

Richard Barnett thinks it was in 1970 that Jackson approached him about political education classes at Breadbasket. It was music to his ears whatever the year, for Barnett believed there could not be enough trained volunteers fighting a political organization whose greatest asset was its patronage army of thirty-five thousand. Barnett told Jackson he would be delighted.

The classes were a great success. Breadbasket, and then PUSH, served as the perfect venue. It lent the program an instant institutional credibility and served as a feeder system for potential recruits. In time, enrollment

---

*The same criticisms would be leveled at PUSH. Despite claims it was an organization with a national vision, in the mid-1970s every one of PUSH's nine officers hailed from Chicago except for baseball legend Jackie Robinson.
**It was later called People United to Serve Humanity.

mushroomed. Trainees became instructors, and eventually PUSH operated several courses concurrently for different levels of expertise. By 1972, when the energies of the black community were focused on preventing Edward Hanrahan's reelection as state's attorney, the PUSH graduates proved critical.

Yet shortly after the Hanrahan defeat, PUSH closed its doors to Barnett and other teachers. "Jesse came to us and said we were going to economics, that the fight wasn't electoral politics anymore but against private corporations for a fairer share," Barnett said. "Jesse cut it out in the middle of a ten-week course, just like that." Jesse Jackson had spoken—just like that.

The complaint about Jackson was that he walked away from any number of unfinished projects, distracted by the promise of the next opportunity. It was as if he couldn't tolerate something happening in the black community if he was not part of it.

Consider 1972. At Amiri Baraka's black unity convention in Gary, Indiana, in March, Jackson declared, "We must form a black political party." Otherwise, Jackson said, we'll forever be in the hip pockets of the Democrats. His proclamation thrilled the convention's more militant delegates.

Back in Chicago, though, a group of party renegades were making headlines challenging Mayor Daley's slate to the 1972 Democratic convention in Miami Beach. Daley's preselected slate, they charged, defied new party rules establishing quotas for minorities and women; locals assembled a second slate, and the issue was taken up by national party leaders. Jackson stopped talking about a black party and joined these Chicago mavericks fighting for fairer representation within the party. The newspapers revealed that Jackson had not voted in the primary that year, fueling talk that these rebels were not genuinely concerned with the Democratic party but with their own agenda. But Jackson was not deterred. He was late to the cause, but that didn't stop him from taking it on himself to cut a deal with Daley—which was later scrapped—though no one had granted him that authority.*

---

*In the end Jackson's contribution proved critical. No other local black leader enjoyed Jackson's national reputation, and none would have been nearly as successful convincing party leaders from around the country to buck Daley. Both delegations went to Miami Beach, where the party's delegates ruled in favor of the renegades. Daley returned to Chicago defeated.

Later in 1972, Jackson did little to help Republican challenger Bernard Carey defeat Ed Hanrahan, according to Don Rose, Carey's campaign manager. But there he was on stage at Carey headquarters the night of his victory, an arm draped over the new state's attorney's shoulder as the television cameras whirred. By New Year's Day, Jackson was telling Richard Barnett and others that economic issues, not electoral politics, should be the black community's priority—precisely the opposite of what he said the previous year. In 1971, in fact, Jackson had launched a short-lived run for mayor.

Economic empowerment was the black nationalist's position, yet Jackson's pronouncement hardly won him favor inside Chicago's nationalist community. "The nationalist by and large saw Jesse as your typical Reverend Leroy–like preacher," said Salim Muwakkil, a writer for *Muhammad Speaks* through much of the 1970s. "A hustler. That venerable black stereotype of the hustler-preacher. In fact, that's one reason I think Jesse embraced [Louis] Farrakhan publicly [in 1984], to give him a kind of black authenticity he lacked among the black nationalists. They questioned his authenticity."

Those focusing on defeating the Daley machine generally regarded Jackson as an effective media spokesperson, quick on his feet and clever. (After Daley delivered a well publicized anticrime speech, Jackson countered with a speech of his own that decried "crimes" that Daley had failed to mention, such as the black infant mortality rate in Chicago that was two times that of the white rate.) Yet fighting the Chicago machine meant more than smooth rhetoric and well-attended press conferences; it meant door-to-door precinct operations and tedious voter registration drives.

Former Alderman Sammy Rayner, one of the first independents elected to the City Council, was among those seduced by Jackson's line. In 1968 when Rayner ran for Congress, Jackson spoke of the army of volunteers he would lend his campaign. "His people promised to work like hound puppies," Rayner said, "but they got as far as the first restaurant and ate hot dogs and drank coffee, and that was it." In 1973 a west sider claimed that a delegation from PUSH talked him into running for alderman but ended up doing little on his behalf.

This same complaint was voiced time and again. People envied the potential for PUSH to play a greater role in the antimachine fight, yet they were forever disappointed. Jackson and those defending him said that if he was never the antimachine organizer people wanted him to be, then that was a matter of unreasonable expectations. The man can't do *everything,* his supporters said; PUSH can't root out all the black community's problems.

Yet Jackson created the expectations that weighed on him, elbowing others out of his way when cameras flashed. Jackson would promise the world and then prove unable to deliver. It seemed Jackson tricked even himself. When he announced he was running for mayor in 1971, he filed just seven thousand signatures, falling far short of the fifty-eight thousand an independent needed that year to earn a spot on the ballot.

Jackson's worst indiscretion, at least in the eyes of his more militant Chicago cohorts, was his use of the white media to best his black contemporaries. The white press, not black people and certainly not his colleagues, crowned Jackson Chicago's top black leader. Yet he began acting like royalty among people who considered him nothing more than one of their own. He communicated through envoys as if in a league above them. A former bodyguard spoke of Jackson's tendency to "call important people to his bedside, where he chairs midnight talks with the pompousness of a prince." "The major media anointed him as the Guru for Black People," a *Defender* columnist wrote of Jackson in 1974, "and he begins to believe his own press notices. Then I worry and so do a lot of other folks."

Jackson placed himself in worldly company—if not the company of the other-worldly. "Pharaoh Daley," Jackson once said, "don't tell me you don't hear. I am telling you, not asking you, not begging you, but telling you to let my people go." When reporter Barbara Reynolds wrote that Jackson was a "demagogue," Jackson called her, livid. "Don't you realize Jesus was a demagogue?" he yelled. His response could leave one speechless, but Reynolds managed to reply, "Excuse me, Reverend, but I fail to see the comparison."

When Reynolds, who published her Jackson biography in 1975, pressed Jackson about his home, a Tudor mansion on the city's south side, he said, "They put the white leader in the White House. Why would anyone expect me to live in a mud hut? At least I deserve a Black House." Another time Jackson complained to Reynolds, "Too many people concentrate on my charisma. They never seem to realize that, without a doubt, I am one of the most intelligent men in this country."

In the 1975 mayor's race a lakefront independent named "Billy" Singer challenged Daley for the Democratic nomination. Jackson endorsed Singer over Richard Newhouse, a black independent who had also entered the race. Perhaps Jackson believed, as the pundits did, that Singer was the stronger candidate, though neither was a formidable candidate next to Daley.

Newhouse and his supporters seemed more bemused than angry. Newhouse said Jackson's failure to endorse him was no big deal; Jackson, he said, was more a liability than an asset. The "few votes" I'll lose, Newhouse said, "will be more than made up by the votes of those impressed Jackson is not endorsing me." Thomas Todd, a Newhouse supporter and a prominent local attorney the nationalists looked upon as an ally, was not inclined to blast a fellow black leader in the white media. Still, Todd mused aloud that Jackson had only one year earlier impassionately appealed to his black brethren to unify behind a black mayoral candidate.

Some might have been impressed with Jackson for siding with a white man in a race that also featured a black candidate, especially in the face of the intense criticism within the black community, except that Jackson reneged on his endorsement. Just three days prior to the election he held a press conference announcing that he was switching his support to Newhouse.

The summer of 1982 seemed, for Jackson, a time for making amends. Where in the past he would have taken it upon himself to announce the ChicagoFest boycott, he first called around to see what others thought. He embraced the unity cause as if it were his own, phoning people with whom he had not spoken in years. Still, at the same time he was tending to the past, he was creating new resentments. Among those he angered were Marion Stamps and Dorothy Tillman.

On and off welfare through much of her life, Stamps lived in the Cabrini-Green housing project with her five daughters. She first began organizing against Byrne when the mayor moved into Cabrini, "as if she's some Great White Hope." Stamps was among the city's more outspoken leaders after Byrne announced her white appointments to the CHA board.

Stamps never cared for Jackson. You wouldn't find her at PUSH on Saturday mornings, and not just because she didn't want to pay the carfare. She didn't take it well when, in the summer of 1982, Jackson emerged as the media's leading spokesperson on the CHA controversy. He didn't diplomatically stand off to one side, like others new to the cause, but instead adopted what one former PUSH staffer called "Jesse's aggressive headline-hunting mode." Stamps said, "We raise the questions. We educate the people. We do the hard work, but then these so-called high-level leaders like Jesse come in and take the credit and compromise our efforts."

Dorothy Tillman watched television that summer with similar frustration. She shook her head when Jackson explained to reporters what the black community would do next in its fight with Byrne. "Ain't that just like Jesse," she said to herself. She wondered if Jackson truly believed he was the only human alive who could make things happen for Chicago's black community.

Had Tillman been inclined to do so, her blasting of Jackson would have carried some weight. She, too, was an SCLC veteran, a member of King's advance team back in 1965. Yet Tillman chose the high road, organizing several carloads of volunteers to walk a picket line with other ChicagoFest boycotters. "We were all ready, singing 'Old Freedom,'" Tillman said. "But when we got over there we learned they had negotiated a deal with Jane Byrne." The protesters would not stand just outside the gate as planned, so as to be in position to persuade people to abide by their boycott. Instead, they walked a picket line off in a corner, away from the entrance. What they received in return were portable toilets, a tent, and assurances that the police would not harass them.

The fervor at the City Council meeting, the arrests outside Byrne's apartment, their scuffle at the CHA meeting—not only was Jackson trying to steal all the credit, he was taming their protest. "We need a careful, organized boycott of ChicagoFest," Jackson had said. "Otherwise, the town's going to start rioting." This was too much for Tillman. It was a legitimate position, but what Tillman, Stamps, and others wondered was who was Jackson to decide?

Around the time of the ChicagoFest boycott a meeting was held in Jesse Jackson's backyard. Soft Sheen's Edward Gardner was there, along with a team of media people working for his company. The conversation centered around concept boards and slogans and other details of a voter registration campaign that Gardner and Soft Sheen were underwriting to assist the campaign for a black mayor.

Jackson offered nothing more than a few token suggestions, but his input was not the meeting's real purpose. Jackson's effort to move the voter registration efforts to PUSH had failed. This was his consolation prize, a gesture aimed at soothing Jackson's feelings. Jesse, a PUSH staffer explained, "needs to feel wanted."

Nate Clay, who became the news editor of the *Metro News* after leaving PUSH, was involved with the People's Movement for Voter Registration, one of several groups popping up that summer in response to Washington's demand for fifty thousand new voters. Clay's group had no phone or office—nothing, really, but energy. Still, they managed some success, such as the weekend they registered nearly a thousand people in one afternoon. A longtime member of the city's Board of Elections said he had never seen so many people registered at a single site in one day.

Jackson phoned Clay to offer his group space at PUSH. If they needed staff support, they could have that as well. They jumped at the offer. Soon afterward Jackson formed his own voter registration group. Aimed at enlisting the support of black clerics, it was dubbed the Praise the Lord and Vote campaign. The staff members Jackson lent Clay's group were reassigned; their phone number became the Praise the Lord number. Clay was among those present at the inaugural meeting of Jackson's new group. Afterward Clay said that Jackson told him, "See, that's how you get something going." It was as if Jackson was telling him, Clay thought, "That little shit you all are doing ain't nothing compared to what I can do."

Clay didn't brood for long. The People's Movement moved to another location and shied away from Jackson, choosing not to respond when Jackson announced a "voter family fever registration drive." "We were used once," Clay said. "We weren't going to fall for the okeydoke twice, because whoever we registered out in the park that day, Jesse would have made sure he got the credit. We were hip to Jesse by then."

Those emerging as leaders in the voter registration drive agreed that drastic methods were required. Though the various groups met to talk strategy, they came together not so much looking for a consensus as to avoid interfering with one another's efforts.

The idea behind a group called P.O.W.E.R—People Organized for Welfare and Employment Rights—was a simple one: set up voter registration tables at the unemployment lines and the welfare offices to draw into the electoral process the most disenfranchised voters. Registration tables were also placed in shopping centers in the black and Latino communities, and outside public housing projects. The challenge in getting P.O.W.E.R. off the ground was the months of haggling with various government agencies for the right to set up tables.*

Renault Robinson appreciated the potential of P.O.W.E.R., but he had fixated on the idea that the radio was the key to any black registration drive. He was thinking about that one day while driving on the expressway when he heard a newscaster mention that Ed Gardner of Soft Sheen had made a nice-sized contribution to some worthy cause. On a whim he pulled off at the next exit and called Gardner. The two had never met, but Gardner invited Robinson to his office, where Robinson told him of Washington's fifty thousand voters challenge. He also mentioned an Urban League study that showed there were at least two hundred thousand unregistered black Chicagoans above the age of eighteen.

Gardner agreed to put up seed money and offered Robinson the services of Soft Sheen's creative department. Their brainchild was the "Come Alive October Five" campaign: a series of slick radio ads that played incessantly on black radio and also brightly colored signs and bumper stickers ubiquitous in the black community. October 5 was the day Chicago residents could register to vote at their polling place.

Churches opened their doors to Washington and his confederates seeking to preach registration. Father George Clements allowed children to register at his parish school only if a parent presented his or her voter registration card. Another pastor announced that a registration card was a precondition of a free meal at his church kitchen. Each effort had its own spirit. Even Nate Clay admitted it was "overzealous" to have registrars walk the wards at Cook County Hospital registering people on their sickbeds. "We didn't bother the comatose," Clay said, "but if they moved, we tried."

P.O.W.E.R. would take credit for adding some 40,000 new voters to the rolls, yet the voter registration figures from October 5 were more impressive still. Usually no more than 10,000 people register on an in-precinct registration day, but that October more than 130,000 new regis-

---

*Election officials tried thwarting these efforts by imposing strict guidelines on P.O.W.E.R.'s volunteer registrars. One of the more absurd rules dictated that a van must be parked just outside each voter registration site, ostensibly so that registrars could get in out of the rain.

trants signed up at the polls, most of them in the city's 17 predominantly black wards, said a spokesman for the Board of Elections.

Nate Clay said Jesse Jackson's Praise the Lord campaign didn't amount to much. "A lot of preachers prayed and shouted and said 'amen' a lot, but they didn't register many voters." Still, the downtown dailies cast Jackson as the linchpin in the black community's voter registration drive. Even academics looking back on the 1983 election emphasized Jackson's role in the voter registration drive above all others.

Just as Byrne inadvertently helped her foes when she appointed three whites to the CHA board just as P.O.W.E.R. was setting up its voter registration tables, Illinois Governor James Thompson also lent a hand, as did Ronald Reagan. With less money from the federal government, Thompson cut General Assistance from $190 a month to $144. Thompson's reelection that November served as an inspiration.

The party regulars also aided those behind Washington in unintended ways. The city agency overseeing local elections initially opposed the idea of deputy registrars out in the streets, but the new party chairman, Ed Vrdolyak, persuaded the Board of Elections to at least allow them a trial period. Vrdolyak even contributed $5,000 in seed money to help P.O.W.E.R. get started.* Eager to revitalize the party, Vrdolyak was looking no further ahead than a strong anti-Thompson showing from Chicago in the upcoming Thompson-Stevenson governor's race. Stevenson was far back in the polls through the summer and early fall; a victory would help revive the Cook County Democratic party's reputation as a machine that shapes state and national politics.

That November, Washington was reelected to Congress with over ninety-seven percent of the vote. Thompson edged out Stevenson, but the closeness of the contest—Stevenson fell just five thousand votes shy of winning, or less than one vote for every precinct in Illinois—still boded well for Washington. Though Vrdolyak would take much of the credit for Stevenson's near victory, an energized black community in Chicago was the primary reason. The voter turnout in the city's predominantly black wards

---

*After the tremendous success of the fall voter registration drive, party sentiments turned against P.O.W.E.R. With cold weather around the corner, organizers asked if they could set up their tables inside rather than outside. They were turned down.

reached sixty-five percent, a record for black Chicago in a nonpresidential year election.

There were other signs that black Chicago was ready for political change, yet Washington still hesitated. He approached Roland Burris, a moderate black politician just reelected Illinois state comptroller, hoping he could persuade him to run in his stead. But Burris was quoted in the *Sun-Times* as saying he wanted to consult first with Vrdolyak, the party chairman, before making any final decision. "I'm not out to create waves," he said.

The night before Washington finally agreed to run, he told a group of black leaders that he didn't want to be their candidate. "But if we don't find someone else in the next twenty-four hours, I'll run," he said. Those there that night were relieved at the same time they were baffled. If one hundred thirty thousand new voters and a renewed vigor inside the black community were not enough of a motivation, there was Richie Daley's announcement several days earlier that he was challenging Byrne for reelection in the Democratic primary. With Byrne and Daley in the race, the machine would be split in two. What better scenario could Washington possibly want?

6

THE

FAMILY

BUSINESS

Reporters working out of the City Hall press room were skeptical. To them, several hundred angry people protesting Byrne's appointments to the Chicago Housing Authority was something that made their jobs more interesting for a few days, and nothing more. It hardly proved that black Chicago was on the verge of a political miracle. Harry Golden, Jr., the City Hall reporter for the *Sun-Times* since the 1960s, didn't look upon the ChicagoFest boycott as significant so much as ironic. White teens showed up wearing T-shirts thanking Jesse Jackson for convincing black people to stay away from the festival. Jackson making friends in white Chicago by allowing them to have a whites–only party: Golden and his City Hall colleagues had a good laugh over that one.

Golden had seen it before. Self-appointed black leaders find some issue around which to whip up black anger; Jesse Jackson calls a press conference proclaiming black Chicago ready for political liberation or some such nonsense; then election day rolls around, and it's just as it had been four years earlier and four years before that: the angry black voters seemed invisible, their leaders all bluster. Elections were about media budgets and war chests, not demonstrations; winning was the art of lining up key supporters around the city. Where were Washington's endorsements? Golden asked.

Golden was more inclined to heed the views of Iola McGowan, a black committeewoman whose star had risen under Byrne. McGowan claimed Washington wouldn't crack even fifty percent in her ward. McGowan was an elected official, put in office by a black constituency. Who was Lu Palmer but a hot-headed reporter who went off the deep end in the early 1970s, ranting about a racist media, flushing a column—a column!—down the toilet.

In the fall of 1982, Washington strategists like Renault Robinson spoke of an "eighty-eighty" strategy. If eighty percent of the black registered voters showed up at the polls and if eighty percent voted for Washington, then Washington could win without a single white vote and only a small share of the Latino vote. Yet no black candidate for mayor had won even a majority of the black vote, let alone eighty percent. Black voter turnout had never exceeded seventy percent. Polls that November showed Washington third behind Daley and Byrne, even among black voters. Why would this same candidate who just six years earlier had lost the black vote to Michael Bilandic suddenly inspire black Chicago? Chicago's most able local political writer, Mike Royko, declared that Washington didn't "have a prayer of winning."

When reporters bothered to consider Washington's candidacy at all, they were inclined to wonder to whose advantage it might work, Byrne's or Daley's. More than one pundit latched on to a view popular among Daley supporters. Washington, it was said, was nothing but a Byrne stalking horse.

The Byrne-Daley story was one they had been writing in their heads for three years, ever since Byrne engineered it so that the party opposed Daley when he ran for Cook County state's attorney less than one year into Byrne's tenure. That election, nasty and mean, was only the first volley in a three-year fight for control among rival party bosses. So entrenched was this notion of a Byrne-Daley showdown that a popular comedy club opened a musical satire called *Byrne, Baby, Byrne II: See Dick and Jane Run*. A *See Dick and Jane Run* coloring book sold in area bookstores.

Both sides in the Byrne-Daley split were driven by self-righteousness, which only fueled interest. The renegade ward bosses aligned with Daley spoke of a vindictive Byrne punishing their wards because of their support for her rival. Those behind Byrne spoke derisively of those acting as if the mayor's seat was somehow "Richie" Daley's by birthright. "An old-style Irish blood feud," Golden said, rubbing his hands together with anticipation.

Richard M. Daley grew up living the life of a prince. He was still in grammar school when his father took control of the Cook County Democratic party. He spent a night in Lyndon Johnson's White House; as a child he had met Queen Elizabeth. In high school the other kids nicknamed him "Mayor." Those from old-world families understood that the nickname was part joke and part acknowledgment of the obligations that fall on the eldest son.

Both father and son grew up in Bridgeport. The son attended the same elementary school as the father. When he was young, the father left the neighborhood each day to attend a well-regarded parochial high school. The son would do the same. In his high school yearbook Richard M. wrote that his ambition was to become "a great lawyer and a politician." The father was both.

The elder Daley was a hard man, strict and religious. His was a home short on books (a Bible, a few other religious books, Kennedy's *Profiles in Courage,* some self-improvement books) and full of religious artifacts. He attended mass nearly every morning, no matter how tight his schedule. Richard J. Daley was a man who seemed obsessed with amassing power, yet the way the story is told, he managed to set aside an hour or two nearly every night to eat dinner with his wife and children. When it came his turn to run for mayor, Rich Daley stressed the themes of family and religion. Old-timers drawn to the almost magical significance of the Daley surname beamed that young Rich was very much his father's son.

The son's first break with expectations came after high school when he left the state to attend college in Rhode Island, but then, supposedly homesick for Chicago, transferred during his sophomore year. He commuted to DePaul University where his father had attended law school and where he, too, would go on to study law. When his father had married, he moved to a house a block from his parents' home. When the son also found an Irish Catholic girl to marry, so, too, did he remain in the neighborhood, in a home two blocks to the north of his father's. The son was married at the age of thirty, the same year he left home and the same year he was elected to the state legislature.

Bridgeport was the cradle of mayors dating back to the Depression. Each of the city's four mayors from 1933 through 1979 hailed from the Eleventh Ward's Bridgeport community, and legend had it that two thousand of the city's employees lived in the Eleventh Ward, in a city where strong ward organizations were granted 400 to 500 city jobs. "[Daley] habitually keeps a fatherly eye on any promising young talent in the neighborhood," Milton Rakove wrote in his book, *Don't Make No Waves, Don't Back No Losers.* "When a young Bridgeporter graduates from college, he is likely to receive a phone call from the mayor asking him to come down to his office for a chat."

The city's budget director, its corporation counsel, its patronage chief, its fire commissioner, the clerk of the circuit court, and countless other top honchos during Daley's tenure were from Bridgeport. The circus would open its annual visit to Chicago twice: once for the Eleventh Ward and then again for the public.

One of Daley's daughters married a man whose father was a doctor; shortly thereafter he was appointed to two part-time city positions at a handsome salary. Daley's son John was just out of college, anxious to try his hand at the insurance business. The firm that hired him soon was handling virtually all of the city's casualty insurance business, worth between $2 million and $3 million. Supposedly, John Daley earned a $100,000 commission. When criticized by the press for steering city business to his son, Daley asked what father wouldn't help one of his own. Anyone not liking the deal, he added, "can kiss my ass."

The Old Man looked after his eldest son with a special eye. He saw to it that doors were opened for his young namesake, doors that would have been closed if not for his powerful father. While waiting to pass the bar, young Daley clerked with a judge close to his father; his next job was as a lawyer for the city. It wasn't long afterward that the city's corporation counsel, a fellow Bridgeporter, stepped down from his city post to go into private practice with young Rich. The clients came flocking, drawn by the name of Clout and Clout on the law office door and the legal miracles that politically connected lawyers can perform in Chicago—miracles beyond the capabilities of even the sharpest legal minds. Rich Daley struggled through law school—the media made snide references to his failing the bar examination twice—but by his late twenties, he was bringing in the kind of money that would make him the envy of even the best and brightest from the country's elite law schools.

Richard J. had begun his political career as a state legislator. Cutting his political teeth in Springfield's back rooms had served him well. Richard M. would be offered the same opportunity.

Bridgeport already had a state senator, but that proved only a minor annoyance. He retired and was taken care of with a well-paying job in City Hall. The same quiet efficiency won young Rich the party's endorsement. Richard M. Daley won his first election by a landslide. The father had always done the community right. Why not vote for the Old Man's son?

In a *Tribune* feature about the Daley clan that appeared in 1977, a man described as an old family friend offered that no one of Daley's four sons was sole heir to their father's considerable political skills. Roll the four into one, and you might have a reasonable facsimile, the friend implied. "All the boys have a part of him in them"—but only a part. The youngest son, Bill, was the one who seemed to have inherited his father's political instincts. Yet in old-country European families, the eldest son inherits the family business, much the way the eldest son ascended to the throne in feudal society. Qualifications meant nothing, age everything.* The other sons were expected to settle for ancillary roles.

From the start it was plain that the young man whose buddies playfully called him "Mayor" was not the dealmaker his father was. His threats and boasts would have been something for other machine loyalists to mock if not for his father. Perhaps rushed into service before he was ready, he would stand to make a motion and then fumble his lines. Whether true or not, the impression was that he carried (in the words of one machine insider) "his

*If a boy, that is: Rich Daley has three older sisters.

daddy's shillelagh" down in Springfield. The wise machine loyalists could not afford to guess wrong, so they took it as gospel that Daley was his father's eyes and ears in Springfield. Before the end of his first term, Daley was named chairman of the Senate's powerful Judiciary Committee.

Some machine colleagues, such as fellow south side senator Tom Hynes, felt compassion. "Rich didn't have the luxury some of us had to cut our teeth down there in semi-obscurity," Hynes said. But even many of those loyal to the father felt resentment. "He didn't impress me as understanding what the hell was going on," State Senator Phil Rock, a party loyalist, confessed in an interview. Rock added that Daley was guilty of "some really off-the-wall comments."

Rich Daley was not humble. He did not behave like an inexperienced legislator with much to learn, but was arrogant, like an important man's son. It was one thing for Chicago legislators to genuflect to the senior Daley; it was something else entirely to bow before Richard M. He hadn't wrecked his weekends working a precinct or kowtowed to climb the career ladder. He hadn't, to draw an analogy with the business world, worked his way up by starting in the mailroom but instead began his apprenticeship as a branch office executive. Whereas the Old Man was a warrior ideally suited to governing in the urban jungle, a street fighter who had scrapped for every opportunity he won, Richard M. had been handed it all on a silver platter. One legislator offered in an interview that when Mayor Daley died, "a lot of people are going to have the shivs out for that kid."

Five years into Richard M.'s tenure, *Chicago* magazine put together a feature on the best and worst legislators in Springfield. Their ratings were based on interviews with legislators, lobbyists, state employees, and beat reporters. In ranking Daley among the "ten worst," the magazine cited his "arrogance," his "sharklike qualities," and his "living off his father's name. . . . If he were named Richard M. Schwartz, he wouldn't even be in the legislature."

The hostility toward Daley occasionally worked its way into the debate, such as the time one state senator took the floor and said, "Those of you who didn't even have to work to get here, just walked in or looked across a dinner table and said, 'Daddy, I want to be a senator,' had better think twice before they start criticizing someone who had to fight like hell for everything he got." That senator, Harold Washington, was always buttonholing colleagues to talk about the uppity kid who acted as if Chicago was truly a monarchy where the king could pass down his throne to the male heir apparent.

Dawn Clark Netsch suffered no illusions about her colleague Richie Daley. He voted the way of any machine loyalist: against open government, against measures to stem election fraud, and against other reforms introduced by antimachine independents such as herself. Even by Chicago's standards the vote fraud inside nursing homes was worthy of note, yet Daley was among those pushing a bill that banned poll watchers from nursing homes.* The only difference between Daley and the other party regulars from Chicago was that he was not simply following orders but passing them on to others.

Both Netsch and Daley were state senators representing Chicago; both were elected to the Senate in the same year, 1972, but Netsch was a lakefront independent at a time when there was war between the machine and antimachine forces. It struck Netsch that if she sponsored a bill, Daley would automatically oppose it. There was the rape-law reform package that Netsch and others put together in the mid-1970s. The bill required police training in rape investigations and prohibited insurance companies from exempting rape from health insurance packages, among other proposals. The bill got no further than Daley's Judiciary Committee. "It got very petty and very mean," she said.

Netsch was a strong advocate of women's rights and gained fame as a leader in the fight for the ERA. Daley's vote on the ERA was mixed, and he opposed a bill to make a woman's past sexual conduct inadmissible in rape trials. He voted to classify abortions as murder and voted in favor of another bill to ban government-funded abortions. "Dirty little Richie," Netsch began calling him.

Yet Netsch saw a different Daley after his father's death, as if he had become free of a great burden. He let his hair grow longer, and laughter came easier. One feature writer offered that Daley seemed more at ease with himself. A son died from spina bifida: that, too, brought about a new Daley.

---

*Daley was confronted years later with these and other votes. His face flushed as he told the reporter, "Vote fraud? I was never for it."

Shortly after his father's death Daley approached Netsch about a bill she was sponsoring to allow for generic drug substitutions. He offered to do anything he could to help pass it. He then worked with the independents on a bill reforming the state's mental health code and another strengthening nursing home regulations. He used his Judiciary Committee and his sway over the machine contingency in Springfield to help pass these and other measures. He was not the creative force behind any of these bills but a politician whose support meant the difference between success and failure.

Since his father's death the media had cast Daley as a top contender for mayor.* The successful courting of the liberal vote, supposedly the brainchild of Bill Daley, was the kind of deft maneuvering that might fulfill those prophecies. Daley surprised people when he showed up at a Netsch softball fund-raiser and even took a few swings of the bat. After passage of the mental health bill, Daley threw a champagne reception in his own honor. A full complement of independents showed up, as did reporters intrigued by this new wrinkle on the political scene. Daley's liberal friends happily told them of their newfound respect for the ex-mayor's eldest son.

Don Rose, who had played a major role in several of the machine's biggest defeats—Hanrahan in 1972 and Bilandic in 1979, among others—was among those who failed to see any great Daley metamorphosis. Daley's support for a few apple pie issues, such as nursing home reform didn't impress Rose as it did his colleagues. They were good measures that offended almost no one and pleased most. He could understand the thinking in the Daley camp—at those prices why not broaden the coalition?—but his fellow independents baffled him.

Even if Dirty Little Richie was never the real Rich Daley but only a role that circumstances imposed on him, the picture presented was hardly flattering: an elected official, representing a quarter of a million people, a man well into his thirties, racks up an awful voting record out of fear of standing up to his father. The idea of toasting Daley at a champagne reception was particularly infuriating to Rose. It was as if independents such as Netsch were celebrating Daley finally choosing *not* to kill a worthy proposal.

*So common was the conception that the man selected to complete the rest of Daley's term, Michael Bilandic, was nothing more than a caretaker that reporters dared to ask Bilandic about it at his first press conference as mayor.

The new Daley was no champion of liberal causes. The Independent Voters of Illinois (IVI) gave Daley a modest plus score in 1973 and again in 1975, yet a minus 16 in 1977 and minus 4 in his final term. During this same period Netsch scored a plus 105. He pushed no reform measures aimed at opening up government; he voted against a state board of ethics, against a bill requiring financial disclosure by Springfield lobbyists, and against countless other measures aimed at reforming Chicago's infamously corrupt election process. He was more open to the ERA but not to other issues important to women. He voted to restrict abortion rights, such as his vote in 1979 for a measure requiring that a woman wait seventy-two hours after "applying" for an abortion.

Rose joked that those suddenly singing Daley's praises, such as Netsch, suffered some variant of the Stockholm syndrome: they seemed akin to prisoners who begin sympathizing with their tormentors. Or perhaps it was like someone living in fear of a Doberman, Rose said. After years of growling and biting, the dog allows you to occasionally pet its head. "You're so grateful, you ignore the fact that it kills an occasional small child."

The slights at first seemed as frivolous as they were petty. Ireland's prime minister scheduled a stop in Chicago shortly after Jane Byrne entered office. The city held a grand gala in his honor, of course, yet the new administration snubbed the Daleys by not inviting them.

Rich Daley spoke on the family's behalf at a press conference. It was bad enough that I was not invited, he said, "but they didn't even have the courtesy to invite my mother." The venerable Eleanor "Sis" Daley, the wife of the late great mayor whose very tenure ensured Chicago a spot on an Irish prime minister's itinerary, was not invited to any of the city's festivities in the prime minister's honor.

Sis Daley never cared for Byrne even when her husband was alive, or so it was said among the machine faithful. Some described the relationship between Mayor Daley and Byrne by drawing the analogy of an affectionate uncle doting on a favorite niece. Others saw them more akin to an indulgent father and his spirited daughter. "Janie," Mayor Daley called her— "Janie Byrnes." Maybe the crude rumors that the two were carrying on an affair fueled Sis's distaste for Byrne; maybe it was just that this Janie Byrnes from Sauganash seemed pushy and privileged.

Byrne's antics at Mayor Daley's funeral seemed to confirm every bad feeling that Sis Daley had ever had about her. The usher walked Byrne to the aisle reserved for the city's department heads, but instead Byrne kept walking, straight to the second pew where President-elect Jimmy Carter, Vice President Nelson Rockefeller, and other national dignitaries were seated.

Byrne tried to tend to any lingering bad feelings after her primary win over Bilandic in 1979 when she appeared in Bridgeport for a rally featuring the Daley clan. She reminded the crowd that she campaigned against Bilandic but carefully avoided any criticism of the man who was her political mentor for so many years. "I hope you'll believe that I know to whom I owe everything," Byrne said, her voice cracking with emotion. Yet not long after Byrne was elected mayor, Daley made a move. He announced he was running for Cook County state's attorney, a high-profile post that would put Daley within striking distance of the mayor's seat. Byrne's sentimentality was eclipsed by more immediate and powerful feelings.

Byrne said she could not support Daley for state's attorney because she had already pledged her support to another Democrat. Who that was, Byrne could not say. After a long and public search that mocked her claim of prior support, she settled on Alderman Ed Burke. The previous year, as a candidate for mayor, Byrne had offered Burke as an example of the evil cabal of men plundering Chicago.

Byrne twisted arms to secure Burke the party's endorsement and came down on any city worker openly campaigning on Daley's behalf. Twenty-eight city workers living in Bridgeport were either demoted or fired for defying the party's endorsed slate. Later, when these twenty-eight sued in the federal courts, the judge on the case interrupted the plaintiffs' case to say he had heard enough. "I share the same outrage that the petitioners do," he said.

Byrne spent over $150,000 in campaign funds on Burke's behalf, to no avail. Daley won the primary running away, with sixty-three percent of the vote. Byrne endorsed Daley in the general election over Republican foe Bernard Carey but then unendorsed him two weeks before election day. She said she couldn't in good conscience back Daley after discovering he discriminated against blacks, but one of those she cited as a supposed black victim was a white real estate agent named Howard Rynberk. "As the one who was running the Carey campaign," Don Rose wrote in the Chicago

Reader, "it is impossible for me to describe the sense of helplessness and frustration that came from watching this loose cannon roll about and undo a finely wrought effort—all the while thinking she was serving her own and Carey's interests."

The prospect of a Daley challenge in 1983 was like an obsession with Byrne. Any alderman or committeeman known to be a Daley sympathizer was frozen out of power. As a consequence, aldermen in the Daley camp found themselves siding with the council independents against Byrne. Several won IVI "best legislator" awards for the first time in their careers. In 1980 Byrne pushed a seven percent raise for thirty-two of the city's thirty-three deputy commissioners; the one exception was a Daley cousin. In 1981 Byrne sent calendars to all City Hall employees. The calendar referred to events taking place at the Civic Center—what it was called before it had been officially renamed Daley Center. Daley loyalists accused her of shortchanging city services to the southwest side communities whose elected representatives had supported her foe.

Byrne's final assault on the Daley camp came in the spring of 1982 when she engineered the dumping of George Dunne, the party chairman since Daley's death in 1976 and a supporter of his son. Jobs were offered to those committeemen who voted against Dunne; Dunne supporters were threatened. Democratic Committeeman John Marcin was one example. A high-paying post was created for his brother George Marcin; two days later John Marcin cast his vote for Byrne's candidate, Alderman Ed Vrdolyak— another candidate Byrne had denounced as an evil caballero.

Daley couldn't have bought at any price the positive PR that Byrne's heavy-handed maneuverings generated. It cast him in the unlikely position of outsider, the victim of a vindictive, power-driven machine. Nothing could have done more to shore up his support among independents. Those whose antipathy for Byrne defined their politics found themselves siding with Daley.

Byrne allowed Daley to distance himself from the worst excesses of the very same machine that spawned him. Byrne relied heavily on a committeeman named John D'Arco to strong-arm the various ward bosses on behalf of Ed Burke in 1980 and then Ed Vrdolyak in 1982. D'Arco was the First Ward committeeman and a man rarely mentioned in media accounts without some reference to "reputed ties to organized crime." Daley made much of D'Arco's involvement, but D'Arco was a solid ally of his father's. Daley would have preferred D'Arco as an ally rather than a foe, yet D'Arco made for a nice foil nonetheless.

When a city inspector threatened a restaurant owner because he put up a Daley poster, an outraged Daley precinct worker telephoned Mike Royko. Byrne didn't invent these tactics; she learned them from an able practitioner whose son now stood as her mortal foe. But Daley, unaccustomed to such coercion, expressed his outrage. Only a "ruthless" administration fires hardworking people over partisan politics; only the pettiest of elected representatives punishes an entire ward for its support of an opponent by denying people vital city services.

A deep sense of bitterness prevailed among the Daleyites. Mayor Daley created Byrne, yet she almost destroyed the organization he spent over twenty years putting together, then she turned against the royal family by trying to cut off at the knees Daley's eldest son. As the 1983 election approached, the Daleys harbored a palpable indignation.

It was with a sense of inevitability that Daley, with his wife and his mother standing on either side of him, announced his candidacy for mayor in early November, right after election day. "My family, my wife Maggie, my daughter Nora and [son] Patrick, my mother, my brothers and sisters, my nieces and nephews are with me today, and they share in my decision," Daley began. "On this day especially I think of my father. He was never satisfied with the progress this city had made. He was always working to make it better because he loved the city. I am a candidate because I share his love." He was running for mayor, Daley said, because the city could not afford another four years of mismanagement and sleaze.

The early polls showed Daley with a commanding lead over Byrne. A poll appearing in the fall showed Daley leading by a comfortable fifty-two to eighteen margin; another had Daley ahead of both Byrne and Washington among black voters, with a projected thirty-three percent of the vote. Some political pundits were already prophesying that he would reign over Chicago for more terms than even his father had served.

7

THE
LIBERAL
APOLOGY

Never had the antimachine movement seemed so ripe with possibilities. Unity, the heart of the machine's strength throughout Richard J. Daley's twenty-one-year tenure, was no longer the organization's greatest asset but instead a potentially fatal weakness. In December, with the election three months away, the Democratic party endorsed Byrne for mayor, to no one's surprise. Yet no longer did the party's endorsement mean the full weight of fifty ward organizations around the city, black and white. Only eleven of the city's twenty strongest ward operations were with Byrne; the other nine were with Daley.

Against this backdrop, an energetic antimachine movement was assembling, led by a black candidate who brought with him an extra hundred thousand voters. But the antimachine forces had problems of their own, largely due to race. In December 1982 there could be said to be two antimachine movements, both agreeing on a common enemy in the Chicago political machine but split along racial lines.

The deadline for filing petitions for the mayor's race fell on the third week in December. Rumors had Bill Singer, a well-known antimachine crusader in the 1970s, entering the Democratic primary as a fourth candidate. Singer hardly had time to assemble a serious campaign, but at the exploratory meetings he called to discuss his chances he voiced his concern: if he didn't enter the contest, then for whom could the independents vote?

Some Washington strategists worried all through the filing deadline. They told themselves that Singer's candidacy would spoil any possibility of the city's white independents joining their crusade. Others, like Lu Palmer, considered Singer's decision with indifference. To them, he was nothing more than another candidate who would further split the white vote.

Bill Singer was thirty-two years old and had served on the Chicago City Council for only three years when he proclaimed he was challenging Mayor Daley in the 1975 Democratic primary. Singer's announcement came at a time when Daley appeared most vulnerable. No less than six prominent Daley aides and allies had been convicted on charges of impropriety between 1971 and the 1975 primary. In 1974, the victim of a stroke, Daley seemed suddenly old and frail. Also to be considered was the fact that thirty percent of the electorate was black. Hanrahan had been defeated in 1972. That same year Ralph Metcalfe publicly criticized Daley for ignoring the police brutality rampant in the black community. The problem was that the ambitious Singer was not the only independent looking ahead to the mayor's race with anticipation.

Metcalfe was Singer's biggest worry. When Metcalfe's feet turned cold, Singer breathed a sigh of relief. But then a state senator, Richard Newhouse, a black independent from the south side, said that he, too, was running for mayor. The announcement hit the Singer campaign with a thud.

Singer and his associates found Newhouse as terribly vain and short-sighted. As they saw it, no independent figure black or white could mount a more formidable challenge than Singer. The newspapers carried a picture of him (and also of Jesse Jackson) smiling triumphantly in 1972 when a band of party upstarts successfully challenged Daley's delegation to that year's Democratic convention. Where Singer cut a citywide figure, Newhouse was only modestly well known inside the black community.

There was also race to consider: what chance did a black man have of winning? Was the main issue race—or beating Daley? Singer strategists suspected that Daley had induced Newhouse into the race as a spoiler.

Paranoia gave way to a righteousness within Singer. He had fought Daley in 1972 not so much for himself—white men weren't the ones underrepresented in the state's delegation to the convention—but on behalf of women and people of color. As alderman he had supported several civil rights initiatives. Didn't they see he had their best interests at heart?

Newhouse partisans didn't necessarily disagree that Singer stood the better chance of winning, but they wondered what difference a Singer administration might make from the perspective of black Chicago. His issues were not those of the black community. He was a corporate lawyer living in a fine home in a wealthy lakefront neighborhood. He spoke out passionately against corruption and waste but was mealymouthed on race. He spoke of a color-blind government, yet many black Chicagoans saw a need for a government that recognized institutional discrimination. Just before election day a federal judge, citing past discrimination, ordered the city's police department to adopt quotas for black and female officers. The ruling was greeted with cheers by black activists but roundly criticized by Singer and Daley alike. Asked about the ruling, Singer offered that he found quotas "repugnant."

Wasn't it always that way with the white liberal, Newhouse supporters told themselves knowingly. Singer expected black support but without the give-and-take of an equal partnership. Beating Daley rested solely on the success of turning out a strong antimachine vote in the black community, yet Singer presumed that a white candidate should lead this coalition. "There are just too many of us to fit into somebody else's car," Jesse Jackson said, explaining his last-minute switch from Singer to Newhouse, "because now we've got the biggest car in town."

Daley won the primary handily. His fifty-eight percent share of the vote nearly doubled Singer's second-place total; Newhouse won a disappointing eight percent of the vote, taking third even among black voters. Black supporters such as Richard Barnett nonetheless saw a silver lining: they had taken important steps toward strengthening the coalition between the white and black independent movements.

The nationalist believed he knew better. The white liberal, the nationalist said, speaks of biracial coalitions only when it is one of their own as candidate. Like the liberal who is for integrated housing—until it means a black living next door. The liberal, the black nationalist predicted, might occasionally say all the right words about racial justice, but he will find any excuse to avoid taking part in a black-led antimachine effort.

Perhaps the *Tribune* was sending a signal to Singer when, several weeks after Washington announced for mayor, the paper mused wistfully on its editorial page about their hopes that "an attractive independent candidate would be lured into the field." It was always that way in the media: though the black community could take credit for the machine's only two citywide defeats, to read the papers and watch the television news was to believe that the antimachine movement was something white and confined to the north lakefront.

Perhaps Singer's star status illustrated this point best. By the time he had served a single term on the City Council, the black community had elected and then reelected several antimachine aldermen as its representatives. The south side's William Cousins was a black independent elected to the City Council before Singer (Cousins's slogan: "Unbowed, unbossed, unbought"). Though he both predated and outlasted his north side colleague, Cousins was never as much in the media spotlight as Singer.

The next generation of reporters shortchanged the black independents in similar fashion. When looking for an antimachine quote, reporters invariably sought out white Alderman Martin Oberman and ignored black west side Alderman Danny Davis. The Obermans and Singers seemed to derive from this coverage confirmation that their every action was the beginning and end of the reform movement.

Bill Singer let the deadline for filing for mayor pass and instead endorsed Jane Byrne. He cited his negotiations with Byrne concerning a new cable television ordinance. A lawyer, Singer had a client in the cable business whose interest he sought to protect. He lobbied Byrne to change the proposed ordinance working its way through the City Council. At her behest he drew up his own plan, which Byrne promptly backed. The *Sun-Times* editorial board spelled out its objections to the plan under the headline, A CABLE OUTRAGE.

After the ordinance sailed through the council, Byrne put the screws to Singer. "I did as you asked," Singer quoted Byrne as saying. "Now you can do for me." What choice did he have but to endorse Byrne? he asked. The same day he endorsed Byrne, the mayor named him to head the city's new cable commission.

Among those who launched Washington's candidacy, few contemplated Washington from the perspective of the north side voter. David Canter was among the exceptions. Canter, a white lawyer, met Washington in the early 1960s. It was a perfect match: Canter, prominent in the city's Independent Voters of Illinois, was drawn to a politician whose ear he could bend; Washington, in turn, welcomed an alliance with a well-connected white ally in a neighboring ward. By 1980 the two were meeting nearly every weekend to pore over the numbers and consider Washington's prospects for mayor.

Canter recognized that it was Washington's ability to inspire black audiences that made him the consensus choice among the black activists and intellectuals. He recognized, too, that if Washington won, it would be the sweep of black enthusiasm that placed him in office. But Canter liked to say that Washington might as well have been chosen because of his appeal as a lakefront candidate, that's how perfect his record was from their point of view.

The way Canter saw it, Washington suffered two big negatives. One was his tax troubles of eleven years earlier. Most media accounts carefully pointed out that Washington was not accused of failing to pay his taxes, but only convicted of a misdemeanor for failing to file his tax forms. But some journalists were not as careful, such as Channel 2's Walter Jacobson, who reported in one of his nightly commentaries that Washington was jailed on tax evasion and disbarred, though neither charge was true. To the extent the Washington campaign worried about the tax issue, the concern was over false reports that left an impression he was yet another tax cheat in a long line of corrupt Chicago public officials.

The perception that Washington stood no chance of winning was his other big negative, but Canter figured that was more of a concern among black voters than the lakefront independents. A futile but noble challenge to the machine, in fact, seemed something of a badge of honor among lakefront reformers.

In Washington the lakefront had a man with a portfolio. He was a lawyer and a member of Congress with twenty years of legislative experience. He was articulate and intelligent. His liberal credentials were almost impeccable. Throughout much of his tenure in the state legislature he stood as perhaps Springfield's most ardent defender of civil liberties. His congressional voting record placed him in high regard with groups such as the Americans for Democratic Action (ADA), the AFL-CIO, and other liberal organizations. Washington's record on women's issues was impressive: he was a key sponsor of rape-law reforms in the 1970s, an unstinting supporter of the ERA, pro-choice, and in favor of public funding for day care centers.*

Washington's record as an antimachine independent was as strong as his two opponents' were weak. The IVI ranked Washington fifth from the top and Daley next to last among all legislators during the four-year period both had served in the state Senate. That same year *Chicago* magazine listed Daley among its ten worst legislators and it honored Washington as one of the ten best.

There was also Daley's record as state's attorney. He stepped up prosecutions in consumer fraud cases, created a special unit to monitor nursing homes, and added another that focused on environmental law. Yet not long into Daley's tenure judges and defense lawyers alike criticized him as a draconian county prosecutor. His office clogged the courts by prosecuting defendants to the full extent of the law for the slightest of crimes, even possession of one marijuana cigarette. Daley successfully lobbied for state laws that mandated minimum sentences. A judge considering the future of a teen found guilty of stealing a television and radio from a neighbor's home was forced to sentence him to a minimum of four years in prison. Similarly, Daley's Springfield lobbyist pushed for mandatory jail sentences for first-time drug offenders, stripping judges of options such as ordering a defendant to serve time at a drug-treatment center.

Washington's other competitor for the lakefront vote, Jane Byrne, seemed to be no competition at all. When she was co-chair of the Cook County

---

*When the National Organization of Women endorsed Byrne for mayor, a chorus cried out that the group should add a second W to its name: NOWW, the National Organization of White Women.

Democratic party, she opposed the Equal Rights Amendment and never fought the machine's antiabortion stance. There were the deals she cut with the likes of Ed Vrdolyak and Charles Swibel and the disappointments of antimachine leaders when Byrne abandoned their prized initiatives. She pressured both the chief of police and the school superintendent for an endorsement. ("The top cop who has become a political prop," Washington said in one debate.) She even attempted to put the squeeze on Mike Royko after he wrote that Swibel was "a notorious political bagman, practically . . . the co-mayor of this city." An old newspaper friend of Royko's worked for the city as a consultant. Royko wrote that a Byrne press aide called with a message shortly after his column appeared: Keep it up, and your friend will be looking for a new client. Byrne fired him, Royko wrote, and then for good measure held up his checks for several months.

Yet the endorsements did not come. Washington won the IVI's support by a vote of ninety-five to two, but that had no apparent effect on the city's white liberal politicians. Adlai Stevenson III endorsed Daley, as did Marty Oberman and another liberal stalwart, State Representative Ellis Levin. Levin, Oberman, and Daley campaign chairwoman Dawn Clark Netsch were probably the three best-known lakefront independents in local politics. Former Vice President Walter Mondale, in late 1982 the Democratic front-runner for president, also endorsed Daley.

Not every prominent white liberal politician was in the Daley camp, however. Senator Edward (Ted) Kennedy, the guiding light of liberal politics in the United States, didn't endorse Daley—he endorsed Byrne.

Only two local white politicians endorsed Washington, Alderman Larry Bloom and State Representative Barbara Flynn Currie. Bloom represented a ward that was eighty percent black and Currie a district with a black majority. Asked how he accounted for this lack of support among white elected officials normally finding themselves on the antimachine side, Washington said, "Maybe it's the way I part my hair."

Perhaps no endorsement was as significant to Daley as Oberman's. Oberman was the highest-profile antimachine figure of the post-Daley era, as Singer had been in the latter half of Daley's career. The Daley campaign had identified the six north lakefront wards as the city's "most fluid." They saw Oberman as key to swinging those wards Daley's way.

Years later, on the defensive, Oberman blamed Washington for his endorsement of Daley. Twice he ventured to the south side, he said; both times Washington told him that he was not running. "Go make the best deal with Daley you can," Washington supposedly told him.* By the time Washington changed his mind, Oberman explained, it was too late. "It would not have been the honorable thing to do to go back on my word," he said. Curiously, though, Washington had already announced for mayor when Oberman called a press conference in December to say that he would endorse either Washington or Daley in the race, but under no circumstance could he support Byrne.

Only when the 1983 campaign was a faint memory did Oberman mention his visits to the south side. During the campaign he said he based his endorsement on Daley's record as state's attorney and his overriding preoccupation to rid the city of Jane Byrne. Daley was inevitable, Oberman told associates. Better he should have some influence inside a Daley administration than none at all.

There was something at once compelling to this logic yet ironic that it was Oberman who was offering it. Over the years he had been associated with any number of improbable causes. His refusal to horse-trade in the backrooms, as if it were beneath him, was something of a joke among the machine aldermen. But Oberman suddenly saw a little bit of influence as better than none. After years of tilting at windmills, Oberman had suddenly discovered pragmatism.

Marty Oberman felt indignant when Washington supporters implied his endorsement of Daley had anything to do with race. "I've done more on behalf of the black community than any other politician in Chicago," Oberman said. The claim was as revealing as it was absurd. Oberman boasted that he endorsed Daley only after first exacting some commitments from him. What this champion of black causes wrangled from Daley was support for two open government measures.

---

*Those close to Washington give a slightly different version of this story. They confirm Oberman's visits, but in their telling, Oberman's preoccupation was whom Washington might endorse for attorney general should he win as mayor. Tired of Oberman pestering him about it, Washington supposedly said, "If you can cut a deal with Daley, go ahead." Oberman acknowledges his ambitions to higher office but said he resents the implication that it intruded on his decision in the 1983 mayor's race.

Daley had not turned out to be the political hack some feared during his campaign for state's attorney. He didn't fire people wholesale, despite eight years of a Republican predecessor. Daley was the first Cook County official to sign the Shakman decree, a federal court order banning the hiring and firing of city employees for political reasons, yet at the same time he used the state's attorney's office to fight Shakman on behalf of other elected officials appealing the decree. His record on issues important to the lakefront independents was mixed.

Others choosing to judge Daley using broader reform standards looked more harshly on Daley's three years as state's attorney. Daley didn't use the powers of his office to fight a city redistricting plan that the federal courts eventually found diluted the voting strength of black and Latino Chicagoans—he defended it. Minority hiring was another sore point. Daley hired more black and Latino prosecutors than his Republican predecessor, but fewer than two percentage points more. The number of women prosecutors rose by three percentage points.*

Missing from Daley's campaign literature for mayor was any sense of commitment to issues dear to black independents. There was no mention that the city shortchanged basic city services in black and Latino communities or any mention of federal poverty dollars spent in white middle-class areas. If this disturbed the likes of Netsch and Oberman, they complained only privately.

The center of gravity of the Daley campaign was not along the lakefront or downtown or in the intellectual environs of Hyde Park but in the regular Democratic organizations. Even Daley strategists admitted that theirs was mainly a Bridgeport-based campaign run by the same Eleventh Ward muckamucks who faithfully served Daley's father. The players atop the campaign, save an exception here or there, were white men who cut their teeth in the old Daley machine.

Earl Bush was an old hand in machine politics who for years served as Richard J.'s press secretary. Old Man Daley fired him in 1973 after he

---

*According to documents Daley's office filed with the federal government's Equal Employment Opportunity (EEO) office, only three percent of the thousand-plus people on the state's attorney payroll were Latino. Of the 723 professionals earning over $43,000 a year, five were black and none were Latino.

learned Bush was the secret owner of a firm that had exclusive rights to display advertising at O'Hare Airport. For his crime Bush was sentenced to one year in jail, but he never served a day in prison; two years later his sentence was reduced to two years' probation, and finally the conviction was overturned by a judge who found the law unconstitutional. Reporters and columnists didn't focus on Bush's presence in the Daley campaign quite the way they did on Oberman's, but that said more about the limitations of daily journalism than it did Bush's significance. Bush sat in on strategic sessions with the Daley inner circle that Oberman only wished he could be a part of. State Senator Jeremiah Joyce could also be counted among Daley's trusted circle of advisers. A machine regular, Joyce was a liberal's nightmare, authoring book censorship laws and a bill that offered a free one-way ticket to any poor person seeking employment in another state.

The Democratic committeemen who years earlier had hitched their wagons to Daley had no cause to abandon him for Byrne. Daley did not declare war on the machine, the way Byrne had in 1979 or Washington had in this campaign. He was anti-Byrne, not antimachine; he was running against the regular organization's endorsed candidate, but if he won, his antiparty stance would last no longer than Vrdolyak's tenure as party chairman.

A Daley administration was likely to be less mercurial and abrasive, and Daley a less vindictive mayor, but there was no mistaking that the key power brokers in the city would be many of the same ward committeemen in power under Richard J. Daley, with a few liberal politicians added to the equation. Yet if the ward committeemen joked among themselves about the pointy-headed liberals scattered throughout the campaign, it was in private. From a PR standpoint, these liberals were too important to hold to public ridicule.

The congressional black caucus met to contemplate Walter Mondale's and Ted Kennedy's failure to support Washington and voted unanimously to express their "utter dismay and extreme disappointment" with Mondale. The presidential front-runner would only say in his defense that he endorsed Daley as a matter of loyalty: "He helped me when I needed his help," Mondale said.

Kennedy wasn't as gung-ho for Byrne as Mondale was for Daley. He permitted a letter to be sent under his name urging black voters and liberals to vote for Byrne, and that was all. He, too, was harshly rebuked by the congressional black caucus.

Kennedy's defense, like Mondale's, boiled down to loyalty. Byrne had endorsed him for president in 1980, and this was the payback. Kennedy had committed to sending out three letters on Byrne's behalf but sent only one. Mondale, by contrast, was the featured speaker at a Daley rally, saying, "Chicago is my kind of town, and Daley is my kind of mayor."

Surely Alderman David Orr preferred Washington over Byrne or Daley. Six years earlier, when Washington first ran for mayor, his apartment served as the campaign's de facto far north side campaign office. The press categorized Orr as a "lakefront liberal," but he was something else—a politician as likely to criticize the liberals as the party regulars. North side activists who had no use for lakefront liberals could be found campaigning on Orr's behalf.

But in 1977 Orr wasn't an alderman representing a mostly white ward. Now, as Orr contemplated his 1983 reelection, he concluded that he had trouble enough without adding Washington to his burdens. Already a foe was exploiting his vote in favor of federally subsidized moderate-income housing in the ward.

The way Orr tells it, Washington understood his desire to play it safe. Orr spoke out against Byrne but did not commit to either Daley or Washington. What most upset Washington partisans was Orr's insistence that campaign volunteers work either for him or for Washington, but not for both. Washington had a hard time finding campaign workers in Orr's ward.

The black nationalists weren't surprised. Harold Washington was black, the lakefront independent white. Case closed.

To them, Washington wasn't just challenging the Cook County Democratic party; he was also running to liberate the black community from liberal paternalism. They wondered when their brothers would learn.

Edwin "Bill" Berry, former executive director of the Urban League's Chicago chapter, was forever taking heat within the black community because of his work with white business leaders he believed were enlightened on matters of race. After the city's west side burned following King's assassination, Berry founded Chicago United, a coalition of black and white businessmen, to work on the yawning gap between the city's black and white residents. For his trouble he was labeled a Tom, a sellout, and worse.

Berry was from Oberlin, Ohio, where his grandfather, a free black man, settled in 1840. His father was a lawyer, and one of his uncles owned a first-class hotel that was patronized by whites. He described his family as "aristocrats" in one interview. Not until he played football in high school against white teams did Berry get his first taste of racism.

In Chicago, Berry frequently found himself uncomfortably sandwiched between the black militants and the white liberals, like the time he was a part of a citywide group debating a black boycott of the public schools to protest the makeshift Willis Wagons set up to avoid integration of the Chicago schools. He recalled with a deep sense of regret the abuse suffered by his friend Virgil Martin, president of the Carson Pirie Scott department store chain. Martin wanted no part of the school boycott, and despite the store executive's work to end race discrimination, several members of the group threatened to picket Carson's. "They were alienating a friend in Martin," he said. He had seen militancy destroy a great many coalitions.

The Washington campaign offered Berry a chance to legitimize his life's work. He could prove the value of the resources he had been cultivating since the early 1960s—prove to the nationalists that the white liberal is open to a black-led coalition when black empowerment also means ridding City Hall of the rapscallions dominating politics for the past fifty years.

Berry, as co-chairman of Washington's campaign, visited his liberal friends downtown, looking for financial contributions. He appealed to those who had given to numerous antimachine causes—those businessmen disgusted with the graft and corruption that drove up the cost of doing business in Chicago. He thought he was speaking their language when he told them that Washington was in favor of self-imposed limits on campaign contributions from firms doing business with the city and against patronage and other wasteful spending. If nothing else, he expected nice-sized contributions from his Chicago United buddies. "Bill had never had fund-raising problems before," said Al Johnson, a black businessman close to Washington who worked with Berry on any number of causes.

Berry had endured disappointments in politics but had never experienced the sense of failure that he felt in those months when he was petitioning his liberal friends for money and their support. He raised barely a dime. "Not even one-half of one percent of the money we raised in the 1983 primary was from whites," Johnson said. The normally optimistic Berry said, "I feel my twenty-eight years in this city have been wasted. . . . I have concluded, sadly, that racism is much deeper than all of my study had led me to believe. Those who said they believed in decency and democracy were phony and lying." Those who had long ago sworn off white liberals just shook their heads knowingly.

Richard Barnett had every reason to feel as deeply wounded as Berry. Barnett, too, had suffered his share of abuse for his work with white independents, such as the nasty comments that dogged him when he chose Bill Singer over Richard Newhouse. "The recent defection of a few Uncle Tom Negroes to support a Jewish candidate for mayor of Chicago, who has never shown any interest in blacks during his tenure in City Council, proves again the stupidity of some white-brainwashed Negroes," columnist Nate Clay wrote in the *Metro News*, a weekly catering to black Chicago.* Barnett also recalled the time he ventured to the Forty-third Ward to help Marty Oberman when he found himself in a tough runoff election for alderman. Barnett had just finished an exhausting stint managing a tough west side campaign while working nights at the post office, but there were two black precincts in the ward that Oberman always lost by wide margins. He assumed Oberman would do the same for a fellow independent in the black community.

Barnett didn't bother confronting Singer. Years earlier Singer had earned a place on Barnett's long list of antimachine sellouts. Singer had made his peace with Old Man Daley soon after the election when he accepted a

---

*The constant reference by Clay and others to Singer as the "Jewish candidate" is offered as proof of a rampant anti-Semitism within the black community. But Clay and others were trying to make a point about the media constantly referring to Newhouse as the "black" candidate. A conscious effort was made to call Singer the Jewish candidate, just as Daley was labeled the "Irish candidate."

city appointment; why he did so became clear a couple of years later when, interested in running for the U.S. Senate in 1978, he appeared hat in hand before the machine's slatemakers asking for their endorsement. Barnett would only say he was "perturbed" by his endorsement of Byrne.

Barnett, though, sought out Oberman to tell him he was as baffled as he was disappointed. It was war with the machine, and independents helped independents. Daley was Daley, a man foursquare in the machine, and Washington was with the independents. For Barnett it was that simple.

Like Barnett, Al Raby put himself on the line for Singer in 1975. He ran for alderman that same year in a predominantly black ward, and Raby, a former King aide, was a strong contender. He knew endorsing Singer would only fuel talk that he was in the back pocket of the liberals—he already had that reputation in some circles inside the black community— but he believed Singer was the stronger candidate. Raby later said he was certain that that decision alone cost him the election.

There was a time in the 1960s when Raby may have felt as deeply disappointed as Bill Berry. But by 1983 Raby looked on his relationships with white liberals like a hardened man who long ago lowered his expectations to make himself impervious to romantic love. "In the sixties and seventies, my expectations were much higher, and therefore my disappointments were much greater. The more experienced I've become, the fewer expectations I have," Raby said. He merely added Singer, Oberman, Netsch, and others to an already long list of partners who had jilted him.

White businessmen were not the only ones reluctant to contribute to Washington's campaign. The lack of big checks written by black businessmen was equally disappointing. Some were blunt in saying that you don't anger a sitting mayor by funding an opponent. Those less concerned with any business arrangements with the city were no less practical: why waste money on a long shot? It was only in the last few weeks, when black businessmen began to fear what it would mean if Washington won and they had given nothing, that they wrote big checks. Washington raised just over $1 million by primary day, far less than the multimillion war chests amassed by Byrne and Daley, especially Byrne.

Businesses with city contracts proved one invaluable source for Byrne. A Milwaukee-based company called Festivals, Inc., which sponsored ChicagoFest and other city events, gave Byrne $67,000; the president of the company claimed to have raised another $50,000 on her behalf.* The accounting firm of Laventhol & Horwath was not doing business with the city when early in Byrne's tenure it contributed $25,000 to her political fund, but that would soon change. Over the next several years Laventhol won ten contracts worth nearly $500,000. By December 1982, Byrne had amassed nearly $9 million in campaign funds, dwarfing the $2 million Daley had raised.

Money helped Byrne close the wide gap that separated her from Daley in the pre-campaign polls. David Sawyer, a high-priced adviser from New York, was perhaps Byrne's wisest investment. Media accounts placed his gross fee at $700,000, but the slick commercials he produced seemed to justify the money. If parochial voices within the Byrne campaign initially complained about this overpriced "outsider," their carping soon gave way to praise. Based on focus group sessions held that summer, Sawyer made Byrne over as a competent chief executive capable of managing a $2 billion city budget.

During the summer Sawyer conducted a series of focus groups to pinpoint Byrne's negatives.** He instructed Byrne to replace her flower-print dresses with suits, change her hairdo, and dampen her rhetoric. She would no longer be "Fighting Jane" but "Executive Jane." Byrne used her war chest to blitz the airwaves throughout December with television commercials that showed off her makeover to Chicago.

Sawyer accomplished the impossible. In October his candidate was polling only thirty-three percent of the white vote and twenty percent of the black vote. Yet by mid-December, Daley's commanding lead had dissipated, and polls showed Byrne slightly ahead. Despite all the fanfare surrounding Daley, Byrne had managed to make a race of it.

---

*Festivals, Inc., could afford to be generous. In 1982 its president said he expected to make $1 million on ChicagoFest alone. Independents charged that a sweetheart deal allowed them to make such profits; for instance, the city, not Festivals, Inc., absorbed the overtime costs of the police and cleanup crews.
**Byrne was reluctant to heed Sawyer's advice until she viewed Sawyer's focus-group tapes. Word has it that she literally shuddered.

8

A
TOWER
OF
BABBLE

Late in December, with the primary election less than two months off, Jane Byrne dumped one of the two white women she had named to the public housing board the past summer, replacing her with someone black. The party's polls showed that, among whites, Byrne was ahead of Daley. It was time to tend to the black vote.

Byrne strategists all but conceded that Washington would win the black vote—if not a clear majority, then at least a plurality. "Whoever wins the primary had to come in second" among blacks, said Byrne campaign manager William Griffin. After all three Democrats had announced for mayor, a *Defender*/WBMX poll showed Byrne capturing only nine percent of the black vote. She had her work cut out for her.

      Byrne's rapprochement began in October when she was a guest on a call-in show on a black-oriented station. Still smarting from her decision to tip the racial balance of the Chicago Housing Authority board from black to white, caller after caller lambasted the mayor. They accused her of not respecting the black community. "When I hear that," Byrne said sadly, "it hurts a lot."

On the day Washington announced he would run for mayor, Byrne held a press conference of her own, boasting of black gains under her rule. She appeared a couple of weeks later at the New Tabernacle Baptist Church on the south side. I haven't "written off" the black vote, she told the congregation. "I know of nothing that I have done in the past three and a half years that would make anyone think that." She added, "I love all of you."

Byrne stepped up her efforts that December with something of a black nominating spree. She named a black executive to fill a vacancy on the Board of Education. Bennett Stewart, the machine's candidate against Harold Washington in the 1980 congressional race, took over as the city's top lobbyist. Just before Christmas, Byrne tended to the racial mess she created at the CHA six months earlier. She announced that Angeline Caruso was stepping aside, and named a black attorney, Earl Neal, to take her place. Caruso was as stunned as anyone by Byrne's announcement, but she told reporters that she would do as the mayor wished. She had already made that pledge to Byrne when she was first appointed in July, when she told Byrne she would "cooperate" should the mayor ever wish to make a change.

If Byrne's aim was to soothe the bad feelings of the black community, she showed how profoundly she misread their simmering anger. Neal was a sharp attorney, but his reputation was based largely on his deftness in defending Mayor Daley when he was stuck in racial quagmires: the 1970 ward remap that civil rights groups charged discriminated against blacks; a racial bias suit against the city over scattered-site housing; the police discrimination suit filed by Renault Robinson.

That Christmas, Byrne spent about $300,000 in campaign funds on hams and Christmas trees for those living in public housing. (Earlier that year the Byrne campaign bought thousands of Mother's Day bouquets for the precinct workers to deliver to loyalists throughout the projects.) Addressing a west side congregation, Byrne explained that hams and trees were a modest gift but ones she felt compelled to give. "You see," Byrne said in a hushed voice, "I know what it's like at the end of the month to be waiting for that bluish green check."

In January, Byrne doubled garbage pickup in the black community and initiated a $10 million jobs program, paid for with federal poverty funds. Most of the jobs were temporary positions that lasted ten weeks—through the general election that spring.

By early January the mayoral campaign had taken on a familiar rhythm. Daley criticized Byrne, and Byrne criticized Daley; Washington attacked them both. Washington's record was vulnerable, yet both Byrne and Daley acted as if he were a fringe candidate. (Daley's campaign literature, for instance, asked people to "compare the records" before deciding—but then compared his record only to Byrne's.) Criticizing the black candidate, strategists for both Byrne and Daley told reporters off the record, could only hurt their candidate among potential black voters. It might also lend credibility to a candidacy they were inclined to dismiss as symbolic. Both campaigns tiptoed carefully around Washington.

The Washington campaign was hardly calling attention to itself as a potential threat. The campaign manager, Renault Robinson, was disorganized and knew little about running campaigns. He also kept insane hours that were driving the rest of the staff crazy. For years exiled to the police force's graveyard shift, Robinson generally slept by day and worked through the night. He didn't hesitate to ring up associates whatever the hour. Washington was himself something of a night owl but, tired of all the complaining, he dumped Robinson three weeks into his campaign, with no obvious replacement waiting in the wings.

Washington sought a new manager who was black but had a reputation as someone who worked well with whites. The new manager also had to be well versed in electoral politics and yet have no ties to the machine. The problem was that those prospective managers with political experience tended to be old machine hands, and those who shared Washington's antimachine bent tended to think in terms of communities and issues, not ward boundaries and constituencies.

Richard Barnett was one exception. Washington, in fact, had asked Barnett to take the job before he offered it to Robinson. But Barnett had recently been diagnosed as having cancer, and the drain of chemotherapy was proving too much.

Al Raby was another possibility. His antimachine credentials were impeccable, and he was a crack negotiator with considerable experience mediating between widely divergent factions. Yet there were as many minuses as pluses beside Raby's name. He had never run a political campaign except his own as an aldermanic candidate eight years earlier, and after losing that race, he left town to find work in Washington, D.C. Raby was out of touch. He also had personal problems that scared Washington.

Yet Raby it would be. The campaign was already proving a Tower of Babel, and the staff consisted of a collection of people sharing a belief in Washington and little else except for bad feelings from years past. When offered the job of campaign manager, Raby admitted to Washington that he didn't feel he was qualified. Among friends he was even more candid—he said he did not think Washington could win.

The campaign's central office was another problem. The rent was cheap and the Washington coffers empty, yet everything about that office troubled Raby. For starters, the building was closed on Sundays. The rest of the week some staffers found it easier to work out of their homes than compete for one of the office's four phone lines. But mainly Raby was troubled by the symbolism of an office at 79th Street and Cottage Grove, on the city's south side. It didn't express an eagerness to expand the base, Raby said.

There were those inside the campaign, hearing this, who grumbled about Washington's choice of Raby, a man they saw as more in touch with white liberal sensibilities than those of black voters. "Fleeing the base," some screamed—fleeing the south side so as to water down the campaign's blackness. But a south side central office struck Raby as a sign that Washington had not yet made the transition to citywide candidate. In January, with the election just six weeks off, the campaign moved into an office downtown.

The Washington campaign was functioning hand to mouth. The previous week's fund-raising helped define the following week's strategy; the money was spent as quickly as the finance people could count the change and dollar bills collected passing the plate at Washington gatherings. Daley and Byrne were running polished television commercials; Washington was forced to rely almost entirely on radio, the poor candidate's medium. There were constant fights over posters and brochures. One neighborhood office would charge that another was hoarding. Staffers complained that sometimes getting up just to go to the bathroom meant that they would no longer have a chair to sit on when they returned.

Lack of money lent a sense of disorder to the Washington campaign. It had the feel of an old-fashioned civil rights crusade: an overworked and underpaid staff managed the best they could without the necessary resources. More than once Raby recalled his days as an organizer for King. "I manage the chaos," Raby said to anyone asking for a job description.

Reporters rolled their eyes when Washington partisans tried to explain that theirs was a crusade, not a campaign. The downtown media did not see the romance of a people's campaign but instead saw euphemisms for incompetence. Appointments were missed; the candidate was perpetually late. An event was as likely to flub as click. It seemed half of the staff wasn't talking to the other half. The Washington campaign had a fragile feel, as if it would self-destruct at any moment.

The *Tribune*'s chief political writer, David Axelrod, was more sympathetic to Washington than most columnists, yet two months into the campaign he wrote that Washington's organization resembled "a bumper car at an amusement park, bouncing from one obstacle to another." Compared to the smooth-running affairs that were the Byrne and Daley campaigns, he continued, Washington's was a "campaign of confusion. . . . One has to wonder whether there is not some lingering ambivalence" about running for mayor. How seriously can we take Washington, one pundit after another asked.

Most boggling of all was Washington's Christmas Day visit to the Cook County Jail. After his brief stay there, back in 1972, Washington had vowed to visit the jail each and every Christmas. Aides tried talking him out of making the visit in late 1982, but Washington wouldn't listen. He felt he should do it, so he did.

Reporters were dumbstruck. It was as if Washington went out of his way to draw attention to his worst negative, as if he wanted to lose. "Today was a homecoming of sorts for Congressman Washington . . ." one reporter began on television that night. Another station flashed Washington's old mug shot on the screen while reporting on his visit. The visit, it turned out, was the best covered event of his campaign since the day he had announced.*

Most disheartening of all from the perspective of the Washington campaign were the numbers. A poll in early January showed Washington with only forty-one percent of the black vote; the campaign's own internal polls

---

*Despite the controversy, Washington made his annual Christmas visit to the jail throughout his tenure.

revealed numbers barely more encouraging. With election day little over six weeks off, Washington had not yet caught on with black Chicago.

At Washington's downtown campaign headquarters, they looked nervously at the calendar at the same time they reassured themselves. People don't think about mayoral politics around Christmastime, they told themselves. With the holidays over, it will all come together. They spoke of getting better organized and of doing a better job ensuring that Washington showed up on time.

On the south side, a group congregated in a campaign office on 47th Street and groused late into the night about Washington's people downtown. To them, the problem wasn't holiday apathy or press accounts characterizing the Washington campaign as disorganized. On 47th Street and King Drive they blamed the campaign's troubles squarely on the suit-and-tie crowd working at the main headquarters. To them, the campaign's top technicians were running scared—scared of anything but the same stale methods of past campaigns. No way Harold's gonna move folks, they agreed—not by attending candidate forums and issuing policy statements proposing structural changes in the bureaucracy. They plotted a coup.

Officially they called themselves the Task Force for Black Political Empowerment. Inside the Washington campaign they were referred to by any of several names: "the Third Force," "the Shadow Campaign," "the 47th Street Crowd."

The Task Force was created a few days before Washington announced for mayor, at a meeting Lu Palmer frantically pulled together to develop a strategy should Washington fail to run. There the Reverend Al Sampson told of his experience in Cleveland when Carl Stokes first ran for mayor. Sampson was a part of a rump group within the Stokes campaign that acted as an independent watchdog against the taming influences of white sympathizers and the black middle class. Sampson suggested they do the same in Chicago. The idea was wholeheartedly endorsed. Two academics espousing black nationalism, Robert Starks and Conrad Worrill, both as much activist as teacher, were chosen the co-chairs of the Task Force. They set up shop at 47th Street and King Drive.

Neither Worrill nor Starks pretended he was an experienced campaign hand—their inexperience was almost the point. Their vision would be broader, their very presence a break from the past. Those trapped by poverty with little hope of better days ahead, those for whom murder and rape were a commonplace of life, those whose babies' odds of survival in their first year were no better than those of third world countries: these were the potential voters, the poor and disenfranchised of the black community, that the Task Force targeted. Yet how many politicians, black or white, had come to them with promises of a better tomorrow?

Conventional wisdom held that these people were apathetic and ignorant, but "alienated" and "angry" were more apt descriptions. These were voters who rejected politics not so much because they could afford to, like many white middle-class baby boomers, but because they saw their participation as meaningless. A great many had rejected politics because they saw it as removed from their own lives. The government they watched on television may as well have been that of a foreign country for all the impact they believed they could make.

Task Force members had themselves rejected electoral politics; between them Worrill and Starks had voted maybe a half dozen times prior to 1983. They felt disenfranchised by black politicians who seemed more intent on proving themselves palatable to white America than addressing black needs. The key, then, as they viewed it, was a campaign that saw Washington constantly pressing the flesh in housing projects and the city's poor communities. Washington could not be afraid to embrace the poor as his own.

The Task Force was largely ignored by the downtown campaign. Washington's schedulers, skittish about these militants, balked each time the 47th Street crew proposed a plan for a rally. A walk through an occasional project was one thing; a series of housing project rallies something else entirely. It meant television images night after night of Washington surrounded by large crowds of black public housing residents. It meant reporters interviewing residents whose slang jangled the white ear and also the black middle class.

Worrill, Starks, and Palmer felt the campaign they helped launch was being snatched away from them. ACTIVISTS FEEL BETRAYED, read the headline over a column by Nate Clay in the *Metro News*. In an attempt at downtown respectability, Clay wrote, "bourgeois professionals with strong ties to the white establishment" were given control of the campaign. The move from Robinson to Raby symbolized that change for Clay. In Robinson, the nationalists and those seeing themselves as grass roots activists had an ally.

Raby by contrast was better connected to black institutions like the Urban League and to liberal organizations.

Downtown they chalked up Clay's article as just one more piece of bad news; on 47th Street they couldn't have been more pleased. "Downtown they were interested in building a campaign," Conrad Worrill said. "We were interested in building a movement."

Downtown they felt superior in their knowledge that electoral politics was more than rousing speeches and bullhorns. They laughed among themselves that these activists who for years dismissed politics as some honkie scam were suddenly experts on winning elections. Even those seeing the Third Force as a godsend—how else would they reach the disenfranchised?—were put off by their stridency. Already the media were marginalizing Washington. Perhaps the campaign's greatest challenge was to be taken seriously by the downtown establishment. Only then would black voters take Washington seriously—so, at least, was the logic downtown. Relinquishing control of the campaign to these grass roots militants, it was believed, was tantamount to writing off the white vote and much of the black middle class as well.

With election day less than two months off, the 47th Street crew grew weary of arguing. The trick, as they saw it, was to persuade the campaign's scheduler to lend them Washington for a day. That way they could show Washington the power of what they were talking about. Starks described their task as nothing short of "the movement side taking the campaign away from the campaign side."

Conrad Worrill had met Harold Washington in 1976 when Washington was gearing up for his run for mayor in the 1977 primary. It was hardly the sort of meeting that would win Worrill a private audience with Washington now, seven years later. Worrill presented Washington with a list of demands that served as a precondition of his support. First he insisted that Washington endorse the rights of the Palestinian people to a homeland. He then demanded that Washington speak out against regentrification—or, in Worrill's words, announce his opposition to "black removal." (According to one colleague, Worrill had tempered his spiel when he spoke with

Washington: "That's when Conrad was advocating that the city seize back land from developers who had moved out blacks.") Their meeting was brief. "Washington told me I was crazy and left," Worrill said.

One of Worrill's most vivid childhood memories was of the death of a fourteen-year-old Chicago kid named Emmett Till. Till's death in 1955 sent shockwaves through black Chicago. Visiting relatives in Mississippi, Till had whistled at a white woman; he was later found dead in a river, his body mutilated. Worrill, who was fifteen at the time, remembered his neighbors organizing protests after an all-white jury acquitted the men charged with the murder. He remembered, too, more than thirty years later, the exact wording of the law that Till supposedly violated—"reckless eyeballing." A few years later Worrill happened to see Malcolm X on a Sunday morning talk show. He didn't quite understand all that Malcolm said, but he understood the emotions sweeping over him as he watched. Influenced by the black power movement of the 1960s, Worrill took to wearing dashikis and pendants honoring his African heritage.

Worrill matriculated at the University of Chicago, where he received his master's degree. The venerated south side institution not more than twenty blocks from his home would have been off-limits to Worrill if not for the financial aid suddenly available to black students in the late 1960s, a by-product of the civil rights movement. At the University of Chicago, renowned for its conservative theorists, Worrill found cause for his growing militancy. It was there that Worrill was first exposed to books heralding the glories of Africa before the white man invaded the continent in search of riches—of an African civilization that predated and precipitated Western culture. These were not just fanciful theories spun by black militants but the scholarly works of respected historians of all races. Any pride Worrill may have felt reading of his ancestors' accomplishments was all but over-whelmed by anger. Why hadn't he been exposed to this in the public schools? He was also excited by the work of black theorists such as Marcus Garvey, whose pan-Africanist movement urged blacks to embrace African civilization as a strategy for bolstering black self-esteem.

To Worrill the esteem problems endemic within black culture could be traced to the failure of the schools and other institutions to respect any-thing that wasn't white, male, and European. Black children were raised believing that they descended from a primitive culture—from savages and illiterate slaves. Public education was a Eurocentric version of world history that celebrated the cultural accomplishments of white Europeans while ignoring those of Africans, Asians, and Latin Americans—exactly what one would expect of a culture dominated by white men whose roots were in Europe. Classic literature as taught by the public schools meant the works of white Europeans; art history, the works of white men. Even Tarzan, king of the African jungle, as Muhammad Ali once pointed out, was cast by Hollywood as a white man.

Worrill was slower to embrace Washington than Lu Palmer and Bob Starks. He took part in the basement meetings—Worrill was for Washington because that's who Palmer was pushing—but his true interests lay elsewhere, far from local politics. He was a leading force in the Black United Front, a national organization that aimed to impress blacks with the richness of African history. It wasn't until the ChicagoFest boycott that he made the 1983 mayor's race a priority. Once aboard the Washington bandwagon, though, he was hooked.

Worrill was out of his mind with anger on a cold Saturday morning in January 1983 waiting well past the appointed hour for a candidate who would never show. The Task Force had learned earlier in the week that Washington was theirs for part of a Saturday. By that morning Worrill was exhausted, his eyes dry and tired from missed sleep. On a street corner stood a crowd of about a hundred who were growing increasingly frustrated.

Worrill tracked down a longtime aide to Washington named Clarence McClain. Either Washington shows up at 35th Street for his next appointment, Worrill yelled into a phone, or we're going to hold ourselves one "goddamn motherfucker of an anti-Washington rally."

By the day's end, though, Washington's blowing them off that morning would be nearly forgotten. Washington showed up only a few minutes late at 35th Street to begin what Bob Starks described as "one of the most emotionally charged experiences I've ever had in my life."

A campaign stop at the Robert Taylor Homes, the country's largest housing project, was the day's highlight. The advance teams had done their job well. A large crowd had assembled by the time Washington and his entourage arrived. When his car came into view, people began chanting, "Ha-rold. Ha-rold." People leaned out their windows and called out enthusiastically; others ran downstairs to be a part of the crowd. A passing bus, Starks said, made an extra stop to allow its passengers to pile out and shake Washington's hand. The streets in front of the Taylor Homes grew so clogged that no cars could pass.

Washington didn't appear uneasy and on edge, as most politicians do when they visit the projects. Instead, he struck Worrill and Starks as more animated and comfortable than they had ever seen him. They practically had to shove him into a car so as not to be too late for the next rally. Similar scenes ensued at subsequent stops. Several times that day Worrill looked at Starks, and Starks looked at him, and they nodded with satisfaction. The Task Force had won over the only person whose opinion really mattered.

The campaign lived with the rift between the Task Force and downtown. Not even Al Raby pretended that the campaign was anything but two separate efforts. "Downtown we had the professionally minded campaign technicians," he said, "who may not have been the city's most experienced election people, but most had some electoral experience. Then you had the crew down at 47th Street doing their own thing, quite separate from the rest of the campaign."

The two camps dealt with each other mainly through Washington's scheduler. Washington allowed strategists to alter his schedule but made it clear that time blocked out for the Task Force was off-limits.

Downtown they tended to get bogged down in detail work, losing sight of the big picture. "Institutional militants," two activists dubbed them. Those working on 47th Street tended to lose themselves in endless philosophical arguments: was class the great divide in our society, or was it race? The Shadow Campaign was never terribly well organized, but then neither were those working downtown. Downtown they dressed in suits and ties for campaign appearances; at the press conference announcing the formation of the Task Force, Worrill wore a three-quarter-sleeved baseball shirt. Downtown the staff was black and white and Latino—so closely mirroring the racial makeup of the city as to seem intentional; 47th Street was almost exclusively a black world. The Task Force targeted several white and Latino neighborhoods, but black Chicago was unapologetically its focus.

When the newspapers revealed that Byrne's south side coordinator, State Representative Larry Bullock, admitted he gave $70,000 in campaign funds to a group organized by the city's most infamous gang, the El Rukns, the Task Force organized a demonstration outside a Woodlawn hotel where the El Rukns were known to congregate. They confronted the gang rather than simply calling a press conference to express their outrage. "We don't issue a whole lot of press statements . . . [and] don't give cocktail sips," Bob Starks told a black reporter. Their aim was nothing short of "an atmospheric change" whereby support for Byrne or Daley was not tolerated inside the black community.

Occasional arguments broke out between the two camps, such as when they argued over the tearing down of other people's posters. To the downtown pros, this simply was not done, if not out of a sense of fair play, then out of fear of getting caught. The Task Force didn't care what some newspaper columnists might say; the presence of so many Byrne and Daley signs in the black community was a constant irritant. Those working down on 47th Street knew instinctively that they could drive through vast stretches of the southwest side without seeing a single Washington poster. Yet on the south and west sides the posters of all three candidates were in evidence. They dispatched squads of workers to crisscross the black community on search-and-destroy missions.

At times this split was comical. Some days Raby learned what the campaign was up to only by watching the television news that night, like the time protesters spoiled a Daley press event showcasing his support among black preachers. On 47th Street they were fed up with black preachers allowing white politicians to use the safety of the church—a white politician was assured a courteous reception—to gain entry into the black community. Like scores of white politicians before them, both Daley and Byrne campaigned in the black community primarily on Sunday mornings, speaking from a different church pulpit each week. Accommodating preachers were as outlandish in their criticisms of Washington's candidacy as they were obsequious in their praise of Byrne or Daley. "If Harold Washington is elected, the city would go down the tubes . . . like Gary," south side preacher Reverend O. D. White said when introducing Rich Daley to his congregation. "We know what happened in Cleveland, Gary, and Detroit. When [Gary's] Mayor Hatcher was elected, the white officials took all the money and ran. . . . Gary is now a ghost town. . . . Can't you see the writing on the wall?" Reverend White asked.

The Task Force couldn't have been happier after they spoiled the preachers' mid-January Daley endorsement session. A group of picketers demonstrated outside the hotel while Starks and Palmer were inside disrupting the press conference. Bob Starks was the chief heckler. "Why won't you speak out against the segregation in your neighborhood?" Starks yelled, interrupting Daley. Why haven't you denounced the racial policies of your old man? he asked. Those preachers gathered to endorse Daley were mainly storefront preachers with small congregations, fueling Starks's outrage. "We talked about the preachers like they were just dogs," he said. A full complement of reporters following Daley meant it was one of the Washington campaign's better-covered efforts. "That really energized us," Starks said. "That energized a lot of folks in the community."

Raby, too, recalled the moment years later; he remembered it as one of those days when he learned of an event from the reporters phoning him for his comments. He had nothing to do with the protest, but there it was on page one of the *Sun-Times* the next day, a photograph of a group of blacks picketing Daley and the preachers. Raby also recalled the incident for the complaints it precipitated about the campaign polarizing under his direction.

There were other fiefdoms inside the Washington campaign. The Finance Committee not only raised money but approved its use. Bill Zimmerman, a California-based political consultant, handled Washington's media; his battles with the Finance Committee were as intense as they were absurd. Because they controlled the money, Zimmerman needed the committee's approval before any radio spot could run on the air. The most vocal, he said—most notably Walter Clark and Bill Berry—were business executives who didn't know the inner workings of a political campaign. "These were people who had never read a script in their life, making changes that were impossible or just plain wrong," Zimmerman said.

It didn't make any difference if Raby had already signed off on the ad—Raby himself was forced to appear before the finance people to plead his case. It was as if a Finance Committee of twenty-five was playing campaign manager.

There were those who saw themselves as part of a black liberation movement and others as part of an antimachine crusade. Still others were drawn to the campaign of a candidate to the left of liberal. Yet they all saw enough of themselves in Washington to ensure they all shared a stake in his election.

The white leftist was as agog over Washington as black children wearing six or eight Washington buttons at once. When slighted, each faction figured the blame must rest elsewhere: with a top aide, with the media, but certainly not with Washington. Only Washington prevented the campaign from collapsing under the weight of its differences.

Washington was fluent in many languages. He could talk Cruse and Fanon with the black intellectual or play hardball like a machine politician. Negotiating through the ambiguities of his coalition was not altogether unfamiliar to Washington. He had stepped carefully through similarly perilous terrain for most of his political career. Washington would not define his campaign as first and foremost a black movement, nor would he downplay its racial implications. The white reformer could venture to the west side and hear Washington say the city work force must be slashed, though black unemployment exceeded twenty-five percent and unemployment among black teens topped fifty percent, just as the black activist could hear Washington speak plainly of black empowerment before a white audience.

Those working out of the 47th Street office could damn Washington for cutting the city payroll, or they could recognize that Washington articulated their issues more forcefully than virtually any mainstream politician in the United States. Anyone who was part of his coalition made that same choice: focus on those aspects that he or she found troublesome or embrace a synthesis of the antimachine movement as defined by Washington.

Washington tolerated the downtown–47th Street split because he saw an advantage in it. Washington needed the likes of Palmer, Worrill, and Starks on the black radio speaking out against the institutional racism that pervaded the Byrne administration and the regular Democratic party. But, as Richard Barnett put it, "we didn't want to go outside the black community with that." The trick was energizing black Chicago without generating a corresponding white backlash.

The city's segregation provided the partition behind which the Task Force could operate a high-profile campaign without drawing the white media's attention.* Radio had played a critical role in the voter registration

*Chicago's segregation has always proven a mixed bag for the black community. The city's Jim Crow practices, for instance, gave rise to a black middle class; for example, the "no coloreds" signs that hung in the city's hotels and restaurants created a need for black-owned hotels and restaurants.

drive the previous fall, yet it remained a secret political weapon. The black community could speak with one another virtually in private simply by tuning to any one of a dozen talk shows on black radio.

Later, the media discovered the black-oriented radio stations and managed to cultivate a few contacts in the black community other than black politicians at City Hall. In 1983, though, reporters covered this most unorthodox of campaigns by traditional means. The media missed almost entirely the role the Third Force played in Washington's campaign.

From the beginning both Byrne and Washington were anxious to debate. Inside the Byrne campaign they were confident that their candidate could easily best the inarticulate Daley. Washington's emissaries, anxious for the free exposure, pushed for as many debates as possible. The problem was Daley.

For a time Daley flat-out refused to debate. The occasional snide column, his handlers figured, was better than a highly public hour-long event that drew attention to his wooden speaking style. But then Daley began to suffer a precipitous drop in the polls, and in mid-January all three Democrats agreed to four debates. The first debate was held the third week in January, five weeks before election day. An estimated two million people watched it.

Commentators rating the candidates' performances split between Washington and Byrne. Those giving the nod to Byrne cited her cool demeanor, despite the double beating she took from Washington and Daley. Those crowning Washington the winner cited his debating skills and also how much he stood to gain. Washington's challenge entering the debate was to prove to voters, especially black voters, that he was more than a protest candidate. On 47th Street they spoke of those blacks so brainwashed by the dominant culture that they needed to be convinced Washington was every bit the equal of a white person. He accomplished that, if nothing else.

Washington's performance didn't quite ignite black Chicago, but it swayed a good portion of voters to his side. Polls taken over the next two weeks showed Washington's support among blacks jumped by nearly twenty percentage points, to fifty-nine percent. (His share of white support, though, remained a steady five percent.) Inside Washington's campaign offices the phones didn't stop ringing. "You can run but you can't hide,"

Washington challenged Byrne during the debate, echoing boxer Joe Louis's famous challenge to white rival Billy Conn. For days blacks enjoyed repeating that line over and over.

The debate's big loser, almost every pundit agreed, was Daley. Not surprisingly, the polls showed Daley's support falling further. Worse yet, his support was slipping among voters living on the southwest side, his base. Polls had him losing or at best tied in each of the southwest side's nine wards—nine wards that Daley must win overwhelmingly, Don Rose wrote in the Chicago *Reader*, "in order to stand a ghostvoter's chance."

Daley was proving that he was not the formidable challenger the experts believed him to be. His trouble was more than an inability to debate; he was equally stiff and uneasy before big crowds. He read most speeches verbatim, rarely looking at his audience. One time Daley, speaking before a large crowd, said, "These three principles *point to sign*—access, opportunity, equity—will guide my administration."

Daley was very much his father's son on the stump. Rich Daley shared his father's jumbled syntax and propensity for stringing together choppy, fragmented sentences that often amounted to nothing but nonsense. From either Daley's mouth, the word *every* sounded like "ev-ee," *administration,* "uh-ministration." The problem was that 1983 was a different era from his father's day. The cliché in Chicago in 1983 was that television replaced the precinct captain as the intermediary between City Hall and voters. Daley's private meetings with a Northwestern University speech professor helped, but that only underscored how far he needed to come to make the grade.

Daley was worse still in sessions with reporters. He giggled nervously and added more than an occasional "y'know." "He behaves like a man in a dentist's chair," one reporter wrote. "He squirms in his seat, checks the clock periodically, and approaches every turn in the conversation anxiously." There were jokes that Daley never exited the same sentence he entered. The press insinuated that Daley was not smart, that his shortcomings transcended a stilted speaking style, and it occasionally reminded the public that Daley had failed the bar twice.

Even supporters unflatteringly imitated their candidate, lampooning their man's limited repertoire of empty homilies inherited from his father. He spoke more about God, family, and the good people of Chicago than taxes or programs. In one campaign advertisement his wife, Maggie, described him as both a wonderful husband and a terrific father. Another ad featured Sis Daley in her living room pointing to her display of family pictures. "That's Rich," she says. "He's the eldest. I'm very proud of him. I'm sure that if his father was alive, he'd be very proud of him."

One precinct worker recalled viewing Daley's debate performance with foreboding. It struck him that Daley trotted out a generic leadership speech to answer nearly every question put to him. "And what, Mr. Daley, would you do about the housing problem?" "The problem in housing boils down to a question of leadership . . ."

Daley's handlers tried limiting the media's access to their candidate. When *Chicago* magazine ran a spread on all three, the Byrne and Washington campaigns welcomed the publicity and agreed to lengthy interviews. Daley declined. Only the friendliest reporters were granted time with Daley.

Daley strategists said out loud that their man wasn't the greatest of public speakers, but they accused the pundits of confusing intelligence with glibness. He's shy, that's all, they explained. (One *Tribune* columnist, Bob Wiedrich, particularly enthusiastic in his support of Daley, pointed out in one column that Richard Nixon and Spiro Agnew were glib. "Are Daley's critics actually paying him a compliment by charging he is inarticulate?" Wiedrich asked.) Dawn Clark Netsch offered in Daley's defense that he was not threatened by bright and able people. He surrounded himself with solid people, people with good ideas. What else mattered?

Early in the campaign Daley said he resented all the attention paid his father, but his brain trust had sense enough to understand the magic of the old man's name. Down in the polls, the Daley campaign did more than put Sis Daley on television. A picture of the elder Daley filled most of a popular campaign poster that read LIKE FATHER, LIKE SON; the junior Daley was relegated to a corner. In his closing statement in the last of four debates, Daley said, "I make no apology for my name. I am proud of my family name, and I'm proud of my father and my mother. From them I learned a love for this city. I look back to my father's life with pride."

Daley impressed both the *Sun-Times* and the *Tribune* editorial boards but not in the same way. The *Sun-Times* gushed over him while the *Tribune* wrote apologetically, but the bottom line was the same: both endorsed Daley for mayor. The *Sun-Times*'s editorial endorsing Daley, *Reader* media critic Mike Miner noted, dedicated fifty-eight lines to extolling Daley and seventy-eight to ripping Byrne. The *Sun-Times* "kissed off" Washington in nineteen lines, he found.

Both newspapers treated the Daley campaign to flattering profiles. The *Tribune*'s Sunday magazine ran cover art of Daley caricatured as a modern-day Lancelot, under the headline, RICHIE THE LION-HEARTED. The *Sun-Times*'s profile ran under the headline, DALEY PROJECTS STRONG IMAGE.

Something was happening in black Chicago. Campaign workers crying for help began complaining of overcrowded offices and a lack of desks. They traded tales that underscored a change within the black community, such as the story of the elderly black man who wrote a letter to every one of his neighbors pleading his case for Washington. Another thirty thousand blacks had registered on top of the hundred thousand-plus that registered just prior to the November 1982 election. The black community's voting strength jumped by more than twenty-five percent in less than one year's time.

There was also word of defections among Byrne's ranks within the black community. Some captains refused to campaign for Byrne; others worked both sides of the street. Washington's good friend Dempsey Travis came across a black man wearing a Byrne button. "Who do you think I'm voting for?" the man asked Travis in a strange whisper. "Byrne, of course," Travis responded. Then, with a wild laugh, the man snapped open his raincoat to reveal a trove of Washington buttons. Blacks who held city jobs could not afford to be seen without a Byrne button, but neither did they want to be seen as Toms.

The ubiquitous Washington buttons were another sign—the "blue measles," Travis wrote. A blue Washington button was suddenly a badge of pride in the black community. At one church the pastor, the entire choir, and a good portion of the congregation attended church services one Sunday wearing their blue buttons. A campaign volunteer's car window was smashed, but all that was taken was the bag of a thousand buttons from the backseat.

Polls in the latter half of January began showing Washington ahead of Daley, yet the media seemed oblivious to the change. When one poll showed Daley regaining a few percentage points, the *Sun-Times* ran the story under the headline, DALEY GAINING ON BYRNE. The accompanying data showed Daley gaining five percentage points on Byrne, and Washington—in second place—gaining six points.

It was the same with television. Long after Washington had moved ahead of Daley in the polls, television stations still treated his candidacy like a side show. Clarence Page, then a Channel 2 reporter who occasionally covered the Washington campaign, said the scene repeated itself time and again. Reporters assigned to the Byrne and Daley campaigns would give their respective reports and then remain on the set to chat with the anchors. If time allowed, the Daley and Byrne reporters would engage in a dialogue. "And when they finished," Page said, "one of the anchors would turn to the camera and say something like, 'And on the south side today, Harold Washington was also campaigning for votes.'" None of the same on-air banter followed Page's coverage.

In early February, with Washington in second place, former U.S. Senator Adlai Stevenson III called a press conference to announce his endorsement of Daley. In his statement he spoke of a choice between two alternatives, that of a candidate who represented "sordid politics" and Rich Daley, "a choice of excellence."

"It is time for a change," Stevenson said, "and Richard Daley is the best and only way to get it." Stevenson mentioned Byrne by name but gave no indication that he was aware of a third candidate in the race.

The Byrne campaign wasn't nearly as slow as the media or the liberals to recognize Washington's rise. In late January, shortly after the first debate, word reached the press of precinct workers going door-to-door to tell voters it was no longer Byrne versus Daley but Byrne versus Washington. Daley was no longer a serious candidate but a spoiler, campaign workers purportedly said. A vote for Daley may as well be a vote for Washington. Finally someone was taking the black candidate seriously.

9

A

RACIAL

THING

The day Harold Washington announced he would run for mayor wasn't quite the illustrious moment Lu Palmer had dreamed it would be. His day began with a shock: Illinois Bell, which had sponsored his radio show for nearly ten years, fired him for becoming too partisan. Palmer wished Washington would address his firing from the podium—the white man had allowed him a forum for speaking out until there was real power at stake, as Palmer saw it—but he understood why he did not. He was not nearly as forgiving, though, of Washington's other supposed sins that day. For Palmer, Washington's press conference was a scene heavy with portent.

First there was Washington's treatment of Jesse Jackson: no place was reserved for him on stage among the dignitaries. A cordon of bodyguards surrounded the podium, assigned the task, Palmer half-jokingly said, of preventing Jackson from upstaging Washington. Jackson, habitually late, ended up sitting with Palmer and Palmer's wife, both of whom scrunched over to accommodate the three of them on two seats. To Palmer, it was as if Washington was flaunting his newfound status as Chicago's number-one black political figure at a time the precarious black unity forming around his candidacy needed nurturing.

There was also the question of venue. Washington chose to declare his candidacy in Hyde Park, an integrated south side haven in an otherwise segregated city. Hyde Park occupied a special place in Chicago's history; it was a stronghold of antimachine dissent dating back more than three decades. Yet it had always been a base of white power, not black. Palmer was incensed.

"We shall see in '83!" Washington boomed after greeting the crowd, borrowing the slogan that Palmer and others had been trumpeting for two years. The place went up for grabs. Then Washington began, "Chicago is a divided city. Chicago is a city where citizens are treated unequally and unfairly." That was music to Palmer's ears, but from where Palmer sat, the speech went strictly downhill from there.

The rest of Washington's speech was anything but sanitized. He spoke of the machine's long history of discrimination against the black community. He spoke, too, of the black community's need to organize itself—to liberate itself from its own political torpor. Yet the speech was also a pantheon to good-government reforms that wouldn't generate the black crusade Washington needed to win. Washington decried the evils of patronage and a system based on spoils for the victor. Palmer couldn't believe his ears when he learned that a first draft of that speech was written by a former alderman, a white man named Dick Simpson. If that didn't beat all, he said to himself, the man trying to become the city's first black mayor let a white man write his speech.

That Sunday, Washington gave a very different talk before a packed house at the Bethel A.M.E. Church on the south side. Washington officially entered the race in the integrated environs of Hyde Park; now he sought a decidedly black pulpit in which to present himself to the "grass roots."

Bethel was Palmer's turf. It was where Palmer held the 1982 plebiscite that crowned Washington the movement's choice for mayor and where Palmer and his cohorts gathered for countless mass meetings. Washington chose Bethel only after careful deliberation. He considered PUSH as an option but then rejected it. Washington was ambivalent about Jackson, and so, too, were those he sought to reach. Palmer rubbed Washington the

wrong way as surely as Jackson did, but Palmer was respected by those people. Bethel it would be.

Washington gave a speech that any of a dozen of those sitting in the
audience could have given. He spoke not so much as a candidate for political office but as an educator laying out the ties between black dignity and
participation in electoral politics. He spoke of the psychological barriers
they would need to overcome to reach many blacks—blacks who were
reluctant to vote for one of their own as mayor because of an internalized
racism. "We've been pushed around, shoved around, beat, murdered, emas-
culated, destroyed," Washington said. "There's been an unfair distribution
of all the goodies. No system works for us. We influence no institutions in
this country except our own. We have no power. We have no land. . . .

"We've been giving white candidates our vote for years and years,
unstintingly hoping that they would include us in the process," Washington
said. "Now it's come to the point where we say, 'Well, it's our turn. It's our
turn!'"

Washington anticipated the criticism that would rain down on him for
his "our turn" comment by offering a quick history of ethnic politics in
Chicago. The Irish were treated like the city's white trash at the turn of the
century; "Paddy Wagons" got their name because crime and the Irish were
closely linked in people's minds, much the same way crime today has a
black face. But the Irish took power, offering no apologies when they
attained representation well beyond their share of the population. Now it
was the black community's turn, Washington said. Two-fifths of the city
were shortchanged in the distribution of education dollars, parks, basic city
services, jobs; even shortchanged was their share of federal dollars meant to
go to low-income communities. The weight of abuse, Washington said,
was overwhelming and should speak for itself. He urged those listening to
"make it unfashionable and uncomfortable" for any black not to vote for
him. It was a suggestion that this particular audience would not have to hear
a second time.

Weeks later a Baptist minister introduced Washington as an amalgamation
of all the good qualities of past mayors. There were no good qualities to be
had, Washington said upon taking the podium, Daley included: "He was a
racist to the core, head to toe, hip to hip, there's no ding or doubt about it.

He eschewed and fought and oppressed black people to the point that some thought that was the way they were supposed to live, just like some slaves on the plantation thought that that was the way they were supposed to live.

"I give no hosannas for a racist, nor did I appreciate or respect his son. If his name were anything other than Daley, his campaign would be a joke."

Washington chuckled at his own abrasiveness and continued in a gentler tone. He spoke of the campaign as an act of redemption for black Chicago: "That redemption is not going to come out in hatred. It's going to come out in positive action toward our fellow man." Blacks, he said, have not only a right but a responsibility to give their best to society, "even if we have to beat 'em across the head and knock 'em down and make 'em take it."

Yet Palmer and others working out of 47th Street were troubled by the multiracial elements of Washington's message. They were not happy when, early in Washington's campaign, he named the Urban League's Bill Berry to head his Steering Committee. A black executive with Inland Steel was named the head of Washington's Citizens' Committee. Again Palmer shook his head in disbelief, though acknowledging that Washington was not going to shy away from issues of race so as to soothe the white community, in the fashion of so many black politicians before him.

Washington's Bethel speech and others like it aroused more than those inclined to the politics of the 47th Street office. Devout coalitionists such as Richard Barnett were equally heartened by Washington's straight talk on race. So, too, were the people in the audience who cheered when he gave the machine what for. Opinion shapers and civic leaders, however, were horrified.

The media vulgarized Washington's Bethel speech. The TV news reduced his thirty-minute address to a single phrase—"It's our turn." The newspapers quoted snippets of the address, but for years to come Washington's Bethel speech would be referred to as his "our turn" speech and nothing more.

Washington could have delivered his speech in the privacy of a segregated setting, but instead he instructed aides to promote the speech as a major address. Washington was angry that Palmer wouldn't disrupt the evening's schedule to ensure that he appeared in time for the six o'clock news. (Perhaps Washington wished he had chosen PUSH after all; surely Jesse Jackson would have been more sensitive to the deadlines of the working press.)

Pressed about the speech, campaign workers downtown explained that by "our" Washington meant all those on the outs under the machine: minorities, the good-government reformers, women . . . anyone not connected to the boys downtown at City Hall. Yet there was no mistaking what Washington said or his intention in a speech to an all-black audience at an event organized by Lu Palmer.

In its endorsement of Rich Daley, the *Tribune* dismissed Washington's campaign as "racially polarizing." The editorial never cited specifics, as if the point was so evident as to need no buttressing.* Nothing more than a "race man," wrote a *Tribune* columnist named Bill Granger. "If something good happened to him, it was a victory for The People," according to a book Granger co-wrote with his wife Lori. "If something bad happened it was because of the White Man denying rights to The People." Another *Trib* columnist, Bob Wiedrich, couldn't understand someone like Washington, with eighteen years of experience as an elected official, resorting to charges that the city's blacks were treated unfairly by the machine. "It is sheer demagoguery," Wiedrich wrote.

Jane Byrne's stock speech was testimony to the greatness of Chicago. When pressed about black political disenchantment, she said that she had been mayor all of four years: what can anyone accomplish in that short period of time? Mostly Byrne assiduously avoided talk of race. Daley also spoke of Chicago's greatness, warning that in Byrne's hands the city would no longer be great. He, too, avoided the issue of race. Washington alone confronted the city's racial problems, but for that he was not praised but damned.

John McDermott was editor and publisher of the *Chicago Reporter,* a highly regarded monthly specializing in racial issues. Charges laid out in the

*"We felt Daley could be more of a healing force than Harold Washington," said James Squires, then editor of the *Tribune.* "We fully expected Chicago to react as it did after Washington was elected the Democratic nominee. We anticipated that his election would divide the city at a time we felt the city was in need of healing."

Reporter carried a certain weight because of its reputation as a publication that painstakingly sifted through evidence to document its points. CHICAGO PARK DISTRICT SHORTCHANGES BLACK AND LATINO WARDS; MORE FACILITIES, PROGRAMS, AND STAFF CHANNELED TO WHITE WARDS, read one *Reporter* headline. PARK DISTRICT SPENDS U.S. POVERTY FUNDS IN WEALTHY AREAS, read another.

Yet McDermott, derided in some quarters (black and white) as nothing but a white liberal with his head in the clouds, took exception to Washington's handling of the race issue. He expressed horror that Washington called Mayor Daley a "racist." "Unnecessary and unfortunate," he said; "fundamentally unfair." Washington supporters, he said, used unnecessarily inflammatory language. OF FOOLS, JACKASSES, AND "KNEE-GROW" POLITICIANS, read a page-one headline in the *Metro News* promoting a column about black politicians who had sided with Byrne. "Traitors" they were called. McDermott disagreed that Washington's charges were permissible as long as they held up to scrutiny, as Washington partisans argued. In an op-ed piece appearing in the *Tribune,* McDermott offered a constricted prescription for black empowerment. First and foremost, he wrote, "race is not a legitimate issue." The last thing Chicago needed was the sort of racially divisive campaign Washington was conducting, McDermott believed.

Over the years their loyalty to the machine made black Chicagoans something of a joke among the pundits, yet when Washington sought to fire up black Chicago by confronting them with their own tolerance of an abusive government, he was roundly criticized. His most effective weapon—the truth about racial politics in Chicago—was deemed out of bounds. Maintaining the calm was, as always, far more important to the opinion makers than the correction of past abuses.

To some, Washington was the black candidate first and the reformer second. Others saw it the other way around. The picture could be complicated further by adding a third definition: he was a candidate to the left of mainstream with a propensity for pragmatism.

The media, however, had no trouble defining the multifaceted Washington. He was the black candidate—as in, "Harold Washington, trying to become the city's first black mayor, campaigned last night in the

Logan Square community." Media accounts identified him as the black candidate as regularly as they referred to him as "Congressman (D-Ill.)."
Neither Byrne nor Daley was identified as the "white candidate."

Rarely, if ever, was Washington described as the antimachine candidate, though virtually his every word was critical of the machine. Byrne had
only broken with the machine months before announcing for mayor, yet in
1979 she was routinely referred to in press accounts as the antimachine candidate.

If any candidate among the three Democratic contenders was portrayed as representing the independents in the machine-antimachine drama,
it was Daley. Daley, after all, had most of the lakefront reformers on his side.

The media perceived Washington's candidacy as a black phenomenon
and portrayed it as such. So often was the complaint made that it became
something of a campaign cliché among Washington's nonblack supporters
to say that the media ignored their presence. The typical campaign shot,
whether on television or in print, showed Washington amid a sea of black
faces. After Washington appeared one evening in Logan Square, a predominantly white and Latino community, a white family of four excitedly
rushed home to look for themselves on the TV news. The two stations
showing brief clips of the campaign stop cut to a small group of blacks in
the audience listening intently to Washington.

Rarely was Washington pictured venturing into the barrio or to a
lakefront stop. Reporters instead pressed Washington with questions that
implied he was nothing more than the black candidate in the race, gearing
his campaign to blacks. Washington appeared more often in white Chicago
than his opponents stepped foot in black Chicago, yet reporters didn't think
of asking Byrne or Daley about gearing their campaigns to whites in a city
sixty percent nonwhite.

At the *Tribune* a black reporter named Monroe Anderson brooded
over his newspaper's coverage of the mayor's race. In early October,
Anderson had written a column arguing that with two popular whites
in the mayor's race, a serious black candidate stood a chance of winning.
The paper held on to his column for weeks, "because from where they sat
the piece was so farfetched as to make it marginal," Anderson said.
Meanwhile, through his contacts in the black community, Anderson
learned on a Friday that Washington agreed to run for mayor. The paper
did not run the article he wrote for its Saturday edition or in the

circulation-heavy Sunday paper. Apparently Washington's entrance into the mayor's race did not strike the paper's editors as much of a scoop.

Anderson was the man white reporters approached when looking for sources inside the black community, yet his editors rejected his request to cover the Washington campaign. Jim Squires, the *Tribune's* editor, said his main criteria when assigning reporters to cover the 1983 campaign were skill and experience covering politics. Squires said he resented Anderson's insinuation that race had something to do with the fact that no one black covered any of the three candidates for the *Tribune*, nor was anyone black, Anderson said, "part of the mix." He covered the "minority" beat, not politics. It was like the occasional restaurant review they asked him to write. "I'd eat lunch with these people all the time, but they'd never ask me to write a review unless it was some soul food place," he said.

To her credit, Jane Byrne went out of her way to stress that hers was a multiracial effort, like her campaign slogan, "Mayor Byrne for *All* Chicago." The campaign's top posts were filled entirely by whites, but her staff was well integrated. Of fifty-four paid staffers, twenty were black and five Latino, according to the *Reporter*. Speaking at a black church the day before formally announcing that she would run for reelection, Byrne said, "I will not let race become a campaign issue. That would be a step backward."

Those behind Byrne did not tiptoe around the issue, however. Even before Washington officially declared for mayor, there was talk of contingency plans. Ed Burke and Roman Pucinski, two Democratic party leaders squarely in Byrne's corner, spoke of running as independents in the general election. Burke was the more candid of the two: "I think it would be important to have an alternative if someone were to be the Democratic nominee who is not competent and capable to be the chief executive of Chicago." In case anyone misunderstood his meaning, he clarified himself in a later interview. I will run, Burke said, only if Washington wins the primary.

Byrne supporters in the black community took an entirely different tack. They assumed a nationalist posture. They exploited, for instance, Washington's endorsement of a white incumbent named Larry Bloom over four black challengers in a ward that was eighty percent black— Washington's own ward, in fact. Byrne precinct workers harped on the

Bloom endorsement as proof that Washington was beholden to white liberal influences.

The city bureaucracy did what it could do to spread fear of Washington. The police chief, Richard Brzeczek, commented that he didn't think the city would be safe should Washington be elected. An assistant in Byrne's press office, Fernando Prieto, said during one radio interview, "We can go to the Department of Human Services and see how dark that department is. Can you imagine how it would be with a mayor with a face of that color?"

Byrne herself was not above naked racial ploys. As mayor, Byrne initiated a monthly publication called *City Edition*. There were two versions of the February 1983 *City Edition*. The one passed out to south and west side residents ran page-one articles about black history month and the appointment of a black woman to head the library. There was no mention of black history month in the *City Edition* passed around predominantly white communities, and news of the library appointment was relegated to page three. Blacks graced the front page of the black-oriented edition and whites the front page of the other. Both editions, however, referred to Byrne's "One Chicago" vision.

In commemoration of Martin Luther King, Jr.'s birthday, the Washington campaign organized a rally downtown. They expected ten thousand, yet only two thousand showed up. Thus it was understandable that there was some reluctance when the idea of a rally at the University of Illinois Pavilion was broached. The campaign needed something to jolt black Chicago, but not a picture in the paper two weeks before election day of a cavernous hall less than half filled.

When it started to snow heavily the day of the Pavilion rally, organizers braced themselves for disappointment. Yet the bad weather only served to impress those using the event as a yardstick to measure Washington's support. The Pavilion, with a seating capacity in excess of twelve thousand, was packed. As Washington stood at the microphone, the crowd chanted a thunderous "We Want Harold." The hall shook from applause and foot stomping, as if a dramatic and important basketball game was tied going down to the wire. A Byrne rally held the previous day drew half that many and lacked the same spirit.

The rally convinced campaign manager Al Raby that Washington could win. It also drew the attention of a black business community generally reluctant to donate a dime to Washington's campaign. In the two weeks between the rally and election day, black businesses donated something on the order of $250,000 to Washington.

Even nonbelievers in the media were impressed. Some revised their take on the election. Washington might even come in second, ahead of Daley.

Fear ran through the Byrne campaign. For weeks Byrne's daily tracking polls showed her holding on to a rock-solid thirty-eight percent of the vote. Washington was inching up but still lagging ten percentage points behind. Ed Vrdolyak was Byrne's main numbers cruncher. Avoid the big gaffe, Vrdolyak told one Democratic committeeman, and she has it sewn up.

Yet a poll taken six days before the election showed Byrne slipping two percentage points, down to thirty-six percent. She dropped another two points the next day. That same poll showed Washington taking thirty percent of the vote, with ten percent of the voters undecided. The key was turnout, Vrdolyak understood. If blacks turned out in large numbers, Washington might win.

At first Byrne's field manager denied reports that precinct captains were casting the campaign as a two-person race between Byrne and Washington. Then he conceded it was true but said the campaign had nothing to do with it. "When we hear about it, I call and tell them to talk to those people, tell them to stop that," he said.

Yet campaign-sanctioned efforts were hardly more subtle. The campaign printed tens of thousands of copies of a letter written on Byrne's behalf by former Republican Governor Richard Ogilvie, distributed on the city's northwest and southwest sides. "Quite frankly," Ogilvie wrote, "the race for mayor is boiling down to a choice between Jane Byrne and Congressman Harold Washington."* Reportedly, hundreds of Byrne campaign workers hunkered down at phone banks in the final days of the election to convince those voters who told Byrne workers they supported Daley that it was no longer a three-way race.

---

*Actually, Daley was making a mild resurgence in those final weeks. One former Vrdolyak ally claims Vrdolyak's poll showed Byrne and Daley neck and neck just ten days before election day.

On the weekend before the election Ed Vrdolyak addressed an assembly of about two hundred northwest side precinct captains gathered in an insurance company cafeteria. "A vote for Daley is a vote for Washington," Vrdolyak told the captains. "It's a two-person race. It would be the worst day in the history of Chicago if our candidate, the only viable candidate, was not elected."

Vrdolyak did not realize that two reporters had sneaked into the meeting. Had he known, he would not have uttered his next words: "It's a racial thing. Don't kid yourself. I'm calling on you to save your city, to save your precinct. We're fighting to keep the city the way it is."

Byrne reacted to the publication of Vrdolyak's comments by scrapping her schedule and making a series of impromptu appearances in the black community. In Chicago's unique party setup, Vrdolyak, as chairman of the Democratic party, was the head of Byrne's precinct operations. Byrne refused, however, to take her chief aide to task. "I've been coughing so hard and have such a cold that I don't even know what he's been saying," she said. She did say she was "annoyed with anybody who makes race an issue"—Vrdolyak or Washington.

Reporters caught up with Washington at Daley Plaza. "Here at the last moment," Washington said of Vrdolyak, "afraid that he will not be able to reign over this city and use this mayor as a puppet, he's gotten excited and resorted to the last defense of demagogues and scoundrels. He's raised the race banner."

An odd sort of pride ran through the Daley campaign. "He's not dividing this town, he's trying to unify it," Daley's press secretary said. On the day he declared his candidacy, Daley appeared at a black church and then at an Urban League dinner. Those in the Daley camp told themselves that Rich could have won if they had succumbed to the temptations of a racial appeal. We could have "put on a white sheet and run around," Bill Daley said. "But that's just not Rich."

Daley spoke of race on occasion, as at his appearance before a gathering of black ministers. "When I fought for legislation against child abuse in the state legislature," he said to the all-black crowd, "I looked at every child. I didn't care about race, creed, or color." He spoke, too, of a deeply felt aversion to racial prejudice. Only modesty, a top campaign aide offered, restrained Daley from scoring political points off his color-blind approach.

Yet a writer assigned the task of monitoring the Daley campaign for the *Chicago Reporter* noticed that where Daley preached brotherly love in front of black audiences, he did not mention race when talking with whites. He claimed when speaking before black audiences that, as state's attorney, he hired a higher percentage of minority staff attorneys than any other big-city prosecutor. He did not make similar boasts in speeches before white audiences.

When in white neighborhoods, Daley highlighted those issues he figured were high on that community's wish list. He spoke of traffic congestion in Lincoln Park and of a library under construction in a southwest side community. Yet before black groups he delivered the same speech, whether appearing before middle-income homeowners in Chatham or the poverty-stricken of Lawndale. It betrayed both a lack of knowledge about the black community and a sense inside the Daley campaign that the black community was some monolith that could be reached with a generic "black speech."

Daley avoided anything but generalities about race, even before black audiences. "His appeals to blacks tread lightly," the *Reporter* noted, "so as to avoid alienating white supporters."[*] When asked for his comments about segregated housing in Chicago, he responded by criticizing Reagan administration cuts in federal housing programs. He spoke as if the city's race problems were Mayor Byrne's doing, laying the blame for any racial strife on Byrne's CHA and school board appointments.[**]

Police brutality, unequal distribution of city services—Daley avoided these and other issues that have historically divided the races in Chicago. Before a neighborhood group on the southwest side, he endorsed their proposal to ban all scattered-site housing in that part of the city. It won him applause but put him on shaky legal ground, given federal court rulings to the contrary.

---

[*]In his book about the city's 1983 election, *Chicago Divided: The Making of a Black Mayor,* Professor Paul Kleppner wrote, "Daley's sensitivity to his white ethnic base . . . simply prevented him from developing any racial strategy to tap the racial concerns of blacks and their anti-Byrne feelings."
[**]Similarly, when critical of a machine practice, Daley spoke as if Byrne herself had invented these concepts. There was a crying need for a freedom of information act, he declared, because the Byrne administration "has built a stone wall between government and the people."

In its editorial endorsing Daley, the *Sun-Times* characterized him as the mayoral candidate who would build bridges of trust to all racial and ethnic groups. It was a depiction that struck many blacks as disturbing or even ludicrous. Daley did not concede the indignities and slights suffered by blacks because to do so would mean criticizing his father. Revering your dead father's memory was a noble trait, but what was the first step in reaching an accord if not at least acknowledging the aggrieved party's hurts? The *Tribune*'s endorsement made no mention of Daley's ability to build racial bridges, but editor Jim Squires would later say that the basis for their endorsement was just that. At the *Tribune* they believed Daley was the best hope for those seeking to rise above the city's divisiveness.

Blacks who were part of the Daley campaign were not blind to his campaign's shortcomings. They noticed that Daley was more nervous and tentative before black groups than he was in front of whites. They were struck, too, by the contrast between the well-organized campaign in pursuit of the white vote and the clumsy affair that was the Daley campaign in the black community. "I have to think that many people here thought they could win this thing without the black vote," one top aide confided. Daley made far fewer trips to the black community than Byrne, and fewer than Washington made to the white community.

The Daley campaign did not defy the city's segregation but instead reflected it. The campaign operations on the southwest side, at the uneasy border between black and white, provided the most striking example. Black workers operated out of a campaign office on the east side of Western Avenue, the Maginot Line between black and white. White workers worked out of a nearby office on the opposite side of Western.

At the main office downtown the mix of white and black Daley workers made for some excruciatingly awkward moments. One black participant working downtown theorized it was just possible that many campaign honchos had never allowed a black in their home, save for nervous encounters with a domestic or a repairman. The Daley campaign, the *Reporter* wrote, "appeared sharply divided into white and black, with separate but equal its unspoken theme." At least one black member of the Daley team wondered about the word "equal."

February 22, election day, saw the Washington campaign riddled with paranoia. Several Robert Taylor Homes residents called the campaign in a panic to complain of a notice from the CHA instructing them to stay home for a spot inspection. "Failure to admit [an] inspector," the letter said, "is a violation of your lease, and your tenancy could be terminated." The letter was the same one sent to Taylor residents on other days, yet there was bitter talk of a machine-controlled CHA attempting to stifle the black vote.

Then at 5 P.M., the height of rush hour, the el line taking commuters home to the south side—where they might vote—broke down. There was more talk of sabotage at the hands of a machine-controlled agency. The campaign claimed the CTA did not offer a satisfactory explanation, but then the CTA never does.

There were the usual complaints about an election run by Democratic apparatchiks: precinct captains meeting voters at the door to the polling place; Democratic committeemen choosing both the Republican and Democratic election judges; charges of vote fraud; and so on.

The weather was unusually warm. By midafternoon the Board of Elections was predicting a record turnout—projections soared as high as eighty-one percent. The final seventy-two percent figure was still astounding for a local election in a country where a fifty percent turnout for a presidential election is considered good. Early returns were showing Washington in a tight race with Byrne.

Newscasters were speechless. Channel 2's Walter Jacobson shook his head, befuddled. How could all of us have been so wrong? Jacobson asked. He then looked around him and, in a rare moment of candor, offered that the problem was evident right there in the studio. Here they were, five white men, trying to describe a phenomenon occurring in neighborhoods about which they knew next to nothing.

The race was close. Washington won with thirty-six percent of the vote to Byrne's thirty-four percent and Daley's thirty percent. Washington won by 33,000 votes out of the 1.2 million cast. Byrne and Daley split the white vote almost exactly down the middle; Washington won eighty-five percent of the black vote.* Black turnout didn't reach eighty percent, as

---

*Washington fared slightly better among middle-class blacks (eighty-seven percent) than those living below the poverty level (eighty-one percent). Byrne received twelve percent of the black vote and Daley three percent. Daley fared best among those blacks sixty-five or older and Byrne among poorer blacks and blacks over fifty.

hoped, but the seventy percent turnout among registered voters was still far higher than the pundits figured. It turned out that Washington could have won without a single white vote.*

At Washington headquarters, speakers biding time while waiting for Washington likened his victory to the civil rights victories of the 1960s. The crowd sang innumerable choruses of "We Shall Overcome," and strangers held hands, the welfare mother linked in solidarity with the black middle-class woman dressed in her finest. People screamed and hugged and didn't know whether to laugh or cry. There were reminders that there was still another election to be won, that Washington had only won the Democratic nomination, but they were ignored like teetotalers preaching abstinence at a cocktail party. An old wino partaking in the celebration told a Washington friend that he had stayed sober for three days to make sure he remembered to vote. A little after midnight someone announced that Byrne had gone to bed. The crowd booed.

It was nearly 2 A.M. when Washington made his way to the podium. The crowd serenaded him, chanting "We Want Harold." "Thank you. Thank you. Thank you." Washington must have said those two words twenty-five times. His next line was one his supporters would repeat over and again in the next few days, still high from the jubilation: "You want Harold? You got 'im."

Rich Daley conceded just before midnight. His was a gracious speech, yet his words echoed bitterly in the upcoming weeks when the general election took on a racial hysteria far worse than anything seen in the primary. Early on, Bill Daley assured Washington emissaries that he and Rich were on board all the way. Washington was the Democratic nominee, he supposedly told them, and the Daleys were lifelong Democrats.

But factors other than party loyalty apparently weighed on the Daleys. There were those inclined to call Daley a "spoiler," blaming him for Washington. A man happening upon Daley at a Bridgeport department store punched him in the face. Many precinct captains balked at going

---

*Most lakefront liberals followed their leaders into either the Byrne or Daley camp. Estimates of Washington's white lakefront vote range from between eight and twenty-one percent. In the seven wards that are ninety-plus percent white, Washington won less than one percent of the vote. Fifteen percent of the city's Latino voters cast their ballots for Washington.

door-to-door for Washington. Quashing the rebellion would have cost the Daleys considerable political capital and would further damage Rich Daley's reputation among the hard core. With future elections to consider, Rich Daley ended up playing a minor role in the Washington campaign.

Byrne was less magnanimous than Daley. She stranded her campaign workers, claiming the race was too close to call, though aides had already told her Washington would win. Her statement the next day was curt. She said all the right things, but her pursed lips belied her words. Byrne did not campaign on Washington's behalf in the general election, but then, his campaign never asked her to.

Who can say why Washington won? Richard Barnett credits those working out of the 47th Street office. They more than anyone else, Barnett said, drew into the political equation those outside his reach and the reach of others who for years preached the vote. "We were the fire that heated the pot," Conrad Worrill boasted.

Perhaps, Al Raby offered. Raby credited the Task Force with bringing about the "environmental changes" that paved the way to a tremendous outpouring of black support. Yet when a candidate wins by a mere thirty-three thousand votes, the campaign manager tends to prize each participant's contribution. "There were a thousand so-called critical events," Raby said. There was Washington's strong performance in the first debate. "If Harold was lackluster in that first debate, we could've kissed it good-bye," Raby said. Weren't those who successfully negotiated the debates as critical as anyone else?

Who is to say that it wasn't the work of people like Richard Barnett finally paying dividends? Or maybe it wasn't the leaders who deserved the credit at all but just plain folk. Countless people freelanced their own role in the Washington campaign. Washington's was not the kind of campaign where a strict manager kept a tight rein on the message and the money. Anyone with a good idea just ran with it.

The campaign's field coordinator would admit she probably didn't know of half the people working on Washington's behalf. People just took it upon themselves to knock on doors. The campaign certainly didn't organize the group of women who worked at 47th Street and Michigan Avenue on election day, cajoling people, men especially, to vote. "Whores for Washington," they called themselves.

There was no single and momentous secret stumbled upon by activists trying to awaken black Chicago; there was no elusive discovery finally made. Lu Palmer, who could claim much of the credit himself, could not say what moved the disenfranchised to show up at the polls for Washington. Maybe, he said, it was like the old cliché that nothing can stand in the way of an idea whose time has come. There were moments during the campaign, Palmer admitted, when he was thinking about giving up entirely, so great was his frustration with Washington. "But you've got to give Harold credit," he said. "When this charming, articulate, brilliant man began to move among the people, man, you couldn't stop it." Washington had claimed the previous summer that it was "the plan, not the man." But even then Palmer was saying that they would have been nowhere without this particular man.

Worrill was a late convert to Washington's bandwagon, but once aboard he couldn't say enough good things about Washington. He could go into any south side bar and know half the crowd, Worrill crowed. "He could relate to everybody," Worrill said. Yet this same candidate ran for mayor six years earlier, and the black turnout hit an all-time Chicago low at twenty-seven percent. Washington didn't even break fifty percent among blacks that year—so the candidate wasn't everything.

Daley strategists explained Washington's victory in terms of their own loss. Rich would have won, they reasoned, if not for the Byrne campaign's portrayal of him as the spoiler. But polls show that those whites making up their minds in the last few days of the campaign preferred Daley over Byrne.

Byrne's media consultant, David Sawyer, blamed the loss on Ed Vrdolyak. Washington's black support jumped something like twenty percentage points in the three days between Vrdolyak's "it's a racial thing" speech and election day. Who knows how many potential black voters would have stayed home if not for Vrdolyak's slip? Byrne didn't mention Vrdolyak when she offered her own postelection analysis. She blamed her defeat on black pride. "They came out in droves," she said. "It was almost like a religious movement. I don't know how you overcome that." Byrne declined any credit, however, for helping to give rise to that movement.

10

POSITIVELY

ANTEBELLUM

The morning after the primary, the networks gave Washington's victory prominent play. All three morning news shows broadcast time and again a snippet of Washington surrounded by a crush of people, mopping his brow and announcing hoarsely that he "proudly and humbly" accepted the Democratic nomination for mayor. The "Today" show beat the competition by securing Washington as one of its guests. The *New York Times* put a picture of Washington on top of page one. The *Times* article stressed that Washington, the sixty-year-old son of a precinct captain, beat the fabled Chicago political machine.

Washington was still groggy the next day when he began meeting with top aides. There was no time to savor triumph—only seven weeks separated the primary and the general election. Jesse Jackson wasn't among those whose advice Washington sought that day, though he was very much on everyone's mind. Again Washington would have to tend to the nettlesome Jesse factor.

Until the night of the primary, Jackson generally abided by the boundaries set down by a business delegation that met with him on Washington's behalf early in the campaign. He gave speeches on the south and west sides and twisted arms among some of PUSH's wealthier black patrons. As hoped, the regular Saturday morning PUSH meetings served as a means of inspiring the shock troops. More important, Jackson didn't call weekly press conferences on Washington's behalf, so his own name would appear in the news. For the most part he shied away from events that would draw the attention of the downtown media.

Jackson's relationship with the campaign was perpetually tense, however. Invariably some Jackson emissary was asking Al Raby or some other campaign official for a few moments of his or her time. Raby would sigh as he looked at the piles of work scattered around his office, yet he would make time for a difficult but important player. Washington was said to be bemused more than anything else by Jackson's meddling. A message reached Washington early in the campaign that Jackson expected him to check in regularly. Jackson had no more than dabbled in electoral politics at that point; Washington, in contrast, had spent his life immersed in politics. Washington let it be known that, no, he would not take the time to stop by PUSH periodically to bow to Jackson's importance.

Jackson's operatives pestered the campaign for weeks about a speaking part for Jackson at the Pavilion rally. Who better to warm up the crowd? they asked. Raby mentioned the idea to Washington, who told his campaign manager to tell Jackson he could "shove his suggestion up his ass." Jackson's operatives still persisted. Even with the rally under way, they still argued that Jackson should introduce Washington—so, at least, Washington operatives claim. The best Jackson was offered was pitchman while volunteers passed the hat. That was still not enough, apparently, for Jackson was there by Washington's side at the rally's climax, grasping Washington's arm triumphantly in the air as photographers snapped their pictures for the next day's papers.

The black columnist Vernon Jarrett was furious with Jackson. "For months it has become clear that Jackson simply cannot tolerate another black man being more prominent in Chicago," Jarrett wrote. "When . . . Lu

Palmer's citywide black poll showed Jackson in third or fourth place as a mayoral choice, I suspect that was too much for Jackson." Near the end of the primary campaign, Jackson called a press conference to talk about a possible run for president in 1984. Inside the Washington campaign there were jokes about Jackson suffering a strange form of the disease that causes depression if one is not exposed to light for an extended period of time. Jackson, it was said, was suffering klieg light deprivation.

Washington, in turn, toyed with Jackson. In early December, Jackson sought an audience before the campaign's Steering Committee. The Reverend, it was said, was troubled by the direction the campaign had taken. Jackson was granted one hour before the committee. He used his time to carry on about all that was wrong with the campaign. What Washington thought of Jackson's speech is impossible to say, for he was out of the room at the time. Washington had excused himself from the meeting, mumbling something about critical matters requiring his attention. Washington killed time in the next room with his issues coordinator, Hal Baron. The two talked about nothing particularly important, Baron said.

Still, Jesse Jackson claimed a lot of credit for Washington's win. He issued a three-page, single-spaced document called "Background and Off-the-Record Information on the Role that Reverend Jesse L. Jackson Played in the Harold Washington Victory." The missive, passed along to select reporters expressly so Jackson would receive on-the-record praise, became something of a joke inside the Washington camp. Jackson claimed raising "more money for Harold Washington's campaign than anyone . . . probably over $350,000 in money and pledges." Nearly one-third of that money was supposedly raised by Jackson during the Pavilion rally while at the mike asking for donations. But he hardly deserved sole credit for the dollars collected there, and Washington didn't raise anywhere near $100,000 that afternoon. By the Washington campaign's calculations, Jackson brought in a grand total of $50,000. "An exercise in 'ego mania,'" wrote Nate Clay, the *Metro News* columnist and former PUSH communications director.

Jackson's strutting seemed minor compared to his impromptu performance on primary night. With hours of air time to kill, television producers scanning the city kept returning to Washington headquarters, where the easily recognized Jackson occupied center stage. The television cameras showed Jackson leading the assembled crowd in a rousing rendition of "We Shall Overcome" and caught him loudly proclaiming, "We want it aaaaalllllllll." He also made himself available for on-air interviews to the reporters assigned to the Washington campaign that night.

Upstairs, Washington monitored the returns with close friends and associates. He was livid. Jackson was the wrong man delivering the wrong message. "What the fuck is he doing?" Washington screamed at no one in particular. Al Raby watched the scene and thought ahead to the general election. He imagined white Chicagoans at home watching their TVs. Raby sent word downstairs that the stage should be cleared.

Jackson was shooed off the stage, yet somehow there he was again on television not more than half an hour later. Once more word came from upstairs: *Get. Him. Off. The. Fucking. Stage.* The stage was cleared a second time.

Later, after his performance had become legendary in black Chicago, he would explain that someone introduced him, the crowd started yelling "Jesse, Jesse," and there he was on stage, swept up by the moment. He meant well, he said. Who else was there who could keep the calm as people hunkered down for a long evening?

Jackson was, if nothing else, cunning. It was shortly before 2 A.M. when Washington slowly made his way to the stage. Jackson was there again, standing at the battery of microphones the media had set up to record Washington's acceptance speech. That was Jackson's trick, to position himself just so. He would slide over to make room for Washington and then end up standing at his side as the cameras captured the moment. Others on stage had done far more to earn that position of honor, but none was as aggressive or as adept as Jackson. One person there that night offered that he was embarrassed watching Jackson elbow people out of his way so as to make it to the stage in time. As Washington worked his way up front, Jackson gave a speech, as if assigned the job of introducing him to the crowd.

When Washington reached the podium, Jackson grabbed his hand. As at the Pavilion rally, Jackson was trying to lift Washington's arm triumphantly into the air. Washington deeply resented the gesture two weeks earlier—it was as if Jackson was the manager raising the glove of his young boxer after a championship fight or like a kingmaker presenting his candidate to the throngs—and he saw to it that this would not recur on this night. He stiffened his arm as he felt Jackson trying to lift it into the air. The crowd cheered, Washington smiled, and the photographers snapped pictures of the two standing together triumphant—while Washington and Jackson were engaged in a bizarre test of strength and ego. Washington waved with his right hand until he was able to tear his left hand free.

Washington delivered his acceptance speech with Jackson reading over his shoulder. When Washington reached the bottom of a page, Jackson leaned over into the camera and turned the page for him. Only discretion prevented Washington from giving him a firm shove off the stage—so, at least, Washington told an aide later on. It's just not something you do when you know the eyes of the country are upon you.

Those watching at home did not know what was going through Washington's mind, of course. What they saw was Jesse Jackson acting as a Washington surrogate. "Our concern is to build," Washington said in his acceptance speech. "Our concern is to heal. Our concern is to bring together. . . . I want to reach out my hand in friendship to every living soul in this city." Yet he offered those words in the middle of the night, whereas Jackson appeared on and off throughout the evening on all the local news stations.

Washington's acceptance speech impressed the *Tribune* columnist Anne Keegan, who was something of a voice for the city's northwest and southwest sides. Yet her column praising Washington focused as much on Jackson as Washington. For her, Jackson's prominence was as disquieting as Washington's words were soothing. "Thousands of TV viewers clicked off their sets after [Jackson's] performance," Keegan wrote. "And thousands more shook their heads wondering how they could vote for Harold Washington, even if he is a Democrat, if Jesse Jackson was going to run the show." The *Tribune* mentioned three times its fears of Jesse Jackson in its editorial congratulating Washington on his primary victory.

Jackson's primary night prancing haunted the campaign in the ensuing weeks. Campaign workers knocking on doors in white communities heard an earful about Jackson, presumed to be the real power behind the throne. Jackson was defining people's impressions of Washington, still largely unknown.

Most whites knew little about Washington, but they knew Jackson. Around the time of the ChicagoFest boycott the *Sun-Times*'s Roger Simon wrote a favorable column about Jackson. The harsh reaction that followed was instructive. "Why do you always give space to that nigger?" one of countless irate callers screamed at Simon. I haven't written a column about

Jackson in three years, Simon informed the man—and in that column he criticized Jackson for embracing the PLO's Yasir Arafat. A Jackson column, Simon wrote, always drew them "out of the woodwork." Simon's colleague, Mike Royko, also recognized this special enmity for Jackson. "Why have I received more outraged mail about Jesse Jackson in the last two weeks since the primary than I received about Charlie Swibel during the four years that he was the most influential member of the Byrne administration?" Royko wrote in early March.

Jackson was not the city's most militant black spokesperson—far from it. Yet white Chicago looked on Jackson with special contempt, born of his success as a media figure. Jackson's desultory jumps from issue to issue were seen by his movement comrades as proof that he lacked a commitment to the less glorious aspects of community organizing. Many whites viewed this same dash from issue to issue as the act of a man exploiting racial tensions for his own gains. One way or another, Jackson was tied to black Chicago's every grievance against the machine. By virtue of his success as a media figure, Jackson became the incarnation of white Chicago's harshest feelings toward a burgeoning black empowerment movement. With twisted logic, Jackson was blamed for instilling race as an issue because he spoke out forcefully against those city policies that slighted black Chicago.

With his Southern Baptist cadence and rolling rhymes, his mixing of politics and God, Jackson was a minister in a religious town who seemed nothing like the preachers white parishioners were accustomed to hearing on Sunday mornings. He struck many as a politician hiding behind a religious title—a blasphemous sin. In the early 1970s, Jackson broached the idea of a black Christmas. He went beyond the usual demand that department stores permit black Santas. Boycott downtown department stores, he preached, and instead patronize stores owned by blacks. Why should white merchants, Jackson asked, be the only ones to profit from Christmas? Many white Chicagoans (and no doubt a sizable share of black Chicagoans as well) found unseemly his casting in racial terms this holiday of brotherly love. Why did Christmas, of all things, have to become racial?

There were those inside the Washington campaign who viewed white Chicago's preoccupation with Jackson as nothing more than an excuse. Those viewing Jackson as some dark and evil eminence did not strike them as potential supporters anyway. If not the taint of Jackson, then someone or something else.

Yet Washington wasn't about to test this premise. In an interview with *Chicago* magazine he said that the view of Jackson holding a special place in his campaign troubled him as much as any other misperception out there. No politician likes to be thought of as another person's man, but it was more likely pragmatic considerations, rather than ego, that weighed on Washington. To have Jackson shape people's impressions of him was disastrous.

There were the southwest and northwest siders to consider and also the city's Jewish population. Jackson was not popular among the Jews, especially since embracing Arafat. Yet the Jews, seemingly Chicago's most liberal white constituency, were critical to Washington's assembling a majority coalition. The Jews were hardly an anomaly. The campaign's own polls showed that reform-minded whites living along the lakefront were typically as hostile to Jackson as their counterparts in the ethnic bungalow belt.*

In the primary Washington had dealt with Jackson through hints and slights. In the general campaign he confronted the Jackson problem more directly. Several delegations let Jackson know he was no longer wanted. Leave town for a while, they told him. Get on a plane and fly around the country. Go act presidential. But stay away from the campaign.

Jackson listened. He avoided the cameras and generally laid low. For much of the campaign's seven weeks he was out of town. He was back in Chicago in time to vote, of course. He spent the afternoon pitching in where he could. Later that night he was at Washington's campaign headquarters. He was there on stage, in fact, standing on the podium as Washington worked his way through the crowd, ready to lift Washington's arm victoriously into the air.

There was already reason for worry. Maybe it was Jackson's antics on primary night. Probably it was much more. The day after Washington's win,

---

*Jackson would draw attention in 1988 for winning upward of thirty percent of the white vote in some presidential primaries. He would win, however, only seven percent of the white vote in his home state.

swarms of volunteers were already descending on Republican headquarters. The procession only intensified in the days that followed, the new volunteers emboldened by those lifelong Democrats making the break before them. The Republican nominee, Bernard Epton, planned to operate three offices but ended up opening thirty.

In the days after the primary, white Democratic officials were suspiciously quiet, refusing to commit to Washington. "The question isn't Epton or Washington," said a man the *Tribune* identified only as a "Democratic insider." "Everyone's for Epton. The question is whether it would help or hurt Epton for [white committeemen] to come out and openly say so."

Washington chose to remain calm. The crowds only proved what he already knew: a percentage of the city's white community would never vote for a black man. Among those who couldn't bring themselves to vote for a black person, only the hard core would bother showing up at the polls; the rest would probably just stay home. A Republican hadn't been elected mayor in Chicago since the days before the Depression. Republicans don't win elections in Chicago, he told himself.

Washington acted like any Democratic nominee would. He pointed to early polls that showed him a comfortable twenty-five percentage points ahead of Epton and kept it no secret that he was already thinking about transition teams and the like. ([WASHINGTON] CAMPAIGN TAKES ON A TWOFOLD PURPOSE—WORKING FOR VICTORY, PREPARING TO GOVERN, read the headline over a Sunday *Tribune* piece.) Washington did everything possible to act like victory was inevitable so as to smother any notion that Epton stood a chance. The credo for his campaign became, It's ours to lose.

Bernard Epton was easy to underestimate. He won his primary race with only 11,042 votes, in contrast to Washington's 415,050. Epton's campaign was even more of a ragtag effort than Washington's. Of the $41,000 he raised during the primary, all but $1,000 came from family members or from his own bank account. His daughter was campaign manager.

Epton harped on his seven terms as a state legislator, yet those fourteen years weren't reassuring so much as they were a quirk of local politics. He was the Republican state legislator from a predominantly black and liberal south side district, elected because for years Illinois required that every legislative district be represented by at least one person from each party.

169

Epton was badly beaten every election but remained in office as the district's top Republican vote getter. When that law was changed in 1980, Epton simply returned to his law practice full-time rather than go down in certain defeat.

The Republican party, as if admitting Epton's limitations as a candidate, ignored him through the primary. Senator Charles Percy, a Republican, held a fund-raiser in Chicago during the primary, yet Epton was not given a spot among the other dignitaries, nor did anyone think to introduce him to the crowd. Ronald Reagan was in town a week later; again, the party's slated candidate in the mayor's race two weeks away sat anonymously at the back of the room.

Until Washington was elected the Democratic nominee, there was no reason for prominent Republicans to believe Epton was anything but another in a long line of sacrificial lambs in a city in which four out of every five voters identified themselves as Democrats. The previous two elections offered unique opportunities for Chicago's Republican party, but they failed to take advantage of either. In the 1977 special election held to elect a replacement for Daley, only a last-minute scramble by party fathers staved off the embarrassment of a professional clown named Ray "Spanky" Wardingly winning the nomination. Byrne's surprise victory in 1979 provided another opportunity. Byrne's Republican foe tried to exploit sexism: Byrne, he said, would be useless several days each month. Yet Byrne won all fifty wards and all but two of the city's three thousand-plus precincts. So it went with the Republican party in Chicago.

Epton further damaged his cause when he immediately made it clear he did not look on himself as some Great White Hope. Epton vowed on television the night of the primary that he would not make race an issue even if Washington won. He also said he wouldn't hire a media consultant or run many television ads because that was never his intention; changing his plans now, Epton said, would only be because his challenger was black. A few days later he told the *Defender,* Chicago's black daily, that he wanted no part of "efforts by white racist Democrats . . . to save Chicago from the blacks." He promised to disavow anyone connected with his campaign who attempted to exploit bigotry.

Epton also spoke respectfully of Washington. The two knew each other from their time together in the state legislature. Washington, Epton said, was articulate and intelligent.

Not long into the new election someone suggested that Washington should appear at Operation PUSH. PUSH was where Ralph Metcalfe chose to announce his break with Daley; it was where Renault Robinson surrendered his badge after he was suspended for speaking out against the racism of his superiors in the police force. Byrne had appeared there in 1979 during her campaign for mayor. PUSH was, if not hallowed ground among black political activists, then at least a place they would insist Washington go if others demanded he didn't make an appearance there. "Harold's going to PUSH," Bob Starks said, "wasn't a matter we considered open for discussion."

The campaign pros downtown could only disparage this latest bright idea from the Task Force types. A PUSH visit would only raise again the specter of Jesse Jackson. Why not dress Washington in prison togs for a rally in the yard at the Cook County Jail? A former black reporter named Grayson Mitchell, the campaign's communications director, argued that an appearance at PUSH would be the campaign's best-covered event. All we need, Mitchell told Washington, is several days of distancing ourselves from an off-the-cuff remark by someone else speaking at PUSH that day. Mitchell went one step further by advising Washington that he should avoid any "all-black anything." Bad visuals, he offered.

The "honkie caucus," it was called: a group of top Washington strategists who believed the white voters living along the north lakefront should be the campaign's prime target in the general election. After one particularly heated debate over a racial issue dividing the campaign, Pat Caddell, an out-of-town political consultant, taped to his door "Chief Honkie Consultant." (After another tense moment, he said he threw a chair because of a disagreement over airing a TV spot.) The group wasn't all white, despite the nickname: Al Raby was among those designated an "honorary honkie." Two other regulars were Tom Coffey and Wayne Whalen, whose apartment served as the group's meeting place. Down at 47th Street there were those who confused Coffey with Whalen. Both were white lawyers working for downtown firms; both were anomalies inside a campaign staff dominated by activists and a range of black players. No one pushed a lakefront-centered strategy as strongly as the Whalen group, and no one more aggressively than Whalen and Coffey.

They remained pretty much in the background throughout the primary, recognizing that they knew little about devising a campaign whose main task was inspiring black Chicago. Yet the general election was different. As they saw it, in order to win, Washington had to sway voters like themselves to his side. Just as they deferred in the primary to those who understood the black community, they expected to be accorded the same respect in the general election.

Neither suggested that Washington avoid the black community altogether. The trick was to have Washington appear all over the city at the same time that his appearances in the lakefront dominated their media strategy. The "media hit of the day," both Whalen and Coffey advised, should highlight the Democratic nominee's lakefront strategy: a lakefront rally one day, a press conference to propose a freedom of information act the next. The lakefront liberals needed to be fussed over so they could see a place for themselves within the black-led movement, Coffey and Whalen argued. Talk reform along the lakefront, preach coalition politics, and for God's sake avoid tripping booby traps like PUSH.

To Coffey and Whalen their point was so obvious as to preclude serious debate. They put their faith in the focus group interviews conducted by Caddell, who found that blacks understood that Washington needed to pursue aggressively the white vote. Washington had the black vote sewed up; the new voters he needed could be found along the north lakefront. Where was the controversy?

Those congregating at the 47th Street office were incredulous. It was as if the honkie caucus was intent on purging the campaign of *anything* black in quest of the white liberal.

The honkie caucus talked of picking up twenty percent of the white vote. Yet what about the twenty percent of the black vote that Washington lost in the primary? Black turnout hit an impressive seventy percent in February, but there was room for improvement. The campaign had fallen well short of its target in the primary of an eighty percent turnout.

On 47th Street they took as an insult the presumption that black Chicago wouldn't notice Washington's suddenly appearing on TV speaking to white crowds, speaking of nothing more controversial than open government. Washington's greatest asset in the black community—an image of someone who wouldn't abandon them in pursuit of white legitimacy—would turn into a liability. Downtown they couldn't have been more pleased with a television ad boasting that Washington endorsed Larry Bloom over four black challengers in a ward that was eighty percent black. On 47th Street they questioned the spending of precious campaign dollars to broadcast that Washington backed a white for alderman in a predominantly black ward. When they thought of this ad downtown, they considered how white viewers would view it. On 47th Street they imagined blacks in front of their televisions.

On 47th Street they recalled Mayor Tom Bradley's race for governor of California the previous year. To them Bradley's big mistake was that he treated black voters as if they were the least of his worries. He spent little money advertising on black radio and failed to place ads in key black publications. As his advisers counseled, Bradley avoided any issue that might stir racial feelings among potential white supporters. Bradley lost by less than a hundred thousand votes. Turnout among the state's three million black residents barely broke fifty percent.

Grayson Mitchell believed in numbers. On leave from his job as a corporate spokesperson for Johnson Publications, which published *Ebony* and *Jet,* Mitchell was anything but a black militant. Yet the pages of data he pored over each day told him that Washington's time was best spent in black and Latino communities, not along the lakefront.

Mitchell's polls showed that Washington scared white people, whether they lived along the lakefront or on the northwest side. Those numbers were how Mitchell convinced Washington to do his own voice-overs for spots running on black-oriented radio stations but use surrogates for advertisements running on the predominantly white radio stations.* Surrogates,

---

*The exception on black radio was a spot aimed at young blacks written and produced by Stevie Wonder. Wonder both sang and spoke his pitch on Washington's behalf in a tape that arrived at campaign headquarters unsolicited.

Mitchell advised, were far more effective for reaching the reluctant lakefront voter than Washington's mingling among them.

The PUSH debate raged for days, waiting for a decision. Yet, if anything, Washington's campaign was more disorganized than during the primary. Early in the general election Washington fired Al Raby as his campaign manager but asked him to stay on for appearance's sake. Bill Ware, Washington's chief of staff back in D.C., was flown in to take over some of Raby's chores, but mainly the campaign functioned without a manager. Resolving an impasse became as difficult as securing fifteen minutes with Washington between campaign stops and convincing him he must make a decision immediately.

The lack of a formal chain of command could be exasperating. A committee of top operatives met every day to discuss strategy, yet the meetings were merely a formality. Arguments were won or lost in the backseat of Washington's car. His top confidants were the half dozen or so aides who took turns riding around town with him, not those meeting daily in a campaign conference room downtown.

If this arrangement caused confusion and some testy moments inside the campaign, so be it, for this was Washington's way of reading the signposts around which he needed to negotiate. "In a sense," said one of his backseat aides, "the question Washington was working out was how he should act as a black man before a white audience."

Around the time everyone was tired of the fight over PUSH, Starks buttonholed Washington, catching up with him at a south side campaign appearance. "It's important that you go," he said.

The way Starks tells it, Washington didn't miss a beat. "I'm going," Washington told him. Washington, Starks claimed, also told him in so many words that he had no intention of making the lakefront the centerpiece of his campaign at the expense of other constituencies. ("Harold was skeptical to the end about the potential horsepower of the white community," one of his backseat confidants said.) Those on 47th Street weren't without their disappointments, though. Washington approved the Bloom ad, and unlike the last few weeks of the primary, he didn't give himself over freely to the

Task Force. Whether or not whites would end up voting for him, he understood that he must project an image as someone interested in all of Chicago if he was to govern as mayor.

The day before Saint Patrick's Day, Jane Byrne gathered reporters around her to announce that she was reentering the mayor's race as a write-in candidate. The city she loved, Byrne said, was still too "fragile" to entrust to anyone else.

Washington said all the right things about Byrne's hurting the Democratic party, but privately he could not have been more pleased. Epton called a press conference and said the obvious, that Byrne would hurt him more than Washington. Two white candidates would again split the city's white vote.

Ed Vrdolyak immediately announced he would have no part of her write-in effort. Two of the party's more visible leaders, Alderman Vito Marzullo and Park Superintendent Ed Kelly, both Byrne supporters in the primary, endorsed Epton. Ted Kennedy endorsed Washington and made a special trip to Chicago to tell Byrne her write-in candidacy would only damage her reputation. On the same day she was booed at a southwest side nursing home, Byrne withdrew from the race. Workers joining her write-in bid complained that they learned of Byrne's decision by listening to the radio. Byrne's revived candidacy lasted only one week.

Alderman Aloysius Majerczyk was the first Democratic official to endorse Epton; Marzullo and Kelly were the second and third. The three were joined by two more Democratic committeemen the day after Byrne bowed out. Another two endorsed Epton the next day.

Fewer than half of the city's fifty Democratic committeemen showed up at the party's official endorsement session. The meeting is traditionally a chance for party officeholders to fawn all over their nominee as they go through the ritual of a formal endorsement. Congressman Dan Rostenkowski was one notable no-show; confronted by reporters, he hemmed and hawed about endorsing Washington. The burden falls on Washington, Rostenkowski said, to convince white voters he's for all the people, not just black Chicago. Only after influential House Democrats reminded him that he needed their support as chairman of the House Ways and Means Committee did Rostenkowski endorse Washington. Still, precinct captains who were part of his ward organization went door-to-door on Epton's behalf.

Epton's staff was no longer the family affair it was in the primary. Republican party officials had moved quickly. Governor Thompson's former campaign manager, James Fletcher, replaced Epton's daughter atop the campaign. Well-known Republican officials were moved into other top positions. Epton had vowed that he would not hire a media adviser or run many television ads, but John Deardourff, one of the GOP's more respected media savants, arrived to handle Epton's media strategy.* Senator Paul Laxalt of Nevada, the new Republican party chairman, hosted a $200-a-plate fund-raiser.

Epton complained that through the primary Donald Rumsfeld, a well-connected Republican living just north of Chicago, wouldn't return his phone calls. Two days after the primary the two met. The national party raised hundreds of thousands of dollars on Epton's behalf. The previous Republican nominee for mayor, Wallace Johnson, recalled with bitterness that in 1979 he didn't receive "one iota of support" from the party.

The challenge facing Epton and the high-priced outside talent advising him was to devise a campaign that exploited racial hostilities while avoiding any mention of race. A man far more adept at managing his career than his personal life, Washington provided Epton with the perfect target. The "integrity" issue, Epton called it when asking audiences whether a man like Washington could be trusted to handle a $2 billion city budget.

In 1966, Early White needed a lawyer because of some hassle he was having in traffic court, so White looked up his old army buddy Harold Washington. "One of the most likable fellows in the unit," White would later tell a Washington biographer. "A brilliant fellow with a sharp mind."

---

*Deardourff was no stranger to racial campaigns. His consulting agency produced the television ads for a Republican running for governor in Virginia against Democrat Charles Robb. Their ads exploited Robb's support of a holiday in observance of Martin Luther King, Jr.'s birthday.

White paid Washington $150 and figured he was getting a real bargain. Washington was a state legislator with a diploma from Northwestern law, impressive credentials for a solo practitioner on the city's south side. White, however, was less than pleased with the services rendered.

The first time Washington was supposed to appear in court on White's behalf he failed to show. He was in Springfield because of some vote and forgot to tell White. The hearing was rescheduled; again Washington failed to show. Washington *was* in court for the third appointment but then missed the date the judge set for pretrial motions. White was technically out on bail, so a warrant was issued for his arrest. That's when White filed a complaint against Washington with the Chicago Bar Association.

There were other complaints already on file. In 1964 Mary Ann Pridgeon complained that she wasted $60 hiring Washington to handle her divorce. The next year the bar heard from Ella Liggens, a housekeeper who said she paid Washington $50 to handle her divorce and never heard from him again. Liggens complained that Washington wouldn't even return her calls. Two more complaints were filed against Washington in 1966, involving a total of $105. These, too, were people seeking a divorce.

Washington admitted he unintentionally ripped off his army buddy. He said he returned White's $150 and felt lousy about disappointing a friend. Yet Washington felt no remorse over the divorce cases. None had paid him what he said was his standard retainer for a divorce back then— $175. It was true he didn't return Ella Liggens's phone calls. But as he asked his secretary to explain to her, he wouldn't do more work on her case until she paid him the rest of his money. Maybe Washington's mistake, one friend offered, was filing papers on their behalf anyway, as a good faith effort.

Washington never responded to the bar association's routine inquiries. Instead he dealt with the problem in his own way, refunding their money— so, at least, he claimed. It killed him to return a dime to Mary Ann Pridgeon. Their countless arguments alone, he calculated, cost him well over $60 in time and headaches, but he thought about the trouble she might cause him in the future and figured it wasn't worth so small a sum.

The Illinois Supreme Court's attorney disciplinary committee receives a couple of thousand complaints a year. All but a dozen amount to nothing but paper in a lawyer's file. Even when the bar association's disciplinary committee investigates, as it did with Washington, it usually means nothing more than a lecture. Typically, only those lawyers bilking a client out of large sums of money have their license revoked.

Around the time Washington missed his first court appearance on Early White's behalf the disciplinary committee wrote Washington asking him for a "brief explanation" of the complaints against him. He ignored their letters, and the committee launched a formal inquiry.

The day Washington was to appear before their committee he sent a telegram telling them he couldn't appear because the legislature was in session. Offering no excuse, he did not show on the next date scheduled, and he ignored the next summons as well. The disciplinary committee recommended a five-year suspension of Washington's law license.

The staff attorney who handled the disciplinary committee's correspondence, John McBride, wondered why Washington was so dumb. Washington's disdainful attitude, which the committee took as a slap, only provoked the committee; the small amounts of money reflected poorly on Washington as well. Why didn't he just pay his clients off and make his peace, McBride thought to himself—not knowing that Washington claimed he had done just that. McBride sent Washington the committee's report and informed him there would be a hearing on their recommendation. Washington could have explained his side of the story there, had he bothered to show up.

Eventually Washington wrote to McBride's committee. He attributed his failure to appear before them to "personal problems . . . too numerous to enumerate in a document." He felt he was in the right in all but the Early White case, but he failed to explain why in his letter. In 1970 the Illinois Supreme Court suspended his law license for one year.

Washington's IRS troubles began in 1971. Criminal charges were filed, unusual in a case involving a mere $500, as the judge who was assigned Washington's case noted at a sentencing hearing. I'm disturbed, he said, that this case ever made it to my courtroom. The IRS typically handles a case like Washington's in the civil courts, if not within its bureaucracy. Normally the agency sifts through someone's tax records, assesses the damage, and sends a bill. The tax code was amended in 1980, in fact, so that the IRS could bring criminal charges only in cases exceeding $2,500.

Those defending Washington in the court of public opinion pointed to the case of Albert Jenner, Jr., a prominent and well-connected Chicago attorney who served as a Republican staff counsel during the Watergate hearings. Jenner did not file *his* returns in 1973, 1974, or 1975, yet Jenner was never prosecuted for failing to file or even charged a penalty. Washington was sentenced to forty days in jail.

Washington's legal troubles were only a minor annoyance during the primary. Mike Royko was the first to mention it, welcoming Washington's announcement for mayor with a pair of columns about his past. Royko exonerated Washington of everything but stupidity. "The real victim was Washington himself," he wrote. "For lack of attention to minor matters, he brought big troubles on himself."

Washington addressed the issue directly in early January in a speech before the Rotary Club. ("We were looking for the absolutely whitest place possible," explained one Washington strategist.) He pleaded no contest in the IRS case, he told the Rotarians, because he was guilty as charged. He was hard at work as a legislator, he screwed up, and that was the long and short of it. "It's just what it was," he said. "Stupid. . . . There is no excuse." After his speech he fielded questions from reporters for about twenty minutes, until the Rotarians started yelling to them to let up. Neither Byrne nor Daley made much of Washington's misdemeanors.

But through the second half of the general election, Epton spoke of little else. The two candidates met in a single debate in the third week of March with election day less than three weeks off. No campaign issue, Epton said in his opening statement, is as important as doubts about Washington's background.* Voters, he said, must ask themselves one question that outweighs all others: "Will he obey the law?" During the debate, Epton held up a thick blue notebook that his aides said beforehand would contain shocking new disclosures. The notebook was nothing more than a compilation of old charges, but it made for a dramatic prop nonetheless.

---

*Somehow questions about Epton's own tax records eluded the glare of the media spotlight. According to Epton's tax return from 1981, he made $241,445, yet paid only $9,051 in federal taxes. He listed his assets at over $4.6 million. Epton broke no law, of course, but a millionaire paying far less than his fair share of taxes seems at least as troubling as Washington's carelessness.

The debate set the tone for the remainder of the campaign. In his standard stump speech, Epton offered no programs or sense of direction—nothing but a recap of Washington's jail term and the law license suspension. Epton vowed he would not raise taxes and then segued into an attack on Washington as a tax evader. A few days after the debate the Epton campaign unveiled seven new campaign commercials; five focused on Washington's personal past. Even Epton's daughter, his former campaign manager, was troubled by the slogan that closed out these new ads: EPTON—BEFORE IT'S TOO LATE. Within the context of the Chicago election, it seemed a not-so-subtle play on white fears.

Epton was a lawyer, so mistakes he made recapping Washington's record were born either of ignorance or malevolence. Epton regularly accused Washington of failing to file for nineteen years, not four, claiming the government didn't prosecute for the previous fifteen years because the IRS was bound by the statute of limitations. Nineteen years was probably closer to the truth than four, according to several top campaign aides; still, there is no limit on how far back the government can investigate once it discovers a taxpayer has failed to file. Washington was convicted on a misdemeanor charge, yet Epton often spoke of his opponent as the "convicted felon."

Epton also attacked Washington for bills still owed from previous political campaigns—money owed to People's Gas, the telephone company, and other creditors. A candidate in debt to a printing company or a public utility long after election day is a commonplace in politics. In 1983, for instance, Bill Singer still owed money from his 1975 run against Daley; that same year Governor Thompson owed nearly three-quarters of a million dollars from his two previous campaigns. Yet to hear Epton tell it, Washington was some deadbeat who couldn't keep up with his personal bills despite the $52,000 salary he earned as a congressman.

Epton ridiculed Washington's worth as a candidate, to the obvious delight of his newfound supporters. The man he earlier had described as an intelligent man was suddenly "not too bright." He asked audiences if Washington was the best the black community could come up with. When Washington headed east for a fund-raiser, Epton suggested he should try to "bring back some brains."

Jesse Jackson was another favorite theme. "Operation PUSH," a *Tribune* reporter wrote, "and its president, Reverend Jesse Jackson, have been frequent targets of Epton's jabs during the campaign." Smear literature slipped by night under the doors of homes in white neighborhoods made frequent references to Jackson. Washington would name Jackson the new chief of police, one said; Jackson would be the true power behind the throne, according to another. The Epton campaign was only a touch more subtle in its characterization of Jackson as a lurking presence on Washington's team. Epton's campaign literature, for instance, listed Jackson first among Washington's "closest advisers."

Washington alternated between outrage and frustration. To him, Epton's assault on his character was nothing but a ready-made rationale for those wanting to vote against him because of race. "God'll forgive you," Epton told at least one audience of white Democrats gathered to endorse him.

Yet partisans had every reason to be as angry at Washington. The Epton campaign released its charges against Washington in small doses, to stretch their impact. It was a simple and obvious trick that nonetheless seemed to stump Washington and his advisers. If Washington reacted at all to any of Epton's charges, it was usually a few days too late to make any difference. He chose to disdain Epton's tactics rather than to counter them.

People inside Washington's campaign understood what needed to be done. Someone would work up a quick response aimed at damage control, but then she'd find that there was no one to sign off on her idea. Washington was a big source of the problem. He would mutter some curse when told of Epton's latest charge but then sit on his anger. Maybe he would offer a public statement a few days later, maybe not. Another problem was those who still believed the campaign was theirs to lose. Those advising Washington to remain above the fray did what they could to sabotage those believing otherwise.

The Epton strategy was as effective as it was simple. The commanding lead Washington enjoyed right after the primary was all but gone by late March, with election day just two weeks off. The erosion was particularly severe on the lakefront. The campaign ran over a dozen commercials aimed at white voters, but as Bill Zimmerman, Washington's media adviser, said, "None could stop the hemorrhaging." Momentum favored his opponent. Looking at the numbers, Pat Caddell saw that Epton just might become the first Republican since 1927 to be elected mayor of Chicago.

About midway through the seven-week campaign, the crowds, reacting to their newfound hero's rise in the polls, began showing up in large numbers, cheering his name, "Ber-nie, Ber-nie." Epton was no longer a desperate long shot but a bona fide contender. The feverish welcome Epton received at one southwest side rally startled even the Epton campaign's own press secretary. "It looks like he just won the war or something," she said. "Do you think they're getting [him] confused with the Pope?"

Whites attending Epton rallies startled reporters with their frank comments about not wanting a nigger mayor. They held up signs calling Washington a "crook" and took to wearing a variety of political buttons decidedly racial in appeal: one showed a watermelon with a black slash through it, another was simply all white. VOTE WHITE, VOTE RIGHT one popular T-shirt boldly proclaimed. Supporters yelled out encouragement at rallies in booming bleacher-bum voices, such as the man who urged him on with the cry, "Attaboy, Jew-boy, go get 'im."

Chicago was provoking something ugly in U.S. politics. It was as if a curtain of civility was lifted that no one bothered to draw down, exposing to bright lights that which resided more comfortably in the dark. The honkie caucus was forever pressuring Washington to appear in the white community, but it reached the point that Washington could not appear *anywhere* on the southwest or northwest side without drawing an unruly crowd of Epton supporters. On Palm Sunday, Washington was scheduled to attend services at a northwest side church. He arrived to find a mob of around two hundred whites, their faces flushed with anger, blocking the church's entrance. The words NIGGER DIE were freshly painted across a set of church doors. The crowd taunted and jeered Washington, successfully turning him away. Chicago, the *Tribune*'s Leanita McClain wrote, was becoming "positively antebellum."

11

A

CITY

DIVIDED

Leanita McClain walked into the *Tribune* the morning after Washington's primary victory expecting a noisy newsroom alive with talk. She looked forward to teasing the colleagues with whom she had been jousting for weeks—colleagues who couldn't believe Washington might actually win. If nothing else, McClain, the first black to sit on the paper's editorial board, expected congratulations. The one thing she didn't figure on was the silence that would begin the seven most agonizing weeks of her life.

For weeks no one could talk about anything else. The cliché about Chicago was true: its citizens follow local politics with the same fervor they do the Cubs and Bears. Despite the great upset the city had witnessed the night before, the newsroom that morning was quiet and sullen, as if someone had just died. "Like attending a wake," said *Tribune* reporter Monroe Anderson. No white, McClain said, could look her in the eye. "There was that forced quality, an awkwardness, an end to spontaneity, even fear," she said. She overheard cracks about declining property values and white flight, jokes she found "unforgivably insensitive." Even "the more open-minded of my fellow journalists" failed me, McClain wrote.

McClain dressed in silk blouses and vacationed in Europe with black and white friends. She was raised in the Ida B. Wells projects, named for a crusading black journalist, but she now lived in a lakefront high rise in a trendy north side neighborhood. She had survived the inner city and made it in the white world, yet she was constantly hustled by old acquaintances from her childhood. Occasionally she bumped into an aunt who worked as a cleaning lady for a white couple who lived nearby. A girl she had shared her dolls with was trapped on welfare with five children; a boy she had been sweet on way back when was in prison for murder. Black militants occasionally accused her of forgetting her roots. "A foot in each world," McClain once described it in an essay appearing in *Newsweek* magazine. "I am a member of the black middle class who has had it with being patted on the head by white hands and slapped in the face by black hands for my success."

McClain shook her head at liberal acquaintances who sought her out as a friend, as if she were some sort of personal affirmative action statistic. She mocked those who believed the world was racially enlightened "because they were the first on their block to discuss crabgrass with the new black family." Yet she wasn't the sort to get into a white person's face. By nature she resided safely in the middle between conflicting points of view. One of her *Tribune* confidants, Monroe Anderson, invariably gave the same feedback whenever McClain asked for it on one of her columns. "You're equivocating, Lee," he would tell her. "Choose one side or the other." But it was as if her unique perspective as someone who understood both sides of urban life prevented her from slighting one world for the other.

She viewed herself as a bridge between disparate worlds. "Whites must stop thinking that every black teenager . . . is a thug," McClain had written during the primary, "and blacks might accept that more than a few whites genuinely understand and sympathize with them. Whites might think deeper about the historic and socioeconomic reasons—not excuses—for black shortcomings and not brush aside a race of people as hopeless and hopelessly all the same, with the exception of a few mutant achievers."

The primary had been difficult for McClain. She laughed bitterly over the *Tribune's* Daley endorsement—an endorsement for which McClain, as one of seven sitting on the *Tribune's* editorial board, was in part responsible, though she had pushed for Washington. "When death finally took the mayor's office away from one Richard Daley in 1976 after twenty-one years," the *Tribune* editorial began, "it was impossible to imagine a set of circumstances under which this newspaper would recommend that the people give it back to a second Richard Daley." "Same old *Trib*," she would say.

Her paper's coverage of Ed Vrdolyak's "it's a racial thing" speech was another sore point. Incredibly, the Democratic party chairman's declaration that the election represented a battle between the races was buried on page eighteen, in the last three paragraphs in an article about the Daley campaign. ("This account ranks as the scoop of the election," wrote journalism professor Ralph Whitehead, Jr., in the *Columbia Journalism Review*, "and there is no reference to it in the headline.") McClain used humor as a shield, those who knew her said, but in February 1983 her armaments were wearing thin.

"My transformation began the morning after Washington's primary victory," McClain would write. Suddenly, Chicago seemed a "sick, twisted" place, oppressive and harsh. She was especially angry at herself for only now realizing how far she had strayed: "I'd be a liar if I did not admit to my own hellish confusion. How has a purebred moderate like me—the first black editorial writer for the Chicago *Tribune*—turned into a hate-filled spewer of invective in such little time?"

The harsh and visceral emotions Washington's candidacy was provoking seemed rooted in something deeper than feelings about a politician's misdemeanor conviction or cynicism about his disorganized campaign. Where the support for Washington was years in the making, Epton went from nobody to white folk hero virtually overnight. Walking the streets of the southwest and northwest sides was startling. One was as likely to see a WHITES FOR EPTON button pinned to the coat of a sixty-eight-year-old woman wearing a babushka as on a rowdy teen's. A white woman wearing a Washington button was told, "He wins, you'll get raped."

The Democratic committeemen endorsing Epton didn't pretend their opposition to Washington was because of his past. Aloysius Majerczyk, the first Democratic committeeman to defect, cited the barrage of calls to his office and his conversations with people in the ward. His constituents, he said, "are giving me a message of racial pride. . . . They're afraid of scattered-site housing. They're concerned about the stability of our neighborhoods." Under Byrne the CHA approved two sites on the southwest side and three on the northwest side, prompting one community group to dedicate five of eight pages in its bimonthly newspaper to Byrne's "double cross." Who knew what a black mayor would do?

Anthony Laurino, another Democratic committeeman, also supported Epton. Laurino scoffed when a reporter asked if his support for Epton boiled down to Washington's legal troubles. "The people in my area," Laurino said, "just don't want a black mayor—it's as simple as that." Another southwest side official, choosing the cover of anonymity, explained for a reporter that whites in his part of the city had been "pushed out of their neighborhoods two or three times by blacks. This is a chance to get even."

It would have sounded foolish had they said their opposition to Washington was due to his misdemeanor conviction. The party faithful had tolerated far worse misdeeds by those within their ranks. The party chairman himself was battling legal troubles with the Internal Revenue Service. In 1980 the IRS accused Ed Vrdolyak of shortchanging them more than $220,000. Vrdolyak settled for much less in March 1983, but the $500 Washington failed to pay in the late 1960s seemed insignificant against the $73,600 in back taxes Vrdolyak ended up owing.

More white Democratic committeemen endorsed Epton (eight) than their party's own candidate (six). The majority avoided any public endorsement. No matter what a committeeman's public posture, ward organizations operating on the northwest and southwest sides were Epton outposts. The northwest side's Richard Mell, for instance, endorsed Washington, yet Mell precinct workers passed out Epton literature door-to-door. When a reporter called Mell's ward office pretending to be a confused voter, the woman who answered the phone said that "all of us here are voting for Epton." A television reporter described the shock on Mell's face when his camera crew caught Mell and his precinct operatives openly working for Epton.

Ed Vrdolyak endorsed Washington, but his support, too, seemed disingenuous. In different circumstances Vrdolyak would have twisted arms to maintain party unity; instead the party chairman made a few perfunctory remarks and left his support at that. When Charles Manatt, chairman of the national Democratic party, came to town for a "unity" lunch, Vrdolyak sent his regrets. Vrdolyak kept in close contact with Epton throughout the campaign—so, at least, a top Epton aide told a writer for *Chicago* magazine after the election was over. But not every precinct captain in Vrdolyak's ward organization campaigned for Epton—the ones working predominantly black precincts pushed Washington.

Roman Pucinski, a former congressman and a Democratic committeeman with a high media profile, defended his endorsement of Epton with a hypothetical statement. If Wilson Frost, a moderate black alderman from within their own ranks, were the party's candidate for mayor, Pucinski said he'd be foursquare behind him. So what made him a racist? And what made him a racist if he opposed someone who used words like "insidious" to describe Pucinski and his lot?

There were no secret meetings such as those in the spring of 1979 when Byrne assured the party regulars early on in the general election that her antimachine rhetoric was all bluster. If anything, Washington had turned up the volume on his antimachine, antipatronage message. "Why should I give him the guillotine with which to chop off my head?" Pucinski asked.

Still, bigotry was very much a factor in the calculus of those white committeemen driven by practical politics. Those white politicians with Epton because they saw a chance to stay in power were parlaying their hopes on white fear, not unlike panic-peddling real estate agents who profited from the dread that accompanies rumors of a changing neighborhood.

"I won't work a day for that man," declared Richard Brzeczek, the city's chief of police. "Under Harold Washington I guarantee that it [the department] will be a circus. Law enforcement will suffer. The general level of competence will go down." Brzeczek mentioned Jesse Jackson first on his short list of those who would really run the department should Washington win.

A northwest side priest named Father Francis Ciezadlo tried to play peace-keeper. He invited both Epton and Washington to attend a Sunday service at his church, Saint Pascal. Maybe that sort of symbolism would help, Ciezadlo figured. Epton declined and Washington accepted, choosing Palm Sunday services for his visit. Former Vice President Walter Mondale was in town on the appointed day to campaign on Washington's behalf, so he joined Washington. Mondale was being touted as the Democratic party's early favorite for president, so a flock of reporters and several camera crews joined the two on their trek north.

Later, Ciezadlo would say that he could pick out only a few regular churchgoers among the crowd of around two hundred Epton supporters who gathered to prevent Washington from entering the church. The crowd grew hostile when the Washington retinue came into sight. Pictures from the scene showed distorted faces, bulging eyes—"faces red hot with hate," Leanita McClain wrote. Video of the scene, stark and evocative, was beamed around the world.

With the Saint Pascal incident the election became one of those exceptional happenings that ceased to be the province of one locale, such as Mississippi in 1964, Watts in 1967, or as Howard Beach would become in 1986. In the remaining sixteen days of the campaign wherever Washington or Epton campaigned he was followed by a mass of reporters that one would expect to surround a presidential hopeful in the closing days of a national campaign. Correspondents descended on Chicago from far-flung regions of the world—a television news team from Australia, a pair of magazine writers from West Germany, a United States–based *Tass* reporter. *El País, Le Monde,* and London's *Daily Telegraph* all featured long pieces on Chicago's mayoral race. Chicago was again making a name for itself globally—not for its infamous gangster wars, not for the outrages of its infamous political machine, but because of race.

Philadelphia, the country's fourth most populous city (Chicago ranks third), was conducting its own mayoral race around the same time; Philadelphians, too, were faced with a Democrat who would be the city's first black mayor if elected. There were ninety-four entries under

Washington's name in the *New York Times*'s index and nineteen under the name of Wilson Goode. The *Times* seemed intrigued by every conceivable angle to the race, such as the article it ran polling the city's business community to hear its thoughts on the election. The *Los Angeles Times* ran fifty-three articles about Chicago's election, compared to seven about Philadelphia's. Chicago even reigned for its Warholian fifteen minutes in pop culture: HATRED WALKS THE STREET, *People* magazine called its feature on the Chicago mayoral race.

The national press fixated on the leaflets and buttons used to promote Epton. "You can either put an Epton sign in your window and support him, or *you can put a for sale sign in front of your house,*" one leaflet read. An "application" for employment to Harold Washington's staff included these questions: "Check machine you can operate: Crow bar? Pinball? Straight razor? . . . Auto: Financed? Stolen? If financed, repossession date?" Elevators would be removed from City Hall, read still another, because *they* prefer swinging from cables.

CHICAGO'S UGLY ELECTION, read the cover of *Newsweek* in late March, introducing an article that was as much a look at racial politics nationally as at Chicago politics. The piece opened with a boisterous Epton rally of twenty-five hundred on the southwest side. The article described Epton as wandering among the crowd in a blissful daze while the crowd serenaded him: "Your record, Bernie, shows you're tough / As for us, we've been PUSHed enough / For Chicago—Epton." The ditty was sung to the familiar tune of "Bye-Bye, Blackbird." Epton described the event as "beautiful."

Those believing that the media were unfairly painting every Epton supporter with the broad brush of racism had the *Tribune*'s Anne Keegan as their champion. Keegan wrote from the point of view of the northwest and southwest side bungalow owner struggling each month to pay his bills. They had every right, she wrote, to react angrily to Washington's careless financial record-keeping. The way Keegan remembered it, Washington declared "It's 'our turn' over and over again." Who could blame white Chicago for seeing Washington as a politician interested only in his own community? There was also Washington's terribly disorganized campaign. It gave one reason to question Washington's ability to run a city.

"I'm no racist, and I resent the way that word is hurled at whites who are voting for Epton," said a white woman featured in one of Keegan's columns. "There are blacks and whites alike that are voting because of race. But there are a lot who aren't. Why are only whites labeled racists?"

Some of Keegan's ire was directed at her colleagues, the political reporters downtown who interpreted events for Chicago. As a group they were almost all white, yet they tended to live along the north lakefront or in the suburbs. Typically, they knew nothing about the neighborhoods of the southwest and northwest sides they were casting as vast bastions of racism. Keegan had lived long enough on the city's northwest side to know that a few hundred hotheads disrupting a Washington campaign appearance didn't typify her neighbors, no more than a black murderer reflected the black community. The media, she wrote, casually threw around the word *racist*—"probably the most common word in the Chicago media today"—with barely a thought.

The out-of-town reporter who booked himself into a downtown hotel was worse. He would drop in on a few local reporters to get himself up to speed, follow the two candidates around for a few days, and then file a story that tried to explain Chicago for his part of the country. Like the local reporters, especially those working for television, the reporter would invariably highlight the outrageous.

Yet the gap between the alienated twenty-year-old showing up to taunt the black candidate and the quiet couple down the block was not as wide as one would have anticipated. McClain renamed the man-in-the-street interviews that reporters conducted to get a feel of the electorate "bigot-in-the-street interviews," for these exchanges revealed the preeminence of race on the minds of many white voters. ("That is what is wrong with this town," McClain wrote. "Being a racist is as respectable and expected as going to church.") There were those who declared that they were not prejudiced, only biased against electing a crook for mayor. But it was just as easy to find a white voter who offered an undiluted bigoted opinion, ranging from the old woman who admitted, "I don't like to see a colored man come in," to the young punk who said, "I don't want no nigger for my mayor." Others struggled out loud with their own prejudices, admitting that race was very much on their minds. The tax issue, one after another said, only clinched their decision.

The *Tribune* tried to quell white fears with an endorsement of Washington, but that only seemed to make things worse. The reaction was intense. Irate whites besieged the *Tribune* with phone calls and letters. Hundreds canceled their subscriptions. "If Harold Washington is elected mayor," one letter writer wrote, "it will be the worst disaster in Chicago since the Chicago fire." That was one of the more polite letters.

Editorial writers were not expected to read every letter to the editor, but McClain took perverse pleasure in poring over them. The middle range of responses, McClain wrote, "had the words 'LIES' and 'NIGGER LOVERS' scratched across the editorial." The third category included those who, she wrote, "besieged the newspaper with letters wishing acts of filth by 'black baboons' on the daughters of its employees." The letters made McClain cry.

Epton was proving he was in over his head. He didn't seem temperamentally cut out for the pressures of a high-intensity campaign—the media spotlight was new for him. His fourteen years as a state legislator were served in relative obscurity, yet he was in the midst of a campaign that had rapidly become a major news story nationally.

Epton was intelligent but also unpleasant, an odd and difficult personality. He was humorous but in a caustic and nasty way. "Volatile and capricious, prone to inexplicable outbursts and fits," the *Tribune's* David Axelrod wrote. Epton won the favor of large white crowds, but reporters who covered his campaign saw him as something of a hard-punching boxer with a glass jaw.

Epton abruptly stormed out of a fund-raising dinner to avoid reporters' questions after lambasting them for their hopelessly biased coverage. When a reporter asked a question, Epton said, "No. You don't get one question tonight. You get zero. You get what I've got from you." With that he shoved several reporters aside and left.*

Epton was fond of asking if Harold Washington was the best the black community could offer. A corollary to that question seemed, "Was Epton the best the white community could do?"

---

*Epton's brittle nature was never more apparent than on election night when he shrilly yelled at his supporters to "shut up," said the race was too close to call, and then stalked out, not to be heard from again until reporters the next day caught up with him at the airport. There he told them, "You make me ill."

In the last weeks of the campaign the media discovered that on at least two occasions Epton took up temporary residence in the psychiatric unit of a south side hospital. His second stay, in 1975, lasted thirteen days. His medical records showed that he was hospitalized for depression and traumatic anxiety, and was prescribed lithium. Epton flared at reporters who broached the topic, and who can blame him except that a stay in a psychiatric unit seems at least as valid a measure of competence as Washington's failure to pay a gas bill in the mid-1970s.

The campaign's low point was a charge that Washington was a convicted child molester and that the media were suppressing the story because of a double standard that favored black candidates for office. Flyers were passed out that urged people to call the local television stations and newspapers to protest this cover-up. Some flyers included a second page—supposedly Washington's rap sheet.

The rap sheet was bogus, but apparently a great many took it to be the genuine article. The *Tribune* received so many calls that the paper felt compelled to address the issue in an editorial. The *Tribune* revealed that they had assigned several reporters to investigate the charge, as had other media outlets, yet no shred of evidence was uncovered. The city's investigative reporters were able, however, to trace the leaflet to a group of Epton volunteers who worked out of a near northwest side office.

The libel took on greater dimensions in the context of all this election meant to black Chicago. A psychologist might say that the Washington campaign functioned as widespread therapy for a people taught to believe they were inferior. Teachers told of compositions written in large loopy letters by black children dreaming of being just like Harold Washington when they grew up. He was a black role model who was neither a sports star nor a drug dealer flashing a thick wad. This was no reason for the average white Chicago citizen to vote for Washington, but it ought to have given one pause before smearing him as a pervert.

Washington was not as impervious to events as it may have seemed from the outside. He confessed that the election was stirring powerful emotions that at sixty years of age had seemed to have been buried forever. He confided in one woman friend that the hate around him both pained him and left him confused. He had dealt with racism his entire life, of course. In politics he knew his share of legislators whom he believed to be racist, based on some gut sense or an offhand comment, but he wasn't accustomed to whites yelling racist trash in his face.

For the most part Washington maintained his cool. He smiled softly when confronted by the mob outside Saint Pascal. A photographer caught Washington grinning when surrounded by a similar crowd at an Albanian church not long after. Twice, feelings lurking just below the surface got the better of him. Once was after the Epton campaign canceled a stop at a south side nursing home out of fear, Epton said; its residents would be punished for allowing him to speak. Epton placed the blame on Washington surrogates: "You only have to go to Operation PUSH on a Saturday morning to see who is bringing up the issue of racism," he said. Washington, in turn, accused Epton of "playing with fire," then foolishly fanned those same flames himself. "Somewhere down the line," Washington said, "it is conceivable that . . . some innocent person . . . may wind up dead."

The other time Washington cracked was when he was told of the child molester leaflets. An aide showed one to him just before he was to speak at a college on the northwest side. After his talk a young man badgered Washington, repeatedly asking him why he never paid his taxes. Washington shot back, "Go to hell. Go to hell. Who said I didn't pay my taxes, asshole?" Back in his car Washington admitted it might not have been the most judicious thing to say but that it sure felt good.

"I would hope that I would allay their fears," Washington told *Crain's Chicago Business*. "But I'm not going to spend all my time trying to prove to white America, business or otherwise, that I'm a nice guy, that I went to school, that I can count. I'm not going to waste my time doing that."

Comments like these drove Tom Coffey to wonder about Washington. Coffey appreciated that Washington embraced the lakefront in the message he put forward, but it was as if Washington, involved in the race of his life, carried some giant chip on his shoulder that clouded his good judgment. He's a different candidate in front of white audiences, Coffey complained; he's like a man half present, going through the motions.

Neither Coffey nor Whalen resigned himself to the campaign's idea of using other means—television ads and mailings, primarily—to win over the lakefront. The mailings were a fine idea, the two could agree. Ted Kennedy signed one, as did Sid Yates, a Jewish liberal who represented the north lakefront in Congress. Southern Democratic party leaders, including Griffin Bell and Bert Lance, sent another, assuring their northern cousins that there was nothing to fear. But to Coffey and Whalen nothing worked like the genuine article pressing the flesh along the lakefront. Whalen thought the notion that Washington's presence hurt more than it helped was rationalized hogwash. To him, Washington simply felt more comfortable campaigning in the black community. Who wouldn't prefer the rousing cheers before black audiences to the reception he was receiving in white Chicago?

Yet with election day less than two weeks off, Washington shifted gears. To the delight of the honkie caucus and others, he virtually took up residence along the lakefront. Some pointed to the child molester charge as the pivotal point. The night of his "asshole" comment he delivered what was perhaps his most aggressive and inspired speech of the general election. He railed against his opponent's "lack of decency" and spoke of Epton's conflicts of interest as a state legislator whose specialty was insurance law. It was as if the child molester charge jolted Washington awake.

Another theory that explained Washington's shift was that the black turnout was no longer a worry with the campaign Epton was running. Others thought it was as simple as strategist Pat Caddell appealing to Washington's pragmatic side. Ten days before election day Caddell showed him the campaign's latest internal poll, which showed him holding only thirteen percent of the white vote. If you don't pick up more white voters, Caddell told him, you will lose.

Still, the honkie caucus wasn't entirely pleased with Washington's transformation. When he was scheduled to deliver an important speech at a well publicized lakefront rally just before election day, the caucus drafted a speech. It was a solid good-government spiel, not unlike a speech that Rich Daley might have delivered in the primary. The activist contingency also drafted a speech for Washington, written largely by Slim Coleman. The tone of Coleman's speech was as challenging as the honkie caucus speech was benign. Washington would address, for instance, a development policy that shifted emphasis from downtown skyscrapers to smaller projects in the neighborhoods—a subject the other speech dared not touch. Coleman's speech pushed its audience to look beyond their own interests as white middle-class professionals.

Washington borrowed liberally from both speeches. He said many of the right things simply because it was the judicious thing to do, but he also broached subjects such as the disputatious development policy he would pursue if elected mayor. He proclaimed his support for all the conventional good-government positions, such as opposition to patronage, but he also stressed fairness and justice as his benchmarks for reform. To Coffey's and Whalen's chagrin, Washington gave his own version of reform, not one the typical lakefront audience necessarily wanted to hear.

Epton also focused on the white liberals in the last days of the campaign. His last wave of television advertisements packaged him in a way that aimed at making him palatable to the lakefront independents. One depicted him as a champion of civil rights throughout his career; another highlighted his support of traditional antimachine positions. "I've done more for the black community in one year than Harold has in a lifetime," Epton said in the final days of the campaign. "I gave more in charity than most people earn." (After the campaign was over, Epton vowed never again to contribute another cent to a black cause.) None of his ads carried the campaign's "before it's too late" tag line.

Epton's approach to the lakefront in the waning days was almost the opposite of Washington's. Where Washington grew more aggressive, Epton softened his criticisms of Washington. Epton also maintained a low profile, choosing a light campaign schedule. "The more I talk," Epton said, "the more people I alienate."

It was an election day like none the city had ever seen. Long lines had already formed before the polls opened in black precincts around the city. An election judge at one south side precinct called the Board of Elections in midafternoon to ask if they should close their doors: every registered voter had already cast a ballot.

Paranoia again reigned inside the Washington campaign. Talk that the machine would steal the election was fueled by an early evening rumor that in the Twenty-fifth Ward the wily old Vito Marzullo had impounded something like two dozen ballot boxes for fear, Marzullo said, that votes might be stolen. People immediately thought of the machine's trickery when John F. Kennedy won Illinois by a mere 8,858 votes and of the long list of precinct captains and election judges who were convicted for vote fraud over the years.

In Washington's suite the mood was grim. Channel 7 declared Washington the winner immediately after the polls closed, but with three-quarters of the votes counted, Epton was ahead. Everyone was nervous, and someone locked the keys in the car that was to take Washington to McCormick Place, where his supporters gathered. Grayson Mitchell placed a frantic call to a political pro named Emmett O'Neill. They needed O'Neill to read the returns coming in from the Board of Elections; they were written in a strange code that no one could read. "Emmett essentially had to tell us we won," Mitchell said.

The election was close—closer than the three-way primary two months earlier. Washington won with fifty-one percent of the vote—by fewer than 50,000 of the 1.3 million votes cast. A record seventy-nine percent of the city's registered voters took ballots. Black turnout was an incredible eighty-five percent—two percentage points higher than white registration.* Washington won over ninety-nine percent of the black vote—or, as one Epton adviser put it, every black vote "except for the accidents."

The Latino vote proved key to Washington's victory. Washington had won only fifteen percent of the Latino vote in the primary despite Latino activists who tried to convince voters of a natural alliance between minorities. In the general election Washington captured around eighty-two percent of the Latino vote. Had the opposite occurred—had four of five Latino voters gone with Epton instead—Washington would have lost. The general election saw Latino turnout reach sixty-two percent among registered voters, an all-time high for Hispanic Chicago.

Washington fared better among white ethnic voters than Epton did among blacks, but barely. The final result was not without its ironies. On

---

*In national politics in the early 1980s, the average voter turnout rate among college graduates was seventy-nine percent, seventy-six percent among those making over $50,000 a year, and thirty-eight percent among those making less than $5,000 annually.

issues of importance to working people, Washington's record was nearly impeccable, Epton's spotty. When the two served in Springfield together, Washington's ratings among labor and consumer groups were as high as Epton's were lousy. Yet Washington won only five percent of the vote in the predominantly white wards of the southwest and northwest sides. Chicago revealed, if nothing else, that race clouded the calculations of self-interest among whites.

The archetype lakefront liberal tried to disassociate himself from the bigotry and intolerance of the southwest and northwest sides, yet the white lakefront vote was the Washington campaign's great disappointment. Estimates of Washington's white support varied, but none showed him gar-nering more than one-third of the white vote along the north lakefront. One poll showed that only thirty-nine percent of those whites identifying themselves as liberal cast their ballot for Washington.

All told, an estimated twelve percent of white Chicago voted for Washington—a figure comparable to that in other cities. Newark's Kenneth Gibson ran for mayor in 1970 against an incumbent on trial for extortion and tax evasion, yet Gibson received an estimated one of every ten votes cast by whites. Maynard Jackson, Atlanta's first black mayor, won in 1973 with an estimated twenty-one percent of the white vote; Jackson's succes-sor, Andrew Young, won with eleven percent white support. Coleman Young of Detroit was elected mayor in 1973 with only eight percent of the white vote. On the other end of the spectrum, Los Angeles's Tom Bradley, a former police chief, was elected mayor in 1973 in a city that is less than twenty percent black.

Commentators drew sharp distinctions between the Philadelphia and Chicago mayoral races, but Wilson Goode, as conciliatory as Washington was contentious, would win no greater a percentage of the white vote than Washington. The racial fighting in Chicago was uglier, politics were more plainly polarized, but in the end that just meant the city offered a starker, more sharply focused picture of racial politics at work everywhere in U.S. political culture. Those living outside the city's borders may have been struck by the news from Chicago during those turbulent weeks, but Chicago was merely a mirror reflecting the racial views of a great many Americans, albeit in particularly harsh light. Chicago, it seemed, was just more frank in its expression of racial feelings.

Black America celebrated Washington's victory as its own. *Ebony* magazine's editors compared Washington's victory to the 1963 March on
Washington, when King gave his "I have a dream" speech, and to Joe
Louis's victory over Max Schmeling. Discussions about national black politics must now be divided into two periods, *Ebony*'s editors wrote: "before
Washington" and "after Washington." ("The presidential candidates for the
1984 election must be viewed in a different light. . . . The world of politics
has been altered by his victory.") A second *Ebony* article argued that
Washington's victory should reopen discussions about a serious black chal-
lenger for the 1984 Democratic presidential nomination; a third featured a
nineteen-picture spread that showed the glittering elite of the black com-
munity celebrating Washington's victory. Among those shown were Lou
Gossett, Jr., Dick Gregory, the poet Gwendolyn Brooks, Urban League
President Vernon Jordan, Ralph Abernathy, NAACP Executive Director
Benjamin Hooks, Jesse Jackson, Coretta Scott King, and her son Martin
Luther King III.

Something was up with Leanita—even acquaintances could see the change.
Everyone knew she was a woman with a dark side, but she seemed suddenly
aloof and distant. And what about that time she and the rest of the *Tribune*
editorial board were watching the television news on the day Jane Byrne
announced her write-in candidacy? McClain spat out a curse word and
abruptly left the room. That wasn't the Leanita McClain people had come
to know.

They could understand how hard it must be for a black woman to listen to this election garbage; they didn't broach the subject that was so
unpleasant, and besides, the wall that she had erected around herself made
it nearly impossible. But some colleagues felt resentful. She avoided eating
lunch with them, avoided chats in the corridors. It was as if she was blaming *them*.

McClain's colleagues would wonder no longer after a piece appeared
under her byline in the *Washington Post*. The headline seemed to say it all:
HOW CHICAGO TAUGHT ME TO HATE WHITES.

Yeah, something was definitely up with Leanita.

The force of the *Post* piece was its intimacy. She wrote of the bouts of sullenness the election provoked. She would stare at her word processor pretending to write as she silently cried. Maybe it was anger, maybe frustration; probably it was both. What do these white people want from us? she felt like screaming. She commiserated with Monroe Anderson, the only black *Tribune* reporter covering the campaign. Anderson was the buoyant sort, McClain explained to her *Post* readers, a devil-may-care type whose sense of humor rarely failed him. Yet Anderson would return from the grim realities of the outside world, slouch in a chair in McClain's office, and just stare at the floor. McClain wrote of another black colleague and the anxiety she felt when she realized she could not bring herself to eat lunch with a white colleague with whom she was close. If the campaign had become a race war, their relationship was one of its casualties.

The reaction of those around her brought about an epiphany in McClain. I'm threatening, she told herself in disbelief. Jesse Jackson, Renault Robinson, Lu Palmer—and also Leanita McClain, moderate but also ecstatic about Harold Washington's victory. *And that makes me threatening.* She wrote of white co-workers cutting off their conversations when a black reporter happened by. "I'm no racist, but . . ." If she heard that one more time, she thought she would explode. She confessed that she suddenly detested the "antiseptic suburban worlds" enjoyed by her editorial board colleagues, narrow and privileged, ignorant and naïve, yet considering themselves informed and progressive on matters of race. There was the white colleague who stopped by to tell her why he could not vote for Washington, as if her office was a confessional.

Worse still were those who equated the white backlash against Washington with black pride. Under different circumstances she might have pointed out the innumerable times blacks supported a white candidate over a serious black challenger, and how rare it was for the opposite to occur.* But she didn't feel like playing the mediator who patiently bridges the gaps of racial misunderstanding.

She could not pretend that everything was okay. She wondered why in the past she had been so quick to offer a strained smile and play along with

---

*One study looked into that very question. There were twenty-two aldermanic races between 1975 and 1981 involving both a black and a white candidate. On average black voters favored the black candidate, but only slightly. In contrast, an average of only four percent of the white voters could bring themselves to cast a ballot for a black candidate.

those who she suspected had cultivated her friendship to prove that blacks and whites in Chicago could get along. Everyone but the bigots confused her. "I distanced myself from everyone white, watching, listening, for hints of latent prejudice," she wrote. She contemplated each long and hard before inviting a person back into her life—or banishing him or her forever.

There was "Kay"—bouncy, smiling Kay who, McClain wrote, "had used me all of these years, like a black pet, to prove her liberalism." She wrote that she would explain to Kay "that having one black person—me— on her Christmas card list did not make her socially aware." And "Clark"— she concluded that Clark was disingenuous. Clark she would bar from her office for no other reason than his white skin. Maybe then he would know a taste of what it was like.

"Nan"—McClain contemplated Nan only a moment before concluding that Nan was sincere. Nan gave of herself to help the poor, and the two always spoke intimately about race. Most whites at work avoided even mentioning race, as if avoiding the topic altogether was somehow progressive minded. "Lydia" also passed, but "Ken"—sensitive, cultured, cerebral Ken . . . she could not make up her mind.

The election, she wrote, left "me torn as never before." The election turned her upside down, leaving her to wonder who she really was. The "double consciousness," W. E. B. Du Bois called it, born of being both African and American. How far can an Afro-American venture into the heart of white society, Du Bois asked, without losing him- or herself? After the election McClain moved to Hyde Park, closer to her south side roots. It was her silent protest against the hypocrisy of her north side neighbors. She dreamed black nationalist thoughts, contemplating the advantages of a "black homeland where we would never have to see a white face again." The election left her confused, she wrote, but clear on one important fact: "I now know that I can hate."

Both Epton and Washington were blamed by the newspapers for ignoring the issues, though it was Epton who could talk about little else but Washington's misdeeds. It was as if objectivity meant nothing more than condemning both sides equally. Worse still was a *Tribune* editorial that declared, "Regardless of the outcome, there will be no cause for celebration. . . . What has made this election such a sorry spectacle is that . . . two candidates [were] so unprepared to handle it." How much better it would have been, the *Tribune* opined, "if the first black . . . had been a widely known and respected community leader."

In conversations with McClain and also in print, colleagues complained that Washington wasn't doing enough to allay white fears. Why wasn't Washington appearing in the white community more? they asked. The columnists hammered at Washington and yet didn't chide Epton for ignoring the black community. Washington made countless more appearances on the northwest and southwest sides than Epton made in the black community. "He hasn't been invited," explained Epton's press secretary.

The local reporters were preoccupied with the national media's characterization of Chicago as the capital of hate and racism. Several columnists blasted these "suitcase journalists" whose views were—as one wrote—"skewed, flawed, and more inciting than insightful." In her *Post* piece McClain parodied the jingoism of these Chicago boosters. "Curses on any outsider who would dare say Chicago has a race problem," she wrote. "What race problem?" The *Sun-Times* ran an election wrap-up piece under the headline HOW WHITE VOTE SPELLED VICTORY, and an op-ed column proclaiming that those white ethnics voting for Washington were the "unsung story" of the election.* The powers-that-be were already busy trying to paper over the stain left by Chicago's election.

Not that McClain believed the national media worthy of praise. *Time* magazine in particular infuriated her. *Time* dismissed Washington as "an undistinguished congressman," despite his leadership role in the anti-Reagan fight. "And because there is otherwise so little to choose between the two lackluster candidates," the newsweekly continued, "the outcome will surely be . . . a litmus test on color." How little *Time* understood.

McClain also suffered the disappointment of Mike Royko. She loved reading Royko. "It would be wonderful," Royko wrote during the primary, "if Chicagoans put their prejudices aside and simply voted for the candidate who appeared to be the most intelligent, thoughtful, and forthright and who presented the best programs. If that ever happened, Washington probably could start planning his victory party." The day after

---

*The op-ed writer's point was that Washington won by forty-eight thousand votes and, of the more than half a million voters on the southwest and northwest sides, forty-nine thousand cast their ballot for Washington. Yet he failed to account for the thousands of black and Latino voters on the edge of many of these wards.

Washington won the primary, Royko wrote, "Washington's credentials for this office exceed those of Byrne, Bilandic, Richard J. Daley . . . and most of the men who have held the office of mayor." He described him as a "smart, witty, politically savvy old pro . . . far more understanding of the fears and fantasies of Chicago whites than we are of the frustrations of Chicago's blacks." Of Epton, Royko wrote, "And, boy, if Epton is anything, he is a perfect example of 'any white candidate.'"

Yet, incredibly, Royko led his April 12, election day, column this way: "If a pollster asked me how I was going to vote today, I'd have to tell him to list me in the undecided column." He lamented the choice between a "kook" and a "crook." The cranky and sardonic persona that McClain had always enjoyed suddenly struck her as callous, cold, and crude. In her mind she crossed a line through Royko's name.

The reaction to McClain's *Post* piece was harsh. Legislation was introduced in the City Council to censure McClain. As usually happens, her long and thoughtful essay was reduced to a single sentence: Chicago's election, she wrote, "would make me feel like machine-gunning every white face on the bus."

The pundits damned her. Hadn't Chicago suffered enough notoriety already? "Good Morning America," "The Today Show," "60 Minutes," Ted Koppel, Phil Donahue, and Charles Kuralt. Television crews from England, France, Italy, Germany, Japan, Australia, and God knows where else. Four reporters and two columnists from the *Washington Post.* Magazine stories in the *New York Times. Time, Newsweek, People;* long features in the *Wall Street Journal* and the *London Times.* The list went on. And now McClain again airs the city's dirty laundry for the rest of the country to see. The article appeared at the end of July, more than three months after the election. Why did it have to appear at all?

Yet Chicago was not in a period of healing but in the midst of another crisis. Following Washington's election there had been no cooling off period. There hadn't been the inevitable drift to the middle that typifies U.S. politics or any sense of the honeymoon period that usually greets a newcomer to office. The network television crews had left, yet the battle over race and community continued. "An evilness still possesses this town," McClain wrote in the *Post,* "and it continues to weigh down my heart."

Nine months after the *Post* piece appeared, McClain, thirty-two, took her life. Some blamed it on the election, citing the *Post* piece as all the proof one needed ("torn as never before . . . a two-headed, two-hearted creature . . . in continual conflict, by turns pitying, then vilifying the other . . ."). But those who best knew McClain scoffed at so simplistic an explanation. Always a troubled soul, she had once before attempted suicide. "Happiness," she wrote in what she called her "generic suicide note," "is a private club that will not let me enter."

Yet as a black woman trying to make it in a white world, there were reasons outside her own personal angst that contributed to her death. "I will never live long enough to see my people free anyway"—that was the final line of her suicide note. A black woman writing in *Savvy* magazine chose McClain as her central subject in an article entitled "To Be Black, Gifted, and Alone." "Her unanswered question continues to haunt her sisters," the author wrote. "'I have made it, but where?'"

Council
Wars
1983–1986

Peace if possible,

justice at any price.

— Jean Baptist Point du Sable,

Chicago's first non-Indian settler

12

THE

BIGGEST

BULLY

IN THE

BAR

There was no longer any need for pretense. At an informal City Council meeting the Friday following Washington's victory, Alderman Ed Vrdolyak broke with his party's newly elected mayor. The chairman of the Cook County Democratic party, Vrdolyak took the council floor and said the election may be over, but it was still war between the party regulars and Washington. He laid the blame on Washington. A Washington aide named Jim Houlihan, Vrdolyak claimed, was passing the word that Washington sought to dump the Old Guard and replace them with aldermen loyal to him. A northwest side alderman named Richard Mell stood to confirm Washington's threat. Later, Houlihan told a reporter that he said nothing of the sort to Vrdolyak or to anybody. Mell confessed he hadn't quite told the truth; he had only repeated the story secondhand, as Vrdolyak had told it to him.

When the meeting broke up, Marian Humes, a black alderwoman on good terms with Vrdolyak, decided she would have a talk with Vrdolyak to clear things up. A loyal machine soldier who had risen through the ranks,

Humes was no more enamored of Washington's victory than Vrdolyak. But she knew that Washington hadn't chosen Houlihan but Wilson Frost, one of their own, to represent him in the council reorganization. Where Houlihan was antimachine, Wilson Frost had been a close Byrne ally through her tenure. Frost and Vrdolyak were allies, perhaps even friends; later, confronted by charges he was antiblack for his opposition to Washington, Vrdolyak said he and Frost used to golf together. They were close colleagues, he said, until Washington's election ushered in a black-white split that destroyed friendships. What Humes couldn't understand is how Vrdolyak didn't know Frost was the one handling things.

Humes stopped by Vrdolyak's office shortly after the council meeting broke up. There she found most of the council's white aldermen. Humes did not know what to think but passed along her message anyway: wait to see what Washington and Frost have in mind. Afterward she was no longer surprised but suspicious.

There were plenty of people advising Washington to do just what Houlihan supposedly said: dump the Old Guard. It seemed each of their plans was bolder than the next. Washington himself harbored grand designs of turning the council on its head. I'll throw the whole lot of them out of power, he boasted to at least one aide. Yet that was when Washington was still high from victory. Not many days later, though, he sobered up, overcome by reason.

Washington recognized that he needed new allies if he was to have a working majority in the council. He would have enough on his mind without a hostile City Council. He figured on singling out only those aldermen most closely identified with Byrne—Vrdolyak, Ed Burke, and Fred Roti. Wilson Frost would have been the fourth name in that group, but Frost was important if only as a symbol to the other Old Guard aldermen.

As Washington explained only after it was too late, he sought to dilute this troika's powers, not strip them of all vestiges of their clout. Burke headed the Police and Fire Committee and Roti chaired Licensing. Washington sought to break Burke's committee into two and allow Burke to keep half of his old post; he was not sure what he would offer Roti except that he knew it would not be Licensing. Vrdolyak chaired the Zoning and Buildings Committee, a plum spot second only to the Finance

Committee. Vrdolyak was also the council's president pro tem, meaning he presided over council meetings in the mayor's absence. Washington sought to bisect Vrdolyak's committee and name someone else the new pro tem. Vrdolyak would not be offered Zoning under any circumstances.

Frost would also lose something under Washington's plan. Frost's committee, Finance, would also be divided. Who would get what committees would work itself out in the next few weeks, Washington figured, before the new council's first formal meeting when they would vote on a new lineup of committee chairs. Frost and other Washington emissaries would dangle the committee chairmanships in the search for new allies.

It seemed a sound plan. Demoting Vrdolyak, Burke, and Roti, routinely described in press accounts as having "reputed mob connections," would send a signal that it was no longer business as usual; at the same time, sticking it to Vrdolyak would seemingly gain him new allies in the council. A great many machine regulars, black and white, resented the hoarding of power under Byrne. Even aldermen loyal to Byrne would mutter off the record that they were left only crumbs while Vrdolyak and a few others feasted on the pie. Diluting this troika's power seemed a good start toward winning new friends—so, at least, Washington figured before he quite understood the role that race would play in his dealings with the council.

Washington and Vrdolyak met shortly after the general election, along with Frost. Vrdolyak told Washington he had no problem stepping down as president pro tem. "The mayor should have his own guy in," Vrdolyak later explained.

Vrdolyak was not nearly as accommodating when Washington told him of his plan to split his committee. Because of your seniority, Washington told Vrdolyak, you will remain a chairman but not over Zoning.

All pretense of civility came abruptly to an end. Vrdolyak felt insulted and told Washington so. Washington, indignant, was equally frank: "You supported Epton, bullshitted me, and you've been organizing since day one. Let's get it out front."

Vrdolyak hadn't broken his back for the Democratic nominee in the general election as he had for his party's endorsed candidate in the primary. But what did Washington expect? Besides, when Vrdolyak offered to host a rally in the Tenth Ward, he was all but insulted for his troubles. "We'll get back to you," he was told, and that's the last he heard from the Washington campaign on that matter. At the time he wondered if Washington really wanted to be mayor.

Vrdolyak couldn't figure Washington. Thirty years in politics, yet he didn't seem to know the first thing about lining up votes. "You're out, Eddie." Does he think it's that easy?

At his meeting with Washington, Vrdolyak assured him that he would not go down without a fight. Washington was equally unyielding. Two weeks before the first City Council meeting, scheduled for early May, both sides went about the business of trolling the council for allies.

Of the fifty aldermen in the council, Washington began with a solid twenty behind him. The council's sixteen black aldermen were sure to side with Washington. At least half of the council's black caucus would prefer throwing in their lot with Vrdolyak, but opposing Washington would be political suicide. The only black alderman who might side with Vrdolyak was Tyrone Kenner. Kenner had been indicted a couple of months earlier for allegedly selling city jobs for as much as $1,200 per. Vrdolyak was helping Kenner pay for his defense.

Washington also counted on the council's small contingent of white lakefront independents. Vrdolyak's reputation as one of the council's more infamous rogues meant they couldn't support Vrdolyak, no matter what they thought of him. There were three or four antimachine aldermen representing the north lakefront, depending on how one read Marion Volini. Volini was aligned with the Daley wing of the party yet presented herself to her constituents as independent of the regular Democrats.

Alderman Burt Natarus would also be a stalwart Washington vote. Natarus was strictly old school, hardly the sort for joining an antimachine rebellion, but he had no choice.* Natarus's patron, the ward committeeman at whose pleasure he served, George Dunne, had thrown in his lot with Washington. Dunne had headed the Democratic party since Daley's death in 1976 through 1982, when he was ousted to make room for Vrdolyak.

---

*"I've never been a reformer," Natarus said on the council floor. "I don't profess to be a reformer. I support the mayor because I've always supported the city's mayor."

Perhaps some dyed-in-the-wool belief in Democratic loyalty was behind Dunne's stalwart support for his party's new mayor; perhaps it was his feelings for Vrdolyak. Counting Natarus and Volini but not Kenner, that put twenty votes in Washington's column—five votes short of a majority.*

Vrdolyak figured on a nucleus of fifteen. There were Burke and Roti, of course, and those who supported Epton, either openly or clandestinely. The fight would be won or lost among the remaining fifteen or so aldermen: the so-called Daley bloc and the incoming freshmen whose allegiances were largely unknown.

Washington counted the Daleyites in his column. Vrdolyak was their archfoe, Byrne's floor leader when the mayor froze them out of power and the party chairman who shortchanged them when it came to jobs and other perquisites. The Daley bloc could blame Vrdolyak for any number of vendettas visited upon them under Byrne.

Vrdolyak, however, put question marks beside their names. Washington's coalition was a ragtag bunch of militants, crusaders, and party irregulars; the Daleyites could not possibly see them as their natural allies. There were also the passions prompting someone to take a swing at Rich Daley to consider. Voters in the ward might not care to hear again about the Byrne-Daley feuding that paved the way to the election of the city's first black mayor.

Seven freshmen aldermen were white, and one was Latino. Several had defeated a machine incumbent, but that did not mean they would throw their support in with the blacks and the independents. Vrdolyak, the party chairman, could help them get elected as ward committeemen, thereby establishing themselves as undisputed ward bosses. Race was another factor. Those freshmen representing white wards were reminded—by Vrdolyak emissaries and by the political pundits—that their constituents would not be pleased should they align themselves with Washington. The Old Guard saw no reason to apologize for this unabashedly racial appeal: it was simply a matter of practical politics, no different from the machine-oriented black aldermen admitting they supported Washington because it was political suicide in the black community not to do so.

Vrdolyak needed the votes of at least half of the nonblack freshmen— or every one of them should the Daley bloc side with Washington. The

*The city's bylaws dictated that the mayor, as the presiding officer over the City Council, break all ties.

211

freshmen, like the Daleyites, were slow to commit. Taking their time only raised their stock, but probably most were more confused and nervous than cunning. The election, harsh and divisive, was over, but the battle over race and community had just begun.

It could be said that Ed Vrdolyak began his political career as an antibusing activist, but that wouldn't be quite right. When he first ran for political office, in 1968, Vrdolyak was an ambitious personal injury lawyer who recognized what a boon to business the ward committeeman post could be. He wasn't driven to run by the antibusing passions sweeping his community, only sly enough to understand its potential. His fervent antibusing stance was something he adopted only for the occasion, a strategy for beating an entrenched committeeman.

Robert Seltzner, editor of an area newspaper called the *Daily Calumet*, planted the idea of an antibusing campaign in Vrdolyak's head when he paid Seltzner a courtesy call. Seltzner took an immediate liking to Vrdolyak, a local kid who had made it. He had earned a law degree at the prestigious University of Chicago, yet returned to the neighborhood—returned to a world dominated by the mammoth steel plants at the Chicago-Indiana border, where soot darkened the sky like a black rain. Vrdolyak bought a home a block from his parents' place and opened a law office on a nearby commercial strip. He was young, barely thirty, but he struck Seltzner as self-assured, aggressive, and smart. As a practicing attorney, Vrdolyak also had an independent source of income, which Seltzner saw as a plus: he couldn't be bought at a cheap price. Vrdolyak struck Seltzner as a perfect candidate to oust the pawn of downtown who served as the Tenth Ward's committeeman. He decided on the spot to help Vrdolyak.

Help came in the form of a tip. The Board of Education was about to announce a trial busing plan, Seltzner told him. A single site, a school on the edge of the Tenth Ward, had been chosen as the guinea pig, yet the committeeman, ever the loyal machine soldier, would not fight the city's decision. Over lunch the two of them "ad-libbed some bullshit suit," Vrdolyak said. "I drafted it there at the table. I filed it after lunch. I was on television and radio that night."

No longtime resident of the Tenth Ward would be surprised that his or her children were the bone the city tossed the liberals and the blacks. The Tenth Ward was on the southeast side, a part of the city that had no place even in the shorthand that people used to geographically place themselves in Chicago: "east side" in a city whose lexicon didn't incorporate the term. Psychologically, one journalist wrote, the east side is "as remote from the Loop as Ulster is from London." So far did east siders live from the center of the city that the closest el stop was forty blocks away.

Most Tenth Ward residents remembered the rioting between blacks and whites at Calumet Park. Over a hundred people fought that day. Yet here the city was intruding on an already explosive situation, choosing a racially changing neighborhood as a test site.

"Instant candidate, that was me," Vrdolyak said. "I had the front page of the *Cal* [Seltzner's *Daily Calumet*] every day. The *Tribune* picked me up, so did the *Daily News*. I was on television a dozen, fifteen times. I had one hundred speaking engagements inside of thirty days. . . . They'd go apeshit. I'd walk in to a standing ovation. I'd leave the same way. It was wild, really wild. Hell, even the mayor called me in during that time."

Vrdolyak knew what he wanted to tell Daley: "I'm only gonna run if you tell me I'm in if I win. There's no sense in my winning if I can't be inside." It was precisely what Daley wanted to hear when he invited this intriguing young upstart to his office.

Vrdolyak's victory as ward committeeman established him as something of a legend by the time he was elected to the City Council in 1971. Beating a sitting committeeman was unheard of back then. Every so often an incumbent alderman lost, but never a Democratic committeeman still in Daley's good graces. Vrdolyak won because the incumbent got caught in the racial crossfire and because Daley agreed to stay out of the race, but he would be celebrated in media accounts as a brash renegade who managed a political miracle.

Vrdolyak was the youngest son of Peter and Matilda Vrdolyak, Croatian immigrants from a tiny mountain village in Yugoslavia. The family lived above Peter Vrdolyak's tavern, a rough place that drew a mix of steelworkers, meat packers, and dockhands. One of Vrdolyak's responsibilities when he was old enough was to help his father and older brothers break up brawls. ("He'd get possessed," Vrdolyak once said of his brother Peter. "He'd rip nostrils, tear ears, jam his thumbs into eyeballs . . .") Vrdolyak was the youngest, so he ended up on a cot in the kitchen. The place shook around the clock, every time a train passed on the tracks adjacent to their flat.

Two of Vrdolyak's brothers were already working in the steel mills when their little brother was accepted to law school. Another brother was a Chicago cop. The University of Chicago was only a twenty-minute drive from the east side, but rare was the kid who grew up in Hegewisch, Irondale, or Slag Valley who ended up attending school there.

The university in Hyde Park opened Vrdolyak's eyes to a world populated by liberals and intellectuals. He relaxed after lunch at school by playing bridge with his classmates; at night he played poker and pool with his east side buddies. During his first year, Vrdolyak said, he seriously considered "calling up my local recruiting office and enlisting."

Between his first and second years at Chicago, Vrdolyak worked a construction job for the summer. The cops showed up one day to arrest him on an attempted murder charge. Seven guys had beaten up a fellow worker over a union-scab disagreement; somehow Vrdolyak was among the seven the police were searching for. A faded photocopy of Vrdolyak's rap sheet was slipped to one reporter or another every time Vrdolyak ran for something, but never was there any mention of the affidavit filed by a law professor that stated Vrdolyak was taking a final exam at the time.

It is with acrimony, even twenty-five years later, that Vrdolyak recalls the university suspending him until the matter was cleared up. Innocent until proven guilty unless you're a Croatian kid from the dirty east side whose parents still spoke with thick accents. Vrdolyak was always sure to point out years later that prejudice was not something that only black Chicago suffered.

During his second year in the City Council, Vrdolyak staged what the press dubbed the "coffee rebellion." Not much of a rebellion, really, it was precipitated by a fight with Daley's floor leader, Thomas Keane, over a pay raise that ended up winning Vrdolyak and his rebels only minor concessions. It was significant, said participant Ed Burke, "because this was at a time aldermen were voting with Daley a thousand percent of the time and wouldn't dare speak in council without permission." One columnist described the rebellion as a matter of "ten or eleven aldermen who say 'yes' to the mayor most of the time and 'no' once in a while."

Yet the gambit established Vrdolyak as an important player in the council. The Young Turks, they were called—the younger machine aldermen led by the impish and brash Ed Vrdolyak. Vrdolyak impressed at least one of his reform foes, Leon Despres. "Vrdolyak didn't focus his hostility on Daley but on Keane," Despres said. "Very shrewd, very shrewd. Because although Tom Keane was Daley's trusted adviser, he was also the man Daley feared most."

Two years later Keane was before a grand jury that was investigating a long list of questionable real estate deals Keane had engineered. The day the grand jury met to decide Keane's fate, the council was in session. It was also an important day for Daley: the independents were threatening to cause trouble over the millions in insurance the city had just steered to his son John's insurance firm. Daley beckoned Vrdolyak to the rostrum. "Keane's in a fog," he reportedly told Vrdolyak. "You take care of things."* Thereafter, Daley frequently relied on Vrdolyak to shepherd an issue through the council.

Winning the party's endorsement for a judgeship on behalf of one favored lawyer was considered a sign of clout in the party; in 1976 Vrdolyak managed to slate two of his people—one a lawyer in his firm, the other a party supplicant in his organization. It was said that for much of Vrdolyak's tenure the Seventh and Ninth Wards were nothing but satellites of Vrdolyak's Tenth Ward. After Daley died suddenly from a heart attack in 1976, Vrdolyak was among the small group of insiders who chose Michael Bilandic as Daley's successor.

Vrdolyak said he was interested in succeeding Daley, but the speculation was that he was not so much angling for the office as trying to force a deal. Only by throwing his hat in the ring could he win something—in this case, the powerful Zoning Committee. Vrdolyak won a backhanded compliment when Byrne specifically named him when lambasting the "cabal of evil men" running Chicago; under Byrne, Vrdolyak's power increased.

---

*Keane was indicted, convicted, and sentenced to four years in the federal penitentiary.

"Fast Eddie" he was called—but not because of his meteoric rise in city politics. It seemed Vrdolyak was always involved in some scam that earned him a headline. "Our Mr. Fastbuck," read the slug over a Mike Royko column dissecting a questionable Vrdolyak deal. A consortium of Tenth Ward women approached Vrdolyak as chairman of the Zoning Committee to enlist his support in reclassifying a parcel of land they had been trying to sell for fourteen years. Vrdolyak obliged the women; in return they sold him a second plot of land for $16,000. Within the year Vrdolyak resold the land to a local savings and loan for $60,000, though it was zoned "residential."

The purchase made no sense: the land was not worth even close to $60,000 as zoned; moreover, the bank was buying the land to house its new offices. A bank official said they simply forgot to check on the zoning status—which, Royko wrote, was "something like a car dealer taking a car on trade without checking to see if it has an engine." The bank applied for a zoning change, which passed through Vrdolyak's Zoning Committee unanimously. There was no proof that Vrdolyak assured the bank prior to the sale that the land would be rezoned—only suspicion.

Someone always seemed eager to do Vrdolyak a favor, such as the time a city contractor gave Vrdolyak $18,000 worth of building materials when Vrdolyak was building his home. A "housewarming gift," the contractor said. A plumber who worked pro bono on his home subsequently became a state representative. After Marina City was built, Vrdolyak's friend Charles Swibel allowed Vrdolyak and several partners to purchase fifty units in the complex—SWIBEL-VRDOLYAK "BARGAIN BASEMENT" CONDO DEAL BARED, read the Sun-Times headline. The next day the City Council considered an ordinance that allowed Swibel to retain ownership of the parking garage facility in the complex. Reportedly, Vrdolyak and his partners doubled their investment in a year's time. When asked about this deal and other seeming conflicts of interest, Vrdolyak pointed out that he has never been indicted.

Vrdolyak always managed to make a good buck as a personal injury lawyer. Two brothers in the police force often meant that a squad car accident or other potentially lucrative lawsuit ended up at his firm. "I always gave the coppers a discount," Vrdolyak said, "so they spread the word for me." His brother Peter, a union official, also steered business his way. Once Vrdolyak represented sixty-two of the sixty-five injury claimants on a single job site. Vrdolyak eventually hired a black sidekick to hustle business in the black community.

His connections broadened as his power increased. Vrdolyak's law firm has handled hundreds of personal injury cases against the city, and eventually he had to hire many more lawyers. Vrdolyak also expanded his police force operations.

The *Daily Calumet*'s Robert Seltzner came to be a good friend of Vrdolyak's. The two were constantly together, so much so, Seltzner said, "I was like a member of Eddie's family." Vrdolyak, Seltzner told a grand jury long after the friendship dissolved, "was constantly paying cops. . . . It was like confetti. Cops dropping Vrdolyak's calling card all over the place. The payoffs were to get referrals for personal injury cases." Vrdolyak denied that he ever paid a single policeman to refer business to his law firm, yet in a diary Seltzner kept he wrote, "Vrdolyak called, 3-hr lunch meet at Club; he paid off line of 4th District cops in cash for injury tips leading to cases."

In 1972 a train crash near downtown killed forty-five and left hundreds injured. A Vrdolyak precinct captain was caught handing out Vrdolyak's business card among the victims. The captain claimed he was acting on his own, as did Vrdolyak. Seltzner told the *Chicago Lawyer*, however, that allegations of ambulance chasing were true. If so, this was ironic, given that Vrdolyak would make much of Washington's law suspension throughout the mayor's tenure.

During the 1983 primary, Vrdolyak chided the *Tribune* and *Sun-Times* for their endorsement of Rich Daley. "Have they ever been to your neighborhood?" Vrdolyak asked. "Have they ever gone to a wake there? Have they ever gone to a christening or a wedding? Have they ever helped somebody who needed help on your block? That's what this organization is all about."

Vrdolyak never looked the part of the old-time ward boss. He did not chomp on a cigar or sport a pinky ring; he was not fleshy jowled and rotund; he fancied Armani suits and expensive shoes. Yet Daley would have swatted Vrdolyak like a pest if not for his skills as a ward boss. There were maybe half a dozen committeemen in the city who ran a ward organization as effective as Vrdolyak's.

Vrdolyak was always dreaming up some extra service to provide residents. In 1977 when the skies dumped record snows on Chicago, Vrdolyak claimed that he spent $60,000 in campaign funds to hire private trucks to clear the ward's side streets. When he grew tired of waiting his turn for one of the two graders the city owned, the Tenth Ward regular Democratic organization bought its own. Vrdolyak was once quoted as saying the alderman was nothing but a glorified ward custodian, yet he also recognized that it was the janitorial services an alderman provided that won people's allegiance.

Campaigning for office in 1975, Vrdolyak stopped at a housing project at the edge of the ward. At the apartment of an elderly black woman, Vrdolyak met with a local pastor to try to gain an endorsement. The woman served the pastor and Vrdolyak fried chicken, but her husband was eating a hot dog. "Go back there this afternoon," Vrdolyak told an aide. "Take her some of our literature to hand out. And bring along six porterhouse steaks for the old man."

There was also the kind of assistance Vrdolyak offered a black woman named Sadie Balfour. Balfour bought a home in an all-white community not far from Vrdolyak's ward office. Neighbors tried to scare her away by breaking her windows. Where in other wards Balfour would have been left to survive or escape on her own, Vrdolyak stepped in. But he didn't use his considerable influence in the neighborhood to explain that the presence of this one quiet woman did not spell the end. Instead he hooked her up with a white family interested in buying the house and found Balfour a home in a neighborhood that wasn't quite so white. He had taken care of things quietly and efficiently—and in precisely the way that pleased most of Balfour's ex-neighbors. Proud of his efforts on Balfour's behalf, Vrdolyak said, "There was nobody else around but me who could help her."

Vrdolyak was always helping out someone in a pinch and was often imposed upon to perform some favor—to speak to someone at City Hall, write a letter on his law firm's stationery. Almost always he obliged. Supposedly he cosigned on dozens of homes around the ward, and he helped people black or white—it never seemed to make a difference.

Where other ward committeemen had a few hundred jobs to hand out, Vrdolyak had well over a thousand. He had at his disposal a disproportionate number of city jobs and control over hundreds of jobs in the private sector. "I've placed as many people in private industry in our area as I have with the city," Vrdolyak said. It seemed he was always scheming to add jobs to his largess.

Robert Seltzner estimated that he wrote somewhere around a thousand articles about Vrdolyak, all of them complimentary, before he came to see Vrdolyak as a "charming scoundrel" who could not be trusted. But the diary in which he logged Vrdolyak's activities indicated that Seltzner was not deluding himself. Vrdolyak's involvement with the Progressive Steelworkers' Union at the Wisconsin Steel Company, representing thirty-five hundred members, offers a good example. Vrdolyak would tell a reporter that he was only lobbying on behalf of a friend running for union president, but Seltzner's diary recounts a different story.

"Vrdolyak called, met at his house 6 hrs.; told about using Atty. Geo. Feiwell to 'get' Mike Drakulich [the union's president]," according to a Seltzner diary entry. In later entries Seltzner wrote about other meetings where there was talk of "destroying" Drakulich through a bogus lawsuit about a "scheme to loot the treasury of the union." Seltzner's job as the editor of the *Daily Calumet* was to "do the discrediting," Seltzner admitted in one interview.

Drakulich was voted out of office in 1973 and replaced with Leonard "Tony" Roque, a Vrdolyak precinct captain. Immediately Roque placed Edward R. Vrdolyak, Ltd., on retainer. Members of Vrdolyak's organization got jobs at Wisconsin Steel; in return the grateful workers were supposed to help out in the precincts. In some parts of the ward Vrdolyak's organization had a precinct worker for every block.

When hard times hit the steel industry, Vrdolyak's meddling took a tragic turn. The mill was about to shut down in the late 1970s when Roque signed away benefits that would have meant $85 million for its members. He did so, he said, as part of a deal to guarantee that the company made good on the workers' pensions, apparently not realizing that most of the pension fund was guaranteed by federal law. The lawyer in Vrdolyak's firm handling the Wisconsin Steel account told Roque that he would be wise to find another lawyer because he was not familiar enough with labor law to adequately represent the union when the company seemed on the verge of bankruptcy. Roque, however, ignored his advice. When Wisconsin Steel closed in 1980, the company announced that it was not liable for $85 million in severance pay and pension benefits that Roque had signed away.

Vrdolyak assured workers that he wouldn't let Wisconsin Steel get away with that. He returned almost half the $136,000 in legal fees he had collected from the union in Roque's eight years in office. He did what he could to secure jobs for those he had put to work in the mill. Yet Vrdolyak received money from Wisconsin Steel, including a $1,000 contribution two weeks before the plant closed. The union contributed $18,000 to Vrdolyak's political funds during Roque's tenure, including one contribution seventeen days before the mill closed.

Another lawyer, Tom Geoghegan, took over the Progressive Steelworkers' case, convinced a federal judge that the 1977 agreement was invalid, and won a $15 million out-of-court settlement from the company. Geoghegan concluded that Vrdolyak's firm "grossly botched" their negotiations with Wisconsin Steel. "He might know workman's comp law, but I don't think he knows labor law," Geoghegan said of Vrdolyak.

"Every year the yard boss would give me ten tickets to Eddie's golf outing," said a former Vrdolyak precinct worker who worked on a ward garbage crew. "It was this yearly thing Eddie put on for all his rich golfing buddies. Tickets were $60 apiece. I was supposed to sell them or eat the cost. Now who do I know around here who plays golf? And during the week. Who am I gonna find to pay sixty bucks and lose a day's pay to play a round of golf?"

A ticket to the ward organization's annual dinner cost another $150. "Every year I got something in the mail about buying a whole table for $1,500," said another former precinct worker. "The crazy thing was, some guys put themselves in hock to do it. That was supposed to be an investment in your future. Eddie really notices a guy who buys a table." The small store owner's burden was the annual ad book. "That meant between $250 and $500 every year just to keep on Eddie's good side," he said.

Apparently the owner of a small east side hauling company profited from his relationship with Vrdolyak but at a price. Shortly after taking office Washington replaced Vrdolyak's handpicked superintendent at the Tenth Ward's Streets and Sanitation yard with a man named Clem Balanoff,

Jr. With considerable pleasure Balanoff told of a conversation early in his tenure with the hauling company's owner.

"He starts off, 'Look, I got a load of concrete out there.'

"So I says, 'Yeah, so?'

"'We want to dump it.'

"'Okay, so bring it to a landfill.'"

To dump concrete, you need to pay a fee to unload at a designated waste site.

"'No, you don't understand. Bob used to give me a place to dump it.'"

"Bob" was Balanoff's predecessor. Bob, Balanoff claimed, was legendary in Tenth Ward political circles for the tens of thousands in fund-raising tickets he sold each year.

"I'm still just looking at him like I don't understand what he's talking about," Balanoff continued. "So he says, 'No, you don't understand, I'm in with Eddie, I buy lots of tickets.'"

Vrdolyak had run the ward for so long that it was only natural people assumed he, not the mayor, hired the ward superintendent.

Vrdolyak wasn't even a year on the job as party chairman when Jane Byrne lost. There was talk that the loss spelled doom for Vrdolyak. With Washington as the new mayor, the conventional wisdom held that Vrdolyak's influence would fall. Vrdolyak understood it differently. He saw the potential to emerge as the election's big winner.

Washington's win didn't need to be an unmitigated disaster. Now Byrne was a has-been, and it seemed that half the white community blamed Daley for Washington. With the city's two top white politicians out of the way, Vrdolyak was both the undisputed kingpin of the party and the best hope of the boys down at City Hall. The organization did not have to be split into a Daley and a Byrne bloc; there would be only a Vrdolyak bloc if he played his cards right.

And who but Washington stood in his way? A lightweight like Bernie Epton received forty-nine percent of the vote against Washington. Imagine how Washington would do against a *real* candidate. The only challenge would be enduring four years without the patronage and other spoils of victory. Maybe he would run himself for mayor, maybe he would put someone up to it. Either way he would bring the black machine loyalists back into the fold, no hard feelings, by offering them a fair share of jobs and other perks. He would be a hero. Washington would probably bomb so badly they'd give Ed a goddamn key to the city.

If dreams of glory were not enough, there was also the motivation supplied by Washington's threats to defrock him. "So I say to myself, I thought this guy was just the mayor," Vrdolyak said in one interview back in 1983. "But he thinks he's the king. So. Did I want a fight? No. Do I know how? You bet." Call it the fighting spirit ingrained in almost everyone growing up on the city's east side. "The mayor read me all wrong," Vrdolyak said. "I'm a fighter. I don't go down easy." It was like a picture Vrdolyak had hanging in his office, showing him screaming at a referee, looking half out of his mind. The picture was taken at the annual softball game between the aldermen and City Hall staffers. "I like to win," he told a curious reporter.

Everyone believed they knew what Washington needed to do to counter Vrdolyak. Play hardball, some said. Threaten to fire key patronage appointments. Tell them that opposing him means they won't get so much as a stop sign.

Others urged Washington to be more accommodating. Why not cut a few deals? Offer a few jobs: let the southwest side aldermen have a say over something like the park district. Wilson Frost wondered if Washington understood that it made no difference if Vrdolyak headed the Zoning Committee when he had veto power. A Frost aide cursed the movement mentality of "off with their heads."

To Washington there was no compromising with the likes of an Ed Vrdolyak—nothing short of selling out. Frost told Washington that he could have his council majority if he kept Vrdolyak as the head of Zoning. Yet Washington was adamant. Paul McGrath, a reporter drawn to Byrne's antimachine message and her first chief of staff, watched as she increasingly sought Vrdolyak's guidance. "It's like walking into a tough bar and either punching out or making friends with the toughest guy in there," McGrath said. "Byrne's way was to make friends."

"I'm not going to pull a Byrne," Washington said.

Jane Byrne sat on the stage while Washington gave his inaugural address. Byrne bit her lip and stared at the floor as Washington assessed the city's problems. Washington didn't offer the usual bromides that such an occasion inspires but instead launched an attack on the waste and fraud destroying Chicago. The *Sun-Times* described the speech as nothing less than a "death sentence on old-fashioned machine politics."

The city, Washington said, was run based more on the needs of the machine than its people. He imposed a hiring freeze and also a freeze on city salaries, and said the city's budget would be cut. He started by proclaiming that the hundreds of city workers Byrne had hired in her last few weeks in office would be fired. He implied race several times, such as when he said, "City government for once in our lifetime must be equitable and fair."

Joseph Kotlarz, an alderman from the northwest side and one of the fence sitters, was impressed. "The people in my ward are excited about what they hear from Washington about cutting the budget," Kotlarz said afterward. "If he does that, they won't care if he's white, black, or pink." He won despite the local ward organization, he said, not because of it. "I have no reason to be with Vrdolyak," he said.

The big council meeting was the Monday after Washington's inauguration. Kotlarz wouldn't say what happened in the few days between Washington's speech and the meeting. Maybe he secured a promise of Vrdolyak's support should he run against the incumbent Democratic ward committeeman—which is what would happen the following year. Whatever the rationale, he signed up with Vrdolyak. "I feel much more comfortable with Vrdolyak than I would have if I was on the other side," Kotlarz told one magazine writer. "Epton beat Washington six to one in my ward. I would have had a lot of grief if I'd been on the other side."

At around eleven o'clock the night of his inauguration Washington phoned Alderman Richard Mell. "Where are we, Alderman?" he began. Mell told him that he would vote with Vrdolyak. "But the split doesn't need to be in stone," Mell told him. Peace was simple: "Eddie's color isn't black or white but green. All you have to do is give Eddie a little green, and you've got everything else you want." Mell also explained to Washington how cheaply his own vote came. "Give me maybe twenty jobs to give my guys," Mell said he told Washington, "and I'd be happy."

Who knows what Washington might have been thinking when Mell added, "Don't make this city suffer for three hundred years of injustice against your people. Don't make me and others pay for it. . . . Let's not make this city another Detroit."

Vrdolyak's best ally was the uncertainty. White aldermen tied to a regular Democratic organization wondered if Washington's ultimate goal was to strip them of all their power. Was it a matter of time before they were as politically beside the point as the independents had been all those years? Vrdolyak offered his own fate as an answer: "If he can do that to a guy like me, what do you think he can do to you?"

Mell may have betrayed the unconscious fears on which Vrdolyak preyed when a reporter overheard him say, "Racism is when the mayor says he wants all the white chairmen out." In fact, under Washington's plan, about half the committee chairmanships were to be held by whites, including many from wards where Washington received no more than a few hundred votes. Still, the fear was real, even if the "facts" were not.

Vrdolyak began with about fifteen solid votes. By the big council meeting he had twenty-nine. Washington started with twenty solid votes and ended up with twenty-one. Of the fence sitters, only Tyrone Kenner ended up falling to Washington's side.

The Daley faction's alliance with Vrdolyak genuinely surprised Washington. He figured they would be wary of supporting a black man but adamantly opposed to throwing in their lot with Vrdolyak. Washington never cared for Daley, but he put aside his personal feelings and wooed Daley and his allies. A few days after beating Epton he announced that he could support Daley's reelection for state's attorney in 1984. It was Washington's way of declaring a cease-fire with the Daley wing of the party. He met with the Daley wing's top ward committeemen: George

Dunne, William Lipinski, Dan Rostenkowski, and Tom Hynes. Frost was told to offer the Zoning Committee chairmanship to the alderman representing Daley's own Eleventh Ward, Patrick Huels.

Daley wasn't biting, though, nor were his allies. Those aldermen serving at the pleasure of Lipinski, Rostenkowski, and Hynes sided with Vrdolyak, as did Patrick Huels. "Rich is not going to be a Ping-Pong ball between the blacks and the whites," a Daley source told one columnist.

The weekend before the big vote a team of lawyers gathered at Vrdolyak's home with all those pledging their support to Vrdolyak. They met for about ten hours on Saturday and then another ten on Sunday. With more than twenty-five votes on their side, Vrdolyak and the lawyers told them, there was nothing Washington could do to stall for time even though he chaired the council meeting. The worst mistake he could make, the lawyers counseled, was a quick adjournment. Should he walk out after a quick gavel, the president pro tem could take the podium and ask for a roll call to show a majority had not approved the adjournment—and Vrdolyak was still officially the council's president pro tem.

Vrdolyak's allies watched, amazed, as this best-case scenario unfolded itself on Monday morning. The meeting began with a standing ovation in honor of Washington's election as the new mayor. Washington then called on an ally who moved to adjourn the meeting. Washington asked for a voice vote and declared that the meeting was over; Washington and his followers then exited. Following the script, Vrdolyak strode to the podium. He lifted his arms triumphantly into the air as he stalked the stage. Later he was quoted as saying, "I've lost a lot of fights in my life, but I've always stayed and taken it like a man."

The remaining aldermen introduced a series of resolutions: one increased the number of council committees to twenty-nine; another put in place the council reorganization plan Vrdolyak and his twenty-eight allies had hammered out among themselves. Alderman Ed Burke of the southwest side was given the plum spot of Finance Committee chairman. Beyond the considerable legislative prerogatives, the Finance Committee meant upward of seventy-five jobs for Burke to fill. Several more resolutions, each aimed at strengthening the powers of the City Council, were introduced and summarily passed twenty-nine to zero. The *Sun-Times* started its page-one article reporting that "Alderman Edward R. Vrdolyak and twenty-eight supporters thrust themselves into command of the City Council Monday in a stunning show of political power that humiliated Mayor Washington."

Wilson Frost took the brunt of the blame among Washington partisans. Washington never wanted Frost as the floor leader, but he had no rapport with most of the machine aldermen. "I had to have a spear carrier in there, somebody who knew the players," Washington said. "I looked down the whole list, and there was only one"—Frost. You can count on at least thirty votes, aides remember Frost telling Washington only a few days before the big City Council meeting.

Those with Vrdolyak believed that blaming Frost was scapegoating. To them, fault rested solely with Washington. In the coming months they spoke time and again of the phone calls Washington never made in April when the council showdown was shaping up. He even failed to return the calls of those few white aldermen who had phoned with their congratulations after the general election. "Harold had surrogates call for him, leaving messages," said one of those surrogates. "But you don't do it that way. It should've been, 'Let's have breakfast, let's have lunch.'" There was also the problem of mixed messages. Only word from Washington himself, several members of the Vrdolyak faction later said, could set the record straight about who really spoke for him, Houlihan or Frost. The closest Washington came to personal cajoling was a unity breakfast he hosted for all the aldermen.

Washington said a few phone calls wouldn't have made any difference, but he did confide to at least one aide that he made more calls than given credit for but did not make nearly as many as he could have. It became for him like a giant chip on his shoulder.* One alderman, an ally, said he once asked Washington why he didn't do more. "Because I wasn't going to kiss their asses," was the response.

Those defending Frost, or at least trying to place the blame on Washington, pointed out that Washington tied Frost's hands. Frost had a few committee chairmanships to offer but no jobs, no clout, no promise of

---

*His second press secretary, Alton Miller, had the habit of wearing sunglasses perched atop his head, even indoors, a fact reporters and Washington insiders never stopped commenting on. Why *do* you wear those glasses, Washington once asked him. No particular reason, Miller said, except now that the glasses had become an issue in the press, he couldn't take them off. That was an explanation Washington could understand. With a smile, he said, "They're the chip on your shoulder. I got no problem with that."

say-so over a few big contracts to appease big-money campaign contributors. Per Washington's instructions, Frost offered nothing to the freshmen aldermen. Vrdolyak was offering chairmanships all around.

The Vrdolyak 29 were ecstatic. Many had given Vrdolyak no chance. He did not have the leverage that a mayor has—the jobs, the contracts, control over city services. Yet they had both underestimated Vrdolyak's drive and misunderstood Washington. His inaugural address, several members of the 29 said, turned them around. Vrdolyak claimed that after the inauguration the Daley-bloc and freshmen aldermen were calling him. "None of this would have happened," Alderman Ed Burke said, sounding like the aggrieved party, "had Harold come to us the way Byrne did."

Vrdolyak's hustle and determination impressed them. He called people once, then again, and then another half-dozen times. He asked those on the fence what Washington had offered. "Oh, he hasn't called yet," Vrdolyak would say. "You let me know when he calls." Among those who had already committed to him, he was like a coach creating among his teammates a sense that they could win.

A verbal commitment was not enough. Vrdolyak asked the aldermen to sign a loyalty oath promising that they would act as a group. There were only twenty committees to go around, so the number was raised to twenty-nine. All but three of the Vrdolyak 29, including seven freshmen, chaired a committee: Kotlarz, who was late in signing his pledge; Vrdolyak; and Richard Mell, named the city's vice mayor. Before the new council reorganization, eight of the council's twenty black aldermen chaired a committee; now only three did.

13

BALANCING

ACTS

The night after the council meeting, the telephone rang at the Vrdolyak home. "Well, Alderman, did you have a good time today?" It was Washington. He extended an invitation to talk—"You and me have to shoot some pool," Washington said.

The two met the next day, Tuesday, in Washington's office. Washington suggested dumping a few of the freshmen as committee chairs as a compromise. He also suggested that Frost be named chairman of the Finance Committee and Burke chairman of a newly created Budget Committee. Vrdolyak balked; he would hear of no plan, he said, that stripped a committee from any ally. Compromise meant adding more committees and leaving Burke at Finance. Vrdolyak offered with a smile that he himself had nothing to bargain away for the sake of peace. "You got exactly what you wanted," he needled Washington. "I'm not a committee chairman anymore."

There was to be another council session that Friday, but on Thursday around midnight a police officer was sent to the home of each of the city's fifty aldermen. The officers carried a message from Washington that he was vetoing the council's call for a meeting the next day. Washington was still hoping that the two sides could work something out before the council met again.

In the meantime, Lu Palmer announced at a press conference that he and other Washington supporters would "utilize continuous techniques of persuasion" to pressure the Vrdolyak aldermen. Five aldermen whose wards Washington won in the general election were aligned with Vrdolyak. His group, Palmer said, would picket their homes. He said he was speaking on behalf of a group called Chicago Black United Communities. Could you imagine, the Vrdolyak aldermen asked themselves, the outrage should a group call themselves Chicago *White* United Communities?

Vrdolyak seized on Palmer's press conference and asked, Is this what the so-called Washington movement is about? Invading one's home because Washington was outsmarted in a legislative fight?

Maybe Vrdolyak was thinking about the threats, the midnight police visit, and all the tensions in the city when that Sunday he cooked up a Mother's Day surprise for his allies. If the other wives were at all like Denise Vrdolyak, they were worried sick about their husbands' safety. Vrdolyak's wife was already nagging him to start wearing a bulletproof vest.

That Sunday morning delivery men bearing red roses arrived at the homes of each of his council allies. "With love, Ed Vrdolyak," the card read. Perhaps, as one writer speculated, "rather than disappointment, there is a quickening in her bosom, her heart races a little faster, and she sighs and says, 'Ohhh, Eddie.'" There were twenty-nine roses to a bunch.

Washington was getting nowhere in his negotiations, so at the next City Council meeting he made a public plea. The city was more than sixty percent nonwhite, yet the council leadership was nearly all white. With the 1983 election Chicago's racial troubles had been broadcast across the land. Hadn't Chicago's reputation suffered enough without further damage? Washington asked from the rostrum.

229

Washington introduced a resolution calling on the council to adjourn for a week to see if they couldn't work things out. The Vrdolyakers balked. Washington's talk of race, they said, is nothing more than the cry of a loser. This is about arithmetic—twenty-nine is greater than twenty-one, the Vrdolyak-aligned aldermen repeated again and again—not race. Vrdolyak, who only four months earlier had said that people shouldn't kid themselves, this election was about race, told one reporter, "This is absolute madness. You can't just keep throwing up race. People don't buy that anymore."

Washington's proposal lost, twenty-nine to twenty-one. Similar proposals were made at subsequent sessions. These, too, lost by a vote of twenty-nine to twenty-one.

Representatives from the two sides met in a series of sessions ballyhooed in the media. A battery of reporters would camp outside their meeting room, waiting for word of any compromise. There was never any news to report.

Some of the twenty-nine assured reporters the impasse would work itself out. The council couldn't remain divided. "Eddie wanted to prove a point, and now he's proven it," one said. "But I don't think he wants to be fighting with the mayor for four years."

But Alderman Ed Burke, Vrdolyak's right hand, saw it differently. Burke said that with time the mayor would figure out that he needed twenty-six votes to get anything done—with time he would soften his hard-line antimachine stance. Byrne's resolve, after all, had lasted all of six months. Burke also boasted that people were calling his office to offer encouragement, saying things like, "Don't give up." We're "heroes" among our constituents, Burke said. Epton had won his ward by over five to one. What reason in the world was there to give in?

Meanwhile, the two sides ceased attempts at a negotiated peace. If anything, they had only dug in deeper. There was the off-chance that a lawsuit working its way through the federal courts would require that new aldermanic elections be held in some wards. The suit charged that the ward map on which the 1983 aldermanic races were based discriminated against black and Latino voters. But what were the odds that a federal judge would declare new elections because a small group of black and Latino activists cried racism? It wasn't long before the pundits were predicting that only the 1987 race would resolve the standoff.

Defections were a constant worry for both sides but never much of a threat. The Vrdolyak 29 were like blood brothers bound by a solemn oath. When a freshman alderman named William Banks, a Vrdolyak ally, announced that he would support Washington when it benefited his ward, regardless of Vrdolyak's stance, hundreds phoned or wrote Banks to complain. An aide to Ed Burke drafted a press release quoting Banks as vowing "never" to support Washington, but Banks declined to accept the release. Still, he tacitly agreed with its sentiment. He never broke with Vrdolyak, not on a single vote.

Occasionally a Vrdolyaker spoke out against some of his colleagues' cruder anti-Washington sentiments. In an off-the-record interview with a *Chicago* magazine writer, one complained of a colleague who always referred to the mayor as "that fucking nigger." "I don't like the 29," Alderman Patrick O'Connor said in that same article. "It's not a coalition set in concrete." O'Connor never broke ranks, however, nor did any of his colleagues.

Vrdolyak was something between the club president and its social chairman. He was forever surprising the twenty-eight men aligned with him in the council fight with special buttons (FREE THE 29), frames for the loyalty oaths each had signed, and group lunches. Roger Simon, a *Sun-Times* columnist, wrangled an invitation to one of these meals. "[Vrdolyak] likes restaurants where he can eat at big tables, family style, restaurants where he orders the appetizers for the whole group as if he were the father," Simon wrote. Vrdolyak also directed the conversation. The group argued back and forth about a politician's future until Vrdolyak weighed in: "No, he's not washed up." There the discussion ended.

"They ate and talked and swapped tales," Simon wrote. "It was like a fraternity, like a sports team, like a family.

"And there was no way to forget who was the head of the family."*

That day freshman Alderman Bernie Hansen had a surprise for his colleagues: a new pinky ring featuring the number 29 laid out in diamonds.

---

*Vrdolyak was not the kindliest of fathers. More than once, Simon, a liberal columnist, was the butt of a sarcastic Vrdolyak gibe. Vrdolyak suggested that Simon order a steak. "Have a steak. Go ahead." When the food arrived, Simon wrote, "Vrdolyak turned to the rest of the table. 'The guy is in a fish restaurant and he orders a steak,' he sneered. 'Can you believe that?'"

Vrdolyak was the one Hansen was most eager to show his expensive bauble. Vrdolyak's minions vied for his attention—to tell a new joke about Harold, to share some inside dope they hoped Eddie had not yet heard. A friend of Vrdolyak's would years later tell a reporter that Vrdolyak could hardly tolerate half the fools belonging to his club of twenty-nine. Soon after his election to the council years earlier Vrdolyak had said, "I held back at first. A few months, maybe. It was pretty clear they weren't a bunch of wizards running around. So I say to myself, 'Don't worry, you can lead these guys.'" Upon this unimpressive lot, however, Vrdolyak's ambitions rested.

About half of the black caucus dreamed of defecting. Like the Vrdolyak bloc, these aldermen beefed that Washington refused to give them a cut of the spoils. Yet these black aldermen were more an annoyance for Washington than a real threat.

Early in his tenure, Washington laid off (along with hundreds of others) the son of one of his allies, Niles Sherman, as part of his plan to solve the $168 million deficit—or $96 million, if one prefers Burke's figures—he inherited from Byrne. Two days later Sherman was on the radio threatening Washington. Some black aldermen, Sherman said, might abandon the mayor if he doesn't start treating them to the privileges enjoyed under past mayors. Washington, in turn, insulted Sherman: "I'm almost certain he could carry a bucket of water across his ward," he said the next day. "He couldn't carry much else." A few months later the Washington administration dismissed the son of another of his allies.

About half of the black caucus longed for neither the days when white power brokers hoarded the spoils nor Washington's reforms. They were neomachinists who hoped that Washington's victory would usher in a new day. "It took forever for us to get here," a black alderman named William Beavers said. "Why change the rules just when we're getting into the game, right when we're where we want to be?"

A former Vrdolyak precinct captain, Beavers occasionally challenged Washington to pony up a greater share of spoils. He threatened one year that unless his ward was granted at least $1 million in community development (CD) funds he would not vote in favor of the CD plan before the council. Beavers did not get his $1 million, but he voted for the measure anyway. Another time Beavers told Washington that he could make no promises about the next election unless he gave him jobs so that he could hire more political operatives. "The mayor just looked at me and laughed," Beavers said. Washington was too popular among black Chicagoans to fret about the likes of William Beavers or Niles Sherman.

Chicagoans quickly grew familiar with the routine and rhythm of their new politics. Washington or one of his council allies—the Washington 21—introduced an ordinance. It failed twenty-nine to twenty-one (or, after Kenner was sentenced to prison, twenty-nine to twenty). The Vrdolyak 29 introduced an alternative, which passed twenty-nine to twenty-one. Washington vetoed it, and there the matter remained deadlocked. It took thirty-four votes to override a veto, yet Vrdolyak could never muster more than twenty-nine. The council deadlocked over the city's $2 billion budget, a new gang crime measure, and a $70,000 outlay to fix up a soccer field in Vrdolyak's part of the city. Rancorous debate followed.

Something—public opinion, maybe, or a past-due deadline—would dislodge the jammed proposal. The long lines to enter the council gallery; the cat-calls punctuating the more vitriolic sessions; aldermen saying to each other, "You asshole" or "You little pipsqueak"—all came to be part of the political landscape. Even a brief shoving match between seatmates, a major news story in almost any other city, was not even that day's top local political story. Chicagoans were by then like residents of a mountain town who long ago had grown accustomed to the splendor of their surroundings. Two aldermen pushing each other—so what else is new?

A local comedian named Aaron Freeman christened the political impasse "Council Wars." He spoofed the ongoing drama between "Harold Skytalker" ("may the clout be with you") and the evil "Lord Darth Vrdolyak." Board games, T-shirts, and novelty records followed. The *Wall Street Journal* ran a page-one feature on Chicago politics that added another term to the local political lexicon. Chicago is no longer "the city that works," the article's authors wrote; is it now "Beirut on the Lake"?

For decades Chicago stood in contrast to other cities where transition from one political order to another was routine. Until Washington, the story line of Chicago politics was how little things changed relative to its mutable

233

urban counterparts. A vigorous antimachine opposition managed an occasional victory here or there, but in the end the Democratic machine was still in complete and absolute charge.

Washington's election transformed that. Chicago was still in the spotlight, but the signature of its politics had changed. The theme was now a city wracked with uncertainty and rancor. With the entire black community on the antimachine side of the equation, the one-time underdogs of Chicago politics had become virtually overnight as strong as the political machine that ruled Chicago for half a century.

The machine-antimachine struggle, though obscured by race, added an urgency to the fight. Daley's political heirs were suddenly in jeopardy of extinction, for if they did not recapture the mayor's office in 1987, it seemed their time would have come and gone. Ward organizations would crumble without access to patronage. Fund-raising would also be a problem without a say in the $400 million in contracts the city gave out each year. The machine enjoyed big business's support because the business elite correctly perceived the machine as the only game in town. Two terms out of office would indelibly change that reputation. The vaunted unity of the Cook County Democratic party was already a thing of the past; the party was really two parties, one white and one almost entirely black. The party would no longer control virtually every aspect of government—it would be merely a political party. Perhaps it was already nothing more.

Vrdolyak revealed one aspect of his strategy in visits to the *Tribune*'s and *Sun-Times*'s editorial boards. Under his leadership, Vrdolyak promised, the council would initiate reforms the likes of which the city had never seen. He railed against a city budget full of fat, and he promised cuts in the city work force. In his twelve years in the council Vrdolyak blocked an array of measures aimed at just that; as a clout-heavy alderman, he had helped shepherd many of these wasteful budgets through the council.

"History is out the window," Vrdolyak said when challenged about his past stances. His posture, at least for the time being, was that the city's future was the only thing that mattered now.

Vrdolyak carried a very different message to the publishers of community newspapers on the city's northwest and southwest sides. When he sat down with them over lunch in early June, he spoke of Washington's plan to "blacken" the city.

Already the Washington administration, Vrdolyak told the publishers, had developed "a three-pronged plan to boost his political power by encouraging and pressuring white Chicagoans to leave the city." He had it on good authority, he said, that Washington intended to use any available CHA funds to construct scattered-site housing in white communities around the city. He said, too, that Washington planned to revive the busing issue. He offered no proof—it was, in fact, perhaps the furthest thing from Washington's mind—except to claim that Washington had already "cut a deal" with the city's school superintendent.

The publishers were astonished. "What he was trying to say," one said in an interview with the *Defender*, "was that Washington is attempting to eliminate the white ethnic neighborhoods . . . to make Chicago more black to ease his reelection four years from now." Louis Lerner, the publisher of a small chain of papers on the north and northwest sides, was the first to go public. He had one of his reporters listen in on a third line as he discussed Vrdolyak's comments with another publisher to confirm his recollection of the meeting. Vrdolyak, however, denied making any such comments.

Washington's first acts in office were aimed at the wary lakefront voter. He signed an executive order creating a freedom of information act and cut his salary by twenty percent. He mothballed the city's limousine, choosing instead to use an Oldsmobile 98. He laid off seven hundred employees in his first year alone*—the first mayor in memory to do so—and refused to cut a deal with Vrdolyak, though it would buy him peace. Washington might as well have been reading from a lakefront independent's manifesto when he promised to professionalize government, computerize city departments using paper accounting methods, and open up the budget process by holding hearings around the city. His predecessors raised tens of thousands of dollars in campaign contributions from individual city contractors, yet

---

*The 29 challenged the layoffs in court, with Ed Burke as their lawyer. At the same time Roman Pucinski proposed a resolution that would grant civil service status to thousands of workers. (A headline in the *Tribune:* PUCINSKI HITS PATRONAGE.) "We're not for the slaughterhouse Republican techniques of lopping off a thousand workers at a time," Vrdolyak said.

Washington announced a self-imposed $1,500 cap on campaign contributions from companies doing business with the city.

Washington made good on another promise to the lakefront when he signed the Shakman decree, which, on paper at least, outlawed patronage hiring and firing. Given black unemployment, this was no small act by the city's first black mayor. Reporters had scoffed during the 1983 election whenever Washington promised to sign Shakman. "Quite candidly," Judge Nicholas Bua said, "I never expected a settlement in this case." "Historic," Bua said.

Alderman Marty Oberman had been pushing these issues since he was first elected to the council in 1975, with virtually no success. It could be said that Washington accomplished more in his first three months in office than Oberman did over his entire political career as an alderman. Oberman, however, did not embrace Washington; instead, Oberman, who represented a north lakefront ward, claimed the council split was not 29–21, as everyone believed, but "29–20–1." In his stock speech back then, Oberman said he was part of no one's camp.

The hangup for Oberman was Wilson Frost. When Washington told Oberman that Frost would be his floor leader, Oberman's jaw nearly dropped. Washington had called Oberman into his office to tell him; Oberman had half-expected that he was going to ask *him* to be his floor leader. He, after all, was the dean of the council independents; Frost was someone the lakefront independents and black reformers alike dismissed as a machine hack. Washington compounded his sin by pushing Frost as his candidate for Finance chairman in his negotiations with Vrdolyak.

For Oberman it was like an instant insight into Washington. He could conceive of no reason other than race behind Washington's choice of Frost. What about merit and competency? Several months into Council Wars, Oberman appeared before a Washington organization in his ward. Confronted by their hostile questions, Oberman grew indignant. He had been part of the antimachine movement long before Washington, Oberman said. "Who was Harold Washington to define what is reform and what isn't?" he asked them.

Still, Oberman was among the more intrepid liberals. Despite his 29–20–1 claim, he voted with the Washington bloc on virtually every issue. In contrast, State Senator Dawn Clark Netsch was downright hostile to

Washington. She openly sided with neither faction, instead choosing to dismiss the entire affair as disturbingly untidy and rancorous.

There were times, Harold Washington admitted to friends, that he wished he had remained in Congress. He had put his sixty-year-old body through the grueling regimen of an around-the-clock campaign for a job that no sane human being would want. Council Wars didn't surprise him as they did many of his supporters. What else would you expect, he liked to ask, "when you grab the tiger by the tail?" It was a forty-thousand-employee bureaucracy that seemed overwhelming. "We were like the Sandinistas rolling into town one day and running the government the next," said one top Washington aide.

He had been elected mayor. But where to start? The day of his inauguration he reminded his friend Mary Ella Smith of an old joke about the first black pilot. After all the speeches and protests there was still the job of flying the airplane. The punch line, particularly apropos to the daunting task he was about to assume, had the pilot asking over the plane's loudspeaker system, "Does anybody know how to get this mother off the ground?"

Exiting Mayor Jane Byrne was of little help. Washington talked about his first morning on the job with the writer David Moberg. He anticipated hours sifting through the extensive files that would unlock secrets to the labyrinth that was City Hall. He searched the mayor's desk and looked into filing cabinets, yet just about all he found was a paper clip. "I sat there and laughed for ten minutes," Washington told Moberg. "There was nothing there, no personnel files, nothing."[*]

Many of Byrne's top aides proved equally useless. Many ignored the Washington transition team's requests for interviews. Of those who were willing to sit down with them, most offered clipped, minimal answers that sounded more like a deposition from a hostile witness. There were unsubstantiated reports of massive shredding parties in the last days of the Byrne administration.

---

[*]Byrne, it turns out, took more than files when she left office: a rug from the Moroccan government said to be worth $15,000 (she said she assumed the rug was a gift to her) and eleven lithographs worth an estimated $11,000 that local real estate magnate Arthur Rubloff insisted he meant as a gift to the city.

Other hindrances were nonmalicious but no less confounding. When Rob Mier, whom Washington appointed to take over the Economic Development Department, reviewed the personnel file on each employee in his department to learn a little about the staff he was inheriting, he didn't find out much. Employees with twenty or thirty years' experience had next to nothing in their file. There were no progress reports or evaluations, usually nothing more than a single letter—a recommendation from the political sponsor who had secured them the job in the first place.

The dead weight of City Hall was oppressive. The departments that suffered the worst neglect seemed those that black Chicago relied upon disproportionately—the Chicago Housing Authority, a public school system whose student body was eighty percent nonwhite, and the Public Health Department. The city's web of health clinics was not based on a rational plan worked out by public policy professionals but one that was implemented by committeemen leaning on City Hall for a clinic to placate protesters in their precincts. High-rise public housing monstrosities that should never have been built now housed nearly five percent of the city.

Middle management posed a great challenge. City Hall was a collection of administrators promoted for their political performance in the wards rather than their accomplishments at the workplace. The HUD report that led to Charles Swibel's forced retirement said that the "vast majority of staff show no professional quality and are incapable of implementing the changes needed to turn the CHA around." HUD deemed only "four or five of the CHA's nineteen project managers" competent. Washington would place top policy people above them, but middle management was not easily fired, especially given the Shakman decree.

Milt Rakove, in his book *Don't Make No Waves, Don't Back No Losers,* told of a man that Democratic Committeeman Bernard Neistein sponsored for a city job. A department head phoned Neistein to complain that the man could barely read or write. "Put him to work, I need him," Rakove quoted Neistein. Yet the department head told Rakove that wasn't so bad. "Bernie Neistein is reasonable. If he sends you five guys to put to work, only two are illiterate. But Matt Bieszczat sends you five illiterates and wants you to take them all!"

From the start Washington took great pains to project himself as the mayor of all the people. Though whites constituted barely ten percent of his winning coalition, the majority of those Washington named to his transition team were white. His inauguration aimed at projecting a multiracial appeal. One reporter overheard this caution about the band playing at that night's party: "I don't want Latinos who look white, Morris. Understand?" Grayson Mitchell, Washington's press secretary, tallied Washington's appearances in the white community to guard against charges that Washington slighted white Chicago because of resentments over the election. Washington took great care to assemble an administration that more closely mirrored the city's racial makeup.* He would be fairer than fair, Washington liked to say: "No one but no one in this city will be safe from my fairness."

Some whites, even those who were part of his government, were uncomfortable with Washington's preoccupation with race. He insisted that certain positions, such as the police chief, should be filled by someone black. Years of police brutality against blacks and court rulings declaring the force guilty of racial discrimination had convinced him of that. There were many more white department heads under Washington than black department heads under previous mayors (including the city's budget director, its chief lobbyist, and the mayor's chief economic adviser). Yet Washington by design named someone black to serve as that department's second-in-command, as a check on the potential for a white appointee's hidden racial blindspots. He was not color-blind as white liberals would have it, he would say, because the world itself was not color-blind.

Washington could get petty in his treatment of white constituents, such as the time he held up the money for a soccer field in Vrdolyak's ward for no reason except as leverage against a foe. Yet five of the six wards receiving over $1.5 million in the administration's first CD plan were represented by aldermen aligned with the 29. The state suggested that

---

*After his first year in office the racial breakdown of those named to top policy positions and to the various boards and commissions reflected almost exactly the racial makeup of the city: forty-three percent of Washington's appointees were black and thirty-seven percent white. Sixteen percent of Washington's appointees were Latino in a city estimated to be between fourteen and eighteen percent Latino.

Calumet, a depressed community in Vrdolyak's ward, be designated an enterprise zone, and yet rather than put his clout behind Lawndale, a black community that several community activists were pushing as an alternative site, Washington stuck by Calumet, which he believed was better prepared for potential investments and thus would benefit more by the designation. Though Police Chief Richard Brzeczek had fanned fears during the election when he said the department under Washington would be a "circus," Washington attended Brzeczek's farewell dinner and said kind words about the departing chief.

Grayson Mitchell was always tinkering to improve the image Washington projected to white Chicago. One time at home watching the television news he noticed that Washington was always surrounded by black bodyguards; the next day he ordered more white bodyguards added to Washington's security detail. When Mitchell's polling revealed that whites perceived Washington as hostile and threatening—in large part due, Mitchell thought, to the harsh scolding look on Washington's face whenever the subject was Council Wars—he pestered Washington about smiling more often.

Washington also muted parts of his persona. A year into Washington's tenure, Joe Gardner, the head of his political operations, noticed Washington "talking less in a folksy vernacular and more in a more formal style." Increasingly he spoke in a style he had in the past reserved for talks before downtown civic groups. "A single misplaced 'right on,'" Gardner said, "and he would lose the fifty-five-year-old white lady living in West Rogers Park." The Washington that mixed street and soul with the intellectual was gone, or at least restrained.

Yet it would never be enough, not even for many whites who were part of his own coalition. In the early days of Washington's tenure, several advisers, frustrated that they were getting nowhere with the mayor, leaked to the press that they were lobbying Washington to name someone white as police chief so as to quell white fears. It struck Washington as somewhere between funny and sad. Wasn't it always that way—that blacks are expected to shoulder the blame for white fears? Never mind the police brutality and the federal rulings: it was up to him to assuage the city's whites as if he were somehow responsible for the hate mobs and vile comments that marred the 1983 election.

Harold Washington

Jesse Jackson

Lutrelle "Lu" Palmer, Jr.

Jane Byrne

Richard Daley

Ed Vrdolyak

Marty Oberman

Ed Burke

Clarence McClain

Jon Randolph

Luis Gutierrez

Jon

Bernard Epton

Dorothy Tillman

Pau

Chicago mourns the death of Harold Washington

Marc

———

Harold Washington, Mike Royko wrote, understands white people far better than whites understand black people if for no other reason than his being a black man operating within a predominantly white world. Yet, for all Washington was intent on heading an administration that reflected the racial makeup of Chicago, he had much work to do tending to his own personal feelings about race.

The 1983 election had a lingering impact on Washington, especially early on. The phone calls he made after his win were one example. Washington was more likely, one top aide said, to return personally the calls of black politicians offering their congratulations than those of whites. "Harold was quick to think back then that all Polish people were against him because of the election," this aide said. He brought Polish people into his administration—a former state legislator named Mike Holewinski ranked among the top half dozen people in the bureaucracy—yet he was not unlike the white person who looks on certain blacks as exceptions rather than the rule.

Just as white Chicago's comfort level with Washington had to be tended to, so, too, did Washington's own comfort level with whites. Among those to whom he turned to sort out his feelings toward whites was Kit Duffy, a chubby-faced Irish woman with strawberry-blond hair whom he had known since the 1960s. He pumped her for information as basic as it was silly. How could one tell if someone was Irish? he asked her. If the name doesn't provide a clue, what then does one look for? What do you mean that someone *looks* Irish? "It was like," Duffy said, "'Explain Irish people to me.'"

Jean Mayer, a white woman who lived on the southwest side, was singularly unimpressed with Washington. The picture of Washington she held in her head was of him standing before a black audience thundering about the injustices of white Chicago. "We black people," Washington would say— and Mayer would cringe. This mayor for all Chicago, Mayer thought, seemed to believe it was only the black community that had suffered over the years.

241

Mayer grew up on the city's south side, in Auburn Park, a neighborhood she later in life spoke of with something between bitterness and outrage. As a little girl she spent afternoons at one of the two movie palaces at the corner of 79th Street and Halsted. She remembered one theater had a pond with swans in the lobby; in the marble bathroom she pretended she was a queen in her castle. One is now boarded up, an empty hull; the other also closed its doors as a theater long ago. It is with a "terrible sense of outrage" that she visits her old neighborhood. Where once it was an ideal place to grow up, it is now an all-black slum that is no one's idea of a dream world.

Mayer never intended to become a political crusader, but in the mid-1970s she was asked to help fight the blockbusting she saw destroy communities like her own. She signed up with a local antisolicitation drive based in the local church. Going door-to-door she heard the horror stories: of mothers who would not let their children walk home from school without an escort, of elderly white women who felt like prisoners in homes they could not afford to sell. She never stopped organizing and, by the late 1970s was director of the Southwest Parish and Neighborhood Federation, the southwest side's most prominent community group. We have our own hurts, Mayer tried to impress on journalists coming to her as a representative of the city's white ethnic voter.

Mayer considers herself far more liberal on racial issues than many of her neighbors. She recognizes that blame for the decline of a neighborhood that quickly changes from white to black rests as much with unscrupulous real estate agents and ill-conceived government policies as the black neighbors moving in. Yet that knowledge does not lessen her compassion for fearful neighbors who have lived through such changes in their neighborhoods. She understood the panicky feeling of her neighbors when the city was on the verge of electing its first black mayor. To Mayer's mind there was cause for worry. "I remember the night of the [general] election," Mayer said. "There was a group of real estate agents down at a bar on 63rd Street handing out their cards. 'Here, you'll need this,' they told people."

Washington spoke before her community group during the campaign. Mayer respected his courage but walked away outraged by his message. He dismissed the scattered-site housing issue even as he mentioned it. A judge had already ruled on the matter, he said, and as mayor he was bound to follow the court's wishes. His next comment left Mayer cold. What was the big deal anyway, he lectured them, about the fifteen apartment units the CHA had slated for the southwest side? The city is rife with crime and drugs and poverty, he said, and your big issue is two modest-sized apartment buildings. Mayer just about lost it.

The day of Washington's inauguration, representatives of Mayer's organization and others like it stood outside the gate to Navy Pier, where Washington gave his speech that day. They had asked his aides to have him stop there to light their "candle of understanding," but the limousine carrying Washington just sped by them.

To Mayer that was symbolic of Washington's indifference to her concerns and her neighbors'. Washington was "playing racial politics with the police department," Mayer's group charged, and later, in a fund-raising letter, she wrote, "Mayor Washington is running City Hall with a vengeance. Either we build a more powerful organization with which to confront this administration or we decide it's not worth it and leave the city."

A new organization was born six months into his tenure, linking Mayer's group with its northwest side counterpart. Save Our Neighborhoods, Save Our City Coalition (SON-SOCC), the group called itself. "Blacks and Latinos have set their agendas," Mayer said at its inaugural press conference. "It's time white ethnics did the same." The organization's new name seemed in poor taste, echoing Vrdolyak's "it's a racial thing" cry. "Save your city . . . save your precinct," Vrdolyak had asked the assembled precinct captains.

At around the time SON-SOCC presented itself to Chicago, the *Chicago Reporter* ran an article exploring white ethnic Chicago's view of Washington. The monthly found that the hostility toward Washington was still palpable; the mere mention of Washington's name still drew boos among white ethnic audiences. Yet in interviews with dozens of northwest and southwest siders, the *Reporter* found that most could not cite any specific instances of neglect. Aside from Washington's failure to light the candle of understanding, the *Reporter* couldn't offer much in the way of criticism. Still, a poll taken just prior to SON-SOCC's formation revealed that three of every four people living on the southwest or northwest side agreed with the statement that Washington was "out to get them." Three-quarters were also convinced Washington would sock them with high tax increases to pay for public housing, the public schools,* public transportation, and other services they didn't use.

"These are extraordinarily trying and dangerous times for Chicago," began SON-SOCC's "Declaration of Neighborhood Independence." "A distressing politics of needless conflict and mindless vengeance has become the order of the day. Responsibility for this deplorable state of affairs rests with the current Mayor of Chicago, Harold Washington. . . .

"Behind the well-crafted, public veneer of the Mayor as Charmer, Healer, and Reformer, there thrives a cynical political opportunist, ready to exploit every racial fear and antagonism without regard to their dire consequences."

Lu Palmer couldn't say he was any happier with Washington's racial balancing act than Jean Mayer. Why is it, Palmer asked with rue, that the city's first black mayor went around town claiming to be "fairer than fair." What had white Chicago done to merit fair treatment?

When whites ran the city, they hogged the best jobs, stole community development funds, and treated their constituents to extra ward services at black Chicago's expense. Yet Washington boasted he had "danced on the grave of patronage." What kind of black man gets up before a black audience and boasts—*boasts,* as if his administration has cured sickle-cell anemia—that he has *cut* the city payroll? Due to cutbacks the percentage of blacks working at City Hall actually *fell* from 1983 to 1984.** "Fuck fairness," Palmer said. Blacks deserved to be "lavished" with services after years of neglect.

Palmer dreamed of what Washington's election might mean for organizations like his own, Chicago Black United Communities: some community development funds for a staff person or two, or maybe funding from Washington's political funds. If nothing else, Palmer was counting on City Hall's lending his group credibility. Yet a few weeks after the campaign Washington sent a letter urging his supporters to join the Independent

---

*During the sixteen years between 1967 and 1983, the number of white children enrolled in the public schools fell from forty-one to sixteen percent.
**The city work force was just over twenty-eight percent black in 1983 but under twenty-eight percent black in 1984. Both numbers fall far short of the forty-one percent of the city's population that was black.

Voters of Illinois—a predominantly white group scorned by the black grass roots. It was as if impressing the white liberals was more important than fostering the growth of a black independent political movement.

Palmer confessed some of his ill will toward Washington was borne of his bad feelings after Washington endorsed someone else in the special congressional race held to fill the seat he had just vacated. Palmer declared himself a candidate after thinking about all he could do for black Chicago with a staff and something like a half-million-dollar budget. He had made extraordinary sacrifices on Washington's behalf, spending his own money though he was perpetually poor, logging hours a man his age should no longer work, yet he would have been happy if Washington had endorsed no one in the race. Washington endorsed a longtime labor organizer named Charles Hayes. A poll appearing in the *Metro News* showed Palmer with a big lead until Washington's endorsement.

The congressional race influenced his feelings, Palmer said, but did not precipitate them. Palmer claimed he was braced for disappointment even before Washington won the general election. The transition, which better represented the north lakefront than the black grass roots, provided one epiphany, while Washington's failure to offer so much as a word of thanks for his efforts, either publicly or privately, provided another. Washington invited more than a hundred people to watch the returns with him in a VIP suite the night of the general election, yet neither Palmer nor his wife Jorja, who had worked on and off with Washington since the 1960s, was invited. It wasn't just him or his wife, either, he said. Others who helped Washington get elected now could not get him to return a phone call.

The first months of Washington's tenure only confirmed Palmer's worst fears. He and his associates spoke of the "Hyde Park Jewish contingency" Washington brought into government. To him, "the Hyde Park Jews had Harold wrapped up when it should've been the black community that had him wrapped up."

About six months into Washington's tenure Palmer finally won an audience with the man. Palmer immediately started in: "Why did you go to such great lengths to defeat me for Congress?" The way Palmer told the story, Washington exploded. Palmer had seen glimpses of Washington's temper but never like he did on that day. "I mean, he got nasty," Palmer said. There was lots of cursing both ways. "Politics is a cold, hard, dirty game, and if you don't want to play it, get the fuck out," Palmer quoted Washington as saying. He was inclined to believe the psychiatrist friend who suggested that Washington treated him coldly because humans tend to resent those to whom they feel beholden.

Yet for all Palmer's complaints the administration Washington put together was unlike any Chicago had known. The infusion of black talent into City Hall was one overt difference. Suddenly blacks held positions of power. The city's top lawyer was black, and so was Washington's chief of staff and his press secretary.

One glaring oversight was a paucity of Latinos, but the presence of even a few in positions of power put Washington above previous mayors. It was also a slight that Washington would address with time. Another quick-glance difference was the increased presence of women in management positions. Women inside the mayor's office complained of the sexism of a sixty-year-old man who was constantly flirting with his female aides, telling them they looked sexy in a particular dress, or commenting on their backside after they left the office. But by 1987, when Washington would run for reelection, just under forty percent of the city's commissioners and deputy commissioners were women. The city's two top financial officers were black women.

The changes were greater than the race or sex of his appointees. Washington hired people who were never before welcome on the premises, let alone offered positions at City Hall. These were people excluded from power not only in Chicago but in just about *any* government in the country. The corporation counsel was a civil rights lawyer renowned for his role as the lead trial attorney in the $1.9 million judgment against the city and county for the raid that left Fred Hampton and Mark Clark dead. A legal aid attorney headed the corporation counsel's housing prosecution division; another top lawyer was active in the National Lawyers Guild. This lawyer's most celebrated case was a suit against the police department's so-called "red squad," which monitored community groups that the machine identified as "subversive." Now, among his other duties, he would defend the police department he had previously sued. In an interview, Washington's choice for the president of the Board of Health referred to a favorite political cartoon from the *Daily Worker* to make a point.

At best the machine ignored community groups that didn't play by its rules; as the red squad suit showed, it often employed Chicago's police department to disrupt or destroy them. In contrast, the director of the city's Department of Neighborhoods was a community organizer who worked for one of the groups the red squad infiltrated. Jane Byrne broke with Chicago tradition, at least for a blink of the eye, when she appointed Renault Robinson to the board that monitors the CHA. Washington named Robinson to head the agency.

In a sense Chicago was a grand experiment with national ramifications, a situation exemplified by the choice of Rob Mier to head Economic Development, one of Washington's more controversial choices. The Economic Development post in any city is invariably filled by someone with a corporate background committed to attracting expensive, large-scale projects downtown. Mier hardly fit that profile. A local university professor, Mier saw himself as more activist than academic. His activity outside the classroom centered around helping community groups fight a city development office more committed to attracting major corporations, big hotels, and high-rise apartments downtown than helping the neighborhoods.

The newspapers and business interests denounced Mier as antibusiness and criticized Washington for allowing himself to be hoodwinked. Yet the problem was Washington's political philosophy, not his choice of Mier. Washington the candidate had promised a better balance between downtown and neighborhood development; he promised he would not allow the city to spend nearly seventy-five percent of its development dollars downtown, as it did under Byrne. Urban development means more than shiny new buildings downtown, Washington said on the stump; it also means the mundane task of maintaining industrial jobs in the neighborhoods and drawing new businesses to depressed business strips around town.

The city would continue to encourage downtown development, of course; the difference was that it would not be the city's top priority. The department would focus instead on the more difficult task of luring manufacturing jobs and the like to the city rather than what Mier called the "low-wage McJobs" like busboy and chambermaid created by a new hotel downtown. In other cities a major corporation contemplating building downtown would be offered tax breaks and other unconditional inducements. Under Washington those seeking breaks from Mier's department needed to offer concessions in return—offering those in the city's manpower training program first crack at a job, for example.

Neighborhood organizations were the beneficiaries of another of Washington's breaks with tradition. With the machine in power, the local ward organizations were City Hall's liaisons to the neighborhoods. By contrast, community groups supplanted ward organizations under Washington as the main power brokers in the neighborhoods. This included wards in which the committeeman staunchly supported Washington.

Still, Washington's administration was not dominated by activists and progressives. Washington chose a conservative, old-school black cop to head the police department. His top policy advisers included an executive from a large downtown accounting firm, two corporate attorneys, and a pair of black businessmen. Washington left in place the commissioners overseeing departments such as Streets and Sanitation, and Water. Washington's first chief of staff, Bill Ware, was a technocrat hired for his administrative skills rather than his political philosophy. Within most coalitions Ware would have been considered liberal wing; within Washington's he was viewed as too conservative.

The black nationalists also had their complaints. To them it was as if Washington was shunting them aside now that he had been elected. They had access to the mayor and to other top administrators, yet they were not among those Washington put in government. They would confess ambivalence—serving in government was in a sense antithetical to their ideals—but still they expected at least the right of first refusal. They were also angry that Washington had gone out of his way to defeat Palmer.

The nationalists proved a tricky issue for Washington. If Washington too closely aligned himself with the black nationalists—if he brought them into his administration and named them to seats on the city's various boards and commissions—that would hurt him among constituencies both inside and outside the black community. Yet shunning the black nationalists meant turning his back on his own 1983 victory and perhaps alienating a critical portion of the black community that he would need in 1987. It was a no-win situation yet one he could not afford to lose, precisely the kind of racial balancing act any big-city mayor must perform.

The good-government liberals were never comfortable with the activists inside the administration—"unprofessional" was among the kinder terms they used to refer to these people who dressed in Hush Puppies, cheap sports coats, and polyester pants. The technocrats were inclined to agree. They were troubled by the lack of management experience among some Washington appointees. Was this the professional administration that Washington the candidate had promised? The liberals were not pleased with a development policy they perceived as hostile to business; the technocrats didn't care except that they wondered why Washington risked alienating the business community.

Too many liberals—that's what the activists and the nationalists said. Too many *bureaucrats.* Washington brought into government scores of people to the left of liberal whose bookshelves at home were filled with works such as *The Political Thought of Mao Tse-tung* and Frantz Fanon's *The Wretched of the Earth.* He was bold in the face of potential red-baiting, yet that did not seem enough. Black businessmen such as Al Johnson, owner of Al Johnson Cadillac-Saab, were among his top advisers; the left-intellectual consequently spoke of the incursion of the black bourgeoisie in Washington's administration.

Some, too, were angry with the presence of so many whites. What did Washington owe the white community? The white liberal rejected him in the primary and then hardly made amends in the general election. When Washington changed press secretaries, hiring someone white, there were those overwhelmed by disbelief. A *white* spokesperson for the city's first black mayor? And the Latinos, who accounted for a seven percent share of Washington's vote in 1983; what had they done to earn Washington's attention?

Washington, the press reported, had in his impasse with Ed Vrdolyak the political fight of his life, but it was the balancing act to keep this diverse group together—to ensure that each element in the coalition shared if not a stake in one another's issues, then a stake in him. That was the true test of his political acumen.

There was the unusual and the radical inside the Washington administration; there were countless breaks with the past. And then there was a top aide named Clarence McClain, a political gadabout who performed various functions for Washington in his short tenure on the city payroll.

From the start one could guess that McClain would mean trouble for Washington before the next election. McClain had earned a high school equivalency degree while in the army and spent a year studying the tool-and-die trade. He spoke in a black colloquial style that no doubt jarred the sensibilities of the average white Chicagoan. McClain might begin a sentence with "what I could've did" or speak of the month of "Joo-lie." McClain said in one interview that his life had been "misconscrewed"; the résumé he submitted when hired stated that he "received in asses of two hundred letters of commendation" while at a particular job.

McClain was flashy in a garish way. He could be boisterous, crude, and indiscreet; his loud cackling laugh made fellow workers wince. The hairpiece he wore—a veritable bird's nest atop his head, a wide Afro wig piled high—so disturbed Chief of Staff Bill Ware that he sought to make its removal a condition of McClain's hiring.

Washington was hardly impressed with McClain at first glance. The two met in 1973 or 1974, by which time, Washington said, "the Superfly look was kinda way out." Yet back then, while making the slow transition from a maverick machine legislator to independent, Washington wasn't about to turn away any willing worker. McClain impressed Washington the more he got to know him; he was diligent and responsible, a man who worked incredibly hard to improve himself. McClain worked the graveyard shift at a local factory, yet several afternoons a week he would stop by Washington's office to work for four or five hours. Since getting out of the army McClain had always worked two jobs, Washington learned. With time he became a mentor to his young aide. "McClain is typical of a large breed of black men who are extremely sophisticated, worldly, and *sharp*," Washington said. "Their lack of grammatical expertise is really secondary. It's just like the farmer who's a poet: you know exactly what the hell he's talking about even if his way of speaking is crude."

By 1982, McClain was among a dozen of Washington's most-trusted aides, yet more than loyalty landed McClain a job in City Hall. It was true that he had received in excess of two hundred laudatory letters while a middle-level manager in a state position (a job Washington helped him obtain). "He was a completely task-oriented person," one longtime member of Washington's inner circle said. "He was brilliant within the context of a bureaucracy. He had an incredible ability to evaluate a project and figure out what needed to be done to get it done."

Whether that brilliance had a place within a reform administration was another question entirely. McClain was a man too willing to cut corners. Once he fixed on a goal, little could stand in his way. During Washington's campaign for mayor in 1977, a north side volunteer mentioned in passing to McClain that they had a lead on a free office but nothing to furnish it with. A few days later a shipment of brand-new furniture was delivered to the office, along with expensive typewriters and other office equipment. McClain never said how he came by the furniture, but there was no need to. He worked for the state then, in the department responsible for furniture and office supplies. The only question in 1983 was what aspect of McClain's persona would backfire on a mayor trying to project a reform image to Chicago.

14

BEIRUT
ON THE
LAKE

Ed Burke grew up dressed in junior-sized suits to attend wakes for people he never knew. One boyhood friend's most vivid recollection of his childhood chum is of Burke, wearing a fedora, consoling a bereaved widow: "He was only eight or nine years old, but he knew what to say and what to do."

City Hall old-timers recall little Eddie Burke in much the same way. He was polite and well mannered, a well-dressed kid whose father, Alderman Joe Burke, brought him everywhere. For a time he told every ward heeler who asked that he planned to become a priest. He did not live the fabled life of fellow southwest sider Rich Daley, but by the time Burke was in his teens he had already shaken hands with Mayor Daley and met a senator named John Kennedy. In 1959, the year the White Sox won the pennant, the Burkes had season tickets directly behind the Daleys.

In 1968, a few months before his death, Joe Burke took the council floor to boast of his twenty-four-year-old son. Many sons and daughters were rejecting all that their parents stood for back then, but not Eddie, his father said. No, he was a police officer and in his final year of evening classes at DePaul Law School; industrious, ambitious, respectful—a remarkable lad, really.

Ed Burke was two months out of law school when the ward's precinct captains met to choose someone to take his father's place as ward committeeman. They chose Burke who, at twenty-four, was the youngest committeeman in Chicago history. ("With all his father did for the people around here," one captain said, "we kind of owed it.") A few months later Committeeman Burke slated himself for alderman, winning easily. At the age of twenty-five, dressed in a smart suit, he took his place in the council, the second youngest alderman in the city's history sitting in the same seat occupied by his father the previous fifteen years.

Ed Burke, more than Vrdolyak, fought Washington on the front lines of Council Wars—in the media. It was Burke on television proposing an alternative budget or calling a press conference to decry a deal involving a supposed Washington crony.

A meticulous man with an eye for the picayune, Burke was well suited to the role as the majority bloc's front man. As a lawyer, he prided himself on his ability to trip up adversaries who failed to dot their *i*'s or cross their *t*'s. Like a technocrat taking solace in his charts and numbers, Burke boasted smugly of his rich command of the arcane and the scarcely relevant. In an interview with a journalist he launched into the story of a 1927 City Council confrontation he saw as similar to the May 2 meeting when Washington left the council chambers. His pride swelled as he embellished his tale with detail after detail. As Finance chair, Burke had both the jurisdiction and the staff to sift through every deal the city entered. If there was a connection to be made between Washington and any organization or business that received so much as a penny of city money, Burke would root it out.

You could taste the vinegar listening to Burke. He carried the baggage of any obedient machine soldier, yet with a straight face he stood before the press expressing outrage over the Washington administration's steering a contract to a business that donated money to his campaign. He had witnessed far worse under previous mayors without uttering a peep, yet it was as if he was sickened by the very idea of a city contract favoring a politically connected black contractor. Moral decay had always been his specialty.

Burke distinguished himself early in his aldermanic career by fighting massage parlors, prostitution, and pornographic bookstores—just as his father had done before him. When a gay rights housing ordinance was proposed in the City Council, Burke scorned the idea: "Next, they'll want the right to marry and adopt children."

Through the 1970s Burke was reviled by foes as self-righteous and hypocritical, but viewed as a man of conviction by supporters. Burke no doubt inspired similar feelings when in 1983 he turned that same crusading zeal to fighting a force he saw as even more insidious: Harold Washington.

The revelation six months into Council Wars that a top Washington aide had a criminal past was the 29's first big break in their PR battle. SERIES OF VICE CONVICTIONS BARED read a headline in the *Tribune*. Clarence McClain, Washington's longtime aide, had a record.

The *Tribune* wasn't quite right: McClain's criminal past was not a series of convictions so much as a series of arrests and dropped charges, with two convictions. The first conviction was on the charge that he patronized a prostitute when he was twenty-four years old. Two years later he was convicted of "pimping" and "keeping a house of prostitution"—a far more serious set of charges, to be sure, but misdemeanors for which he was fined only $50. McClain was arrested five more times over the next four years, but in each case the charges were dropped.

The last entry on his record was an arrest for "contributing to the delinquency of a minor." A *Tribune* reporter who tracked down the story discovered that it was a case of mistaken identity. The arrest was expunged from McClain's record, yet it was there on page one anyway. The *Tribune* article failed to mention that the police had arrested the wrong McClain, though the paper found room to mention twice that the victim was an underage young male from Grand Rapids, Michigan.

Inside City Hall, Washington and his senior aides gathered to decide how to react to the *Tribune* story. Only two people did much talking, Press Secretary Grayson Mitchell and James Montgomery, the city's corporation counsel. There's no question McClain has to go, Mitchell began. The middle-class sensibilities of a great many blacks was one consideration; those of potential white liberal supporters another. There were, too, the contradictions of a mayor who put more women into management positions than any of his predecessors but who also chose a convicted pimp as one of his top advisers. "Our goal here," Mitchell told the group, "is a lead that says that, 'Upon disclosure, Clarence McClain's resignation was requested.'" A former reporter for the *Los Angeles Times, Washington Post,* and *Newsweek,* Mitchell sought to stop the story from taking on a life of its own.

Montgomery, a criminal defense attorney by trade, disagreed. What kind of evidence are we talking about here? he asked. A few misdemeanor convictions more than fifteen years ago? And what about the larger issues involved? Are we going to dismiss any black man with a police record? he asked. McClain had muttonchop whiskers and a crazy wig and was known to dress garishly flashy. Montgomery looked around the room. We all understand, he said, what goes through a cop's mind when he sees such a black man.

Montgomery was only getting started. There was also the issue of rehabilitation. Do you know the percentage of black males in Chicago who have had a run-in with the law? he asked. Who out there will take rehabilitation seriously if *we* won't? Sweat appeared on Montgomery's face as he continued with his impassioned plea on his client's behalf. He was ripping apart his case, but Mitchell was impressed. He remembers thinking that Montgomery was every bit the highly touted defense attorney he had sized him up to be.

Like a judge listening to opposing counsel, Washington said little. "I'll prepare a press release," Mitchell suggested at the end of the meeting. Washington said okay, yet twenty minutes later Mitchell found Washington in his office in a foul mood. "Fuck it," he said. "I'm not going to do it." He wouldn't fire McClain.

Mitchell took a moment to gather himself. Washington was, if nothing else, a practical politician. Mitchell tried a different tack, appealing to the side of Washington that loved chess. "You're a few moves away from mate, Mr. Mayor. You need to sacrifice a rook."

With that Washington lit into Mitchell. "Goddamn it, look at you," he snapped. A Brooks Brothers suit and buttoned-down shirt—things handed to you. Washington ran down McClain's history: worked two jobs at once; thrived when given a white-collar job; dedicated, loyal, hardworking. He struggled his way to the top rung by rung, beating the odds with every step he took. There were certain worlds in which McClain would never be accepted despite his skills—and not just white worlds, either. "McClain never had a goddamn thing handed to him in his whole life," he said.

Washington vented some more before giving in to his better judgment. Within the hour he stood before the cameras reading the prepared statement, Mitchell said, "with utter insincerity." At the end he ad-libbed a few more sentences, staring into Mitchell's eyes as he said them: "A fine, fine gentleman . . . in a class by himself. . . ."

One month later Washington again praised McClain when he acknowledged that he was helping him as an unpaid political adviser for the upcoming spring primary. "Clarence McClain is a worthy adviser," he said. "My hope is to work with that young man all the remaining days of his life." A week later Washington commented that *friend* would have been a better word than *adviser*. By then, however, the damage had been done.

McClain submitted a letter of resignation as requested but maintained his innocence. He never contested the pimping charges, he said, because paying $50 seemed far simpler and cheaper than a legal fight. "I was a kid," he said. "How were these piddling charges going to hurt me?"

He was managing a south side apartment building then when a couple of white cops came to the door looking for the apartment of two women living there, two women McClain had always figured to be prostitutes. He tagged along behind the cops and intervened when he thought they got out of line with some of their comments. The two cops got angry and arrested him as their pimp. That, at least, was McClain's version.

Ed Burke seemed nauseated by Washington's relationship with McClain. He mentioned McClain often, always describing him as either a "pimp and a panderer" or "an arrested child molester." McClain's record led Burke to conclude during one television interview that under Washington, City Hall was "run by pimps and panderers."

Burke was a guest on a radio talk show one Sunday morning when the subject turned to the upcoming primary race between State's Attorney Rich Daley and Larry Bloom, a white alderman aligned with Washington. Burke described McClain as a child molester, then added, "When the Washington-Bloom-McClain political caravan comes around to your neighborhood, the mothers and fathers of Chicago children better lock them up and keep them out of the way."* In another radio interview Burke said, "If you talk to some of the police officers who used to arrest McClain practicing his profession, you'll find that they will tell you the way he enforced the rules over the prostitutes who were working for him . . . was to whip them with wire coat hangers."

It was an absurd notion that Bloom or Washington might bring McClain along on a campaign swing when he had just left the administration under a cloud. So, too, was Burke's coat hanger story far-fetched. Most media outlets quoted Burke's lurid comment about McClain's penchant for coat hangers, yet no reporter bothered to press Burke for the names of any officers with whom he might have spoken.

Ed Vrdolyak also expressed his horror over McClain. How can one trust Washington, he said, when "he surrounds himself with ex-cons, including a convicted pimp"? Yet in 1971 seven organizers of a Vrdolyak fund-raiser were convicted of raffling off prostitutes. (Rooms were reserved at a local Ramada Inn; winners were provided a key and a woman.) Vrdolyak's brother was among those convicted. A topless dancer named "Miss Boo Boo Loo the African Queen" provided the entertainment at a later Vrdolyak political function. When in the early 1970s a columnist dressed down Vrdolyak for these taints, Vrdolyak got indignant. Sounding very much like a Washington loyalist defending McClain, he said, "Those newspaper guys downtown'll never understand what it's like to come up in the Tenth Ward."

McClain was regarded by the black middle class with the same anguish and sorrow with which Italian Americans might regard the discovery of a high-ranking official cavorting with a reputed mobster. The hate literature passed around during the 1983 general election anticipated a Washington administration run by "black baboons." Gang leaders would run the police department, pimps the Department of Human Services. And here was McClain the bogeyman in the flesh. "With his muttonchop sideburns and outlandish style," *Tribune* columnist Clarence Page said, "McClain was a tailor-made media caricature."

---

*A reporter on the panel that day, Mike Flannery, swears Burke warned Chicago parents to lock up their "little boys" not their "children," as the newspapers reported. Media accounts quoted Burke characterizing McClain as an "arrested child molester" without setting the record straight.

McClain wore platform shoes and a diamond stickpin, prompting *Sun-Times* columnist Tom Fitzpatrick to write, "I thought that had the right touch of nostalgia. McClain started his career as a south side pimp. The flashy stickpin is just the kind of thing they think has class."

McClain was on the city payroll less than three months, yet to hear Burke and Vrdolyak tell it, he was the archetype Washington appointee. Another top official, Joe Gardner, had been convicted of carrying a concealed weapon when he was a community organizer working in one of Chicago's more treacherous neighborhoods, but to the political opposition Washington's was an administration seething with ex-cons.

In 1984, Washington failed to file on time an annual ethics statement as required by law. Burke called a press conference and damned Washington for his failure to meet a simple deadline. At the council meeting later that day, the 29 crowned Richard Mell, the city's vice-mayor, the new mayor.

The next day's *Sun-Times* carried this headline on its front page:
"WASHINGTON: 'I'M THE MAYOR!'"
"ALD. BURKE: 'NO, YOU'RE NOT!'"
"CITY HALL BRAWL HEADS FOR COURT"

"None of us really expected me to become mayor," Mell later confided. "But we sure did make Harold look silly, didn't we?" Anything to portray Washington as a bumbler in over his head.

Ed Vrdolyak staged a press conference beside a heap of uncollected garbage to drive home the point that even the most basic municipal tasks were beyond the grasp of this new administration. He told the reporters assembled that Washington promised sweeping reform but couldn't even pick up the city's garbage. "This guy doesn't have the foggiest idea of what the job is about," Vrdolyak said.

A few days later Mike Royko wrote about a businessman who had witnessed the strangest thing in a vacant lot across from his establishment. A city truck dumped a load of garbage in a perfectly clean lot, and a crew of workers spread the rubbish around. Cameramen and reporters arrived, listened to Vrdolyak, and then everyone left. The garbage, however, remained.

The story that television anchor Walter Jacobson featured three nights in a row in his regular "Perspective" commentary sounded very much like a tale from the city's past. Jacobson, whose newscast was the city's highest rated, told his listeners of the millions the administration steered to a politically connected black-owned bank that wasn't paying the city interest on the money. "A sweetheart deal," Jacobson called it, that cost taxpayers $250,000 in lost interest annually. Jacobson used his most effective tool, his voice, like a good chef who knows his cutlery uses a knife. Particularly sharp was his distinctive laughing lilt that mocked its target: won't they ever learn, the voice jeered. Jacobson was pleased with himself. He was a political muckraker who had to admit that Washington was bad for business.

Ed Burke followed up the first day's report with a press conference. "Another example of cronyism and favoritism and manipulations of city business to benefit friends," Burke said, a perfect "display of the bungling ineptitude" of this administration.

The story seemed indicative of another kind of ineptitude, however. The numbers Jacobson provided were off by a multiple of twenty-five—the lost interest would have amounted to something like $10,000 a year, not $250,000—except that the culprit, the Seaway Bank, *did* pay interest on these accounts. Had Jacobson bothered to check, someone there could have shown him the bank's records. Seaway's board of directors included Washington campaign contributors, but there are only four black-owned banks in Chicago, and officers at all four contributed money to Washington. Excluding all four from doing business with the city for appearance's sake seemed a drastic step, especially when most of the city's money was deposited in downtown banks whose white officers were generous contributors to the Old Guard. The switching of this particular account to Seaway—a holding account for the checks Chicagoans wrote to pay parking ticket fines—was no sweetheart deal: it provided Seaway with an average yearly balance of about $250,000 plus about $50,000 in annual fees as remuneration for the paperwork nightmare.

Jacobson confessed his main source for the story was a document called "A Report and Analysis Submitted to Alderman Edward M. Burke from the Committee on Finance Staff Regarding the Washington Administration's Opening of a Secret Bank Account in the Seaway Bank."

Vrdolyak's media adviser, Joe Novak, had called to say he had a great story, along with all the documentation Jacobson would need. A journeyman media consultant, Novak had already earned a reputation as a rapscallion of Chicago politics before going to work for Vrdolyak. He was a man who pursued the planting of dirt as a single-minded endeavor—"the kind," a former client said, "who thinks jugularly." Jacobson was aware of Novak's reputation but said that he did not care where he got a tip as long as the story was a good one. A few calls, and Burke's report seemed all the proof he would need.

Jacobson's colleagues at the NBC affiliate picked up the story as well. They played it as the lead news story the night of Burke's press conference, then followed their report with a harsh rebuke by on-air commentator Jim Ruddle: "Maybe it's time the mayor sent his spotless garments of reform to the cleaners. He's probably got a friend in that business, too."

Reporters didn't see much story potential in a Finance Committee meeting held in the dead of July 1984. On the agenda were some contracts that needed the committee's approval, a few personnel matters—the usual array of dull items. An $820 million bond was also on tap, but even that seemed to lack promise. The money was for various public works projects already under way, including the $1.6 billion expansion work at O'Hare Airport that had been approved under Byrne. It seemed worth a paragraph or two in the next day's paper, tops. Still, the reporters for the daily newspapers, the all-news radio stations, and even a couple of TV stations sat through every Finance Committee meeting. They had learned early on in Council Wars that they could take nothing for granted.

The Washington staffer who read the wording on the bond proposal before the committee had apparently learned the same lesson. It read like the typical boilerplate proposal except that a word had been changed: instead of granting the City Council the right to "review" all contracts, it granted them the power to "approve" all contracts over $50,000. With a council majority the Vrdolyak faction could hold up hundreds of deals each year, which gave them enormous leverage in their fight with Washington. A fight erupted.

Burke said he was seeking to keep in check an administration rife with cronyism, and he wouldn't budge. The Finance Committee approved the proposal as is, and the City Council approved it twenty-nine to twenty the next day. Washington vetoed the proposal, Vrdolyak couldn't muster the thirty-four votes needed to override the veto, and there the two sides remained, deadlocked as the media frantically reported on the pending shutdown of the entire O'Hare project. The impasse showed what could happen to every contract over $50,000 that the city tried to enter into unless Washington was willing to toss some contracts to the Vrdolyak forces.

With time the 29 backed down. The business community applied pressure, albeit begrudgingly, pushing the 29 to drop its push to approve contracts. Yet who won in the end is not clear. The 29 tried the exact same scheme several more times, and others like it. Washington remained resolute, but each event prompted more headlines about a city mired in political conflict. No doubt a great many people were growing increasingly wary: it seemed *everything* was a fight with this mayor.

The established practices and traditions that seemed to work for years in Chicago were suddenly being reconsidered with Washington as mayor. Shortly after he named a black cop to head the police department, one of Vrdolyak's allies pushed legislation that stripped the executive branch of its jurisdiction over police beat boundaries and manpower deployment. The measure would have required council approval to initiate any "major changes" in police operations.

In 1977 the *Chicago Reporter* had revealed that police posted in black districts handled roughly one and a half times more calls per officer than those working white districts. BLACK DISTRICTS LOSE OUT IN POLICE DEPLOYMENT POLICY, read the headline over a later *Reporter* piece. Yet by the 29's logic this new black administration couldn't be trusted to handle police deployment in a fair and equitable fashion. The council majority tried to exert the same control over the city's fire department.

For years Chicago was known as a city where a mayor's powers bordered on the omnipotent. Suddenly, one of Ed Burke's favorite themes was original language in the city charter that called for a strong council–weak mayor system. Wasn't it about time, he asked, that power was shifted back to the council where it belonged?

Council Wars were about power and control, but also race. And within its racial context, the Vrdolyakers weren't just subverting any mayor but the city's first black mayor and a symbol of black hope nationwide.

Chicago's government was a $2 billion corporation that would rank 183 (above Uniroyal, Upjohn, Corning Glass Works, and Polaroid) on *Fortune* magazine's yearly listing of the country's top corporations. No black CEOs run a Fortune 500, so one could say that Washington, Los Angeles Mayor Bradley, and Reagan's Secretary of Housing and Urban Development Samuel Pierce were then the nation's three top black chief executives. One in nine Americans is black, yet no black sat in the U.S. Senate in the mid-1980s, nor was there a black governor. As both a former congressman and Chicago's mayor, Washington ranked high among the country's black political elite.

One heard black Chicago's anger and frustration when listening to any one of several black radio talk shows. Though the Vrdolyak bloc was driven in large part by political survival, most callers saw race as the 29's true motivation. And who could blame them? It was, to borrow from a notable baseball first, akin to throwing a hard fast one at Jackie Robinson. It was part of the game, sure, but who could be surprised when the black community, highly protective of their own, cried race, especially when at least a few batters were known to sharpen their cleats just before games with the Brooklyn Dodgers?

Washington's sexuality was a strange preoccupation for the 29, Vrdolyak in particular. Numerous times Vrdolyak insinuated that Washington was gay. One time during a council debate Vrdolyak, seeking to speak, fluttered his arms and said in a high voice, "To someone of your gender I should say 'pretty please.'" Another time a feature writer asked Vrdolyak about his early love life. ("Believe me," Denise Vrdolyak told the interviewer, "when we were first dating, he wasn't 'Fast Eddie' back then.") Annoyed by this line of questioning, Vrdolyak snapped: "Ask Harold that question! Ask Harold about *his* dating."

Vrdolyak was always criticizing Washington about his past legal troubles. "Because I pay my taxes," Vrdolyak said during a budget debate, "the schools, the police, and fire stations stay open. But the mayor never filed income tax for over twenty years, and if other people were like him, you wouldn't have any police or fire houses or public aid or mental health clinics . . ."*

Even the machine's own discriminatory past proved a handy weapon in the 29's arsenal. Washington's attempts to treat the entire city to the same amount of garbage pickup and street sweeping meant taking from those communities, mostly white, that enjoyed a disproportionate share of services—and Vrdolyak or one of his allies was there to drive the point home. "There's a deep fear among the white people," said Donn Bailey, a black professor at Chicago's Northeastern Illinois University. "I can understand it. They think we're going to treat them the way they've treated us."

"Incidents of racial violence against minorities in the Chicago area escalated in 1984," began an article in the *Chicago Reporter*. Racial violence had not been so intense in years: "Firebombings throughout the Chicago area and a six-hour stoning attack on the home of a black family in 'The Island,' an all-white enclave . . . highlighted a year of racial violence."

Cardinal Joseph Bernadin, among others, blamed it on the political fighting. "The conflict, even though not intended, perhaps, gives aid and comfort to racists, white and black alike."

They were dubbed the "hostage appointments"—Washington's appointments to various boards and commissions that required council approval. The Vrdolyakers didn't invent rationales for opposing them as unqualified; instead they simply refused to consider them. The names were submitted but never found a place on the agendas of appropriate committees, all run by members of the 29.

An editorial would occasionally excoriate the Vrdolyak faction for refusing to act on the appointments. Vrdolyak would promise to do so, but the appointees still languished—two hundred days later, four hundred days later, six hundred days later.

---

*That Vrdolyak was making this charge was ironic. In 1974 the newspapers carried stories about Vrdolyak being $36,000 behind in his property tax payments. In 1983 Vrdolyak settled his own problems with the IRS, paying $73,600 to settle a claim that he owed the government more than $220,000.

The Library Board had eight lame-duck members at a time when the city was making plans for a new central library projected to cost around $100 million. Millions in neighborhood development projects were pending before the Urban Renewal Board, which could not assemble a quorum. Because the 29 refused to consider those people whom Washington appointed to the Park District Board, a machine regular maintained control over its two thousand–plus jobs. For Vrdolyak and his allies it was a critical beachhead in the bureaucracy, with City Hall temporarily dry as a source of jobs.

Explaining the hostage holdup, Ed Burke said he and his allies weren't about to allow Washington "to put his buddies and pals and cronies in positions presently held by buddies and pals and cronies of the City Council."

For Burke that was a rare moment of candor. Usually Alderman Richard Mell was the Vrdolyak ally sounding off on matters that colleagues believed were better left unsaid.

Mell was first elected to the council as a reformer in 1975. His campaign's central issue was opposition to a proposed crosstown expressway. A pet project of Daley's, the expressway was slated to cut right along his ward's edge. The way Mell told it on the radio, his opposition to the expressway did not run nearly as deep as his ambitions. After he was elected he was offered the ward committeeman's post in exchange for his vote on the expressway. "From then on I thought it was the greatest idea that ever was," he said.

There was nothing remarkable about the story—politicians are always betraying their own vows—except that Mell publicly admitted it without anyone even challenging him. "I may have been a rubber stamp," Mell said another time, reflecting on his first two terms in office, "but at least the ward got something out of it."

To Mell, Washington was somewhere between incompetent and greedy. He tried working with him, but "with this guy there's no middle ground; either he gets a hundred percent of what he wants or he vetoes it." He imagined out loud what would happen if Vrdolyak were elected mayor in 1987: "The next day an air-conditioned bus picks all the blacks and dissidents up, and they all go up to Eddie's farm. There at his farm are new Seville Cadillacs sitting there with an alderman's name on each one. Fight's over! Fight's over! Working majority. . . ."

"If I'm the mayor of Chicago, and I can't get forty-eight votes on every issue, I don't belong there. With everything going for him, for all you could help people, why have anyone against you?" There's the park district, the Port Authority, and the Board of Elections, and a city bureaucracy with forty thousand jobs and $400 million worth of contracts. There's a lot a mayor can offer in exchange for a vote. There's also the city's yearly share of community development funds that the federal government has slated for low- and moderate-income communities. Mell offered this hypothetical example: "Say I have $100 million in community development money. I'd give each alderman a million and let him do what he liked with it. That way I still have $50 million for myself."

But like everything else with Washington, Mell said, community development money meant more fighting. Every year Washington would introduce his own spending plan for the approximately $100 million in development funds and then ignore the 29 when they drew up an alternate plan that differed by $5 million or so. There was never any money slated for someone like Roman Pucinski, who represented a middle-class ward on the city's far northwest side, so the 29's plan fixed that. The money would be spent in middle-class wards but the city would "hire the minorities and the poor" to perform the task of fixing up sidewalks and other "blight" in the nicer parts of town. Besides, there was a category called "preventive" spending.

"There are problems in Pucinski's ward," Mell said. "Why shouldn't he, in fact, be entitled to some of the CD money? It's community development money. Why shouldn't he be given money to develop his community?"

Years later one of Mell's council allies, Alderman Patrick O'Connor, would credit Washington with providing what he considered a fair share of community development funds for the poorer areas in his ward. The *Tribune* and *Sun-Times* editorial boards credited Washington with finally heeding the advice of the city's Community Development Advisory Commission and with spending a much higher percentage of the money in the neighborhoods—seventy percent more in 1984—than on administrative costs. Yet the six o'clock news stories reporting on the community development fight focused on Mell and his colleagues accusing Washington of discrimination against their wards: the black mayor was not giving the white wards their fair share. "Let's call it for what it is," Mell said during debate. "It's fashionable today to be black. And this is the blackest man in the city of Chicago today."

By mid-1984 there were more than a few inside the 29 as fed up with Washington as Mell. Let's give him nothing, the more hawkish members of the 29 said. Thus when Washington introduced a $95 million bond measure to fix the city's crumbling streets, sidewalks, and sewers, there was no eagerness among the 29 to lend their support.

Later Mell would regret his candor about his opposition to the bond proposal, but in a talkative mood one morning he confessed to a journalist that there was a lot about this bond measure that made sense. He said it was exactly the kind of project proposal that in years past would fly through the council without debate. "I could use the four miles in [street] resurfacing," Mell said. "We definitely need it here in the ward, and it wouldn't cost that much." The problem, he said, was that Washington's plan favored the city's black communities.

Mell or one of his colleagues was always making this claim. The Eighth and Ninth Wards "get theirs," Mell said once during council debate, while the Tenth and Eleventh Wards get nothing. The Seventh and Eighth Wards are black wards, the Tenth and the Eleventh Vrdolyak's and Daley's respectively. In a letter his captains distributed throughout the ward, Mell implored voters to stand up against Washington's "policies of neglect to our community." Only if Washington is put out of office, the letter continued, will "we, as taxpayers, be in a position to demand our fair share of city services and projects that have been nonexistent since the election of Harold Washington."

Yet a listing of projects that Washington sought to fund with the bond proposal showed that sixty-three percent of the bond money was designated for wards represented by the majority bloc, though the twenty-nine constituted fifty-eight percent of the city's fifty aldermen. Vrdolyak's Tenth Ward was in line for more money than thirty-nine other wards. Three of the four wards slated to receive the most money were represented by an alderman aligned with Vrdolyak.

When a journalist confronted Mell's claims that discrimination was behind his opposition to the bond measure, Mell leaned in and spoke more softly, as if needing to physically prepare himself to be frank. Sure it's a good proposal, he said, fair and equitable. "But the sad situation is, in fact, it is naïve to ask why isn't this being done or why isn't that being done just because they're good-government positions. There are some who believe that to get rid of Harold Washington is good government because we simply can't take four more years of him. Maybe . . . two years of not having this [bond] is worth ten years of political stability in this city. It's a legitimate position; arguably, not voting for this bond *is* in the best interest of the city." Mell and his allies opposed the proposal precisely because it would make Washington look good.

15

BLACK REFORM, WHITE REFORM

Harold Washington didn't take it well the time Ed Vrdolyak fluttered his arms and sang out "pretty please" in falsetto. "You're about to get a mouthful of something you don't want, mister," he said, pointing his gavel at Vrdolyak. Ed Burke jumped out of his seat: "Is that a threat? If it is, come on down here on the floor."

Washington understood that threatening to punch a rival in the mouth ensures the kind of notoriety he did not need. Responding to Burke would only make matters worse. Yet Washington motioned to Burke and said, "No. You come up here. You come up here." Alderman Wallace Davis, a Washington ally, leaned over toward Burke: "Sit the fuck down or I'll knock you down."

The council floor exploded into a cacophony of voices. Above the din one could hear Washington's gavel and his call for a recess. Ironically, an issue on that day's agenda was a proposed Plexiglas barrier between the aldermen and the gallery to protect the politicians from the general public.

Burke more than Vrdolyak typically set Washington off. Washington was forever ranting about Burke. "Ever shake hands with the guy?" Washington asked at least one aide. "Just repulsive." He spoke of a physical feeling whenever he noticed Burke staring up at him during a council meeting. "It's like the man emanates a raw hatred," Washington said and shuddered.

Washington could go either way with Vrdolyak. He could be furious with Vrdolyak yet find his antics amusing nonetheless. The two had something of a relationship before the 1983 mayor's race; always recognizing the importance of maintaining good relations with the city's black politicians, Vrdolyak would every so often stop by Washington's congressional office on Saturdays, dressed in a polo shirt, to shoot the breeze for an hour or so. Washington respected Vrdolyak as one of the sharpest minds in the Democratic machine and viewed him as an equal putting up a good fight. There was nothing friendly between Washington and Burke, but in contrast the mayor and Vrdolyak occasionally engaged in joking repartee, such as the time Vrdolyak thanked Washington because he had recently parlayed a $10 bet on a horse named Sweet Harold into $250.

"A better gesture," Washington said from the rostrum, "would be to divide the profits."

"I've been trying to tell you that for eleven months," Vrdolyak shot back.

An "engaging rascal," Washington said of Vrdolyak in one interview; the "lovable bandit," he said in another. "He's the kind of guy you like. I wouldn't play poker with him, but I might have a drink with him." Another time Washington likened Vrdolyak to a poolroom hustler who "shoots dice in the alleys." Then he apologized for the comment—to the pool players and dice shooters of the world.

Yet there were long stretches when the rancor of Council Wars overwhelmed any feeling of respect Washington might have for Vrdolyak. When presidential candidate Walter Mondale was in town for a rally, which forced Washington and Vrdolyak to be together for an evening, a journalist witnessed the two of them speaking through intermediaries though only feet apart. In an arrangement not unlike a child's game, Vrdolyak spoke but Washington pretended not to hear; instead he waited for an aide to repeat for him what Vrdolyak had just said. Washington responded by whispering in the aide's ear. The aide then repeated aloud what Washington said. Only a few days after Vrdolyak's "pretty please" gibe, the chief of police informed Vrdolyak that his police bodyguard detail would be trimmed from five to two. Washington did not mind if people made a connection between the two incidents, for that was exactly how he meant it. "I'm a man, goddamn it," he complained to his press secretary.

A group of moderate black executives with whom Washington met regularly were always chiding him about the role he played in Council Wars. Be less combative, they advised him; don't step into the traps the 29 sets for you. They insisted that it was beneath him as mayor to be calling names or threatening people. MAYOR: GET SMART, NOT MAD, read a headline over a *Defender* editorial a little over one year into the Council Wars. The black daily warned that otherwise Washington would be the city's third one-term mayor in a row.

Be mayoral, be more statesmanlike: Washington heard it all the time from all quarters. His top lobbyist and a press aide came to him with a plan designed to remove him from the day-in, day-out fighting. You shouldn't respond to Vrdolyak's charges, they told him; instead it should be one of your aldermanic allies. They drew an analogy to national politics: a senator defends the president when a senator from the opposition party criticizes his policies, not the president himself. Washington listened silently, giving no indication of what he thought of the idea—until the next Council Wars outburst. Washington called the Vrdolyak 29 "scurrilous hooligans" and a few of the dozen insults that were part of his repertoire.

"It's all right to say anything about Harold," Washington would growl to no one in particular. "Sure, beat up on Harold, he can take it." Washington resented that he was expected to endure silently anything his foes might do or say. I'll stop fighting only when Vrdolyak backs down, he snapped at those belaboring the point, his brow sternly frowning to punctuate the point. He reminded them that he was not elected to accommodate the status quo. "I'm not Monty Hall," he said, "and this isn't 'Let's Make a Deal.'"

He muttered under his breath about the dirty "sonsabitches" in the council. "Vicious bastards" he called Vrdolyak and his ilk, correcting a writer who described them as "merry pranksters." Yet nothing turned Washington on quite like politics. A former girlfriend said her most vivid memory of Washington was of the two of them out at a restaurant, Washington's eyes afire as he excitedly told of some parliamentary trick he had used to outsmart a foe in the General Assembly. It was his love of the game that struck her. "That was his life," she said, "politics."

"Washington needs politics the way other people need families and ordinary social things," Bill Harris, the black man whom Washington pushed as president of the Cook County Young Democrats, told a biographer. "He needs politics the way other people need sleep and food." Fun for Washington as mayor was Sunday afternoon sessions at his apartment with close associates, pulling apart political conundrums for hours on end. He didn't have close friends so much as political associates with whom he felt intimate enough to reveal stray parts of himself. It was no coincidence that three of his longest-standing friends—Bennett Johnson, Gus Savage, and Charles Freeman—were themselves politicos. As if for efficiency's sake, Washington chose for friends those also in his political life.

Washington, the feature profiles usually pointed out, loved to read, but mainly books about history and politics. One visitor to his apartment noted some of the newer books lying around: a biography of Booker T. Washington, Seymour Hersh's *The Price of Power*, about Henry Kissinger, and Ken Auletta's *The Streets Were Paved with Gold*, an account of the New York fiscal crises. His favorite novel, Washington once said, was *The Gay Place* by William Brammer—a political book about the seamy underbelly of Texas state politics, written by Lyndon Johnson's press secretary before Johnson was elected president.

There was the Washington who didn't bother balancing his check book and another who, engaged in a political contest, found no detail of the battle too small. He could consider a political decision from twenty different angles. He was always that way, said those who knew him back in his Springfield days when he studied his fellow legislators with the discipline of Ted Williams sizing up a rival pitcher. Several times Charles Freeman noticed elaborate charts on his friend's desk—what Freeman called "personality charts"—plotting possible ways of gaining a recalcitrant legislator's support on a bill he was championing.

After Washington was elected mayor his security detail asked him to move to another, larger apartment in the building. From then on Washington paid the monthly charges on two units because he never could make the time to go through the stacks of papers left behind. Washington routinely worked eighteen hours a day because that is what it took to get something done, but he never seemed to have time for trivialities such as his own life.

He was the kind of politician, aides said, who could see around corners. One top aide was constantly amazed at how often she sat with Washington, figuring on walking him through some issue, and found herself being hand-led. She approached Washington with what she thought was a sensible course of action about something he knew little about and left realizing how thoroughly Washington had apparently thought through a host of political problems that hadn't even dawned on her. Another aide, hearing this story, believed his associate misunderstood. Washington probably hadn't pondered the issue for even a moment prior to their meeting; it was that his political instincts were remarkable.

Grayson Mitchell recalled a moment early in Washington's term when things were happening so fast there was never time for such luxuries as briefing notes. Mitchell was walking beside Washington to a meeting with the CEOs of several major Chicago-based corporations. Another meeting had run over, so Mitchell had only a minute or two to prep him on the business meeting they were already late for. Mitchell threw out a few terms to help Washington set the correct mood and tone: "fiscal prudence . . . act deferential . . ." He likened it to a manager pumping up his boxer as they entered the ring.

"Of course Harold pulled it off remarkably, as he invariably did. . . . All you had to do was lay out a concept for him one or two times and he'd have it forever."

Mitchell described Washington's life as a "political bubble." He woke in the morning thinking of politics and went to bed with the topic still on his mind. Mitchell figured that during the two years he served as Washington's press secretary, the mayor must have called him at home an average of four or five times a week. Yet he never bothered to learn his wife's name or those of his children. Alton Miller, who replaced Mitchell as press secretary, told the same story. Washington spoke fondly of a few relatives still living in Chicago but rarely ever saw them.

Washington phoned Mitchell on Christmas Eve his first year in office. "Can you stop by my place for a while?" Washington asked. When Mitchell mentioned that it was Christmas Eve and he was busy assembling new toys for his children, Washington seemed embarrassed. Mitchell hung up thinking Washington hadn't even realized what day it was. "For Harold, politics was his universe," Mitchell said, "and things that occurred outside that universe didn't seem to concern him much."

Those who saw the hours Washington kept were furious with the media characterizations of Washington as a mayor only half-committed to his job. He routinely called aides after midnight or received calls from them at that hour; aides were confident they could call Washington as early as 7 A.M. without fear of waking him. Usually he didn't arrive home until after 11 P.M., jamming several events into a single evening. He treated himself to working at home on Friday afternoons—"so I can take my shoes off," he explained.

Yet in press accounts, Washington complained, it was "the mayor is five minutes late" or "the mayor didn't show up at some hotdog fest." Washington complained to Al Miller of a media double standard. Where Daley made it a point to make it home for dinner each night so he could eat with his family, rarely did Washington treat himself to a sit-down dinner. The evening meal for him was usually some food gobbled down because he was running late for an appointment. Yet somehow the prevailing impression was that Washington was lazy and remiss in his duties.*

When a journalist asked if this had anything to do with racism, Washington responded, "You're damn right it's racism." In a peevish mood

---

*"Though not publicly confirmed by either Vrdolyak or Washington," one *Tribune* reporter wrote, "the story is reliably told about a meeting Washington requested with his archfoe in the mayor's Hyde Park apartment at 9 A.M. one Sunday morning. Vrdolyak appeared on time, but despite persistent knocking on the door could rouse no one inside. Finally, just as Vrdolyak was about to leave, Washington appeared at the door sleepy-eyed and dressed in a bathrobe. He had forgotten about the meeting he had asked for."

There could be no doubt about the source of the story, and no doubting its inaccuracy. The desk monitor on duty in the foyer or the police guard sitting in a squad car out front would have called the "command post" in the apartment across from Washington's. If Washington was in fact still asleep, one of Washington's bodyguards would have been there to meet Vrdolyak long before he arrived at Washington's door. Even if Vrdolyak had somehow managed to slip in undetected, one of the bodyguards would have heard Vrdolyak's "persistent knocking." Still, one was always hearing about the shiftless and lazy Washington not up to the task of being mayor.

one day he announced publicly that he was restoring his salary to its original $60,000 because, he said, "no one gives me any credit anyway." He also began using the stretch Cadillac limousine at his disposal—the same vehicle he proclaimed "obscene" when campaigning against Jane Byrne for mayor.

Washington worked from early morning until well past midnight for weeks on end, yet then, abruptly, he would ditch his entire schedule.

A great deal of planning went into the city-sponsored black-tie dinner in 1984 honoring Ray Meyer after forty-two years as the basketball coach for DePaul University's Blue Demons. "An excellent opportunity to have a nice love fest with the city's Roman Catholic population," Grayson Mitchell said. "An opportunity to get in touch with the city's Irish." The engraved invitations proclaimed Washington the evening's host.

An hour before the dinner Mitchell phoned him at home. Mitchell and Bill Ware, Washington's chief of staff, had gotten into the habit of doing so, especially on weekends. "We'd wrestle with him to make sure he got there on time," Mitchell said. When on this evening Washington fumbled around about being ready, Mitchell grew worried. He called one of Washington's bodyguards, which made him even more concerned; despite the Meyer dinner, he had told them he wasn't going anywhere that night.

Mitchell called Washington right back, but Washington didn't answer the phone. He called about ten more times before Washington finally picked up. "Fuck it, I'm not going," Washington said. Mitchell reminded him that there would be hell to pay. He didn't need to explain to Washington that they were constantly fighting the perception that he was a good-for-nothing, forever late. "Fuck it," Washington repeated. "Who's mayor anyway?"

Mitchell rushed over to Washington's apartment thinking he'd personally escort him to the dinner, but Washington was already gone. The dignitaries there that night included the governor, Cardinal Joseph Bernadin, and several U.S. congressmen, but not Washington, who left no word as to where he was going.

For the next two days neither Mitchell nor Ware had any idea how to reach Washington. When Washington finally called, Ware asked him, "Where the fuck are you?"

"I'm riding around, looking over my city." That's what Ware told Mitchell that Washington said. Ware was livid. He was like the parent who is worried sick—until the child finally arrives, and then is utterly furious.

Mitchell fretted over the potential press fallout. What if a reporter learns Washington had checked out for a couple of days? Mitchell remembered hearing once that when Daley was off in Michigan at his summer home, his limousine driver would drive to City Hall anyway, park in its usual spot, and then feign driving the mayor back home sometime in the evening. In the future when Washington disappeared, Mitchell would automatically instruct Washington's driver to do as Daley's had done.

Ware and Mitchell looked after Washington like mother hens. He was their mentor and their leader but also their charge. Keeping Washington to his schedule was one concern, his style of dress another. Washington invariably came to work wearing a tie that was either terribly outdated or stained, if not both. Several times Ware had a secretary buy Washington a tie or a shirt because he didn't think Washington looked the part of a big city mayor. Ware was horrified when he glanced over at Washington standing beside Italy's prime minister, his shirttail hanging down past his suit jacket.

Ware persuaded Mary Ella Smith, Washington's companion (his "fiancée," during his years as mayor), to help Washington pick out new clothes. Yet nothing, not even the finest fabrics, would compensate for Washington's rumpled look. Pictures of him with sunglasses shoved in the breast pocket of his suit jacket and a rolled-up document sticking out of another pocket appeared in the paper. Mitchell made it his business to acquaint himself with Washington's wardrobe so that when he wrote up Washington's briefing notes, he could suggest specific outfits. When it came to Washington's clothes, the idea was to leave as little to chance as possible.

Those who knew him from way back noticed changes in Washington. The Washington who called political foes names wasn't the man they knew. "I'm so popular," Washington was fond of saying, "they're going to bottle and sell the air I breathe." The old Washington always had a strange humor, but it was subtler and cleverer than this slapstick ego stuff. Kit Duffy called to confront him about the name calling after she heard him on a radio talk show. "It's beneath you," she said. Washington immediately grew defensive. "Where I'm from, it's whatever works."

One could see the toll the Council Wars were taking on Washington: the fatigue on his face, his ballooning weight, his short fuse. It was apparent in his relations with the City Hall press corps. Whereas Washington at first had seemed to enjoy his repartee with reporters, his exchanges with the predominantly white press corps grew increasingly surly and unpleasant. He mumbled his way through press conferences when feeling resentful; his peevishness was plain in every answer. He cursed those in the media who gushed over his struggle with Vrdolyak, like hypesters working in network sports—"selling soap," he'd say.

Washington smoked two to three packs of cigarettes a day for years, then gave up the habit almost completely. I'm a role model to so many young people, he said. Yet it is doubtful that quitting prolonged his life. He chugged Coca-Cola at ten in the morning; aides told of triple cheeseburgers he devoured between meals. He would eat a modest lunch of soup and crackers, and then later gorge himself on all the wrong foods. Late at night he would stop at a favorite Chinese restaurant that was willing to serve him after hours the plate of greasy egg rolls he always ordered. He gained around fifteen to twenty pounds a year.

He maintained the pace of someone running for political office. The only vacations he allowed himself were trips overseas that combined sightseeing with business. He brought with him a contingent of city officials and aldermen; a small complement of reporters were permitted to tag along.

In late 1984 flu laid him out for nearly two weeks. His resistance, intimates said, was way down. Washington partisans were inclined to blame it on Vrdolyak and Burke. "They're killing him, you know," they said among themselves.

Watching Washington respond to crowds made it difficult to recall a time when Washington didn't want to be mayor. He seemed to love making the rounds as mayor, meeting people, having them react to him. He happily donned sombreros and yarmulkes; he was a Cleveland Browns fan, but with the city alive with Bears fever, he was one of their more energetic cheerleaders. Washington adopted as his own a group of overweight women calling themselves the "Refrigettes" in honor of the team's hefty rookie sensation, William "The Refrigerator" Perry. He might think the whole thing silly, but the pictures and his grin as he posed in formation with them told a different story.

His old associate, Kit Duffy, spoke with Washington just after a visit to the Taste of Chicago—an annual all-week eating festival in Grant Park downtown. "There were a million people down there, most of them white, and they loved me," Duffy quoted Washington as saying. "He was like a little kid over the phone, thrilled that there were all these white folks downtown and he was having a good time with them." Another time Washington told Duffy about an evening spent barhopping with Congressman Dan Rostenkowski. He had such a good time visiting Polish bars on the northwest side, he told her, "I think I'll try Italians next."

There was the open and garrulous Washington who seemed born to the job of mayor, yet also the Washington who was still the loner, spending his days locked in his room with only a book as his companion. He had an inviting personality—even Burke and Vrdolyak would grant him his charm—but was, by all accounts, a private man who acted as if personal facts about himself should be rationed. "A subject that didn't unfold his secrets easily," wrote Al Miller, a man who, some believed, observed Washington like an author studying his subject.

Personal questions were to him a great intrusion. "He worked rather hard at distancing people," a former girlfriend said. "It bothered him if you got too close. It was like he resented the intimacy." Charles Freeman was described as one of Washington's two or three closest friends throughout the 1960s, yet during that period Freeman said he saw Washington's apartment maybe three times, and then only long enough for Washington to fetch something that he had forgotten. The two spent a great deal of time in Springfield where each preferred the same hotel. Yet Washington rebuffed all Freeman's attempts to see him socially down there. It was as if he had a Chicago life and a Springfield one and had no interest in introducing one to the other.

As mayor, Washington impressed his staff with the attention he gave to their issues and concerns. He listened, they said, not with the preoccupied air of a busy man but as someone actively taking in what they were saying. He amazed those around him with his absorption and recall. Yet what he might be thinking—what decision he might be leaning toward—was more often than not a complete mystery. He nodded his head and asked questions, yet shared nothing more than he had to, like a poker player who didn't show his hand if everyone else in the game had folded. When he made his decision, he didn't explain himself to those around him so much as inform them of what he was doing.

The white reformers were up in arms when Washington enlisted Ed Bell as a political adviser. Bell was Old Guard. A loyal Finance Committee staffer dating back to 1961, he was a protégé of Alderman Tom Keane and had served as chief of staff to the previous two Finance chairs, Michael Bilandic and Wilson Frost. Washington could have explained that Bell was hired as a "translator" who offered a vast pool of indispensable inside knowledge—a man who knew both the players and the rules. Yet Washington said nothing. If the white reformer did not understand that hiring Bell made sense, then that was the reformer's problem.

The first few times a mayoral aide invited Conrad Worrill to a meeting at Washington's apartment, Worrill had to wonder if there was a mistake. He had played a key role in the 1983 victory and had earned the visit, yet he wondered why an avowed black nationalist was in Washington's apartment arguing with City Hall technocrats, white liberals, and wealthy black businessmen he believed were more concerned with making their next $100,000 than the issues of poverty that so concerned him. With time Worrill recognized that this was Washington's way. He brought together a mix of people to stage debates on prickly political matters. Worrill was there to play the part of the nationalist.

"His thinking was," one longtime associate said, "that if you threw together all the ingredients, out of it would come soup, and that that soup would be right." That was his gift as a manager, loyal aides said: building in tensions among his top advisers so as to facilitate creative solutions. Mier was his top economic development official, but Washington chose a Republican hostile to Mier's theories, Ronald Gidwitz, the president of Helene Curtis, Inc., to chair the city's Economic Development Commission, and Barry Sullivan, the CEO of the First Chicago bank, was among those Washington met with regularly.

Washington was someone who hadn't changed his home phone number in more than ten years. He shared that number far more often than anyone around him would have advised. Shortly after starting with the city, Mier was contacted by a man claiming that he had spoken with Washington at home the previous night. The man explained that Washington liked an idea he had mentioned at a campaign stop, had given him his home number, and had told him to call later that night. Mier was dubious; big-city mayors don't go around giving out their numbers to every Joe they meet on the street. Yet Washington confirmed the man's story. "I think he's really on to something," Washington told Mier matter-of-factly. "You ought to hear him out."

His consensus-building approach irritated more than a few people inside the administration. Decisions were always being put on hold so that Washington could hear from some faction. It drove Tom Coffey crazy.

Coffey, the city's top lobbyist, had been a lawyer for the downtown law firm of Kirkland & Ellis; he had experienced his share of meetings. Decision making meant gathering three people into a room and throwing around some ideas. Yet Washington was not a man given to a small group of advisers who brokered government by fiat. A top aide during the campaign, Coffey recalled with sarcasm "the twenty different levels of advisers" upon which Washington relied—a style, he believed, at the root of the campaign's disastrous disorganization.

Chief of Staff Bill Ware was a guest on a Sunday morning talk show early in Washington's administration when during a break he boasted that the mayor would prove the cynics wrong. The Washington administration, Ware vowed, would be devoid of cronyism, the corruption of the past, and will remain a government above petty political concerns. "You'll see," Ware said. "By the time this administration is done, we'll have a political Camelot here." Reporter Mike Flannery didn't doubt Ware's sincerity, only his sense.

Washington knew even before he was elected that he wanted Ware to head up the bureaucracy, yet convincing him to move back to Chicago was no easy task. He had moved away years earlier, disgusted with the politics, and had no intention of ever moving back. But Washington challenged the side of Ware that would embrace as the ultimate challenge the reformation of Chicago's City Hall like a missionary sent to Sodom.

Washington saw Ware as the perfect candidate for getting hold of government. He was obsessed with details, a workaholic, and autocratic in pursuit of his aims. He was incredulous, Ware said in one interview, that the city didn't know the number of light posts within its borders, so someone was hired to count the light posts. He was straitlaced and humorless, a man steeped in corporate culture and well versed in memo-speak. Whereas everyone around him referred to Washington as "Harold" (at least when out of earshot), Ware alone called him "H. W."

Washington would be responsible for the political piece, and Ware was entrusted to handle government. Yet while the division of labor made some sense on paper, government and politics were a married pair. Ware often made policy decisions with profound political ramifications without thinking of clearing them with Washington. Ware may have been the perfect chief of staff for a U.S. congressman, but he was out of his element in Chicago's City Hall. He was the type for getting caught up in the rhapsody of a good idea, missing entirely its impracticality. He did not believe in shortcuts, only proper channels. This man in a highly political job in the most political of cities found politics dirty, the antithesis of reform.

It was an oversimplification, but inside City Hall the word on Ware was that he was not apolitical but antipolitics. To him, politics intruded on the serious task of professionalizing government. "There was this prevailing sense in the first year or two," said Joe Gardner, Washington's political director, "that we had to meet after work in a dark corner to talk about using the government to push our political agenda."

Ware embodied all that was good and noble about the lakefront reformer, but his shortcomings were also characteristic of the breed. On no issue was this clearer than on the yearly fight over the city budget.

By most measures Washington's first two budgets should have won him new converts around the city. He proposed two thousand layoffs in his first two years. Where in the past the city budget wasn't released until the last moment allowed by state law, and then passed with barely any debate, the administration released it at least a month early and organized budget hearings around the city. Ware's rigorous timetables of long-range planning forecasts and his proposed efficiency measures mostly met with complimentary editorials. Yet, incredibly, Washington ended up losing his first two budgets where it counted most—in the court of public opinion. His second budget, hammered out in the fall of 1984, must have proven particularly frustrating.

The trouble began when Ware discovered that Chicago's police-to-citizen ratio was about the highest in the United States, at least among big cities. In Chicago there were 4 cops for every thousand people, New York City had 3.4 per thousand, and Los Angeles 2.3. According to a second study, 911 calls had dropped fifteen percent in the previous five years. Where candidate Washington promised to beef up the police force, Ware saw a department ripe for cutting. Washington learned only after it was too late that the new budget included a proposal to allow five hundred city police officers to retire without replacing them.

A trial balloon floated through a leak could have saved Washington the hail of criticism that followed—except that Ware did not believe public opinion was a legitimate criterion for judging the merits of a policy decision.

Others inside the administration were amazed. Hadn't Ware seen the hate literature in 1983, declaring Washington unconcerned about crime? Police protection had always been a matter of public perception, and tops on people's minds, at least among whites, was the fear that Washington would be soft on crime.*

Later that same year Ware compounded Washington's PR problems when a couple of weeks before Christmas he ordered the crèche removed from the City Hall lobby. Ware cited complaints from religious groups and spoke of a recent Supreme Court ruling that barred cities from underwriting the cost of overtly religious scenes. Ware was on the right side legally and maybe morally, but the decision placed the administration on the wrong side politically.

Maybe Washington made a bad call, but Ware, ever the loyal soldier, took the bullet. Yet the point was moot, for Washington took the media blows that followed. "The grinch who stole Christmas," Burke said of Washington.

"Bottleneck Bill" Ware was dubbed. In part because his boss believed all parties should be heard from on politically sensitive issues but also because he was cautious and controlling, a routine matter could remain on Ware's desk for weeks as he pondered again and again its every facet. The consummate bureaucrat, Ware ran the bureaucracy scared. One associate, hardly more than an acquaintance, recalled Ware calling her

---

*Not long after, the budget hearings ended a petition drive to recall Washington. Dips in the police force were not entirely novel; its number fell by nine hundred in Byrne's first two years, for instance. Byrne, however, was accused of "jeopardizing the safety of many neighborhoods," as Washington was.

out of the blue to bare his soul after firing a holdover from the Byrne administration. He was unsure, insecure. Did he do the right thing? he wanted to know.

In 1984, Washington told Ware and Jim Montgomery to develop an affirmative action plan for minority and women contractors. Washington placed Ware in charge of the project, yet Montgomery made sure it didn't die a slow death in a file on Ware's desk. "Every time we went to Bill to talk about it," Montgomery said, "he put us off."

Montgomery sought an aggressive affirmative action policy. A city audit revealed that in 1982, Byrne's last full year as mayor, ninety-four percent of the dollars let through city contracts were in the hands of white male businessmen. The numbers in Washington's first year were hardly better. An aggressive affirmative action policy, he argued, was both justified and a valuable offering to the black businessmen who would underwrite the 1987 election. Don't be afraid to help your allies, Montgomery would say: "Be fair and play favorites." Government, Montgomery argued, should be an engine of change. In a country where eleven percent of the population is black, only three percent of the businesses are black-owned. Montgomery sought specific goals for both minority-owned enterprises (MBEs in the bureaucracy's shorthand) and those owned by women (WBEs).

Yet Ware was worried. The legal ramifications were one concern; the impact on Washington's reputation another. How would it look if this self-proclaimed reform administration was sued for reverse discrimination? What about charges of impropriety? Ware preached caution. We should encourage department heads to seek out qualified MBEs and WBEs but not commit to any numbers—just like a white liberal administration might offer.

Top aides met after hours to plot around Ware. They wrote a speech for Washington, leaving blanks instead of specific goals. Montgomery and a few others approached Washington and suggested goals of twenty-five percent for minority contractors and five percent for women-owned enterprises. Washington said that sounded fine.

Ware was sitting in the audience the night in the spring of 1984 that Washington delivered the speech before a group of white businessmen. Ware, it was said, just about fell out of his seat. Montgomery, for one, learned a lesson about how things are accomplished in the bureaucracy.

Few areas in city government were as lucrative as bond counsel work. A bond lawyer's fees were calculated as a percentage of the total amount of the deal; a $100 million bond transaction, for instance, gained a firm between $50,000 and $300,000 in legal fees for relatively routine work. The bond world had been closed to black lawyers in Chicago. For Jim Montgomery, control of City Hall meant rectifying that.

A lawyer who worked with him said that Montgomery "is the lawyer you want if you're guilty." He was sharp, quick, and savvy, a formidable foe in any setting. He was an accomplished defense lawyer who could use a velvet touch or scrap in the mud. The day after the crèche was removed from City Hall, Montgomery approached Ware: why not tell reporters a work order had gone out by mistake? "But Bill said, 'No, I am on civil libertarian grounds, this is a matter of principle,'" Montgomery said, speaking Ware's part in a loud and noble voice meant to mock his associate's moral stance. When the press was all over him for hiring a messenger convicted several times for armed robbery, Montgomery fibbed. In private meetings, one top Washington aide said (and Montgomery later admitted), Montgomery readily confessed he knew the man had a criminal background; before reporters he denied knowledge of the man's past.

Montgomery notified the city's established bond counsels: if you want future work with the city, you'll choose a new counsel from a short list of black attorneys I've established. The city would not pick up the extra cost of taking on a black partner. Instead, the bidding firm would absorb the extra cost themselves as a kind of affirmative action tax. "I informed them," Montgomery said, "that should they not like these conditions, they could feel free not to bid on any new work with the city."

Montgomery proved no more patient about integrating the city's court reporting duties, for decades an Irish bastion. In early 1984, Montgomery switched over to an outfit operated by Joseph Bertrand, a bank executive and also a former city treasurer under Daley. Bertrand had no experience in the court reporting field; he had started the business for the express purpose of landing a contract with the corporation counsel's office, joining forces with the white-run operation that always handled the city's court reporting. Washington's lakefront allies were furious, though none more than Bill Ware.

Marty Oberman was out of town when he learned of the Bertrand deal, but he phoned Washington, more concerned, he said, than angry. No other company was invited to submit a bid; the deal was just announced one day, with no pretense that the process was heeded. Oberman laid out a solution for Washington over the phone. Cancel the contract. Don't necessarily rebuke Montgomery publicly, but at least leak word of your displeasure to the gossip columnists. He reminded Washington that the bidding process was sacrosanct to those pushing for reform.

Washington was unhappy with the Bertrand deal—others remembered him angry over it—but Washington did get into it with Oberman. He mumbled his thanks, suggested he talk with Montgomery, and hung up. Oberman called Montgomery to express his disappointment, but all he got was a lecture about how the Irish ran everything in Chicago. Why, Montgomery asked, did he have to apologize for giving the court reporting business to a black man when an Irishman had profited all these years?

Oberman worried that a reporter would press him for a comment on the Bertrand contract. What would he say? What could he say? He didn't want to aid Vrdolyak by exposing Washington publicly. He could envision it: DEAN OF COUNCIL INDEPENDENTS BLASTS WASHINGTON ADMINISTRATION—but he had his integrity to maintain.

Affirmative action was something he could live with, but Oberman felt the process was above all else. Fairness was the administration's watchword—Washington loyalists literally wore the word pinned to their clothes. Yet Oberman viewed the Bertrand deal as anything but fair. If confronted by a reporter, he could explain that the Washington administration was somewhere around ten or twenty percent the old way and eighty percent a break with the past. But that would get swallowed up in the coverage. One bad deal, Oberman said, could wipe out a year's worth of good deeds. "The problem with Harold," Oberman later confided, "is that he gave us too much to apologize for."

It wasn't just the Bertrand deal, either. Montgomery's dealings with the established bond counsels troubled Oberman as well. There were the hardball tactics Montgomery employed and the fact that the corporation counsel authorized only four black lawyers to serve as potential co-counsel. Richard Newhouse and Carol Mosely Braun, state legislators firmly allied with Washington, were two of the names on Montgomery's list of four. Another was an attorney who in the past shared office space with Montgomery. "I was appalled," Oberman said. "Jim Montgomery is a civil rights leader. What did he think the civil rights movement was about all these years?"

Montgomery was hailed as pragmatic, a man of action in an administration weighed down by procrastination, cautiousness, and fear. He fought to win—unworthy of note, perhaps, except so many inside the administration fought the good fight even when certain to lose. Montgomery also proved one of the more effective progressive forces inside the administration. His political counsel, by most accounts, was about the best advice Washington was hearing. Yet Oberman was not impressed. To him, Ware, not Montgomery, represented all that should be respected and emulated in the Washington administration.

Oberman was also upset with Montgomery's boss. Why didn't Washington fire him? It wasn't just Montgomery's actions or those of other appointees. There was the deal Washington worked out with Vrdolyak late in 1983 to buy himself some peace. Washington proposed increasing the council committees from twenty-nine to thirty-seven. Twenty-nine committees was already ridiculously high; eight new committees only meant further waste. There was already a Committee on Housing, but this new plan added a Committee on Buildings; there would be a Committee on Streets and Alleys and one for Traffic Control and Safety. Each new committee meant a staff and a budget—precisely the sort of profligate spending a self-proclaimed reformer mayor should oppose. Oberman lodged his complaint but was ignored.

Oberman could only imagine how other lakefront whites viewed deals like these. It may not be fair, he said to Washington more than once, but you carry an extra burden. Most whites expect the worst. He advised a safe and cautious approach to affirmative action especially. "You have to be like Caesar's wife," he explained to Washington. "You have to be above reproach."

To Montgomery the priority was opening City Hall to those locked out. Perhaps he displeased the genteel sensibilities of the reformers living along the lakefront, but wasn't fairness as important (if not more so) than the process? The south side's Seaway National Bank was the nation's largest black-owned bank, yet only the 2,003rd largest overall and not even among the top hundred in Illinois. Should the city further retard the growth of banks like Seaway because a few lakefront liberals worried that it would reflect poorly on Washington?

Montgomery thought he had shown restraint integrating the city's bond business. He could have given business directly to any one of dozens of talented black attorneys whom he felt were deserving. But instead of relying on inexperienced lawyers, which might place a deal at risk, he built into the system an apprenticeship. That same philosophy was at work in the entire MBE/WBE program: established contractors were told their chances of a city contract improved if they linked themselves with minority or women subcontractors. What Oberman saw as foolishly aggressive, Montgomery saw as prudent and judicial counsel. He brought about an important reform without jeopardizing city operations.

It was as if there were two distinct reform traditions in Chicago, one white and one black. "White" reform was about process and efficiency; open and honest government was among its hallmarks. The reformer was typically liberal and white but not necessarily so: a government based on a corporate model of efficiency was something conservatives could get behind; and Chicagoans like Bill Ware were fiercely behind this brand of reform.

"Black" reform was more expansive. This tradition equated reform with fairness; it was also more political in content. Black reformists weren't in favor of inefficiency and corruption, of course; it was mainly a matter of priorities. Government was not merely something to be run more efficiently, as the Bill Wares and Marty Obermans would have it, but an engine of change. Redistributing government benefits was just as much a priority as rooting out petty corruption. Where white reform was based in corporate culture, black reform sprang from two traditions, the civil rights movement and the black church.

There was always enough overlap between the two movements to link them in political battle. The city's handling of its community development was one example. For the liberal reformer, the integrity of the process mattered most; the black reformer sought change in a program in which money earmarked for depressed communities ended up underwriting the patronage army at City Hall.

Yet the points of contradiction between the two traditions were equally significant. Cutting the city payroll was a fine idea for those living in comfort on the lakefront, but it was another matter entirely in the black community. History bore out the contradictions between these two reforms. Ed Kelly was a Depression-era mayor who allied himself with organized crime and ruled a political system rife with corruption; the good-government reformers loathed Kelly. But he was also a New Deal Democrat who cut blacks in for a share of the action. Martin Kennelly was the "reform" mayor who succeeded Kelly. Kennelly's vision of government was purer than Kelly's, certainly, but this "reformer," one historian wrote, "ran race-baiting campaigns and destroyed a well-run, integrated CHA. His actions set the CHA on its disastrous course of concentrating poor blacks in new ghettos."

If there was one overriding resentment among Washington partisans toward these lakefront reformers, it was that theirs was the only legitimate brand of reform. The press followed them, adopting white reform as their yardstick for measuring Washington against his reform claims. When money was placed in a black-owned bank, this was not viewed as a kind of reform but a continuation of the old politics; reform was not redistributing city business but ridding government of political influences. The *Sun-Times* in particular was inclined to report on Washington's affirmative action policy as if it were scandal. Every time Burke's Finance Committee discovered the Washington administration bypassing a low bidder to award a contract to a black-owned company, an article appeared in the first few pages of the *Sun-Times,* written in the tone the newspaper reserved for dirty deals it had unearthed.

Who is to say which kind of reform was more important? The city's Economic Development Department was shifting the city's priorities from downtown to the neighborhoods. Was this shift in development policy any less worthy a reform than those put forth by the lakefronters? These were the sort of philosophical differences that were rarely debated yet which nonetheless wracked this diverse and unusual coalition allied behind Washington.

"If I was his political director from day one," Marty Oberman said, "I would have made reaching out to whites my number-one priority. When you win a divisive election like he did, you bend over backward to bring in the opposition. You kill the opposition through kindness."

287

Yet Washington ignored this man who so much wanted to play more of a role. People who knew Washington well couldn't imagine for a moment his entrusting political leadership to the querulous and demanding Oberman, a man disliked by most of his colleagues, but whom the mayor saw as well meaning if sanctimonious and righteous.* "There was so much more Washington could have done to make his a broader-based coalition," Oberman said. Instead, "It was like we were just there as adjuncts. Like whites were just a necessary evil."

In 1984, Washington dumped Wilson Frost as his floor leader and replaced him with Alderman Tim Evans. To Oberman, Evans was an improvement over Frost but hardly the ideal choice. "Tim was chosen because he was the best choice in the black caucus," Oberman said. "*I* was the senior member of the reform caucus."

Tom Coffey, the city's top lobbyist, was, like Oberman, always pushing Washington to do more to broaden the coalition. This man, part of the so-called honkie caucus during the election, continued to push Washington at every opportunity to pitch his strategy to the lakefront. Yet, as in 1983, Washington usually ignored his advice. Coffey was inclined to read some deep psychological problem into Washington's resistance. He spoke of Washington's "internal confusion" over wooing voters he didn't believe would ever accept him anyway.

The tensions within Washington's caucus of City Council allies reflected the strains on the coalition. A stranger sitting in on their sessions might think he was among bitter foes when he heard: You're an opportunist. You're a liar. You're a know-nothing fool. Anything proved fair game: an embarrassing item in the papers, any piece of bad news. Alderwoman Marian Humes was supposedly the worst, the loudest mouth and also the nastiest.

Humes's favorite targets were the white reformers. The white reformers aligned with Washington looked on themselves as bold and principled,

---

*"Often sanctimonious," Don Rose wrote in a 1983 column critical of Oberman for paying himself a salary of $2,000 per month from funds he raised for his short-lived campaign for state attorney general. It's not illegal, Rose wrote, but the kind of ethical breach for which Oberman would take others to task.

supporters of Washington despite constituents who were generally hostile to the mayor—and despite snide remarks by commentators such as the gossip columnist Mike Sneed, a former Byrne press secretary, who dismissed Oberman in one *Sun-Times* column as a "barking lap dog" of Washington's because of his support for the mayor. Yet they did not feel appreciated by many of their black colleagues but scorned. It was as if those black aldermen hostile to Washington's reform stances blamed his posture entirely on the white lakefront aldermen. If we take this course of action, one of the white aldermen might say, it will prove unpopular on the lakefront. That would prompt Humes or any of a half dozen others to launch into a diatribe about how little difference it makes when Washington reached out to whites.

Oberman was a favorite target. So, too, were Larry Bloom and David Orr. Alderman Danny Davis, who was black, put forward similar arguments to the white reformers but did not receive similar treatment. After a time Marion Volini and Burt Natarus, the two other whites who were part of the Washington 21, stopped attending the sessions regularly. Who needed this aggravation?

At the root of these tensions were profound disagreements over what Washington's election meant. The progressives would see a challenge firmly to the left of Ted Kennedy; the liberals seized those pieces of Washington's message that favored government reforms; the black nationalists saw Washington's election as a matter of the blacks usurping the Irish. The "beauty" of 1983, Bob Starks offered, was that "the very expression of being part of the Washington camp was an expression of nationalism." Oberman considered such opinions with a plaintive sigh.

Racial tension weighed on the administration. Personality conflicts between a black and a white were often viewed in racial terms. Blacks mocked white officials who, walking into a meeting where there were, say, five blacks sitting around a table, seemed ill at ease. It was the kind of scene a black professional deals with daily in the work world, yet the same scene in reverse seemed to give many whites the jitters. Blacks high in the administration worked out for themselves those whites who were sensitive to race and those who they believed were not. Top appointees of all races were disgusted with the white liberals. Washington could do twenty things for the liberal community, yet it would never be enough.

At Economic Development, Rob Mier wondered if the MBE program was much more than a more equitable version of the conservative's trickle-down solution. At one meeting he said that the city should go beyond MBE; the city should place greater emphasis on job training. Mier believed he was arguing for a more progressive solution to the problems of poverty, but it struck him, the only white in the room, that others felt he was arguing that true economic power should remain in white hands, with blacks as only the hired help. In Mier's department a black deputy fought with a female colleague who advocated a separate affirmative action category for women. To his mind, white women were a privileged group no more in need of special breaks than white men.

Under past mayors several black contractors built prosperous businesses handling employment training for the city. When one of Ware's internal audits found that these businesses were not producing much in the way of tangible results, the decision was made to rely more heavily on community-based organizations operating in low-income areas. The black contractors raised hell. At cocktail parties they took to calling Washington antiblack. Washington's director of employment training was a Latina, fueling ugly rumors. "Our contracts are going to the Latinos," it was said.

Countless similar conflicts strained the wider coalition outside City Hall. Washington named the city's first gay and lesbian liaison, supported a controversial gay rights ordinance, and was the city's first mayor to speak at a gay pride rally. Yet in a community where the church fuels much of the activism, more than one Washington supporter was rankled by the mayor's outspoken support of gay rights. Issues such as gay rights and feminism exposed the deep cultural divisions between black and white activists. Chicago's Gus Savage was one of the few reliable progressive votes in Congress, but Savage's use of the term "faggots" underscored that Washington's was an improbably broad coalition.

Washington appointed a man named Paul Igasaki to serve as the city's Asian-American liaison to give his community more of a presence in Chicago politics. Soon thereafter a local organization calling itself the Black Solidarity Movement made a point of condemning the congressional committee named to consider financial reparations for those Japanese-Americans placed wholesale into internment camps during World War II.

Why the Japanese, a leaflet asked, when blacks were never compensated for all they lost at the hands of slavery and Jim Crow?

It was standard fare at nationalist gatherings to criticize Washington for hiring too many Jews. There was also talk he gave Latinos more than their due. At the same time there were Latinos who believed Washington was doing less for them than for blacks, though both communities were equally in need. The journalist Nate Clay, who had played a critical role in the voter registration drive prior to Washington's election, was a part of the multiracial coalition that met to discuss voter registration strategies of several upcoming local elections. Clay continuously used the term "illegal aliens." At least one participant cringed every time Clay said it; in a group that included several Latino participants, the politic thing to do, if not simply the right thing, was to use the term "undocumented."

The voter registration group also had to tolerate the Reverend Al Sampson. Sometimes he would pretend not to hear anything said by someone white. A white reporter called Sampson to ask his comments on a particular issue. Sampson asked the reporter to hold and set the phone down, allowing the reporter to hear that he was chatting with a friend about nothing in particular. A couple of minutes later he picked up the phone and stated that the white press was a racist press and that he had nothing to say. "Al's always playing games with white folks' heads," said one black ally. Washington nominated Sampson to sit on the city college's board of trustees.

Too many Jews.

At first it was just talk. Operating within the milieu of City Hall, the alderman heard secondhand references to the displeasure in some quarters with the number of Jews whom Washington had brought into government. The alderman faithfully attended the 21's caucus sessions, so he had heard his share of garbage about how the "Mexicans" were getting too much from Washington and about the gays having something on the mayor. Still, the first time he heard Alderman Allen Streeter talk about "Harold's Jews," this alderman was, he admitted, stunned "in a naïve sort of way." Streeter just raised the subject out of the blue, starting in about how the Jews placed pressure on Washington and how Washington, afraid, had caved in. Streeter went on to list the Jews in top positions in the administration. I'm on their hit list, you know, Streeter confided to the alderman—although he wouldn't answer inquiries about it years later.

"He'd be telling me this thinking it was all cool," the alderman said. "And I'm thinking to myself, 'Where the fuck did he get *that* from?' This guy's an alderman, and he's talking the most ignorant bullshit."

There were times during the Washington years that this alderman believed himself blessed. To live in Chicago and share a certain political bent was to glow with pride about Washington. Around the country there were those looking to Chicago as the hope for all those who believed in the potential for a multiracial coalition formed around shared interests and concerns. Yet there were also those times he endured Streeter's comments about Harold's Jews or about the gays or the Latinos or the Asians. It was at moments like these that he would wonder whether the idea of a rainbow coalition was anything but impossible. Chicago demonstrated the power of this multiracial progressive alliance, but it provided a clear look at its inherent limits as well.

16

THE
CHICAGO
EXPERIMENT

Nate Clay looked out on Lake Michigan believing he knew the answers to many of the questions the national press was asking about Jesse Jackson in 1984. A former PUSH communications director, Clay likened him to Alexander the Great—a man, Clay said, "after conquering the world sat down and cried because there was nothing else to conquer. . . .

"With Harold's election, Jesse would no longer be the black community's top figure. With no mayor to criticize anymore, his piece in Chicago was over. He had to do something different, and where was there for him to go except up?" Complicating Jackson's life, Clay said, was that "Jesse and the mayor he had helped elect were at arm's length."

Black leaders from around the nation gathered throughout 1983 to consider Chicago with foreboding. Congressmen, civil rights leaders, and others who were part of what might be called the black leadership family sought a strategy for the 1984 presidential election. More local white party officials publicly endorsed Washington's Republican foe than supported their own party's nominee. The two stalwarts of liberalism, Walter Mondale and Ted Kennedy, sided with opponents of Washington in the primary. What did this augur? they wanted to know.*

The Democrats had not won a white majority in a presidential election since 1964—not since Lyndon Johnson and his Great Society programs, which identified the Democrats with the poor and the blacks. With an eye on the 1984 election, the moderates and even some of the party's liberal leaders were blaming their failures on the so-called special interests. Those part of the black leadership family were astute enough to read between the lines.

Some argued that defeating Reagan was the priority. Nothing should impede that goal, they said. Others spoke seriously of backing a black candidate for president. Those taking this position put forward a variety of arguments, yet time and again they returned to the topic of Chicago. Atlanta Mayor Andrew Young was still angered by Mondale's rebuffing of Washington in the 1983 primary and warned of "a mass defection of blacks from the Democratic party that might cost the Democrats the presidential election."

Washington won despite—or in direct opposition to—the white liberals. For many that was the lesson of Chicago: power is not given through liberal goodwill but taken. In June 1983, at a meeting held in Chicago, the group endorsed the idea, despite the risks, of a black presidential candidate.

The black leadership group did not slate any particular candidate, but thoughts turned to Jackson. Jackson, who sat among them while they pushed around the idea of a black presidential candidate, had already declared his interest.

Jackson said Chicago hit him like a vision. He witnessed the crusade-like spirit of the Washington campaign; he saw hopelessness, frustration, and anger harnessed into a spirited voter registration drive. Perhaps Chicago was a bellwether of a mood swing across black America, Jackson said in speeches. The idea of running hit him during the primary, he told *Playboy,* when the Democratic leadership snubbed Washington. "If it had

---

*A study by the Institute of Policy Studies, a think tank specializing in policy analysis from a left perspective, wrote that one of the two factors bringing about these meetings was "the widespread defection of white Democratic party leaders and voters from Chicago mayoral nominee Harold Washington."

been left to them," Jackson said of Kennedy and Mondale, "the rise of the black political movement would have been stopped, stillborn." Challenging these same leaders in the presidential primaries seemed to Jackson a natural next step. Influenced by Washington's stunning upset, Jackson initiated a national voter registration campaign shortly after Chicago's 1983 general election. "It's a particularly important victory because it signifies to the world that a new inspiration is at work right here in Chicago," Jackson said.

The Washington campaign aided the Jackson effort in another way, albeit an ironic one. When Jackson was asked to stay away from Chicago during the mayoral election, he occupied his time crisscrossing the country speaking of the potential for replicating Chicago on a national scale.

Jackson was not the only one projecting higher possibilities on Washington's 1983 win. Writers for publications to the left of mainstream—publications such as *The Black Scholar, The Nation,* and *In These Times*—reported on Chicago with enthusiasm. "The agenda for the 1984 presidential election has changed suddenly and drastically. What happened was Chicago," began an essay in the magazine *Dissent* in the summer of 1983. Chicago, the *Dissent* writer offered, is a "promising harbinger of better things to come on the nation's political stage." Manning Marable, renowned within black intellectual circles, voiced much the same viewpoint in an article he wrote following Jackson's announcement for president: "What has changed has been the overall national political climate since the victory of Harold Washington in Chicago."

Those disheartened by the Democratic party's rightward shift pointed to Chicago as confirmation that the Democratic party's problem wasn't pandering to special interests but the lack of a coherent philosophy. More than two-thirds of the city's black voting age population voted in 1983 in a country where only fifty percent of the electorate elects a president. The disaffected could be awakened but not by the watered-down mush the party called its message.

Black-oriented publications such as *Ebony* and *Jet* treated Washington as if he were mayor to all black America. *The Black Scholar* wrote of Chicago as a model to be studied. In its index one year, the magazine classified its articles on local politics in one of two categories—those about Chicago and those not. There was also the retrospective importance of Chicago with

Jackson's rise. Two academics writing on Jackson's 1984 campaign included a chapter on Chicago titled "The Trial Heat."

The country's left publications also claimed Washington as their own. One week after Washington's 1983 victory, a headline in the *New York Times* read, KOCH TO FILL MORE CITY JOBS WITH BLACK AND HISPANIC WORKERS. This was evidence, one New York journalist wrote, that the tremors of Chicago were felt well beyond its borders. The optimist saw Chicago pointing toward the future, signaling the emergence of a third force in U.S. politics. For them, studying Chicago politics was akin to looking at Jerry Falwell's rise in Lynchburg, Virginia, to understand the rise of the New Right.

Chicago was not entirely original. The vigor of Chicago's black community was there in Cleveland in 1967, for instance, when Carl Stokes was elected the first black mayor of a major U.S. city. Yet it had been a long while since the black community crackled with the electricity found in Chicago in 1983, and Chicago's influence in rekindling the spirit of unity dormant since Amiri Baraka's unity convention back in 1972 was appreciated. Washington, too, stoked the imagination of blacks living outside the city's border. "Something fundamental separates Harold Washington from other black mayors, who are often manipulated to blunt the potential militancy of the Afro-American community—Philadelphia's Wilson Goode is a notable example," Manning Marable wrote.

The highly acclaimed "Eyes on the Prize II" public television series used Chicago's 1983 election to end its documentary. Henry Hampton, the series' producer, spoke of Chicago's special role in U.S. politics and the city's significance in black politics nationally. Chicago embodied the black movement's conversion from civil rights to civic power, he said, and also the slow shift to coalition politics. After the dismal days of the 1970s when the civil rights movement seemed stuck in neutral, it was only fitting that so inspirational a series should end on a hopeful note.

National publications such as *Time* had cast the race as nothing but an election between an anonymous black man who spent time in jail and an anonymous white man, significant only because of the overt racism expressed in the campaign. Yet several nationally syndicated columnists saw great significance in Chicago's 1983 mayor's race. William Raspberry wrote a column about the implications of Chicago on national politics ("Chicago Race Important to Dems"), as did Rowland Evans and Robert Novak

("Chicago and the Presidency") and David Broder ("Chicago Election Can Shape Presidential Race"). Broder's column began, "Chicago's mayoral election Tuesday is the exception to the rule about the national insignificance of local contests. . . . [The Washington-Epton race] can shape the climate for the 1984 presidential contest as profoundly as any event in this year."

Perhaps nothing underscored Chicago's significance in national politics like the parade of party officials and Democratic presidential hopefuls that arrived in Chicago during the general election. The party, worried about the black vote in 1984, recognized that the party split in Chicago was a dilemma with national ramifications.

Chicago lent credibility to Jackson. The coalition that rallied around Washington had cracked a tough nut in defeating the vaunted Chicago political machine. The cliché in movement circles was that if it could happen in Chicago, it could happen anywhere. And Jackson was never shy about taking credit for Washington's victory.

To Jackson, Chicago was nothing short of the start of a "renegotiation" between the Democratic party and black America. No longer would black representatives allow themselves to be taken for granted; the crumbs of white liberal power were no longer enough. Before black audiences Jackson spoke of Chicago as testimony to what an invigorated black community could accomplish.

The time seemed ripe with possibilities. Lu Palmer's leadership role in Washington's campaign, the successful enlisting of Conrad Worrill and other doctrinaire nationalists—these developments portended a widespread willingness to accept electoral politics as a legitimate path to black empowerment. Perhaps Jackson could be The One who bridged the ideological chasms that split black leadership, as Washington was in Chicago. It was a role Jackson had coveted throughout his career. If ever he was to make the jump, if ever he was to be the leader accepted by the diverse elements that encompassed black political culture, 1983 seemed the time for a career switch. On November 3, he announced he would run for president.

In Chicago they understood the precariousness of the Rainbow Coalition that Jackson envisioned himself leading. A black-based movement predicated not on nationalist sentiments but on coalition building; a progressive platform that in one stroke inspires blacks of all political stripes and also reaches beyond black borders; a coalition of those outside the pale in Democratic circles; the crusadelike fervor inherent in a campaign seeking to draw together divergent movements—those considering themselves part of the Washington coalition saw their own reflection in the Jackson campaign. The simple wisdom of Jackson's campaign was the wisdom of their own. The problem was that in Chicago they knew Jackson. He was never about rainbow politics or well versed in coalition politics.

Everyone had his or her story. There was the black woman earning her living working for not-for-profit groups who spent evenings and weekends working with the Coalition for Illinois Divestment from South Africa. Jackson spoke frequently about South Africa, imploring people to get involved, yet PUSH was rarely around to help with efforts like the weekly pickets at the South African consulate in downtown Chicago. "You would think PUSH would be one of the groups at the forefront at the South African work here in Chicago, or at least that's what I thought before I got involved," she said. "But they never have been." For several years she and other organizers tried enlisting PUSH's help. "What you find out is that PUSH doesn't get involved in things unless they can call the shots. After a while we would just call PUSH headquarters and say, 'Well, here's what we're doing in case you're interested. If you want to send a representative to be a part of it, go ahead.'"

Prexy Nesbitt, a leading antiapartheid activist in Chicago, related pretty much the same story. He added that if a dignitary passed through town—a leader of the African National Congress, say—PUSH would pressure various groups to have the event held there. "If they weren't successful, they'd usually refuse our requests for help," Nesbitt said. Another black Chicagoan active in politics said, "Jesse—well, let's say he was new to the concept of coalition politics." Ironically, this activist dates his political awakening back to Jackson's aborted 1971 run for mayor.

Jackson's realm had always been the black community. People did not offer this as a criticism so much as a statement of fact appropriate to judging someone seeking to lead a multiracial coalition. He didn't have Washington's historic ties to the trade unions, for instance; in fact, in his role as the head of PUSH, he angered union leaders, running roughshod over their concerns during any number of his campaigns to integrate an industry. "He finds it difficult to make significant new coalitions," Don Rose, Jackson's former publicist, wrote in the Chicago *Reader,* "because he is largely not trusted by his peers in labor and other social action groups; and he finds it difficult to gather a strong, intellectually capable group around him for sustained periods because he, like many, requires blind loyalty and grows jealous of those who challenge or pose a vague threat."

Washington would have no trouble putting together campaign literature establishing his credentials on issues important to women. In contrast, Jackson had to defend himself against things like his antiabortion stance in the 1970s. "Black genocide," he called it, ascribing to a perspective then in vogue among the black nationalists. He would have to explain PUSH's longstanding refusal to respond to gay and lesbian groups that sought its support, and the civil libertarian would have to weigh Jackson's crusade against recording artists such as Billy Paul, who sang about an illicit affair in "Me and Mrs. Jones (We Got a Thing Going On)," when his big issue was the black family.

Reaching out to the Latino population proved a similar challenge. Where Washington could point to his support while in Congress for issues such as bilingual education, Jackson had to explain his poor relations with Latino groups locally. In the late 1970s, Jackson was publicly rebuked by several Latino leaders for initiating negotiations over a school desegregation plan under consideration without inviting any Latinos to participate in the discussions. Jackson called a press conference to patch things up and ended up further aggravating his Latino counterparts. He promised to invite a contingent of Latino leaders to PUSH to form a "Black–Spanish coalition." Weeks later *Tribune* reporter Clarence Page phoned several of the Latino leaders whom Jackson specifically mentioned by name; they said they had never heard from PUSH. A PUSH spokesperson explained that the staff didn't have their phone numbers, so Page suggested he look in the phone book, where he had found their names listed. Yet neither Jackson nor his staff phoned, because Jackson was suddenly offered a higher profile opportunity. "Within a day or two," Page wrote, "Yasir Arafat invited Jackson to the Middle East, and the agenda was eclipsed again."

Lu Palmer was foursquare behind Jackson. So, too, was Conrad Worrill. Jackson was black, and he was one of their own raising the issues on the national level; it was that simple. If nothing else, Worrill said, the Washington era had "heightened our political maturity, heightened our willingness to work together with people we might not have worked with before." Palmer was "pissed off" over what he called Jackson's "Rainbow Coalition crap"; like Washington he was kowtowing to those for whom black liberation was secondary at best. But Jackson wouldn't back away from Louis Farrakhan's endorsement, despite the considerable pressure to do so.* To Worrill and Palmer, Jackson had placed above all else the historic rifts between the nationalists and those on the civil rights side.

Both were also impressed with Jackson's drive. A frequent visitor to Jackson's home, Palmer said that with Jackson it was always business—not even a few minutes first about football or the kids. "He's a man obsessed by movement politics," Palmer said. The man worked grueling hours.

Vernon Jarrett, the black newspaper columnist, was no less committed to black unity or black empowerment. Because of his unstinting commitment to writing about black issues, he was labeled a "militant," but that revealed more about his white critics than his politics. He was more coalitionist than nationalist. In 1983, Jarrett, like Washington, would take heat for supporting an incumbent Jewish progressive against five black foes in a ward with a black majority. He worked for the white press—first at the *Tribune,* then at the *Sun-Times*—an unmilitant act in itself.

Jarrett couldn't support Jackson; he couldn't toss aside the numerous columns he had written exposing Jackson's sins over the years. ("Perhaps . . . the Reverend Jesse Jackson's toughest critic in the media," a fellow black columnist wrote of Jarrett in the *Columbia Journalism Review*.) In one column about the 1984 elections he asked if Jackson's commitment would survive the six months of fame his crusade would bring him. He may have been thinking about a column he wrote in 1979 after Jackson announced PUSH was organizing marches against unemployment in twenty cities across the country to commemorate the historic 1963 March on

---

*The Farrakhan endorsement took place in Chicago's City Hall at the Board of Elections. Salim Muwakkil, a former Muslim, wrote a humorous account of the endorsement in the Chicago *Reader*. Jackson attempted to lead the crowd in a version of "We Shall Overcome." Muwakkil wrote, "The nationalists may have broken tradition and registered to vote, but it was another thing altogether to get them to sing a song they've long derided as a 'slave melody.' Jackson soon abandoned the effort."

Washington. Plans were made, committees formed, press releases sent out—but then the idea was dropped.

JESSE'S CHARISMA NOT ENOUGH, was the headline that ran over one Jarrett column in 1984; in three other columns Jarrett offered the rationale of various elected black officials supporting Mondale over Jackson.

Harold Washington always grumbled about the spineless liberals in Washington, D.C.; pressure from the left might just do some good. Yet he wasn't ready to publicly embrace Jackson, especially considering the considerable political cost of doing so. "We do not have the political luxury to be in any campaign behind a black candidate who can't win," Washington said. "The task at hand is defeating Ronald Reagan."

Washington announced that he would run his own "favorite son" delegates in Chicago. He expressed a "preference" for Jackson but would not endorse him. Carl Officer, the mayor of East St. Louis and chairman of Jackson's Illinois campaign, tried twisting Washington's arm for an endorsement, one top Washington aide said, "but Harold basically threw him out of his office." He would endorse no one, the mayor said, until the convention.

Things came to a head between Washington and Jackson after a ceremony at City Hall in Jackson's honor. Jackson had just returned from Syria, where he won the release of a U.S. Navy officer being held prisoner there. Jackson and Washington were pictured smiling together afterward, but Jackson was not happy. He thought the medal would be conferred on him in a public setting like the City Council chambers; instead, a small ceremony was held in the mayor's conference room. The event was closed to the press except for the staged photograph.

"I was willing to step out of the picture," Jackson reportedly told Washington afterward. "I did what I was asked." Jackson threatened to run a slate of delegates against Washington's. "It got very nasty," said someone who tried to serve as an intermediary between the two. "Jesse was pissed, and it was like Harold didn't care."

Washington didn't blink. He was having enough trouble in Chicago without adding Jackson—and with him the baggage of "Hymietown" and Yasir Arafat—to his list. That night there was a Jackson rally at the Arie Crown Theater. Washington did not show. Still, Jackson took that opportunity to endorse Washington's slate of favorite-son candidates.

Mostly, though, there was a closing of ranks around Jackson among the city's black activists. This wasn't about personalities but politics, one heard time and again. For much of the country Jackson ironically came to embody all that Washington's movement stood for. For better or worse, he was the stentor spreading the gospel of Chicago. Boycotting Jackson meant boycotting their own success.

Perhaps he was an opportunist, only an impostor pretending a belief in this rainbow coalition. Yet what presidential hopeful wasn't a political chameleon? Maybe it was all ego trip. "Any presidential candidate without a strong ego would be a national security risk," Jackson offered in one interview. It was a strange quote—but nonetheless true.

Maybe Jackson's propensity to jump from issue to issue, as he had done for so long in Chicago, was actually a plus. What was a presidential candidate except a two-minute expert on every subject under the sun?*

That summer's Democratic convention offered another opportunity for Vrdolyak to one-up Washington. Washington had boasted in the winter that he would line up enough Democratic committeemen in the spring's primary to vote Vrdolyak out as party chairman. The mayor didn't come close.

Washington immediately learned what it meant to be a maverick out of step with the party. He arrived in San Francisco still uncommitted to Mondale—he was unsuccessfully trying to use his thirty-six delegates to broker Mondale's support of a jobs bill— and also without proper credentials for his bodyguards and staff. Vrdolyak, in contrast, had the papers to get his people in.

Vrdolyak's whispering voices made sure that reporters back home heard the story of Washington's foul-up. Perhaps Vrdolyak, too, pulled every string he had to make sure that the party or Mondale's people didn't come to Washington's rescue. Tormenting the mayor seemed Vrdolyak's

---

*Jackson captured seventy-nine percent of the black vote in Illinois, which wasn't as good as New York (eighty-seven percent), New Jersey (eighty-six percent), and several other states, but respectable nonetheless. Yet in Chicago, Jackson received only sixty-seven percent of the black vote in those wards with a black population of ninety percent or more, according to the Chicago *Reporter,* and only about five percent of the white lakefront vote.

main task in San Francisco—at least that is how it looked when invitations to a Washington breakfast were slipped beneath the doors of the Illinois delegates, though there was no breakfast. Vrdolyak's aide, Joe Novak, was blamed for the prank.

Washington brought bad press on himself when he blew up while being interviewed on live television by CBS's Ed Bradley. Bradley had asked Washington if he thought the party rift in Chicago would hurt Mondale's chances in Illinois. Washington said he couldn't answer that, it was up to the party chairman. Bradley then turned to Vrdolyak, who was standing off-camera nearby listening to the interview, and asked him what he thought. Washington was visibly angry over Bradley's attempt to set up a three-way dialogue. He dressed Bradley down for "stooping to such a thing" and yelled at him to turn off the camera.

The exchange between the two was a top news story in Chicago for several days. "Mayor-in-a-snit," one columnist called him.

The political year 1984 presented Vrdolyak with another opportunity. That year Louis Farrakhan called Judaism a "gutter" religion and said that Hitler was "a great man, but wicked, wickedly great."

The weak points in Washington's coalition had proven fertile ground for Vrdolyak and his allies. Alderman Miguel Santiago, the council's sole Latino and Vrdolyak's only nonwhite ally in the council, was forever trying to stir anti-Washington sentiments among the city's Latinos: "It's the south side and the west side who benefit from this administration, not my community," he said on occasion; Washington was concerned with helping "only the right minorities." Santiago called a press conference after the release of a study that he said proved Washington favored black business people over Latino ones at the O'Hare expansion project. Santiago said that Latinos, who made up around seventeen percent of the city's population, were receiving less than two percent of the dollars spent there.

The reporters quoting Santiago that night and in the next morning's newspapers failed to check with the professor who conducted the study, so they couldn't know that he thought Santiago "seriously misrepresented" his work. Latino-owned businesses received 9.8 percent of the contracts at O'Hare, his study found, compared to the 13.7 percent received by black-owned firms. Given that there are 2.5 blacks for every Latino in Chicago, black contractors were actually getting *less* than their fair share of the O'Hare project when compared to their Latino counterparts.

The 29 also did what they could to goad the frustrations of the machine-oriented aldermen. In 1984 Ed Burke compiled for his fellow aldermen a ward-by-ward listing of every city worker hired during Washington's tenure. The machine-oriented black aldermen were incensed. Scores of people had been hired in their ward, yet they recognized few, if any, of the names.

The tensions between the city's blacks and its Jews also lent themselves to Vrdolyak's tactics. When the incumbent sheriff, Richard Elrod, a Jew, lost his bid for reelection, Vrdolyak blamed it on anti-Semitism in the black community. There was a multitude of reasons that the black community might have opposed Elrod, including the memory of his father Arthur, one of the white political bosses who lorded over a predominantly black west side ward. Still, with Washington's endorsement, Elrod won over ninety percent of the black vote, faring better in the city's black wards than in its white ones. The press reported on Vrdolyak's charge but never counterbalanced it with election data.

Another time, the director of the Midwest Anti-Defamation League felt compelled to publicly criticize a Jewish Vrdolyak ally named Jerome Orbach who made the "outrageous" claim that Washington was unfair to the Jewish community. Orbach, he said, was "using the Jewish community as a political tool."

Farrakhan's ministry, dating back to the mid-1970s, had been based on the city's south side. His face was familiar to anyone living there, for it gazed out from countless posters announcing a forthcoming sermon. His had always been a modest-sized organization; its membership was estimated at between five thousand and ten thousand members nationwide. Yet in 1984, with one of its own suddenly a household name across the country, Farrakhan became a useful tool. Burke even blamed the removal of the City Hall crèche on Farrakhan. "Mr. Ware," Burke explained, "is jumping through Mr. Farrakhan's hoop." Bill Ware was hardly the sort for jumping through the south side minister's hoop, yet when pressed, Burke would only say, "I have my sources." Vrdolyak went a step further when he drew up a resolution calling on Washington to denounce this Chicagoan who was suddenly public enemy number one.

Washington refused. "The whole point of this guy," Washington told his press secretary, Al Miller, "his whole message is that black politicians are getting their strings pulled by whites—bankers, corporations, the media. So am I going to prove Farrakhan right by jumping up and denouncing him because the bankers and the corporations and the media say I have to? Because Eddie Vrdolyak says I have to? Shit." Washington cited his good relations with Jews and Jewish organizations dating back forty years. He would denounce all bigotry in general but not Farrakhan individually.*

Marty Oberman understood that Vrdolyak was only trying to make trouble between blacks and Jews, yet he was furious with Washington. "It was this 'base' crap again," Oberman said. "As gutsy a guy as Washington could be, he was sometimes a real coward." To no avail Oberman pointed out to Washington that Los Angeles's Mayor Tom Bradley had denounced Farrakhan.

The issue dragged on for weeks. Alderman David Orr, one of Washington's allies, introduced a rival resolution that called on Washington to denounce bigotry and anti-Semitism generally, but Orr's proposal went nowhere. Vrdolyak chose his issue wisely: the vote was the first to break neatly along racial lines. Every white voted in favor of Vrdolyak's resolution, and every black voted against it. The resolution passed, but Washington never signed it. In 1987 a great many Jews who had voted for Washington in 1983 were still angry.

---

* Ironically, the City Council had once sung the praises of Farrakhan's Nation of Islam when it passed a resolution that read in part, "The Nation of Islam has served the community with a solid program of social reform which has been responsible for assisting black people all over America and [it] has exalted the basic family unity and developed an education system which teaches dignity, self-respect . . ." The resolution, signed by Mayor Daley, proclaimed February 26, 1975, "Nation of Islam Day in Chicago."

17

A
MIDTERM
BLUNDER

Everything was going well for the 29, mainly because things were going so poorly for Washington. As the midpoint in his term approached, the prevailing image of Washington was of a terribly outmatched bumbler up against craftier, more politically shrewd opponents. Washington was portrayed in media accounts as well meaning but in way over his head, ineffectual and uncompromising. One political writer likened him to Jimmy Carter, sincere but inept, a good-hearted man unable to find the levers of power to actually accomplish anything.

Washington could cite the breadth of problems confronting any big-city mayor or rant about the underhanded methods of his foes. But that further ingrained the image of an oversized Vrdolyak manhandling a child-sized Washington, as if Vrdolyak were able to lean a hand against Washington's head and hold himself just out of reach so that poor little Harold flailed wildly, throwing aimless punches this way and that without ever being able to tag his opponent.

Things were not going well inside the administration. Snafus such as Washington's missed deadline on his ethics statement seemed all too common. A fairer mix of people inside government—more women, more minorities, and more protesters mixed in among the career bureaucrats and ward heelers—meant, among other things, that government was bogged down by inexperience and internal feuding, as well as sabotage born of resentment. Art Vasquez, a deputy in the Economic Development Department, drew an analogy to a newly married couple: "We had to learn to get along but, maybe more important, we also needed to learn how to fight." Perhaps government was no more or less efficient in Washington's first two years than under previous mayors but merely subject to an unprecedented scrutiny given all that was at stake; still, the unmistakable impression left by the media was that under Washington foul-ups were suddenly endemic.

The Council Wars were another impediment. The administration was making progress in overhauling government, but it was all but overshadowed by an emotional and persistent political fight. Politics, not government, dominated the media's attention. "No one wants to deal with that nitty-gritty stuff of government," Washington said to a *Reader* media columnist. "The news is not Vrdolyak calling me a bastard and me calling him a son of a bitch." Without media attention to the real issues of government, Council Wars seemed like nothing but loud and meaningless fights between the two strong personalities of Washington and Vrdolyak. Yet only through his performance as chief executive could Washington win new white converts.

At the corporation counsel's office, for instance, Jim Montgomery and his top aides initiated a series of sweeping changes. Once known as "the worst law firm in town," according to a former *Sun-Times* beat reporter writing in *Chicago* magazine, "[law] has made perhaps the biggest improvement, with almost half the 160 lawyers replaced by merit hiring." *Chicago* credited Montgomery with bringing in "first-rate litigators" and initiating a number of other much-needed reforms.

This was the stuff of small-type sidebars, however, unlike a trip Montgomery took to France, paid for by the city. Ostensibly he traveled overseas to look into a huge deal the city was considering for a light-rail system at O'Hare, though it was never satisfactorily explained why the city's top lawyer needed to travel abroad to study engineering designs. A family trip to Mexico arranged through Waste Management, Inc., was headlined. Montgomery claimed he repaid Waste Management for the entire cost of the trip; still, a vast disposal firm doing business with the city seemed an odd travel agent.

These and other examples of petty corruption among Washington's top managers caused a variety of problems for Washington. It buttressed the 29's point that Washington was no more about reform than his predecessors. Deals such as Montgomery's Waste Management trip caused bad feelings among those in Washington's black caucus who wished that his election meant a bigger cut of the pie.

Another problem was the extraordinarily high expectation in the black community at a time of shrinking federal dollars. ("Being the first black mayor," Maynard Jackson, Atlanta's first black mayor, once said, "is what you wish on your worst enemy.") Reagan's reelection in the fall of 1984 only meant further cuts. Staff and single-issue policy groups floated innovations that were pointless without money. Washington's transition team had found that Chicago's health budget was not only near the bottom among all major U.S. cities but that its per-capita expenses were half that of the *median*. AIDS was only beginning to add its burden to an already overstretched budget. Yet could Washington survive a tax hike?

It seemed the administration was always on the verge of firing someone, and then Bill Ware, the chief of staff, would worry. Ware was preoccupied by Shakman—the antipatronage ruling that Washington signed after taking office—and the possibility of lawsuits should they move too fast. The judge hearing the Shakman case had deemed 925 positions "Shakman-exempt"—meaning they were policy positions or sensitive political posts that a mayor could fill entirely at his discretion. Yet any fired employee, even those in Shakman positions, had the right to sue.* Incredibly, nearly

---

*Vrdolyak had always opposed Shakman, but with Washington's election he was suddenly eager to see its rigorous enforcement. He petitioned the judge hearing the case to lower the number of Shakman-exempt positions from 925 to 250. Vrdolyak's brother was among those suing the city, claiming he was improperly fired for political reasons.

two years into Washington's term, the mayor had replaced only 200 of the 925 Shakman-exempt employees.

Washington was the first black mayor, Ware argued; he needed to be purer than pure. But while this logic no doubt pleased the Marty Obermans, it meant that a new purchasing agent was named but the staff working under him was almost to a person the same who served under Byrne. When Joe Gardner was still commissioner of the city's Department of Neighborhoods, several of his top deputies were Old Guard, including a Vrdolyak appointee. After one closed-door meeting of the department's managers, Vrdolyak called to complain about something Gardner had just said to his staff. Gardner sought to fire this deputy and filed the paperwork to do so, per Montgomery's instructions, but his request sat forever on Ware's desk.

The press office was entirely Shakman-exempt. Yet at the midway point of Washington's term, most were still Byrne holdovers. It seemed nothing went wrong inside the press office without its making the newspapers. "Shit, except for one or two people," Washington himself said nearly two years into office, "that whole shop ought to be cleaned out. Half of them . . . aren't working for us anyway."

Political connections were easy to ascertain; in many cases a committeeman's letter of recommendation was still in an employee's personnel file. Yet sorting through the existing personnel proved a challenge. Which ones were there to do a job and who among them held an overriding allegiance to the old machine? Firing willy-nilly any and all Shakman-exempt employees might make the New Guard feel good, but with them would go valuable institutional knowledge.

Some suggested firing anyone in government brought in through Vrdolyak or Burke. But that would have included an Inspections Department employee who secured his job through Vrdolyak but who was considered by at least one top Washington aide, a woman, as a man of integrity. Frustrated by all the ne'er-do-wells on the payroll, this employee shared with her the lowdown on several of the more dishonest characters operating in his department.

The majority of the city's forty thousand employees were connected to one local ward organization or another, so sabotage was constantly suspected though difficult to prove. "We get reports of people calling in to ask a question and getting a snotty answer on purpose," Washington said. "Or they'll say, 'You don't like it? The mayor did it. You elected him.' And hang up. Or some inspector will harass someone and say it's on order of the mayor."

There were reports of worker slowdowns among city crews from the Streets and Sanitation yards working in white communities. Supposedly they were telling people that, under Washington, city services in that part of the city had gone to hell. There was also the suspicion among Washington partisans that special services such as bulk garbage collection lagged because out in the white wards city employees saw ousting Washington as their primary task.

Rob Mier, Bill Ware, and William Spicer, the new head of Purchasing, were at breakfast one day discussing ways to open up the department to minority and women businesses. Spicer said he was frustrated and told of the great lengths he had gone to in order to attract MBEs and WBEs to handle road resurfacing. In the past, City Hall broke the city into three areas; each of the three traditional contractors was a well-established white-owned company. So Spicer broke the city into dozens of sectors to allow smaller companies to enter the bidding. He went one step further by assembling a list of MBEs and WBEs who he figured would be able to handle the work and then sent a letter to each. He was dumbfounded when not a single one sent in a bid.

Mier asked him, "Who sent the letter?" The question didn't dawn on a relative newcomer like Spicer, yet it was the first thing that popped into Mier's head. Spicer shrugged. "Whoever does the mailing in my department." The way Mier told the story, he could see the shock of recognition on Spicer's face.

In the scorecard, "who's ahead, who's behind" journalism that substitutes for political analysis in the U.S. media, Vrdolyak was leading comfortably as the first half of Washington's term came to an end. "If Chicago's 'Council Wars' can be viewed as a political wrestling match," a *Tribune* political reporter wrote late in 1984, "the titleholder, Mayor Harold Washington, is being badly outpointed in the middle period by quicker and more agile opponents." This same reporter wrote one month later, "Nearly two years into his term, Washington is in trouble. As the city budget fight showed, his political instincts are slow and questionable. Time and time again he has been routed by shrewder and more calculating foes."

Even the mayor's staunchest allies were beginning to express their doubts. Things were moving more slowly than anyone expected. Even Washington admitted as much. "I'd say we've pretty much been kept on our heels for the first two years," Washington told one interviewer. Maybe the chaotic campaign of 1983 *was,* as the pundits had said, a symptom of more endemic problems. It seemed in the winter of 1985 as if there were two groups within Washington's coalition: those who were disenchanted and those worrying about a spreading disenchantment. Vrdolyak may have been a rascal, but maybe he also had a point: perhaps Harold Washington was in over his head.

The big news in February 1985 was that a conversation between the mayor and a political functionary had been bugged and that during their talk he had said some unflattering things about an ally named Dorothy Tillman. The news leaked out that the *Tribune,* which obtained a copy of the tape, would print excerpts the next morning. Excitable anchors reported on the latest controversy at City Hall. "Dorothy is not a likable person," Washington was caught saying, ". . . she's abrasive and crude and insecure . . ." Reporters shook their heads over an anonymous deputy foreman from the city's sewer department who had hidden a tape recorder in his jacket and caught Washington off-guard. It seemed the administration was going to have to endure yet another public relations thrashing.

Compounding potential disaster was that the story broke on Al Miller's first day on the job as press secretary. Miller had managed a dance company in Washington, D.C.; he had no formal political experience. Told he would be granted an interview, he purchased several books to see what he might glean about being a press secretary. Even Miller figured he stood no chance at the job.

When a *Tribune* reporter broke the news to Washington to allow him a comment, no one thought to inform Miller that a potential PR disaster was upon them. He learned that the administration had held a press conference by watching the ten o'clock news that evening. Miller thought of calling Washington at home but realized he didn't have the number.

Dorothy Tillman was the favorite in a special election being held in the Third Ward to name a replacement for Tyrone Kenner, who had been sentenced to jail. Only the year before, Tillman had been elected the ward's Democratic committeewoman with sixty-four percent of the vote. She was the ward's acting alderwoman, appointed to the post by Washington. With his support she was certain to win.

Yet Washington saw significance in the Tillman race and was certain the media would judge her vote totals as a midterm test of his standing within the black community. Polls were showing his support slipping, and he sought to stem speculation that his popularity was waning in the black community. The most serious challenger was a sewer department employee named James Burrell who was trying to put together Kenner's old organization. Washington invited Burrell to his apartment one Sunday morning to convince him to drop out of the race.

Later, with reporters crowded around him to record his every word, Burrell said it was Kenner who suggested he protect himself by secretly taping his conversation with Washington. Who knew what threats Washington would use to strong-arm him out of the race. The word in the City Hall press room was that Burrell gave the tape to Kenner and that Kenner, in debt to Vrdolyak for having underwritten his legal defense costs, slipped the tape to the Vrdolyak camp. Several weeks later the tape ended up in the hands of a friendly gossip columnist at the *Tribune*.

Al Miller drove to Washington's apartment the morning the *Tribune* story appeared. He expected to find some kind of council of war deep in discussion; instead he found only Washington, in the last stages of getting dressed. Washington grinned while knotting his tie, shook his head, and said, "Ain't this a bitch." The mayor tried stretching his memory to recall what he might have said to Burrell, with little success. "You know how it is," he said. "You're talking all up and down the wall, it's all bullshit, but you put it in print, and it looks like a goddamn indictment."

Washington's strategy was to ignore whatever he might have said to Burrell and instead stress the incredible fact that his conversation had been surreptitiously recorded. (The taping of a conversation without permission, Montgomery reminded a gathering of reporters, is a felony in Illinois.) The

Washington forces also sought to tie Vrdolyak's name to the incident by mentioning his name at every opportunity. On this morning the usually dubious press corps did not roll their eyes when Montgomery referred to the controversy as "Vrdolygate." In fact, the term appeared in bold letters on page one of the *Sun-Times*. Someone had the foresight to arrange it so that Tillman and Washington walked into the City Council side by side, all smiles in a picture that belied any talk of discord. The administration was learning about spin control.

The *Tribune* provided an invaluable assist when it revealed that its source for the tape was a "Vrdolyak associate." Probably the Vrdolyak brain trust figured on nothing more than a few squibs aimed at sowing a bit of dissension inside Washington's political family. Certainly there was never to be any mention of a secret tape. But the *Tribune's* editor commandeered the story, placing the news of the bugging on page one. The following day the *Tribune* ran a four-page transcript of the entire conversation. Nothing Washington said, it turned out, was as bad as first reported—a fact the *Sun-Times* was more than happy to point out.

The story lasted several more days, by which time there was little left to say except how badly the trick had backfired on the Vrdolyak camp. Tillman overwhelmingly won her election, inspiring several columns about Washington's immense popularity among black voters. It constantly amazed Washington partisans that Vrdolyak was seen as deft and clever rather than something between sleazy and fiendish. Perhaps the bugging incident would prove a turning point in his public image. If nothing else, there was now talk that Vrdolyak and his minions weren't infallible. "The Vrdolyakers," *Sun-Times* columnist Basil Talbott, Jr., wrote in the wake of the bugging incident, "have caught a case of infectious ineptitude from the Washingtonians."

No one could mention the Burrell tape to Washington without a frown immediately appearing on his face, even months after the fact. Yet the tape came to be regarded as a landmark in the media's estimation of Washington. The mayor tried flattering Burrell out of the race. He appealed to his sense of black solidarity, and he dangled the possibility that he would support him for some future office, but he didn't come down on Burrell with the power he could have as mayor. Several times Burrell pushed Washington to spell out what would happen should he not drop out of the race. "Nothing nasty," Washington said. "I got no problem with you." When Burrell again pressed the point, Washington grew testy. "You asked me if I'm going after you," he said. "The answer is no."

"How sweet can you get?" a *Tribune* editorial asked. "The mayor couldn't have handled it better if he had seen the tape recorder peeping out." Al Miller would point out that Washington even corrected himself once when he said "girls" rather than "women." The tape was a perfect chance to examine Washington with his guard down, and the worst thing revealed was that he was a mayor who swore a lot.

From Washington's standpoint, about the only down side to the affair was the media attention paid Dorothy Tillman. Tillman could be an imposing presence. She was a big-boned woman with large angular features and partial to wide-brimmed hats. Her brown almond-shaped eyes burned with intensity. She was the sort who would as soon knock down a door as use the knob. Her trademark pose showed her jutting her jaw defiantly forward.

Tillman first drew citywide attention when in 1981 she and a small group of parents occupied the principal's office in the school that three of her five children attended. She was protesting low achievement scores, she said, and a white principal she believed to be unconcerned and "racist." Tillman was again in the news in the summer of 1982 when the black community was waging its war with Jane Byrne. If white Chicagoans were polled on the local black leader they most loved to despise, Tillman would give Lu Palmer and Jesse Jackson a run for their money.

Tillman was of a world far from Chicago. She was born in Montgomery, Alabama, where her parents were heavily involved, she said, in the Montgomery bus boycotts led by Rosa Parks. She recalled talk of an uncle who had been lynched. In high school she periodically pulled the school fire alarm and then marched students downtown for a civil rights rally. At the end of her senior year, she said, her school principal placed her diploma in an ashtray and, as she sat watching, set it aflame with a cigar. Within the year Tillman was among those who were part of the entourage that traveled north to make preparations for King's arrival in Chicago. "Seeing how bad things were, how could I leave?" she asked.

Washington waited more than six months before choosing Tillman as the Third Ward's acting alderwoman. In the end he felt he had little choice.

He said as much to Burrell: "Look at the situation. She represents a coterie of activist people not just in the Third Ward. . . . And that group had been helpful to me."

To Ed Burke, Tillman was a travesty. He would jump out a window, he claimed, before voting for her confirmation in the council. He expressed his disgust when his staff discovered that a part-time worker on Tillman's staff was an ex-con (sentenced ten years earlier to three years for armed robbery), and that three others had outstanding warrants for their arrest.

Perhaps, then, there was an up side to the inadvertent broadcast of Washington's criticisms of Tillman. The *Tribune* editorial board, for instance, found "something reassuring" in Washington's "astute assessments."

The 29's media backfire could not have come at a worse time for them. With the midterm approaching, the media would weigh in with their half-time assessments of Washington. The midterm provided a chance to recap the crèche fiasco and again pay disproportionate attention to appointees such as Clarence McClain. But suddenly media accounts cast Washington ahead of Vrdolyak in the all-important battle for momentum. The same *Tribune* reporter who three months earlier wrote that a flat-footed Washington was being badly outpointed by Vrdolyak, offered in his midterm review that the mayor's "City Council opposition appears to be in retreat," while Washington "is on a roll."

The media's reviews did not glow, but neither were they dour accounts of an administration stuck in neutral. Reporters at least for the moment paused to look at the dry realm of government—what the *Tribune* called "numerous unheralded achievements . . . within the largely unseen bureaucracy." Washington was credited with cutting the payroll by twelve hundred jobs, saving millions through innovative money-borrowing techniques, and installing a "cadre of respected professionals" to run the government. "Washington has made some stupid mistakes," Don Rose wrote in the *Reader,* "but in context they seem almost frivolous compared to the things Ed Vrdolyak does every day of his life, on purpose, as a matter of policy, and as a perfect expression of everything he stands for."

The press could point to cases such as David Canter's, who went back twenty years with Washington. Canter was a lawyer out of work in 1984.

Washington, Canter admitted, "rescued me"—rescued him with a one-year contract worth $37,000 to study the city's deployment of trucks. Canter knew nothing about the topic, nor was he trained to serve as a deputy commissioner in Streets and Sanitation, where Washington placed him when his contract ran out. The joke inside the administration, though, was that Canter would do no harm there; with all the political tasks he performed on Washington's behalf, he would have no time to cause problems at work.

Yet the media seemed generally impressed with the lack of cronyism inside Washington's government. "To a remarkable degree," *Chicago* magazine reported, "he keeps politics out of appointments and contracts." Business executives said in interviews that negotiations with the city tended to go more slowly, but at the same time they were fairer and generally more professional. Though it was not necessarily viewed as progress, Washington was also credited with funneling more city money into the neighborhoods. Prior to Washington the city devoted just twenty-five percent of its housing budget to low- and moderate-income housing, according to the *Tribune*. In two years the Washington administration was devoting nearly three-quarters of its housing budget to affordable housing. By midterm the city had added hundreds of beds for the homeless. In his first full fiscal year in office, Washington shifted $14 million in federal community development block grants from administrative salaries to community groups and social service agencies.

Still, despite the generally positive reviews, the era of Old Man Daley and absolute power loomed over Washington. "Maybe we've asked Harold Washington to do the impossible," *Chicago's* editor offered by way of introduction to his magazine's midterm assessment. "We expected him—a reformer opposed to the old patronage network—to run the city the way Mayor Daley did, at a time when no mayor can possibly have the kind of power Daley had."*

Dissension thrived among Vrdolyak's council allies. Once friendly strategy sessions at which General Vrdolyak gave the troops their orders, the 29's

---

*One urban consultant displayed more cleverness than insight when he diagnosed the Council Wars as a case of a city that still had not gotten over the loss of its father.

caucuses grew increasingly boisterous. There were the hardliners who, if anything, thought Vrdolyak too soft in his dealings with Washington, and then there were those who believed Vrdolyak too heavy-handed and intransigent.

Bernard Hansen and Patrick O'Connor were among those fed up with the hawkish ways of their allies. "You heard it every time we discussed a proposal," O'Connor said. "'We can't pass this. If we do, it would make Harold Washington look good.'" The problem, both O'Connor and Hansen said, was that the hawks outnumbered the doves. Another problem was that both were first-term aldermen.

Hansen said that the title of "staunchest foe" was a tie between the Twelfth Ward's Aloysius Majerczyk and John Madrzyk of the Thirteenth. Alderman Richard Mell, who placed himself among the hardliners, also singled out Madrzyk and Majerczyk, though he also added Alderman Bernard Stone. Madrzyk was most vocal in his dislike of Washington, but Majerczyk was the most aggressive in pursuit of strategies aimed at undermining Washington at every turn. Of Majerczyk, Hansen said, "If Harold Washington took a step, he was against it." Asked to provide an example or two, Hansen simply replied, "Everything."

Certainly the number two man, Ed Burke, was no tempering influence. "If it was up to him, Eddie Burke wouldn't have given Harold the time of day," said one alderman. "Vrdolyak was a hawk, but he was at least concerned every once in a while with our public image."

Yet both Hansen and O'Connor were as committed as the next man to Washington's defeat. Their beef was reduced to strategy. Vrdolyak was waging an overt war of obstruction when nearly the same results could be accomplished through covert action. Searching out waste and corruption was one way. It may have been hypocritical, but it was a valid and defensible stance nonetheless, and an effective means of gaining support. Refusing to consider the so-called hostage appointments was another thing entirely. Why not instead haul the likes of the Reverend Al Sampson before the council so that the city could hear from this outspoken black nationalist whom Washington chose for the board overseeing the city colleges?

Vrdolyak and most loyal minions did not finesse a point when they could hammer it home. The 29 did not just simply draw attention to this self-proclaimed reform mayor failing to file an ethics statement on time ("And once again," one could hear Burke say, "we see an administration unable to handle even the most basic functions of governance . . ."). Instead they declared that Washington was no longer mayor. For months the council refused to consider Washington's appointment of William Spicer to head the Purchasing Department. When a year later Washington withdrew the nomination, the majority immediately confirmed Spicer—with Spicer's consent. The editorialists slammed the 29 for their mischief.

Vrdolyak seemed entirely of the moment, incapable of grasping the big picture. Bernie Hansen recalled the day Vrdolyak excitedly told the caucus of a tip that Clarence McClain had a criminal past. Let McClain operate for a while, several aldermen argued; let him involve Washington in some deals that reflect poorly on the mayor, then reveal his police record as the pièce de résistance a few days later. "You should have seen the two of them," Hansen said of Vrdolyak and Burke. "As soon as they left that room, they were all over each other fighting to get to a phone." That day the *Tribune* was tipped off to McClain's record.

Yet, except for the occasional off-the-record comment, the 29 maintained a united front. Creating a third faction was something that neither O'Connor nor Hansen ever stopped to contemplate seriously. "It would've killed any of us politically to jump around from faction to faction," O'Connor said. "We already alienated those siding with Washington, and we would've committed political suicide siding with those we endeared ourselves with by siding with Eddie." The realities of racial politics back in the ward, he said, trapped them inside the 29.

Vrdolyak understood that he needed to tend to his image, so late in 1984 he downplayed his street-fighter style, and Joe Novak spread the word that his boss was thinking of running for mayor. He was now an earnest public servant, conciliatory and statesmanlike. He turned the other cheek when attacked; he remained above the fray. During council debate Tillman once likened Vrdolyak to Satan himself. Vrdolyak responded, "We are all God's children, and I love you."

After the midterm, Vrdolyak began talking of Council Wars as a matter of ideology, not race. He donned a white tuxedo and gave a speech in which he laid out his prescription for all that ailed the national Democratic party. He spoke of a party "more concerned about victims than criminals." He denounced racial quotas and joined a chorus of national Democratic leaders calling for an end to the caucuses representing minorities, women, and others. His message didn't differ much from the right-wing populism of Reagan, whose fabled "welfare queen" supposedly lived in Chicago with her "eighty names, thirty addresses, twelve Social Security cards . . . and a tax-free income over $150,000." Vrdolyak came out against abortion, in favor of prayer in the school, and spoke of assigning police to classrooms in rough neighborhoods. He called for drug testing among students. Copies of his speech were sent to national commentators. His people were trying to promote him as a national voice for the disaffected white ethnic voter.

Maybe Vrdolyak's new outlook was nothing more than a politician seeing an opportunity in the wake of Walter Mondale's crushing defeat in 1984. Yet, though Vrdolyak was never an ideologue, he had during his career revealed a wide conservative streak. In 1979 he was among those leading the fight against a gay rights resolution aimed at adding the words "sexual orientation" to the city's civil rights codes. This legislation, he said, "is against God, against nature, and against family." In 1972, the year of George McGovern, Vrdolyak said in an interview with his friend Robert Seltzner, editor of the Daily Calumet, "The kooks took it over. . . . Today they're trying to put in a plank to cover homosexuals. I'm a Democrat, but I am going to do some very serious soul-searching."

Whatever his motivations, Vrdolyak spoke a truth about Chicago politics when he said the city only mirrored the philosophical battle dividing the party nationally. The Reagan Democrats on the city's southwest side were not much different from their counterparts in New York or Boston, or white moderates throughout the South. The two sides in the Council Wars were split along the same fault line that divided the national Democratic party. On the one side were the blacks, on the other the more conservative-minded white ethnics, with other minorities and liberals somewhere between the two. Council Wars were merely more candid versions of the same fights—except, of course, that those on the outs in the national Democratic party were those in power in Chicago. "If the South has become all but lost to the Democratic party in national elections," Thomas Byrne Edsall wrote in the New York Review of Books, "Chicago has become the battleground for the party's northern soul."

For years Vrdolyak personified the Chicago machine. He was an outspoken opponent of the kind of reforms the lakefront aldermen pushed with little success. He advanced a line that would have put him in good stead among those in the conservative wing of the Republican party. Yet Vrdolyak, a smart politician, didn't write off the lakefront.

Vrdolyak had a valuable ally along the lakefront in Bill Singer, the man who in the 1970s came to symbolize the city's antimachine movement. After he was defeated for mayor in 1975, Singer cut his deals with the machine, but it wasn't until 1985 that he began describing himself as a top Vrdolyak adviser. "A good friend," he said of Vrdolyak.

Singer was no longer a chubby-faced idealist named "Billy" running against Daley for mayor. In the interim he had divorced his wife, taken up jogging, lost forty pounds, and accepted a six-figure position with a major downtown law firm, Kirkland & Ellis. He wintered in Colorado resort towns and began collecting Native American artifacts during trips to Santa Fe. He claimed he hadn't changed, the world around him had, as if he were like a cynical character reading lines from *The Big Chill*.

The Vrdolyak-Singer relationship would dissolve by late 1986 when Singer began speaking of himself as a potential mayoral candidate, but in 1985, Singer needed Vrdolyak's pull in the council. His political connections and his abilities as a lobbyist were critical to Kirkland & Ellis. Though he tried through liberal emissaries to tie himself to Washington, the mayor would have nothing to do with him. Vrdolyak, then, would be his point person in government.

Once Singer approached Vrdolyak about helping a client that manufactured smoke alarms. Singer drafted the bill, and Vrdolyak introduced it into the council. Reportedly, Singer balked when Vrdolyak suggested that a black alderman named Perry Hutchinson introduce the ordinance. "You mean you told your client that Vrdolyak himself would introduce it?" Vrdolyak was quoted as saying. The ordinance, had it passed as initially written, would have proven quite a windfall because the technicalities spelled out in the ordinance favored the alarm manufactured by Singer's client. Smoke alarms save people's lives, Singer said in his own defense.

The white middle-class audience that gathered in a gymnasium at the exclusive Lincoln Park private school was representative of the lakefront voters who might swing the election in 1987. You don't really know Ed, Bill Singer said when introducing Vrdolyak. He's reasonable, a graduate of the University of Chicago Law School, and a real family man who cares for

320

all Chicago. A political reporter named Ben Joravsky, there to write about the event for the *Reader,* couldn't quite believe Singer's "obsequious" reaction when Vrdolyak had entered the room. He said Singer jumped up upon seeing Vrdolyak and said: "Ed, Ed, do you need help with your coat?"

Vrdolyak understood his audience. While in the council, Vrdolyak was pure James Cagney, Joravsky wrote, before this group he was something closer to Jimmy Stewart. "An administration trying to do the best that it can," Vrdolyak said of Washington's government. And later: "It took Daley three years to solidify. In the first term you're still trying to learn the names of the players."

The crowd, at first polite but uncertain, seemed impressed. The man standing before them did not seem the kind whose associates slip a bugged conversation to the *Tribune.* "Eddie Vrdolyak may be a son of a bitch, but he's a roll-up-your-sleeves kind of guy who'll make these trains run on time," a big-bellied man said to his wife and anyone else who might be listening. "He's wonderful," a middle-aged woman said to her neighbor as the crowd bathed Vrdolyak with warm applause.

The midterm media polls generally brought good tidings for Washington, yet there was also the discouraging news that Washington was making little progress along the lakefront. One poll showed that Washington's approval rating among northwest siders was thirty-five percent, yet only thirty-four percent among north lakefront residents. Asked to choose between Washington and Vrdolyak, most lakefront voters indicated no preference. More than a few liberal voters were inclined to agree with Ed Burke, who explained the 29–21 stalemate as an attempt by Washington to "distract attention from his utter lack of accomplishments." Vrdolyak might not be winning new supporters himself, but it looked as if his heavy-handed opposition might just lead to Washington's defeat nonetheless.

In 1987, Edwin Eisendrath III would win election as the new alderman of the Forty-third Ward, following in the footsteps of Bill Singer and Marty Oberman. In 1985, though, he was only another ambitious Lincoln Park resident who believed Chicago couldn't afford another four years of Washington. He didn't need to bother with focus groups to test the efficacy of a campaign based on an anti–Council Wars platform. He understood instinctively that it would be a winner in his ward.

Eisendrath looked on Council Wars with the mien of a disapproving aunt. Little Eddie said Harold started it, and Little Harold pointed his finger at Eddie, yet all this kindly aunt saw was the mess that the two of them had made. "Harold's so preoccupied with Eddie and this black–white fight that he's ignoring the real issues of vital importance to Chicago," Eisendrath said. Lines like these played well among voters.

Eisendrath was someone who looked on himself as a liberal on issues having to do with race, yet he sympathized more with Vrdolyak. Washington, he said, was "a master at playing the politics of hate." Washington had said, "Vrdolyak must go, or black people can't support the party." It was lines like these, Eisendrath said, that caused him to believe Washington was appealing only to the black community. To him, Washington "created Vrdolyak as his enemy and then gave him every evil characteristic possible. . . .

"That's the last thing Chicago needed: some politician playing the race card because it was easier to run against this bogeyman than to push for a reasonable agenda."[*]

CITY FACTIONS SWAP JABS, read a *Sun-Times* headline that could have run any of a hundred other days. MAYOR STALLS MCCORMICK LOAN; MAJORITY BLOCKS PATROL DEAL. The Council Wars casualty list included a $300 million project to rehabilitate the city's Navy Pier in the style of Boston's Faneuil Hall. The 29 killed that project, flushing away the nearly $1 million already invested, but what difference did it make whose fault it was? The city was suffering. The general sentiment along the north lakefront was that Washington needed to compromise.

Eisendrath, Singer, and countless other white lakefront voters gravely pondered the city's reputation in light of the Vrdolyak–Washington fight. There was the occasional feature piece decrying the decline of Chicago's reputation. OTHER CITIES BENEFIT FROM COUNCIL WARS, read a headline

---

[*]"It annoys me to hear white liberals say that Washington is, well, you know, kind of racist himself," a writer named Thomas Geoghegan wrote in a cover story about Chicago in *The New Republic* ("America's Greatest City"). "They feel that if Washington were really such a great liberal reformer, he would turn the city over to them to run. White liberals feel somewhat irrelevant. All they can do is sit on the sidelines and sniff that Washington and Vrdolyak are on the same level, and that both succeed only by making appeal to their racial constituencies."

over a *Sun-Times* piece quoting prominent business people and urbanologists. CHICAGO'S STATUS ON THE SKIDS AS CITY THAT WORKED, read a headline over a similar piece in the *Tribune*. Washington's angry pout on national television at the 1984 Democratic convention; the BEIRUT ON THE LAKE headline on the *Wall Street Journal*'s front page; the countless articles in the national press depicting a city out of control. Even some of those sympathetic to Washington questioned the advisability of supporting him. The garbage was being picked up; there was no appreciable rise or fall in the crime rate; yet maybe the city would be better off without Washington, no matter how well intentioned he was. How else to put an end to the Council Wars wracking Chicago?

Hearing this argument, one white Washington supporter, a man who much preferred the label "progressive" to "liberal," likened these erstwhile machine foes to the Jews with Moses who preferred the familiarity of the Pharaohs to the uncertainty of a future in the Promised Land. In a speech before the city's Executive Club, Washington chose a different analogy to make the same point: "They said, 'Bell that cat.' And I said, 'All right. Got the bell. Got the mandate. There's the cat.' And so I crept up behind this cat, and the closer I got to this cat, the more it meowed and screamed and kicked and clawed. And as I put this bell around that cat's neck, the people who asked me to bell it said, 'Don't do that, the cat's making too much noise. Back up. The cat's keeping us awake.'"

Lu Palmer was so upset with Harold Washington by the midterm that he even began making himself available to white journalists. He wasn't impressed by some set-aside program that would benefit a few black businessmen, nor did he think the black masses would put much stock in that change. The argument was as old as it was relevant: Was it more important to push for more black MBAs or fix the lousy ghetto schools crippling black youth? Did it make a difference that there was a greater black presence in the city's health department when the black infant mortality rate was still more than fifty percent higher than it was for white babies? Where were the tangible gains in areas like Health and the Chicago Housing Authority?

In 1984 a black man named Roland Burris entered the Democratic primary in a bid to become one of Illinois's two U.S. senators. To Washington, Burris was a competent manager ideally suited to the post he held as state comptroller, but he didn't think much of his political skills or his moderate politics. Washington instead endorsed Paul Simon, whose politics more closely matched his own. Palmer was incredulous. There wasn't a single black in the U.S. Senate, yet Washington endorsed some white liberal over a serious black contender.

In the bugged conversation between Washington and James Burrell, Washington said of Tillman, "She comes out of that active black nationalist group."

Burrell: "She's a racist."

Washington: "Shit, most of them are."

Never the sort for quietly nursing his disappointments, Palmer expressed his criticisms over the airwaves. He told blacks that they were growing restless with Washington. "If the election were held tomorrow," Palmer told a white journalist with the Chicago *Reader*, "Harold would be hard pressed to get a sixty-five percent turnout. There would not be the same crusade happening today that you saw in 1983."

Most of Palmer's cohorts, however, believed Palmer had fallen terribly out of touch. "You walk up and down 47th Street," said one, "and you got dope fiends and wine heads and prostitutes and folk hanging on the corner discussing the damn city budget or who was appointed to sit on some board. That's the level of politicalization we're talking about." Bob Starks, co-chair of the Task Force for Black Political Empowerment, offered that "you can't underestimate the impact of street sweepers and snowplows cleaning the side streets in the black community. That was something that people had never seen before Harold." Some, including Washington, blamed Palmer's anger on his wife Jorja. Jorja Palmer, Washington believed, was the bee in Lu Palmer's bonnet.

Palmer was convinced that Washington was responsible for the building code citations he and his wife were hit with after he publicly broke with Washington. The building—the coach house behind the Palmers' home where countless voter education meetings were held in preparation for 1983—was technically owned by "Jorja English," her name by a previous marriage. Yet all the citations were sent to Lu and Jorja Palmer, not to Jorja English.

Palmer was also convinced that Washington intervened when a black-owned radio station was on the verge of hiring him as one of its regular talk show hosts. Everything seemed all set, he said, until several sponsors backed out at the last minute. He had no proof that Washington had anything to do with it, only suspicions, but when in 1985 Palmer was searching for the perfect term to describe Washington, he settled on the word *diabolical*. Washington was, Palmer came to believe, a vindictive man who retaliated against him in the fashion of an old-style political boss.

It got to the point that if Palmer knew Washington would be at a banquet, he refused to attend. He didn't want to place himself in a position where he had to stand and applaud him. Yet Palmer found himself increasingly isolated within the black community. The same radio listeners who in the past hung on his every word called in to dismiss his criticisms as nothing but sour grapes over the congressional race. To Palmer, black people were not able to hear the truth about their precious Harold: "No one else would criticize Harold because he was considered God in the black community. And no one wants to hear someone criticize God."

The midterm was a chance for Washington to take stock. The mayor told his staff the time had come for taking risks. Byrne holdovers running departments like Streets and Sanitation were replaced. He encouraged city managers to rid their respective departments of disloyal deputies. We can't operate government in fear of Shakman lawsuits, he said. Washington also invited his cabinet to a retreat near O'Hare Airport to lecture them on reform. We've made progress in areas of "structural reform," he said, changes essential to a smooth-running city government. But equally important were what he called "social reforms"—reforms based on a fairer redistribution of the city's resources.

Bill Ware's death may have represented the most significant change inside government. At the end of 1984, Ware was in and out of the hospital hoping that doctors would make sense of the strange disorder that seemed to be killing him. In May 1985 his doctor announced that Ware, thirty-seven, died of a rare pulmonary infection. Washington was broken up by the death of a man who was described inside the administration as something of a son to Washington, yet the mayor was also said to be surprised when he learned that his top aide died of AIDS. Among Washington's top aides, Ware's homosexuality was an accepted fact, yet it seemed to say a great deal about Washington that he enjoyed a close working relationship with Ware for years without knowing the first thing about him personally.

In Ware's absence, Jim Montgomery emerged as the de facto number-two man in government.

Joe Gardner, Washington's political director, marveled at his boss's patience. "He accepted losses early on in the game with no sense of panic," Gardner said. "He realized, unlike the rest of us, that this was a four-year battle and not something that could be won through a few quick moves." Near the midterm people around Washington began talking of the mayor's skill at chess, offered as a metaphor for their growing appreciation of his political skill as a politician. Before becoming mayor he played the game for hours at a time; supposedly he was a genius-level player.

The administration followed up the bugging incident with a string of victories, including passage of the bond measure aimed at dealing with the city's crumbling infrastructure that had languished for months in committee. The media scheme the Washington brain trust devised to sell the bond seemed until then beyond their capabilities. The mayor visited southwest and northwest side wards to speak with residents about the proposal. He laid out for them the projects slated for their wards and then threw in the kicker: it would cost the average homeowner only an extra $12 in property taxes a year. With the mini-cams rolling and pens scribbling, the residents said it sounded like a great idea. Each ward's alderman, invited along for the visit, hemmed and hawed and then endorsed the proposal.

Ed Burke had said in 1984 that he was against the $95 million bond proposal because it was too great a burden on the homeowner. But after Washington successfully wooed the support of several of Burke's allies, Burke sent out a press release announcing his support for a bond measure that had been upped to $180 million so as to satisfy the demands of aldermen on both sides of the political fight. Inside the administration they had a good laugh over that one, even if the press didn't pick up on it. There was a great deal of laughter in the latter part of 1985; momentum, at least for the time being, was on their side.

18

THE CONTINUING SAGA OF CLARENCE McCLAIN

And like that, the momentum shifted again. Late in 1985 the city learned that several black aldermen and a Washington appointee were videotaped accepting money from an FBI informant who was posing as a businessman. Then within the week it came out that the FBI's link to City Hall was Clarence McClain. With Washington's bid for reelection barely a year away, McClain, the official whom Washington had banned from government after it was discovered that he was convicted on a pimping charge in 1967, was again dominating the news.

The years following his expulsion from City Hall were not good ones for McClain. He stayed on Washington's political payroll for a few months, helping Washington set up a citywide political operation apart from the regular Democratic party, then quit to make a run for Democratic ward committeeman in the Sixteenth Ward. McClain lived in the Fifth Ward—it was a celebrated fact within political circles that he lived in the same Hyde Park building as Washington—and his name recognition wasn't the kind an aspiring newcomer covets, yet somehow he convinced himself he stood a chance at victory. He asked for Washington's endorsement, but Washington refused. Even James Taylor, the former Byrne aide who said he was only "bull-jiving" when he asked two businesswomen to bed with him in exchange for a liquor license, received more votes than McClain. Thereafter, McClain mostly tended to his wounds.

McClain didn't quite know what to do with himself. He was cut off from politics, his world for the previous ten years, and also from his social circle, for he was a workaholic who did little with his life outside work. Washington's victory in 1983, McClain said, "was the major achievement of my life."

Suddenly idle, he gained thirty pounds. Old associates worried about his drinking, especially after he was arrested for driving under the influence. He spoke incessantly—and at times incoherently—about the newcomers to Washington's inner circle who were suddenly occupying his prized spot as a trusted top aide. He focused much of his enmity on his old rival Bill Ware who had gotten stuck with the chore of informing McClain that he was out. Those on the other end of the phone tried to explain that Ware wouldn't have fired him without Washington's say-so, but McClain didn't believe them. "I was too valuable," he said.

There had been no one more important to Washington than him—so, at least, McClain believed. "If you want to get a guy, there are usually two places to go," he explained in one interview long after he left City Hall. "His wife or his mother. Harold didn't have any of the two of them. So where to go? Let's go get McClain. McClain is the cog that makes the political machinery work, McClain is the nuts-and-bolts man." The way McClain saw it, the mayor's foes didn't go after him to harm Washington's reputation but to eliminate Washington's number-two man.

McClain had spent only two months in government, but he invented for himself a glorious and extraordinary tenure. He told of the time Washington introduced him at a meeting of the Washington 21. This is the man to see with your complaints, Washington told them. "They stood up and for ten minutes clapped in harmony, bar none," McClain boasted. Several aldermen remembered the meeting. They recalled McClain but no standing ovation. "Maybe there were a few seconds of polite applause," one offered.

Looking to put his life back together, McClain sought a business that took advantage of his political know-how. He decided he would help fledgling minority-owned businesses get a leg up through the city's affirmative action program. "Should I have gone back to being a tool-and-die maker?" McClain asked. "Should I have gone back to being a janitor? A bus driver? Should I have wasted all this experience and my vast knowledge?" With an eye on the pot of available affirmative action money, he also considered starting up business ventures of his own.

McClain recognized what the downtown media would say, that they'd look suspiciously on his activities. But which was more important, he asked, something the press might write or helping "a small black-owned business find its way." In late 1984 he set up his own business as a consultant.

McClain was soon bragging about all the money he was making—$140,000 in 1985 alone, he told one reporter. It was remarkable, he commented, how quickly his enterprise had gotten off the ground. People paid handsomely for his assistance in performing the simplest of chores. He packaged himself as a well-connected man. "I'm the mayor's close friend," he told potential prospects. Yet in interviews McClain said that it was a client's problem if she thought he would provide anything more than basic technical assistance for her money.

There was something familiar in a figure like McClain popping up in the shadows around town, presenting himself as the one to see at City Hall. It was a story as old as machine politics. A potential contractor hires the clout-heavy insider for his "expertise." The businessman secures his contract; in appreciation he throws some money to the mayor's political fund. Maybe it was like the Vrdolyakers said: black reform is really nothing more than replacing a Charles Swibel with a Clarence McClain.

MAYOR'S FRIEND SEEKS CITY MINORITY CONTRACTS, the *Tribune* reported on its front page in the fall of 1985. Headlines like these were beginning to appear regularly in the Chicago press. "McClout," Mike Royko dubbed McClain.

Yet there was something inherently circular to the McClain story. McClain's claims of influence would appear in one gossip column or another (". . . a tipster told us that McClain indicated in corridor chats that he wielded considerable influence in Chicago parking matters"). In turn, Vrdolyak, Burke, and others spoke of McClain's clout at every opportunity. They made much of the fact that McClain and Washington lived in the same building.

After a time reporters took as a given that McClain was a key influence inside Washington's government. This man who was no businessman at all—his business track record until the mid-1980s was a series of failed ventures—was described in the *Tribune* as one of the "most politically influential black businessmen in Chicago." One potential McClain business venture, the *Tribune* reported, "appeared to have all the necessary ingredients for success": ingredient number one, the article stated, was "McClain's political connections." He was "Washington's Pal" in headlines. Eventually both dailies described McClain as "one of Washington's closest friends."

People came to treat McClain as someone influential whether his claims were true or just empty crowing. Business was so good, McClain said, he was turning down more opportunities than he accepted. He was invited to join a support group of black business people. "If you want to assure that your message gets to the right ears," one participant remarked, "you have got to ask yourself, would you rather have him [McClain] there or not?" Several white-owned companies also sought out his assistance, dangling attractive deals before him. McClain had next to no business experience, yet a white steel executive sought him out as a partner in a joint steel supply venture.

Within one week of each other, the *Tribune* and the *Sun-Times* marked McClain's return to the news pages with lengthy McClain profiles. The *Tribune's* ran on a Sunday under the headline MEET SLICK CLARENCE MCCLAIN: "I'M THE MAYOR'S FRIEND." "I know who to talk to and how to talk to them," McClain explained. "That's what I do best. That's one reason I'm the mayor's friend." The *Sun-Times* profile (MCCLAIN: CONFLICT, CLOUT, CONTRADICTION) opened this way: "Street smart and calculating, manipulative and ambitious, he is considered one of the most influential blacks in Chicago's political backrooms." In *Lords of the Last Machine,* a book co-written with his wife Lori, Bill Granger, a *Tribune* columnist, summed up Washington's 1983 victory this way: "This singular man whose best friend at the time was Clarence McClain, a convicted pimp whom he made his legislative assistant, was the great hope of the black community." It had all gotten terribly out of hand.

There was a time when Washington felt only sympathy for McClain. "A man striving for legitimacy his entire adult life," Washington said of him, "who attained a certain high level until his past caught up with him." For a precious few months McClain was at the center of a political movement that stood as the envy of black activists around the country until his police record was revealed. For a crime committed almost twenty years earlier, McClain was hit with the worst sentence imaginable: to be rendered beside the point.

Washington confessed that he spoke periodically with McClain through much of his first two years in office. He was one of dozens whom Washington relied on to serve as his eyes and ears in the black community. When in 1984 a group of wealthy black businessmen pressured him to cut off all ties with McClain, Washington ignored them. When pressed by a white department head who didn't think much of the inarticulate McClain, Washington described him as a misunderstood "political genius." Washington found it funny, one associate said, that McClain was making money lining up white clients who believed he held the key to City Hall.

With time, though, Washington grew increasingly incensed with his old associate. Only later would McClain admit that in late 1984 the mayor let him know in no uncertain terms that he was to keep his nose out of city business. By early 1985, Washington spread the word among his top aides that McClain was persona non grata. "Mr. McClain is not involved in city business," Washington informed his revenue director in mid-1985. "Mr. McClain is not involved in politics. Mr. McClain is nonexistent. Period."

Yet Washington seemed angrier with the media than McClain. He was troubled by the presumptuousness of reporters who believed McClain was among his most intimate friends. As if these white reporters knew the first thing about his personal life. To him reporters were stupid if they assumed that anyone throwing around his name was, in fact, telling the truth. Washington's description of McClain as "a worthy adviser" was offered in media accounts as proof that McClain was some dark and evil eminence inside his administration. Yet that, too, struck Washington as ignorant. "The man had taken a shot right in the chops," Washington said. "His past had caught up with him. What am I going to do—kick his ass?"

Eventually Washington stopped offering denials that McClain served him in any capacity. Instead he stared down any reporter who pressed him on the issue. The media badgered Washington with a simple solution: say publicly and unequivocally that this man does not speak on behalf of your administration. The suggestion was offered in the form of a question ("Why don't you denounce McClain, Mr. Mayor?" one reporter or another invariably asked) and also as an accusation, as in the countless articles and television pieces pointing out that Washington still refused to denounce his controversial former aide. It seemed to say a great deal about both Washington and his relationship with the press that he didn't simply inform them he had told McClain and top administrators in no uncertain terms that McClain did not speak for him.

In mid-1985, McClain spoke with a bureaucrat frustrated with the countless delays that threatened the city's O'Hare expansion project. McClain later admitted it was the mayor's wish that he should stay clear of these kinds of conversations, but at issue, he said, was "the potential collapse of the biggest project in the history of the city." Years later in a courtroom a business associate of McClain's testified, "He indicated he was going to go ahead, that the mayor was preoccupied with so many things that he didn't know what was good for him." His boss and mentor was engaged in the political battle of his life, McClain reasoned; it was no time to abandon him.

MCCLAIN TALKS REVEALED, read the headline over a *Sun-Times* article stressing the contradiction between Washington's claims and McClain's actions.

Reporters were themselves more than a little disgusted with Washington. They were accustomed to politicians blaming them for their own bad press, yet with Washington everything seemed to boil down to race. Early in the Council Wars, Washington didn't mince words in a speech before a gathering of radio, television, and newspaper reporters: "Half the Caucasian reporters in the city don't understand who I am, where I come from, or what I'm saying." In another speech Washington said that when it came to covering women's or minority issues, reporters have "brains made of concrete, encased in steel, and submerged in water, impervious to sound."

By 1986, Mike Flannery, the Channel 2 (Chicago's CBS affiliate) reporter assigned to City Hall, had had his fill about race. He heard it in phone calls to the station after reporting a story that cast Washington in a negative light. He heard it when he was buttonholed on the street by some zealous Washington supporter: the White Press was out to get

Washington. The media's coverage of McClain seemed every partisan's prime example.

Flannery confessed to problems with the coverage of Council Wars. Despite the endless waves of words he and his colleagues spewed out, the newspapers and television crested over the issues, he conceded, like a movie so intent on showing action that it quickly passes from scene to scene. One morning over breakfast, bleary-eyed, he explained to a cohort that he had been up past 1 A.M. editing a satellite feed for that morning's network news. There had been another council blow-up the previous day. It was 1985, but it may as well have been 1983, 1984, or 1986. "New York eats this stuff up," Flannery said, adding that his network colleagues "can't ever get enough of the Harold and Eddie show." A *Sun-Times* reporter for eight years before taking a job as Channel 2's political editor, Flannery was irritated by the ambiguity in television between news and entertainment. But long ago he had made his peace with his profession. "There are alternatives for those wanting a more in-depth look at the issues," he said.

To Flannery, the media's handling of the McClain issue was nothing deeper than an aggressive press looking into signs of corruption within government. Yet Council Wars had gotten so out of hand that people spoke of "some buried need that white reporters have to find"—here Flannery spoke in a throaty whisper—"the evil black person pulling the strings."

It grated on him that the mayor's foes harped on McClain. Yet there was enough evidence to justify going on-air with their accusations. One incident that stuck in Flannery's mind was Bill Ware's reaction to McClain. The quiet and contained Ware, Flannery said, "was suddenly an entirely different person when the subject turned to McClain." There was also the way McClain introduced himself to Flannery—"I'm the mayor's new patronage chief," he said. When he heard that, Flannery reminded himself that it was at least two years before all the dirt started coming out about Byrne, another self-described reformer.

Washington's strange reaction also fed his suspicions. "Here you had the mayor insisting that McClain had no role in government when there were insiders and McClain himself saying otherwise," Flannery said.

On Christmas Eve 1985, news of the FBI's undercover sting hit the city. FBI GRILLS 3 ALDERMEN IN PAYOFF PROBE, shrieked the front page of the *Sun-Times*. $40,000 BRIBE TO McCLAIN TOLD the tabloid reported two weeks later. McClain, it turned out, had taken money from the FBI's undercover agent, introduced him to several black aldermen, and served as the middle man for a $10,000 "loan" to a city official. Flannery and his colleagues felt vindicated. Washington grew angrier still.

Among those impressed with all he was hearing about Clarence McClain was a wheeler-dealer type who went by the name of Michael Burnett. Burnett was an alias, one of at least a half dozen Michael Raymond used. In March 1984, Raymond introduced himself to McClain as a representative of a company called Systematic Recovery Services (SRS), a New York-based bill collection agency bidding on two city contracts. In July of that year the FBI discovered Raymond and another man in a van in Nashville after being tipped off that the pair was planning to rob a wealthy local businessman. They were caught with a loaded machine gun and an automatic pistol, but while in custody Raymond told the FBI, "I'll give you Chicago . . . if you turn me loose." From that point on, Raymond wore a microphone as an FBI informant.

It's hard to say who conned whom. The media would stress the tape recordings of McClain bragging to Raymond of his close friendship with Washington. I'm so close to the mayor, McClain told him, that "I am the mayor." McClain dropped the names of other top officials. Raymond called his boss in New York. It's unbelievable, he told him: "Bernie, I'm gonna be in the mayor's lap very soon." A few months later he was telling his boss it was practically a done deal: "In three months we're gonna do a couple of million dollars' worth of business." McClain apparently had assured Raymond that he could count on a lucrative contract to collect past-due parking tickets in Chicago. For his troubles Raymond paid McClain $35,000.*

But not long afterward the FBI captured on tape a heated argument between Raymond and McClain. Raymond told McClain that he felt taken. He had passed around something like $300,000 in bribes on SRS's

---

*In July 1989, McClain was found guilty of taking $35,000 in bribes. In September he was sentenced to eight years in jail. In setting his sentence the federal judge labeled him a "habitual liar" who at some point lost the ability to discern truth from dishonesty.

behalf. He had the supposedly clout-heavy McClain doing his company's bidding. Yet the "done deal" ended up no deal at all. SRS didn't get its parking ticket contract.

Somehow this critical fact was swallowed up in the ensuing coverage. No one inside the administration knew of any FBI probe; a contract was signed with one of SRS's rivals well over a year before the FBI's cover was blown. Raymond had lined up, in addition to McClain, four aldermen and several other seemingly influential officials, including the chief clerk of the circuit court. Yet the media stuck to their characterization of McClain as an influential behind-the-scenes player who pulled strings at City Hall.

PROBE REVEALS McCLAIN KEPT HIS CLOUT, the *Tribune* declared one Sunday in a headline appearing on its front page. The article went on to tell of conversations between McClain and several city officials in 1984. A top Washington adviser named Ira Edelson, responsible for the parking tickets contract that SRS coveted, was set to sign a deal with Datacom Systems Corporation when McClain intervened. He told Edelson of a soon-to-be released study that was supposedly harsh in its criticism of Datacom. On top of that several black aldermen were pressuring the administration to avoid any hasty decision in Datacom's favor. John Adams, a deputy director in the city's Revenue Department, was also preaching caution. Later it came out that these aldermen and Adams had accepted money from Raymond. It was also learned that the seemingly objective study damning Datacom was actually paid for with SRS money. Yet in 1984 the fear they were about to bungle a major deal seemed real. The administration heeded McClain's caution and suspended its negotiations with Datacom while it investigated the charges against the company.

Meanwhile, SRS landed a similar contract in New York City to collect on its past-due parking fines. New York officials (it later came out that Raymond bribed many of them as well) were touting SRS. When it appeared that the city was still sticking to its choice of Datacom, McClain switched tactics. He tried to convince Edelson and others that the two companies should split the contract. In mid-December, a few months after McClain alerted him about the study, Edelson went to Ware to say he was angry and puzzled over McClain's involvement. No sooner had he uttered those words, Edelson said, than Ware "went off the wall." A few weeks later the city signed an exclusive deal with Datacom.

In the end SRS secured a relatively minor contract to serve as one of three companies collecting on past-due water bills; it received no piece of the prize it sought, a parking ticket collection contract worth millions.

Thirteen days after news of the FBI probe first broke, Washington invited the entire press corps into his office for a conference. They were told that he would remain as long as they had questions. McClain was the central topic of discussion, of course. As always, reporters were preoccupied with Washington's refusal to denounce McClain. If he is only pretending to speak on your behalf, one reporter asked, why don't you "just pick up the phone and say, 'Clarence, cut it out'?"

"You've got to be kidding," Washington responded.

To Washington, the city's first black mayor didn't denounce black figures simply because the white lords of the media demanded it, if not because of racial pride then because of practical politics. "The media has its moral standards, and I have mine, which are very much influenced by the fact that I'm the city's first black mayor," Washington said several months later. "I'm not saying that my standards are any better than the media's, I'm just saying that I have my own that I must live by." He passed the word among top aides to ignore McClain and instructed one to "hound" McClain to pay the past-due taxes he owed to the city. Still, Washington didn't share this information that day. How would it look, he asked, if I jumped every time some white institution demanded I do so?

Yet Washington was asked again, maybe for the tenth time that day, why he didn't just "get the word to McClain to shut up if he's throwing your name around." Washington responded by repeating the reporter's own words: "Mr. McClain. Shut up. Don't throw my name around. Stop it." He laughed and said, "Isn't this getting a little ridiculous?"

Washington was being facetious, but the big news that night was that Washington had finally rebuked his controversial former aide. MAYOR DROPS HOT POTATO MCCLAIN, the *Tribune* reported the next day on its front page.

Mike Royko, for one, felt cheated. The sting operation was at best a three, he said, on a scale of one to ten. The administration's piece in the scandal was, Royko wrote, something on the order of a two, "despite the panting of the press." He seemed particularly disappointed in Adams, who had taken only $10,000 from Raymond. "Why, the great grabbers of City Hall lore used to pocket more in one week than this amateur took in his one breathless, sweaty venture into pocket-stuffing. It's almost embarrassing to think of this as a true Chicago scandal," Royko wrote.

About the only bad thing one could say about the Washington administration was that it acted the liberal in firing Adams. Top officials didn't go public when learning that Adams had accepted a "loan" from a potential city contractor, and then, told that Adams's wife was pregnant, gave him several months to find a new job.

James Montgomery, the mayor's controversial corporation counsel, was among those who knew about Adams. The FBI probe signaled the end to his tenure, though for another reason. To his chagrin, Washington decided he would name a special prosecutor to investigate the media's charges of corruption. The idea was to find (according to one strategist) "the squeakiest cleanest, whitest, most blue-ribbon lawyer we could find"—Thomas Sullivan, a former U.S. attorney and a Republican. Sullivan insisted on complete independence; Montgomery, responsible for the negotiations, balked and sought another lawyer. When Washington heard over the weekend that talks with Sullivan fell through, he hit the roof. That Monday, Washington contradicted reports that Sullivan was out; that same week Montgomery tendered his resignation.

The political damage to Washington's reputation was significant. The media reported that each of the aldermen nabbed in the sting operation was a Washington ally yet failed to point out that each had no more use for Washington's reform than the Vrdolyak 29. Press accounts gave the impression that Washington's coalition was rotten to its core.

As often as not, in the court of public opinion the accusation that someone is guilty is as good as a conviction. Living in a white neighborhood, one couldn't help hearing time and again that one needed to consider nothing more than Clarence McClain to conclude that Washington was no good. The only question was whether it was McClain's rap sheet or this seemingly nefarious influence peddler's prominence in a self-described reformer's administration that they found more troubling.

Michael Raymond, despite his boasts, never climbed onto the mayor's lap. The U.S. attorney prosecuting the case made a point of saying that the mayor was in no way implicated in its sting operation. Yet a *Sun-Times* editorial cartoon depicted McClain and Washington in an alley peering into a

337

trunk loaded with money. The *Tribune* compared the scandal to Watergate. MAYOR ECHOING DALEY IN DODGING THE SCANDAL, according to a *Tribune* headline.

Reporters made numerous comparisons between McClain and Charles Swibel. "We're not treating this mayor any differently than any other mayor," television reporter Andy Shaw offered in defense of the media's coverage. "Byrne died by Charles Swibel." If McClain was indeed Washington's Swibel, the mayor misunderstood how the game was played. He instituted a self-imposed $1,500 campaign contribution cap and other reforms counterproductive to the kind of role that Swibel played. The supposed "emergency contract" was one handy means for subverting the bidding process on behalf of a generous political friend, yet under Washington they dropped dramatically, from 1,261 in Byrne's last year to 622 in 1984 and 14 in the first ten months of 1986.

Still, most pundits were not impressed. The probe, the political editor of the *Sun-Times,* Basil Talbott, Jr., wrote, proves that the Washington administration is infected by clout. Talbott was most disturbed by the role "mayoral pal" Clarence McClain still played in city government. Those "disreputable twins that have haunted every recent administration"— cronyism and coverup—"roam" this one as well. Talbott's piece carried the headline, CHICAGO REFORM STUMBLES ANEW.

McClain wasn't one of those issues dividing Washington's coalition along racial lines. The nationalist was as frustrated with McClain as the white liberal. MCCLAIN DESTROYING MAYOR & BLACK MOVEMENT, read a headline over a column in the Chicago *Metro News.* The columnist Vernon Jarrett labeled McClain "the Great White Hope." It seemed every Washington partisan's greatest wish was that McClain would somehow just fade away.

But McClain seemed to do everything he could to remain in the news. He sued the federal government, claiming their news leaks spoiled any chance at a fair trial, and spoke of plans to write a book exposing the FBI and the Justice Department. "My name will be known nationwide," he boasted. He sued Ed Burke as well as two white aldermen aligned with Washington for defamation of character. He spoke of running against Rich Daley for state's attorney—forgetting, perhaps, that not only did he stand no chance of winning but that one must be a lawyer to qual-ify for that office. McClain hired an assistant to help him index and synop-size every article written about him and help him organize something like ten boxes of materials that would, McClain said, "prove my innocence ten times over."

When two women he had just met in a Milwaukee hotel ripped him off for $1,600—while he was in the bathroom, his pants draped over a chair—he reported the crime to the Milwaukee police. Virtually any man, especially one whose every misstep generates headlines, runs from that kind of publicity. Clarence McClain went out of his way to report the robbery. The incident seemed emblematic of all that was illogical about the media's estimation of McClain's influence: one had to hold Washington in particu-larly low esteem to believe that McClain was Washington's intimate and trusted consigliere.

Incredibly, McClain continued to imply with a nod and a wink that he was still Someone to See at City Hall. Six months after news of the FBI's sting operation broke, McClain was asked if he still met with Washington. "We don't have to see each other," he responded. "What for? I can get a message to him without talking directly with him." He paused for a moment, then added, "Of course, not that I do. I'm just outlining the pos-sibilities." Later in that same interview he said, "If Harold's got to say, 'I'll never talk to Clarence McClain again in my life,' if that's the game plan to achieve the goal, what difference does it make? As long as Clarence McClain knows the difference." With that statement McClain let loose a devilish and guttural laugh.

At the *Tribune,* Clarence Page, who took Leanita McClain's place on the newspaper's editorial board after her suicide, was disturbed by the drive with which some of his white colleagues took aim at Washington. Page was as moderate as Leanita McClain had been through most of her career. Hired by the *Tribune* in 1969, he was only the second full-time black reporter ever to work there. The first was hired the previous year, in the paper's one hun-dred and twenty-first year. On his predecessor's first day on the job, a white reporter asked him why he was there. "I'm a reporter," the new man responded. "Porter," Page says the white reporter said. "What do we need with a porter here?"

He worked television for a while, but by 1984, Page was sitting on the *Tribune*'s editorial board and writing a twice-a-week column. Things had improved vastly since his days as a journalistic pioneer, yet not so much that there weren't similar tales to be told. He noticed in several white colleagues, he said, a "certain eagerness that the mayor be no better than the rest." He then ticked off several reporters by name. His colleagues' coverage of McClain was a prime example.

Clarence McClain's media image was simple and uncluttered: he was a stick figure devoid of complexity or subtlety. The McClain profiles that appeared in the *Tribune* and *Sun-Times,* presumably meant to provide a glimpse of the McClain that was missing from the episodic nature of the daily news, were a case in point. The *Sun-Times* piece opened by casting doubt on McClain's claims that he badly injured his left leg after a car accident, portraying him as a kind of con man who buys a neck brace after getting tapped at a stop sign. Yet had the article's two authors asked to see his leg, they might have been persuaded to McClain's side. The calf muscle was clipped off small bits at a time, McClain said, until the doctors concluded it was of no use; McClain's scarred skin is shrink-wrapped to his bone, his lower right leg a thin dark club. The *Tribune* profile opened in similar fashion, placing McClain in a nice restaurant with starched white tablecloths yet in every way acting the lout. The piece was written by a reporter who invited Ed Vrdolyak to his wedding. Neither profile explored McClain's considerable skills as a bureaucrat—skills that won him recognition as a state employee and a high position in Washington's government.

"In Chicago," Clarence Page said, "there are people who love Washington and people who hate him. Not surprisingly, a newspaper's staff reflects that range of opinion." The problem was that the *Tribune*'s staff, as in every downtown media outlet in Chicago, did not reflect the racial makeup of Chicago. Consequently, myopia pervaded the newsroom, as when the *Tribune* reported in its midterm assessment of the mayor: "Washington has had little incentive to expand his political base beyond the black community and reach out to ethnic whites. He won without them in 1983, and he thinks he can win without them in 1987." Ironically, Washington was far more diligent about putting together a government mirroring the city's racial makeup than the newspaper making this accusation. The *Tribune* editorial staff covering a political fight the media itself cast as inherently racial was only seven percent black.

When Washington first took office, reporters praised him as the most open and accessible mayor they had known. Yet where once he permitted reporters to call him at home and granted impromptu press conferences, at around the midterm he began limiting their access. He had grown frustrated with the media. It was not the long-awaited showdown between the machine and antimachine forces, or a pitched ideological battle within the Democratic party between its progressive and conservative wings, but little more than a continuous clash between blacks and whites. Chicago had been a divided town for at least fifty years, yet only with his election was there a pressing concern on the editorial pages for "reunifying the city"—as if it ever had been. Early in the Council Wars, Washington bought something like twenty copies of a book about the differences in the ways blacks and whites communicate. He gave them as gifts to reporters and then later wondered why he even bothered.

"Unarticulated premises" was Washington's buzz phrase for what he saw as the latent biases among most of those covering city politics: "They're operating on so many unarticulated premises," he would say, "they're blind to their own racial hangups." To Washington, the McClain coverage boiled down to a white press's presumption that his administration would never be more than an "Amos 'n' Andy" show.

Channel 5's Paul Hogan, who reported his share of McClain stories, confessed it was McClain's outlandish appearance that first stirred his suspicions. "I was real curious about him because he was strange looking," Hogan said. "It was that hair of his." The question was whether Hogan and his colleagues would have been equally dubious of a political operative named Wochinski in polyester and a cheap toupee who spoke of dese guys and dose.

Al Miller told of countless arguments with his boss over individual reporters who, because they were white, Washington believed were hopelessly biased against him. Miller did not doubt there were reporters who fit the description, but he assigned fewer reporters to this category than did Washington. Washington looked on Mike Flannery and Channel 7's Andy Shaw as irredeemably biased. Miller couldn't disagree more. He was as frustrated as

Washington by countless Flannery and Shaw news reports, but Miller, who was also white, did not see race as the issue. Shaw, for instance, had been fired from his job as editorial director at Channel 5 because he pushed management too hard to endorse Washington over Epton in the 1983 mayor's race.

There were two theories among the City Hall press corps to explain Washington's harangues about the white media: he was either thinner-skinned than other politicians, or he was using them as a means for galvanizing the troops. Most seemed inclined to believe the latter. "Race and racism," the *Sun-Times's* Basil Talbott wrote, "are winning issues for Washington." Yet columns like Talbott's served to make Washington's point. Only a white columnist could possibly believe that racism, the single greatest barrier in Washington's way, was actually an asset.

Washington at times cried racism when the true enemy was nothing more than the media's usual fare of sensationalism, superficiality, and uninspired reporting. Vrdolyak's charges that Washington was lazy; the impression that City Hall was now as black as it used to be white; the mayor was shortchanging the white wards in favor of black ones—where the readiness to believe these myths might have boiled down to white perceptions and fears, that they hung in the air until digested as truth was simply the way of the media. If a prominent opponent makes a charge, whether true or absurd, it makes headlines.

But there was no denying that Council Wars was a story being reported largely through a white filter. The city had a nonwhite majority, but of the twenty-five or so reporters who gathered in the City Hall press room on days the City Council was in session, only three were black. One worked for the *Defender,* one for the local public radio affiliate, and the third for an all-news AM radio station. The dailies assigned two reporters full-time to the press room, but not until 1986, when the *Sun-Times* made a personnel switch, was one of the two slots filled by someone black. None of the television reporters regularly covering city politics was black, nor were the television producers who helped them package the daily news. "TV," Washington once said, "is a bunch of white people discussing blacks and Hispanics."* Could you imagine if the reverse were true, Washington

---

*A national survey conducted in 1984 found that eleven percent of the staffs of the country's big-city dailies were minorities. Both of Chicago's dailies fell below that mark.

asked in a speech—what the white reaction might be if virtually every reporter covering Council Wars was black?

There was a camaraderie between the white reporters and white politicians that did not exist between reporters and black politicians. When a black politician entered the City Hall press room, it was a safe bet that he or she was there in search of Chinta Strausberg, the *Defender's* City Hall beat reporter. Fred Roti and Bernard Stone regularly held court in the press room. Strolling from desk to desk reading over shoulders as reporters worked on their articles, they offered comments and arguments. Both had far more influence over the media's daily coverage of Council Wars than, say, Alderman Danny Davis or Dorothy Tillman. Davis and Tillman simply didn't enjoy the same chummy relations with the reporters assigned the City Hall beat.

Washington was careful not to blame the FBI probe on race, instead blaming it on a Republican administration in D.C. out to get any big-city Democrat.* Yet a top mayoral aide acknowledged that Washington, fearful of the probe's potential damage inside the black community, sought the assistance of people like attorney Thomas Todd, a prominent black with whom Washington met regularly at his apartment. Washington knew full well how Todd would cut the issue, but it gave him an air of innocence. Could he help it if Todd and others characterized the probe as nothing more than white institutions attacking a black politician?

Vrdolyak didn't deny that Council Wars was being reported largely through white eyes, but he believed this served Washington's interest rather than his own. So fearful were white reporters of being labeled bigots, Vrdolyak argued, that they gave Washington a free ride. "You are all very weak-kneed when it comes to taking a position against this administration," Vrdolyak chided reporters. He compared the media's treatment of Byrne, a woman, to Washington's. Had Byrne had a Clarence McClain in her administration, he said, "the press would have buried her long ago." When

---

*An unnamed Justice Department source told the *Sun-Times* that with all the charges going back and forth in Council Wars, his office figured that "where there's smoke there's fire." There was smoke in City Hall before Washington, of course; there was smoke in City Hall long before Washington was born. Yet remarkably, despite Chicago's reputation, this was reportedly the first undercover sting operation the feds had set up inside Chicago's City Hall.

Washington talks of race, it is the black man standing up for his rights. When Vrdolyak or anyone else white raised the issue of race, he was a racist. "That's how crazy it's all become," Vrdolyak said.

Mike Royko was inclined to agree. He believed that reporters were influenced by the storm of protest they could count on should they attack a black politician. When a reporter criticized Vrdolyak, Royko wrote, he did not fear a torrent of phone calls from the city's Croatian community. Yet a column about a black politician would elicit exactly that reaction. "No matter how deserving the slam," Royko wrote, "I'll be accused by some of his supporters . . . of being racist." To Royko, Washington was a smart politician who capitalized on the widespread belief among black Chicagoans that a biased and unfair media reported the news.*

In 1986 Vrdolyak commemorated the fiftieth time a *Tribune* editorial slammed him since Washington took office. John Madigan, a well-known radio commentator, offered that in 1984 alone the *Tribune* editorial page made something like forty unfavorable references to Vrdolyak without a single word of praise for his efforts to increase the size of the police force or serve as a watchdog over the Washington administration. "Whatever the reason," Madigan said, "and there's some evidence that it has to do with the color of his skin, Mayor Washington is treated far more gently than his predecessors."

*Royko may have been thinking of an incident in 1983 when Washington declared that a column Royko wrote "whetted the appetites of racists." James Hoge, then the publisher of the *Sun-Times,* asked Washington about the charge. "Oh, Mike knows I don't mean that," Washington reportedly said. "He has to write his column. I have to say that."

Something Less Than Hate
1986–1987

When I first visited Chicago, I
thought there was one in a thousand
chances of reform succeeding here.
Now I think the chances are one in
two thousand.

— William Stead, *If Christ Came to
Chicago,* 1894

19

THE

RECKONING

Latinos had been ignored for so long in Chicago, a city that so emphatically defined itself in black and white, it seemed entirely improbable that they would come to dominate local politics as they did in early 1986. A suit filed before there was a Council War, charging that the city's ward map discriminated against black and Latino voters, was finally adjudicated. The judgment required that special elections be held in seven of the city's fifty wards; all seven were represented by allies of Vrdolyak. Suddenly the council standoff might end.

There were really two separate suits, one filed by a group of black plaintiffs and another filed two weeks later by a like-minded set of Latinos. Both sued the city on grounds that the redistricting plan drawn by the Byrne administration and then approved by the City Council violated the federal Voting Rights Act.* The judge hearing the case enjoined the two

---

*The redistricting plan approved by the council cut the number of wards with a black majority from nineteen to seventeen, though the city's black population had increased by more than a hundred thousand between 1970 and 1980. The numbers were even more telling among Latinos. One of every seven Chicagoans was Latino, according to the 1980 census on which the new map was based, yet in no ward did Latinos constitute a majority.

suits, a bone of contention with Al Johnson, a top adviser to Washington and a wealthy black businessman. "The Latinos didn't spend fifteen cents," Johnson said "They just showed up when it was time for court."

The judge ruled in 1982 that the city was guilty of discrimination. New boundaries were drawn in time for the 1983 local elections, but a U.S. appellate court ruled in 1984 that the judge's remedy did not go far enough. "Super-majorities"—majorities of at least sixty-five percent—should be established, according to the court. Three wards should be at least sixty-five percent black, and four at least seventy percent Latino. Lawyers appealed the higher court's ruling all the way to the U.S. Supreme Court.

The 29 tried various means to pressure Washington to underwrite their appeals with city funds. They threatened that they would oppose the $180 million infrastructure bond proposal that proved so difficult to dislodge from committee unless he set aside the money. But Washington stood firm. The city had already spent nearly $1 million fighting the case by the time Washington took office, according to numbers put together by his administration. Vrdolyak arranged for the Cook County Democratic party to pick up the additional legal costs. Party officials refused to say how much they spent defending the map, but their foes estimate that the party spent at least $700,000. Eventually the legal battle boiled down to the Washington administration's petition to establish their lawyers as the defense attorneys for the city, rather than the 29's lawyers. The judge ruled in Washington's favor, and the city quickly dropped all appeals of the case.

If nothing else, the appeals had seemed an effective way of delaying the possibility of special elections. Each month the case remained in limbo, the less likely it seemed a judge would rule in favor of so extreme a solution as new elections. "It's just not significant enough to warrant all the effort," the 29's chief lawyer said.

But when the judge ruled that the special elections would be held concurrently with the March 1986 primary, Vrdolyak shifted his strategy. The aim now was to impress those Latino voters who would decide his fate. "A welcome development," Vrdolyak said of the judge's decision.

There was a time not long ago that the big-city machine was a refuge for the immigrant population. Mayor Anton Cermak gave rise to the political machine that would come to bear the name Daley. Cermak, elected in 1931, had two years of formal schooling and used to sell kindling from a horse-drawn cart. The scorn of Wasps, who continued to dominate city politics though no longer a majority, was captured in the derisive nickname given to Cermak—"Pushcart Tony." The ruling Wasps spoke paternalistically of protecting for their own good these beer-swilling urban ethnics who didn't seem to know better. How could they trust their city to the dirty rag salesman and the ignorant masses rallying behind him?

The machine's strategy was to court the various ethnic groupings once their numbers demanded representation. The Irish, the Poles, the Italians, the Bohemians—each group had its war lords, each was represented in the party's central committee where the spoils were divvied up. But it was different with the new Spanish-speaking immigrants. Earlier waves of immigrants were given a place at the table long before their numbers reached the magnitude of those arriving from Mexico and Puerto Rico, but when these latest newcomers challenged the ward bosses who lorded over their communities, such as Vito Marzullo, they were told they did not know their place. "These people better learn something about America or go back to Mexico where they belong," Marzullo said in 1983 when a Latino man opposed him for alderman. Where once the machine was a vehicle for the empowerment of the disenfranchised, now it was a vehicle for locking them out.

Until the 1980s the extent of Latino representation consisted of a single socialist alderman named William Emilio Rodriguez who served only one term around World War I. No Latino represented a Chicago district in the state legislature; of the hundreds of Cook County judges, three were Latino in 1980. Juan Andrade, Jr., the executive director of an Ohio-based Latino empowerment organization called the Midwest Voter Registration and Education Project, could name no place where the problem of underrepresentation was as severe as Chicago. There were more Latinos in a single Chicago neighborhood than there were in several midwestern states that had a Latino serving in the state legislature. Chicago's Latino populace didn't even rate the sort of Uncle Tom politics that plagued the black community throughout the machine's tenure.

Latino Chicago is concentrated in two communities that stretch along the border of the black west side. The city's Mexican Americans are concentrated in a barrio sandwiched between the west side and the city's southwest side. Those living in the barrio bordering the west side to the north tend to be Puerto Rican, those to the south tend to be Mexican. There are those in either barrio who will tell you it's no coincidence that they live in a sort of buffer zone separating black from white. A Mexican-American family wasn't as desirable as a Ukrainian one, but they were not nearly so bad as one that was black.

Only after the 1980 census demonstrated that Latinos accounted for fourteen percent of the population did political operatives on either side of the racial barrier recognize the potential power of Latino Chicago. In 1983 when the Latino vote secured Washington's victory, political reporters followed suit. Until then there were only two categories of Chicago voters, black and white, with Latinos counted primarily among the whites. Even Roger Simon, a white liberal columnist, as late as 1983 referred to Chicago as sixty percent white when, in fact, precisely the opposite was so. Only by lumping the Latinos (and also the Asians) in with the whites could Simon have made such a statement.

A Latino presence in City Hall came late in 1981, as sudden as a whim, after Byrne was attacked for her redistricting plan. Like an imperialist rigging a colonial election, she offered the incumbent white alderman a city job at twice his aldermanic salary and chose an attorney in Ed Burke's law firm named Joseph Martinez to serve as the acting alderman. Martinez confessed he could point to little community involvement but said he planned to change that with his appointment. He had always gone by the name of Joseph, but he asked in his first press conference for people to call him Jose.

To the community activists who would join the Washington coalition, City Hall was, at the start of the decade, still some gringo world downtown that was not relevant to their lives. The low Latino registration figures proved that these activists were not alone. The 1980 census was a key turning point. The Latinos inclined to the sort of politics espoused by Washington were angry with Byrne, but some realized they also had themselves to blame. Their own indifference to Chicago politics had made them easier to ignore.

Soon after the 1980 census Latino community organizers and like-minded blacks began meeting to consider the future. Their aim wasn't anything as bold as an alliance to run the city but a shared strategy for fighting a school system that was predominantly black and Latino yet run by whites. The possibility of joining forces in legislative districts where the two communities constituted a majority came next. If a legislative district was more Latino than it was black, then as a group they would endorse a Latino for state senator and a black for state representative. The same would hold true where the numbers were reversed.

The two communities shared a common foe in the machine and also profound problems such as gangs, drugs, and infant mortality rates that matched those of third world nations. Together they constituted somewhere around fifty-seven percent of the population, yet a black-Latino coalition would not be easy. There were tensions between these two communities living side by side. From the Latino perspective there was, according to Jesus Garcia who would emerge as the ranking Latino in Washington's coalition, "the bigotry and stereotypes inherited by a people trying to assimilate into U.S. culture." There was also a question of identity. Many Latinos, especially those of Puerto Rican descent, viewed themselves as nonwhite. Others, especially Mexican Americans, sought to identify themselves as just another ethnic group like the Italians, the Irish, and the Poles. The last thing they wanted politically was a place reserved for them within a black movement. On the black side of the equation, the naysayers stressed priorities. Why should the problems of these relative newcomers be equated with the discrimination suffered by black Chicago dating back seventy years?

Yet by 1983 those who were part of this fledgling partnership could already claim success. Had Washington fared badly in the Latino community rather than winning more than eighty percent of the vote, he would have lost his race against Bernard Epton. The city's 1983 general election saw Latino turnout reach an all-time high. The black vote didn't put a Latino independent into office, but not for a lack of effort. If Latinos had fared half as well in Latino precincts as they did in black precincts, Latino representation would have come sooner to the barrio than it did.

"Folks around the country are watching to see if the Hispanic-black coalition works here," Juan Andrade said of Chicago. "There have been isolated incidents around the country in the last ten or fifteen years of blacks and Hispanics working together, but never has it occurred as dramatically as it did in Chicago on April 12. We brought their man over the top. Harold acknowledged that himself. Now it's time to see if he's going to make winners out of us."

Washington's Latino record had its soft spots. Only after considerable pressure did Washington follow through on his campaign pledge to create a Commission on Latino Affairs. But where he envisioned a benign city agency that would collect statistics showing he was in every way the ideal mayor from the Latino perspective, his Latino allies had in mind an independent commission that would serve as the Latino community's advocate within the bureaucracy. Every six months the fifteen-member commission graded the bureaucracy's performance, printing the result in a newsletter sent to the press and Latino leaders. The commission routinely singled out those departments with poor Latino hiring records, irritating the offending department heads. Once the commission gave Washington a "D" grade when not one of the new twenty-six managers he named during his midterm shakeup was Latino.

Yet no Latino stumping on the mayor's behalf would have trouble making a case for Washington. Washington could be criticized for not hiring Latinos at a fast enough pace or for not giving Latino contractors their due, but the numbers Washington posted far outdistanced those of previous mayors. Dollars to Latino contractors increased tenfold between 1982 and 1985. The administration was more aggressive in hiring blacks than Latinos, but the Washington administration was hiring Latinos at a higher rate (eleven percent in 1985) than Byrne's (seven percent). By the commission's count, twenty-seven Latinos served in what could be called decision-making positions; under Byrne there were only three. Twenty percent of all Washington's appointments to the city's boards and commissions were Latino. "They've tended to be better choices," Juan Andrade said. "They have been proven community leaders rather than people with little community experience but who previous administrations knew would be loyal."

The fact that the commission was granted liberty to publicly criticize its boss was the most dramatic break with the past. That was the greatest dif-

ference between Washington and his predecessors. He empowered the outspoken community activist whom previous administrations had tried to
silence.

Alderman Miguel Santiago, part of the 29, was never impressed with
Washington. The mayor's Latino allies, he said, when asked about
Washington's improvements over past mayors, are nothing but "puppets
who say whatever Harold Washington wants them to say." Yet Santiago had
strings of his own to explain.

Santiago was an eighth grade schoolteacher who took Jose Martinez's
place in the council. He had served for four or five years as assistant
precinct captain when he was plucked for advancement. In 1985,
Santiago's council allies cut twenty-nine of the thirty-six Latino community groups from the mayor's community development funds plan. Most of
the organizations were long-standing social service agencies, yet Santiago
voted with his council allies. Three times the question of special elections
came before the council. Twice Santiago failed to show for the vote. The
third time he sided with the rest of his colleagues in the 29, voting against
a resolution that would in effect increase Latino representation in the
council from one to four aldermen.

The arithmetic of the special elections was simple. Washington needed to
pick up four new allies to win a council majority; the magic number for
him was twenty-five.

From the start Washington could count on two new allies in the
three court-ordered elections held in black areas of the city. In the
Third Ward the new boundaries were drawn in such a way that blacks constituted a majority but accounted for less than fifty percent of the eligible
voters. The white incumbent seemed certain to retain his seat, especially
since there remained only a few months for any challenger to mount a
campaign.

Washington conceded the Santiago race. Santiago might prove vulnerable, but Washington figured attacking the council's only Latino representative could backfire. Santiago won with fifty-seven percent of the ward's
Latino vote and fifty-eight percent of its white voters.

There were no surprises in the two special elections held in the largely Mexican-American communities sandwiched between the west and southwest sides. Jesus Garcia, the incumbent ward committeeman, and Juan Soliz, the state representative, won their elections. Garcia was an early pioneer in the efforts to build a black-Latino coalition as well as one of its beneficiaries. The two black precincts in his ward proved the difference in 1984 when Garcia beat the incumbent Democratic committeeman by only 59 votes. He outpolled his opponent 267 votes to 33 in one, and 211 to 13 in the other. Garcia took a job as a deputy commissioner with the city. He was certain to be Washington's twenty-fourth vote.

Juan Soliz, too, was both an early proponent and a beneficiary of this black-Latino alliance. Soliz first ran for state representative as an antimachine candidate, railing against the "thugs" and "goons" in Vito Marzullo's organization. In that same campaign, he described Marzullo as "an old man terribly out of touch with our people." Soliz beat the machine incumbent in 1984; by odd coincidence he also won by fifty-nine votes. Soliz won his race by overwhelmingly defeating his opponent among that twelve percent of the district that was black. Yet Soliz's victory in his special election proved a victory for Vrdolyak. Vito Marzullo was no longer the alderman from the Twenty-fifth Ward, but he was there at Soliz's side the night of his aldermanic victory. Soliz watched the returns at Marzullo's headquarters, where he described Marzullo as a "fine man" from whom he had a lot to learn. Soliz won with forty-five percent of the Latino vote and seventy-four percent of the white vote against three Latino foes.

Soliz spoke of creating an independent Latino bloc in the council, but media accounts listed him squarely on Vrdolyak's side. Soliz would not prove the media wrong. Control of the council, then, swung on the contest in the Twenty-sixth Ward, a predominantly Puerto Rican ward on the city's near northwest side.

From the start the Twenty-sixth Ward's race was billed as the premier battle. Just as nothing was ambiguous in the Council Wars, there seemed nothing ambiguous about the loyalties of the two candidates, Manuel Torres and Luis Gutierrez. Torres was unequivocally with Vrdolyak, Gutierrez with Washington. Which of the two would win was anyone's guess.

Torres got his political start in Alderman Richard Mell's ward organization. He was, by all accounts, a hardworking and effective precinct captain, and a few years earlier Mell rewarded him by pushing him as a replacement for a Cook County Board commissioner who was convicted of extortion. The Mell organization, from the neighboring Thirty-third Ward, served the Torres campaign as its backbone.

Where Torres was the prototype machine candidate, Gutierrez was a housing activist who had only recently discovered electoral politics. Gutierrez had never bothered registering to vote until the fall of 1982 and then only "because I needed a tree torn down," he said. On the "euphoria of Harold Washington's victory" Gutierrez challenged Congressman Dan Rostenkowski for ward committeeman. He drove a cab to make enough money to mount a decent campaign but won only twenty-three percent of the vote. Shortly thereafter Gutierrez took a job as a deputy superintendent with the city's Department of Streets and Sanitation.

Their personal styles couldn't have been more different; Gutierrez was fiery and effervescent and spit sparks when in front of a microphone. Torres was ill at ease in crowds and during press conferences; feature pieces used words like "wooden" and "taciturn" to describe Torres. Even their appearances served as a means for contrasting the two. Gutierrez was small and wiry, Torres husky and square-jawed. His campaign made much of his background as a body builder.

Torres chose to frame the election as a referendum on Washington's treatment of Latinos. The tactic was a strange one, given the machine's own appalling record, but Torres nonetheless pursued it with gusto. He spoke at every campaign stop of how little Washington had done for Latinos, always stressing how much the mayor had done for blacks. On a candidate's survey filled out for the *Sun-Times*, Torres wrote, "Of course we are not getting our fair share on contracts, jobs, and appointments. Blacks are getting more than their fair share."

Gutierrez beat Torres among Latino voters and scored big among the eleven percent of the ward that was black; the white vote went overwhelmingly for Torres. The final results had Gutierrez ahead of Torres by a scant twenty votes. The official tallies showed that a man named Jim Blasinski, a school crossing guard running as a write-in candidate, won eleven votes—nine short of the twenty that would have denied Gutierrez a majority—yet a couple of weeks later Torres's lawyers announced they had in hand thirty-one affidavits signed by voters claiming to have written in Blasinski's name.

The affidavits alone were not enough to bring about a runoff, but they convinced a circuit court judge to order a recount. The election's fate was in the hands of the Board of Elections, which Washington partisans were quick to point out was still run by a machine loyalist put in office by Mayor Bilandic. At the board, workers claimed to find—voilà—nine more Blasinski votes, bringing his count to a perfect twenty, not a single vote to spare. The missing votes were discovered in ballot boxes left unsealed and unattended at the board's warehouse. After several weeks the courts found that a runoff would need to be held. Gutierrez's new buttons read RE-ELECT GUTIERREZ.

The initial Torres-Gutierrez race had been nasty. Gutierrez was depicted as a radical who consorted with terrorists, Torres a dim-witted puppet of Mell and Vrdolyak. The rematch was worse. Gutierrez mistakenly accused Torres of a cocaine arrest in 1971 and then retracted the charge because he had the rap sheet of the wrong Manuel Torres. Torres was behind in his child support payments—a fact reporters learned from Gutierrez. Torres complained that the "goons" at City Hall stole the first election from him—a charge that brought a sour smile to the face of old-time machine foes.

Torres went to great lengths to portray Gutierrez as the candidate of carpetbaggers and tie him to various black politicians. Well-known whites and Latinos also traveled to the Twenty-sixth Ward to campaign on Gutierrez's behalf, but in speeches Torres focused on only three—Harold Washington, Jesse Jackson, and Alderwoman Dorothy Tillman. When reporters pointed out that Torres, too, had outsiders visiting the ward on his behalf, pointed out that Jane Byrne was standing beside him at that very moment, Torres replied that in this case it was different, Mayor Byrne had always shown a keen interest in Latinos. Though both Vrdolyak and Mell aggressively fought against the special election that permitted Torres this chance, their contribution was somehow different from that provided Gutierrez by Jesse Jackson and Harold Washington. Torres's most memorable line from the campaign, "We've got to get that monkey in City Hall off our back," was never quoted in either of the city's two main newspapers or on channels 2, 5, or 7.

On the eve of the runoff, a Spanish-language television station sponsored a debate between Torres and Gutierrez. Torres introduced himself in Spanish but then spoke English for the remainder of the debate. Gutierrez had portrayed Torres as a pawn of those behind his candidacy; Torres's own bad Spanish seemed to drive that point home. Torres lost the runoff by just under a thousand votes.

Later, when his closest allies would become his bitterest foes, they grumbled about the endless hours they had spent helping him get elected in 1986. They took to calling Gutierrez a *vendido*—a sellout—and also a "Napoleon," because of his small stature and sizable ego. Yet in April 1986 there was only euphoria. Ten months before the end of his first term, Washington had a council majority.

The first big rift among Washington's council majority was Ed Burke's fate. Dorothy Tillman was adamant about dumping Burke as Finance chair. Tillman threatened to withhold her vote—the critical twenty-fifth vote—from any reorganization proposal unless Burke was out. "Why show a racist like Burke an ounce of sympathy or respect?" Tillman asked in caucus. White Alderwoman Marion Volini from the lakefront was equally adamant. In my community, Volini said, Burke is seen as the only thing between Washington, tax increases, and widespread cronyism. She wouldn't vote for any reorganization plan that dumped Burke.

The Burke question also split Washington's advisers. There were those like Tillman who saw this as their chance to rid themselves of Ed Burke. Washington could sympathize—if he indulged his true feelings for Burke, he would be leading the anti-Burke charge—but he could see the potential dangers. Ousting Burke would portray Washington as an old-style boss. Instead he created a new Budget Committee. Burke would remain the chairman of the Finance Committee but one divested of much of its traditional power.

Washington would disappoint his more strident supporters in other ways. Washington chose a white ally, Alderman Larry Bloom, to head this new Budget Committee. The council's two most powerful committees, with one hundred jobs between them, were headed by whites. Washington's council reorganization plan also allowed thirteen of Vrdolyak's allies to remain as committee chairmen. Still, not everyone was convinced that

Washington was any different from the standard-bearer of the office, Richard Daley. "Washington," wrote Basil Talbott, political editor of the *Sun-Times*, "was as ruthless as Mayor Richard J. Daley."

Twenty-five of the sixty-three appointees pending before the council were put up for a vote in the first meeting after the special elections. Several were confirmed by the slimmest of margins, such as the white liberal board president and militant black women named to the politically sensitive Park District Board; in other cases members of the old Vrdolyak bloc switched sides to vote for a particular nominee. Only eleven aldermen, including Burke and Vrdolyak, voted against every one of them.

With two Latinos part of the equation, the dynamics of Washington's council caucus shifted slightly. The white independents were given a bit of respite, for they were no longer the sole targets of the black machinists' frustrations over a lack of spoils. The Latinos heard their fill of Marian Humes. "Marian was always mouthing off during caucus about how much the fat-cat Latinos were getting from this administration," Jesus Garcia said. "We were getting too many jobs, too many contracts, too many appointments—all at the expense of her constituents. Marian would needle your ass," Garcia said.

Every vote was close, so more than ever the black community turned up the pressure on those black aldermen known to be soft in their support of Washington. Humes missed an important vote—left the meeting early because of personal business, she said—prompting Washington partisans to picket her ward office. Alderman Perry Hutchinson was another Washington supporter looking over his shoulder ever since attorney Tom Todd had named names at Operation PUSH, listing Hutchinson along with Humes and others as potential traitors to the cause. After arousing anger when claiming a doctor's appointment prevented him from attending an important council meeting, Hutchinson made sure to be at the next meeting: he was transported there in an ambulance, wheeled into the council chambers in a wheelchair, and sat through the session hooked up to an IV drip. He said he was there in defiance of his doctor's express order to rest because of heart trouble, yet he deemed the political risks worse than the health ones.

Aaron Freeman, the comedian who coined the term "Council Wars," dubbed the new City Council "Master Harold and the Boys."

Washington used his new council majority to pass, among other measures, a tough new ethics ordinance, a Tenants' Bill of Rights ordinance, and a new set of taxi regulations designed to end the near-monopoly enjoyed by Yellow and Checker cabs. It also proved invaluable in killing efforts to change the way Chicago elected a mayor.

The plan was to elect a mayor in the same fashion that the city elects its aldermen—it would be nonpartisan. If one candidate received over fifty percent of the vote, he or she would be the winner; if not, a runoff would be held between the top two finishers. In 1983, Washington and Byrne would have faced each other in a runoff. A nonpartisan election would eliminate the possibility of two white foes splitting the white vote.

The nonpartisan election was an old idea that the independents floated from time to time. After the 1983 election the regular Democrats adopted it. Petitions were passed out on the southwest and northwest sides; among those supporting the drive were Dan Rostenkowski and fellow Congressman William Lipinski, both allies of Rich Daley. "It's the only way Rich can run for mayor," a top Daley adviser, requesting anonymity, told the *Tribune*. Petitioners had collected enough signatures to put the measure to a vote on the November 1986 ballot.

Illinois law stipulates that each city can consider a maximum of three referenda, so Washington's council allies concocted three local referendum questions and filled the ballot before the nonpartisan measure could qualify. Rich Daley denounced Washington for denying Chicagoans a chance to debate the question—"pandering to politics," he said. The *Tribune* and *Sun-Times* were also critical, but Ed Burke seemed impressed and offered his compliments.

The mayor's foes were not without their weapons. One effective advantage still enjoyed by the Vrdolyak faction was the widespread fear among whites that any black politician will push for higher taxes.

Unlike most cities, Chicago had no fixed property-tax rate. The city's yearly budget was conceived, and the property-tax rate was figured after the fact. For several years running Washington sought a fixed property-tax rate; with his slim council majority, he was able in the fall of 1986, with the 1987 primary only a few months off, to push the idea through the council, set-tling on a three percent rate. Predictably, the mayor's foes carried on about a home-destroying property-tax increase. "The policy of this administra-tion is, if it moves, tax it once," Vrdolyak said during debate. "If it stands still, tax it twice." Vrdolyak and his other allies dubbed Washington "High Tax Harold."

Three percent was higher than the previous year's figure but not nearly as high as it was in 1980 when Vrdolyak, Burke, and others approved a Byrne budget that called for a three and one-half percent property-tax rate.* To compensate for inflation and federal budget cuts, Byrne raised taxes and fees by $500 million during her term, compared to the $400 million Washington raised during his. Alderman Richard Mell was able to explain the apparent contradiction: "Just because I was stupid enough to pass some-thing before doesn't mean I'm dumb enough to do it again."

The sight of the old-machine aldermen posing as cost-cutting advo-cates would have been humorous were it not so effective. In the headlines and shorthand of television broadcasts, the plan was described as a tax hike. (A headline in the *Sun-Times:* WASHINGTON SEEKS RECORD PROPERTY TAX INCREASE.) No less a reporter than the esteemed Harry Golden, Jr., of the *Sun-Times,* whose mastery of the budget was so great that Mayor Bilandic once offered him a deputy-level job with the city's budget office, was taken by the Vrdolyak bloc's rhetorical claims. In one article Golden referred to the "ardent economy advocates" and "cost-conscious" aldermen fighting Washington's "record-setting budget hike."

"We simply cannot afford another term of Washington," began a leaflet sent to a number of Chicagoans by an organization calling itself the "Save Chicago" Task Force. The brochure, which went to residents on the northwest and southwest sides shortly after the property-tax fight, was in the form of a letter from the organization's president, Ed Vrdolyak.

---

*Because the aggregate worth of the city's real estate increased, due to both inflation and a downtown development boom, the rate fell each year after hitting a high of three and one-half percent. The logic behind the administration's tax plan was that a fixed rate would allow the city's tax rolls to keep pace with the downtown boom, which placed greater stress on city services.

It should also be noted that a three and one-half property-tax rate does not mean a straight three and one-half of the worth of one's home or business. Through a complicated weighting system meant to tax private homes at a lesser rate than business properties, a homeowner pays taxes on one-sixth of the assessed value of his or her home. The assessed value is generally well below the market value of one's home. Chicago had the second lowest property rate in the state in 1987.

"Harold Washington says he has big plans for His city," Vrdolyak wrote. "The question is, Can we afford HIS PLANS?. . .

"If he is reelected, the sad fact is there won't be another chance for us. Then Harold's tax plans will all come true—his dream—our nightmare! You've probably never believed this could happen—well it has—and it's up to you to end this nightmare. The fight is your fight. Join us! Together we can win."

20

ANY
WHITE
WILL DO

Before speculation began that she would run for mayor again, there were rumors that Jane Byrne was sincerely searching for another line of work. Items in the gossip columns had her weighing offers as a television analyst, a teacher, and a consultant. Byrne busied herself by doing a little of this, a little of that: she sang a line in a *USA Today* commercial, promoted a chain of Mexican restaurants, and gave an occasional speech. She was frequently spotted dressed in fur from head to ankle, shopping the Michigan Avenue boutiques. But a small squib announcing that Byrne was studying Spanish was one of many clues that revealed what was really on her mind.

As early as 1984 Byrne was discreetly putting out feelers about running for mayor. Early in 1985 she confessed that she was considering a run on the Republican ticket; by mid-year she had hired a press secretary. At a press conference that July she announced her intent to run for mayor in 1987. She could no longer sit on the sidelines, she said, while petty politicians were destroying the city she loved.

Others were also thinking of challenging Washington—Vrdolyak, Mell, Roman Pucinski, Dan Rostenkowski—yet only Byrne had the temerity to announce so unfashionably early. The cunning behind her decision was not lost on those whom she preempted. The first white candidate to announce, they understood, meant anyone following her into the race risked the spoiler label. The challenge, then, became to convince her to drop out.

Byrne was saddled by a ward remap that the federal courts declared racially biased. There were the enormous campaign contributions from city contractors that might sour the pivotal lakefront voters, Charles Swibel, and Byrne's one week as a write-in candidate after the 1983 primary. (ABORTIVE CAMPAIGN DIMS HER ONCE-BRIGHT FUTURE, a *Tribune* headliner wrote back then.) There was also her hiring binge in her last months of office, when her fate was decided.

The Latinos would prove key to any Washington challenger, but so, too, would unity among all those opposed to him. Byrne, a lightning rod of ill-feelings, fell short. In particular there were the residual bad feelings among the Daleyites; they were not about to side foursquare behind Jane Byrne. Those seeing the need for a unified front saw Byrne as perhaps the worst possible choice.

Vrdolyak did what he could to convince Byrne to change her mind. He had an aide spread rumors about the lawsuits pending against Byrne over old campaign debts. Vrdolyak also hinted at dark secrets he might reveal should Byrne remain in the race—"truth-slinging," Royko called it.

But Byrne was dogged and tough—and in the driver's seat. It would take more than a nuisance suit and rumor to scare her out of the race.

Actually, Vrdolyak seemed indifferent to whom he supported for mayor against Washington. In 1985 he was asked if he could support either of two Republicans mentioned as possible candidates for mayor, U.S. Attorney Dan Webb or former Illinois Governor Richard Ogilvie. Webb is a good administrator, Vrdolyak remarked, and responded "of course" when asked if he could work better with Ogilvie over Washington. "I could work better with you," Vrdolyak said to the reporter asking the question. In other interviews Vrdolyak said he could support "anyone in the entire universe against Harold."

Among the many who viewed themselves as potential candidates, few seemed better qualified than Byrne. Those who wanted it in the worst way—those pushing themselves at every opportunity, such as Richard Mell and former Parks boss Ed Kelly—were not worth taking seriously. The more formidable contenders, such as Webb and Rostenkowski, were ambivalent and uncertain. Washington seemed vulnerable, but Chicago politics had become a racial obstacle course that one might be wise to avoid. Rich Daley's chances were dashed when the nonpartisan election idea fell through. There was no possible way he would risk re-creating another matchup with Byrne and Washington.

Another possible candidate was Vrdolyak himself. His aide Joe Novak, who once boasted he spoke to Vrdolyak as many as fifteen times a day, was planting stories that his boss might run. Certainly no one had earned that honor any more than Vrdolyak.

In November, Vrdolyak decided he had had enough of politicians scared to challenge Washington. He would run. "It's going to be war out there," Vrdolyak said with characteristic bravado.

There was talk that Washington might skip the Democratic primary altogether and instead run as an independent against the Republican and Democratic nominees, virtually ensuring himself two white foes. Washington had hinted as much when Byrne announced for mayor. If Washington skipped the primary, Vrdolyak would run against Byrne. Otherwise, Washington and Byrne would square off in the primary, and Vrdolyak would run as an independent. Byrne had dropped all talk of running as a Republican.

Washington chose the Democratic primary. Speculation was that the independent route looked less appealing because no serious Republican entered the race.* Washington's advisers insisted that their man never seriously contemplated a run as an independent—the ploy was only meant to keep his foes guessing. As expected, Vrdolyak announced he would run in the general election to avoid hurting Byrne's chances. The chairman of the

---

*The announced Republicans included Bernard Epton; a professor at Northwestern's business school; and perennial candidate Ray "Spanky" Wardingly. Epton was knocked off the ballot because he failed to gather enough valid signatures.

country's largest local Democratic organization would run as a third-party candidate against his own party's nominee.

The Democratic party did not bother with an endorsement. Chairman Vrdolyak sent a letter to the ward committeemen decreeing it "meaningless," and that was that. It was the first time in over fifty years that the local party would forgo an endorsement session for mayor, and presumably one of the rare times in U.S. politics when a party chairman actually declared his own party's endorsement meaningless.

There was a chance that Vrdolyak might face Byrne in the general election; still, he announced that he was lending the Byrne campaign two thousand workers. He also declared that he was running as a third party rather than as an independent because, under an obscure state law, anyone signing the nominating petition of an independent candidate forfeits his or her right to vote in the primary. "I would not dare to have sixty thousand or seventy thousand signatures challenged and have people not allowed to vote for Byrne versus Washington," he said. "I will not be a spoiler in the primary." Vrdolyak was saying, in effect, that he would not dare spoil the chances of any white person challenging Washington, yet such was the inured state of Chicago that Vrdolyak's comments went virtually uncommented on.

Shortly after Vrdolyak announced for mayor, another lifelong Democrat, Cook County Assessor Tom Hynes, declared his candidacy. Hynes was the Democratic committeeman from the Nineteenth Ward, but he, too, announced he was skipping the primary to run as a third-party candidate. Hynes would not endorse Byrne. He also assured voters he would lie low until after the primary races.

Vrdolyak greeted Hynes's announcement with the kind of insults he usually reserved for Washington. Vrdolyak reminded voters that Hynes was aligned with the Daley faction—the same people who supposedly split the white vote in 1983. "It's rule or ruin with these folks," Vrdolyak said. Hynes, he said, was nothing but a "spoiler."

Meanwhile, Washington gloated. His foes should have been holding hands and singing sweet songs of unity, dancing around a single candidate they proclaimed their savior. Instead, several candidates were in the race, vying for dollars, precinct workers, and political talent. The fabled Chicago machine seemed suddenly feeble. Washington likened his situation to the so-called bum-of-the-month who challenged Joe Louis for boxing's heavyweight title. Like Louis, Washington said, he felt he was waiting for the next Great White Hope.

There were the predictable battles within Washington's camp over how he should handle the race issue. There were those urging Washington to stress the machine's racism, past and present, and those who said he should not even mention the word. The former group argued that only by attacking Byrne's record could Washington rekindle the emotions of 1983.

Yet Washington saw nothing but negatives in a strategy that stressed race. Perhaps he couldn't repeat the crusadelike fervor of 1983, but he had new weapons on his side—money (he raised $5 million for the 1987 election including nearly $1 million at a fund-raiser that summer) and all the advantages of an incumbency. The biggest challenge back in 1983—convincing black Chicago he stood a chance of winning—was no longer an issue. He was more experienced and no longer an underdog. The media's polls showed Washington with a solid twelve-to-sixteen-percentage-point lead over Byrne.

This time there was no Task Force for Black Political Empowerment operating as a second brain center; leaders such as Conrad Worrill instead sat among the other campaign strategists. Lu Palmer would play next to no role in the campaign by mutual consent. Whereas in 1983 Washington had described Daley as "a racist from the core," on the occasion of the tenth anniversary of Daley's death, Washington said, "He was not a perfect man, but he was as perfect as you can be in an imperfect world." Washington was criticized for his "Great White Hope" crack but generally steered clear of any mention of race. "Our approach this time," Deputy Campaign Manager Jacky Grimshaw said, "is more intellectual than emotional."

Yet there was still something emotional in the support behind Washington. If nothing else, Ed Vrdolyak and his minions had seen to that through three and one-half years of Council Wars.

On a cold Sunday evening a few weeks after he kicked off his campaign, thousands packed a large auditorium downtown. The event had more the feel of an old-fashioned religious revival than a political rally. Washington stepped into view, and the balcony shook with the stamping of feet. The crowd chanted its ubiquitous mantra, "Ha-rold, Ha-rold," a woman sang gospel accompanied by a band, and onstage Washington danced to the beat by himself. People looked to their neighbors, sharing a familiar, welcome feeling, like greeting an old friend with whom they hadn't spent time in years.

Washington avoided the thorny Jesse Jackson issue as best he could. Jackson was offered no role in the campaign, a decision full of ironies. Jackson put forward a message of multiracial politics, yet precisely because Washington sought to present his campaign as a rainbow effort, that forced him to minimize Jackson's role. Perhaps only in Chicago in 1987 would a black politician use a photograph in his recruitment brochure only after cropping out Jackson.

In the old days the regular Democrats took care to run a slate that reflected the ethnic makeup of the city. The Washington campaign effort was similar except that they thought in terms of race, not ethnicity. In its ubiquitous campaign picture—Washington smiling, his arms outstretched, standing before a crowd gathered around the Picasso statue in Daley Plaza—great pains were taken so that a multiracial crowd served as the picture's backdrop. The group was refigured when someone noticed that no Asian was in plain sight. No one monitoring the shot wondered, however, whether among the whites there might be a disproportionate number of Italians or not enough Poles. In the past the dream ticket might have someone Irish, a black, and a Pole. Inside the Washington campaign there was wistful talk of the perfect "tricolor ticket"—a black man for mayor, a Latino for city clerk, and a white liberal for city treasurer.*

Lu Palmer was incredulous when he learned that Washington would downplay race in the 1987 campaign. Race was an element in virtually every problem confronting Chicago. The manufacturing jobs that fled Chicago disproportionately hurt blacks; the problems of the public schools and economic development were largely black problems. The Urban League had found in 1983 that the economic disparities between blacks and whites in

---

*The tricolor ticket never worked out. Washington endorsed a Latina named Gloria Chevere to run for city clerk but did not dump the incumbent city treasurer, a machine-oriented black man named Cecil Partee, and no white independent emerged as a challenger for that post.

Chicago were far greater than any of the eleven metropolitan areas with a population over 2.5 million. The 1980 census had revealed that Chicago was home to ten of the sixteen poorest communities in the country. All ten were black neighborhoods, but, Palmer said, "Harold's so afraid of what white people might say that he agrees he won't talk about race." Washington had tried healing the rift between the two by hosting a fund-raiser to help Palmer retire his congressional campaign debt, but the mayor's perceived sins as mayor stood in Palmer's way.

Palmer was also outraged by the campaign's multiracial approach. A black man named William Walls had already announced for city clerk before Washington allowed his Latino allies to find a qualified Latino to take that post. "Our communities are in competition for political advancement," Palmer said. "We both want to make up for past abuses. You have to make up your mind who comes first."

Washington knew Walls. He was a former aide who was something of a traveling valet for Washington in 1983—the man who took care of the tab, for instance, when Washington and a few aides stopped off for lunch—and then handled his schedule for his first couple of years in office. Washington grew frustrated with Walls's propensity for passing himself off as more important than he was, and fired him in 1985. He didn't consider for a moment supporting Walls for clerk. When asked on a radio program about Palmer's comments, Washington waved them off by dismissing Palmer's organization, BIPO—the Black Independent Political Organization. "BIPO-Shmipo," he said.

Crime was a centerpiece of Byrne's campaign. One Byrne ad showed a child holding a razor blade, cutting lines of white powder. Under Washington an announcer intoned, "Drug arrests are down nearly eight percent." In another spot, crime statistics scroll the screen. Each of Byrne's four crime commercials ended with the same message: "The more you think about it the more you know—Chicago can't afford Harold Washington."

It was true, as Byrne's ad claimed, that drug arrests dropped eight percent between 1985 and 1986, but that was due to the banner year for drug arrests the police enjoyed in 1985. Actually, drug arrests were up compared to the Byrne years, even taking into account the drop-off in

1986.* Byrne took advantage of a similar statistical blip to portray Washington's Chicago as one overwhelmed by murder. In 1986 there were a reported 666 murders in Chicago, the lowest figure since 1968. The next year the murder rate rose by fifteen percent. So Byrne's ad cited a fifteen percent rise in the murder rate under Washington. The 740 people murdered in 1986, however, were still fewer than the average 816 murders per year during Byrne's tenure.

One need look no further than Washington's cuts in the police department, Byrne said, to see that he did not care about crime. "While drugs and crime are out of control," one Byrne television commercial claimed, "Washington reduced police protection by almost 1,000 officers." Yet there were 12,565 uniformed police in Chicago at the start of 1987, compared with 12,581 when Washington took office. That was a drop of 16, not 1,000.

Black Chicago, not white Chicago, is hardest hit by crime. An estimated two-thirds of the city's crime is black on black. Federal crime statistics show that black Americans are twice as likely as whites to be robbed or raped, and stand a four times greater chance of being murdered. Nearly ninety percent of the whites who are murdered or raped were the victims of other whites, not people of color. Yet the white community in Chicago and elsewhere has always acted as if it has a monopoly on the issues of crime and fear.

"You will be robbed or killed," the hate literature said back in 1983, contemplating Washington as mayor. "White women will be raped. With a black police chief there will be absolute chaos in the city." Four years later the terminology was much tamer, but the message was the same.

Any criminologist can tell you there's little connection between fluctuations in the crime rate and the size of the police force. Innumerable studies have shown that other factors, such as the weather (a mild winter is certain to chase the crime rate up), are better indicators of the incidence of crime than the number of police on the beat. Moreover, a rising crime rate does not necessarily reveal something bad. Improved relations between police

---

*From 1979 through 1982 the police averaged 15,641 drug arrests per year. From 1983 through 1986 they averaged 19,814 per year—a twenty-seven percent increase.

and the people they serve is a positive development that drives up the number of reported crimes.* Short of eradicating poverty, drug addiction, and other factors, there is only so much a mayor can do.

Nonetheless, a crime-centered campaign is an effective strategy, especially against a black incumbent. Reporters at the *Reader* and the *Tribune* presented a thinly disguised hypothesis for several political strategists. If you were putting together a no-holds-barred campaign against an incumbent black mayor, what issues would you hammer at hardest? Crime was the consensus choice. It's a winner, one out-of-town media consultant said, because "it stirs up racial feelings. It's a good issue to yell about to whip whites up." At the top or near the top of any survey of voter concerns, crime is a legitimate campaign issue. The trick, then, was to emphasize it with propriety.

Between elections a group formed calling itself CONDUCT—the Committee on Decent Unbiased Campaign Tactics. CONDUCT was to be an impartial arbiter to decide what was proper and when candidates were resorting to bigotry, a strictly blue-ribbon panel that reflected the racial makeup of the city but whose members were described in press accounts as "civic leaders." Seven of CONDUCT's twenty-nine members were business executives, six were clergy, and five were college presidents. John McDermott, who had been editor and publisher of the *Chicago Reporter* for twelve years before taking a job with Illinois Bell, headed the group.

CONDUCT was well meaning, yet its usefulness was another matter entirely. It made no mention of Byrne's handling of the crime issue, nor did it see fit to comment on white politicians who freely threw around the word "spoiler" as code for two whites splitting the white vote. Nor did CONDUCT opine on a *Sun-Times* article that ran just prior to the final day for registering to vote. VOTER APATHY LIFTS MAYOR'S PRIMARY HOPE, read the page-one headline. The figure cited—a projected turnout of seventy percent among whites—hardly revealed apathy, however. In the body

---

*Wesley Skogan, a noted Northwestern University criminologist, found that between 1984 and 1986 citizen complaints against police for excessive force decreased by twenty percent. "Complaints against the police are down," Skogan said just prior to the 1987 election. "Police shooting of civilians is down, the total discharge of firearms [the number of bullets fired] is down . . . there's been a real civilizing of police behavior."

of the article, Vrdolyak's pollster readily acknowledged he provided his polling data to the *Sun-Times* precisely to spur registration.

CONDUCT instead focused on the conspicuous. Jacky Grimshaw was reprimanded for using the term "right-minded whites," as was Byrne for using the phrase "from the Gold Coast to the Soul Coast" (a favorite of Jesse Jackson's). CONDUCT declared "excessive and inflammatory" a quote by Washington supporter Tom Todd, who said, "I'm sick and tired of the pinstripe bigots. I'm sick and tired of the racists who have changed their white sheets for blue suits." CONDUCT would wade no deeper. By way of explanation, McDermott plaintively asked if one understood how difficult it was to reach a consensus in so diverse and unwieldy a group as was under his charge.

CONDUCT was able to agree, though, that the 1987 election was a far more agreeable experience than 1983's had been. At least there were no watermelon buttons this time.

The most publicized racial incidents of the primary involved two zealous Washington supporters, Dorothy Tillman and Eugene Pincham. An Illinois appellate court judge, Pincham was speaking at PUSH about a month before the primary. It was a passionate and moving speech that included one line in particular that drew media attention: "Any man south of Madison Street [the dividing line between north and south] who casts a vote in the February 24 election and who doesn't cast a vote for Harold Washington ought to be hung." Washington did not denounce Pincham, as some commentators demanded, but instead defended him: "It was slang. He is a very peaceful, honest man, one of the best judges in the world."

The Tillman incident occurred two weeks later. Tillman was at a news conference for a group calling themselves Women Embarrassed by Byrne when she began extemporizing on Washington's record from the standpoint of the lakefront: he cut the city payroll by something like fifteen percent; signed the Shakman decree; passed an ethics ordinance, despite opposition on both sides of the council fight—in other words, he initiated a host of cost efficiencies. To her mind, Tillman said, she could see no reason other than the color of Washington's skin that would stand in the way of lakefront liberals voting for him over Byrne. Tillman's remarks were featured prominently in the media, as were Pincham's two weeks earlier.

The media quoted Tillman with proper horror, never pausing to weigh her statement. It was a point worth debating. Whites along the lakefront carped that embracing Washington meant embracing Clarence McClain and Renault Robinson, yet the alternative was Jane Byrne, who sold out the lakefront reformers and surrounded herself with the likes of Charles Swibel, John D'Arco, and Ed Vrdolyak. The *Sun-Times* and the *Tribune* endorsed Washington. The *Tribune* extolled Washington for budgets that were "balanced without hidden deficits and other traditional City Hall voodoo."

What few lakefronters said, at least publicly, was that they feared Washington because he was too black—too black in style or too black in his language, or maybe just too black to avoid noticing that he was black. It was not at all unusual to attend a gathering at a pricey condominium in Lincoln Park and hear the highly educated host and hostess and their lovely friends talk about the nigger mayor. Mike Royko, himself a Lincoln Park resident, wrote of the white liberals who "hyperventilate if they find themselves on the elevator with a black delivery man." Tillman was summarily pilloried for having the audacity to say that the emperor wore no clothes.

Jane Byrne was not faring well. Polls showed Washington holding on to a solid fifty-four percent of the vote and Byrne barely at forty percent*— though there were developments worth celebrating, such as Alderman Juan Soliz's endorsement. Soliz, who had once described Byrne as a "travesty," and accused her of "shortchanging Latinos their due," stood beside the former mayor and said he was "delighted and thrilled" to give her his "undivided endorsement." But her triumphs were few and far between. Either her attacks were falling on deaf ears or her aim was off. In the closing weeks of the campaign she jumped with fervor on Pincham's and Tillman's remarks and anything else that struck a racial nerve among voters.

---

*One Gallup poll, done for the *Sun-Times* and Channel 7 and released in late January, showed the mayor's race neck and neck. But Gallup based that poll, its pollster admitted, on the assumption that blacks would make up thirty-six percent of the electorate when in 1983 blacks accounted for something like forty-two percent. After realizing that his numbers were way out of whack with other polls (and after both the *Sun-Times* and Channel 7 ballyhooed the poll as if announcing the election's winner), he chose the forty-two percent figure, and again Washington was winning by over eleven percentage points.

Byrne's next rotation of television ads highlighted Pincham's comment. Pincham, not Washington, said what he did, but Byrne acted as if there was no difference. In the ad she ran, Pincham's injudicious remarks were used as an example of Washington dividing Chicago. Washington had immediately disavowed Tillman's words, but Byrne blamed Washington for those remarks just the same.

"We must end the polarization of the Washington administration," a Byrne mailer said. "We can make government work for *all* the people again. . . . We must restore the simple principles of merit and fairness to government." References like these crept into Byrne's literature and into her standard stump speech in the last weeks of the campaign. The implication of her slogan, "A Mayor for *All* Chicago," was clear even if her own campaign did not reflect this multiracial sentiment. She bothered with few appearances in the black community (she cited intimidation), and there were no blacks among her downtown campaign staff.

Her campaign put together a slick thirty-minute video that ran on one of the city's television stations—a paean to the racial unity and feeling of safety that people had felt when she was mayor. In Jane Byrne's Chicago the paid advertisement said, "People loved their city." She called for a return to saner days when the city wasn't split in two. In another ad Byrne stared sincerely at the camera and said, "Love. Unity. Pride. Sharing. Hope. I want Chicago to smile again."

In their respective tenures, Byrne did more to incite black Chicago than Washington to incite white Chicago, yet a Byrne press aide named Andy Bajonski said in one interview that it's "a schmuck like Washington who's racially polarizing this city."*

Near the end of January, Byrne made a campaign appearance at the Cabrini-Green housing project where, as mayor, she had lived for two weeks. Byrne drove her dark blue Lincoln through the project, the *Sun-Times* reported, but left her car "just long enough to visit the Chicago police outpost that is housed in one of the Cabrini buildings."

---

*Five months before the 1983 primary election, Byrne commissioned a study of Chicago's neighborhoods. Blacks, an early draft of the study reported, perceived that Chicago was "a racist city which has sharp divisions between the haves and the have-nots" that could be dealt with only through the election of a black mayor. Byrne canceled the study after seeing the early results. The report was not made public until the Washington administration asked its author to send a copy of it to prove he actually earned the money he was paid.

The labor bigwigs who gathered to endorse either Byrne or Washington shouldn't have wasted much time with debate. Both of the candidates had served a single term as mayor; from labor's standpoint, the two terms could not have been more different. Byrne's relations with labor were tense, to say the least. Stormy strikes, handshake agreements later betrayed, arms twisted to force a campaign contribution—those were the Byrne years. As a candidate for mayor she had promised to fight for the right to collective bargaining, but that was one of the many promises Byrne broke after she became mayor.

In Washington, labor had a lifelong union man with a strong labor voting record. After he was elected mayor he endorsed a long-term traditional unionist to take his place in Congress. He had a wall's worth of awards and plaques from the Illinois Federation of Labor and similar groups. Only the most moderate labor leaders were welcome in the typical legislator's office; in Washington's, labor activists less accommodating to the bosses gathered to plot legislative strategy with their ally, Harold.

Washington's supporters in the labor movement were generally pleased with his performance. As mayor he proved to be a hard-nosed negotiator, yet he abandoned the traditional handshake agreements in favor of collective bargaining and cleared the way for the unionization of ten thousand white-collar workers. Besides, Washington was an incumbent mayor. The labor council always endorsed the incumbent mayor.

Yet the labor council voted to endorse neither candidate. Perhaps there were motivations other than race, but it seemed that the truth was no more complicated than the facts that he was black, his opponent white, and the labor council's majority was white as well.

Near the end of the campaign a caravan of people calling themselves "reverse freedom riders" arrived in Chicago to campaign on Washington's behalf. Most were from the South, though the group's leader, the Reverend Benjamin Chavis, Jr., was the executive director of the New York–based Commission for Racial Justice. The commission was run under the auspices of the United Church of Christ.

Predictably, the Byrne campaign went into high gear, figuring that a great many white Chicagoans would resent southern blacks pointing an accusing finger at the city. Reporters quoted anonymous Byrne aides offering that Washington may just have committed the gaffe they were hoping for. It may have been the issue their candidate needed to spur a big turnout among white ethnics and sway lakefronters.

Byrne spoke of these reverse freedom riders the day of their arrival, the next day, and the day after that. "A very, very important negative factor entering the city," Byrne said of these "outsiders. . . . We'll still live with the taxes and the high crime when they are gone again," she added. At a rally two days after the group's arrival in Chicago, Ed Burke decried these "carpetbaggers" among us, led by "fly-by-night, two-bit reverends from Selma, Alabama." Burke also reminded the crowd that Washington had once dismissed Byrne's limousine as "obscene." "What do you think that big, fat, 250-pound frame is riding around in today?" Burke asked, to the crowd's delight.

Byrne harped on her divided city theme through election day. The night before, the Byrne campaign sent word that Byrne would stop at Holy Name Cathedral for a moment of prayer. Outside the church she told reporters that she prayed "the city comes back together again and moves forward as the great city that it is."

For most of the primary it was a muted Harold Washington versus a hard-hitting Byrne. Washington rarely took the bait, instead straining like a dog pulling against a short leash. Though Washington might have taken comfort in the comfortable cushion between him and Byrne, instead he groused about the game plan as each day the media reported more Byrne charges.

The dampened image of Washington was reminiscent, ironically, of Byrne's 1983 makeover, yet Washington wasn't quite as willing a subject as Byrne. "Unless [campaign manager] Ken Glover called him early in the morning to remind him," press secretary Al Miller wrote, "he was likely to show up with the same soup-stained paisley cravat, finger-stained at the knot, that he had worn the day before."

The plan was to stick to the issues, yet on several occasions he allowed his instincts to get the better of him. The worst time came when he said that Byrne "reminds me of Hitler. The Big Lie." Byrne immediately expressed her outrage, but her former campaign manager, Don Rose, was around to remind people that in that election, Byrne had likened *her* foe to Hitler.

Byrne captured almost all the undecided vote—maybe her eleventh-hour exploits made the difference. Washington, though, held firm to his bedrock fifty-four percent of the vote.

Washington won something like 99.6 percent of the black vote. In 31 precincts Byrne failed to receive a single vote; in 110 others she won only one vote; in nearly one-third of all the city's precincts she received fewer than 10. Black turnout fell from 1983 when an astounding sixty-eight percent of all those blacks old enough to vote in the general election showed up at the polls; it fell by eleven percentage points.* Yet white turnout dipped as well—by eight percentage points, to fifty-eight. The *Sun-Times* had its own view of Byrne's loss, despite the numbers: VOTING PLUNGES IN WHITE AREAS, the headline over one of its postprimary pieces read.

Washington won few new converts in six north lakefront wards. Against Epton, residents there gave Washington forty-two percent of their vote; against Byrne, Washington inched up to forty-four percent. That number was less impressive still when considering that twenty percent of the lakefront is nonwhite. Washington fared worse still among those living on the southwest and northwest sides.

SON-SOCC, the coalition of northwest and southwest side community groups formed shortly after Washington's election, learned to live with the mayor just as he learned to live with them. In 1985 Washington gathered with SON-SOCC leaders at a City Hall press conference, where he said, "One of the greatest challenges of my administration is reaching out and appreciating the special needs and concerns of the predominantly white ethnic middle-income neighborhoods. . . . This coalition once asked me to

---

*Registration figures are most commonly given as a percentage of registered voters rather than as a percentage of the voting-age population. To use that more standard measure, eighty percent of the registered black voters showed up at the polls in the 1983 general election, compared to seventy-two percent in the 1987 primary. In the 1983 general election, eighty-five percent of black Chicago was registered to vote, in 1987, seventy-eight percent.

light a candle of understanding of their communities. I want to light a candle of understanding in each and every community in our city until the city is blazing with enlightenment." Jean Mayer, one of SON-SOCC's two co-chairs, said she was so pleased that day she nearly cried.

Jean Mayer came to respect Washington. He treated her community group, the Southwest Parish and Neighborhood Federation, with greater respect than previous mayors, especially Jane Byrne. Certainly under Washington her group had greater access than ever before. Where the local Democratic organization had been hostile to neighborhood groups, Mayer credited Washington with providing community groups access to the information they needed, such as police beat statistics and housing court records. She also had positive things to say about Rob Mier, Washington's director of economic development. Perhaps it was only because housing dollars were scarce, but Washington didn't push a sudden influx of scattered-site housing in white areas, as SON-SOCC's membership feared.

The issue dearest to SON-SOCC leaders was their home equity proposal. Under their plan every property owner would pay a small annual fee—something like $20—to provide insurance against property loss should a neighborhood change racially. SON-SOCC's logic was that this would blunt the panic if a black family moved into a neighborhood. At least this would assuage the well-meaning homeowners' fears of financial ruin, guaranteeing them the market value of their homes. Washington secured on SON-SOCC's behalf the $90,000 they sought to fund a home equity research project. When Washington announced his support of home equity, SON-SOCC leaders were thrilled.

A black attorney named Tim Wright was the administration's liaison to SON-SOCC. Of SON-SOCC, Wright said, "I worked with some of the bitterest, angriest, meanest, disrespectful folks imaginable." When Washington spoke before their group, Wright overheard comments such as, "Get your fat ass home." So, too, did many inside the administration, those derisively calling the home equity plan "insurance against black folks." Yet Wright found Washington's patience amazing. "He kept coming to their conventions," Wright said, "no matter how narrow a viewpoint they took."

There was a softening in attitude toward Washington among the city's white ethnics. There was no frenzied opposition as there had been in 1983. White voter turnout fell between 1983 and 1987, causing a Washington pollster to write, "Whites appear to be much less hostile at the notion of another four years with Harold Washington as mayor."

Yet those living on the northwest and southwest sides still did not vote for him. The anti-Washington sentiment on the southwest side was still high, where a Republican named Robert Raica first won election as state senator in 1986 after handing out leaflets with a picture of Washington and the headline, LET'S WIPE THE SMILE FROM HIS FACE! Jean Mayer did not campaign on Washington's behalf in 1987, nor did any of the other SON-SOCC leaders who favorably compared Washington with his predecessors. SON-SOCC leaders spoke with a hatred for Byrne, yet Mayer said it was a safe assumption that few SON-SOCC members voted for Washington.

In Mayer's ward, the Thirteenth, a candidate named Art Jones ran for alderman. Jones was formerly a spokesperson for the Nazi group that insisted on marching in the heavily Jewish suburb of Skokie a decade earlier. By 1987 he headed a group that he described as pro-white, pro-Christian, and anti-Zionist. Jones received 1,055 votes to Washington's 1,298; in twenty-four precincts, Jones actually outpolled Washington.

Washington fared better among voters on the northwest and southwest sides than he did in 1983—two-tenths of a percentage point better. He got only one in twenty votes from these once-loyal Democrats of the southwest and northwest sides. Still, had all those whites who voted for Epton in 1983 turned out in full force for Byrne, Washington would have lost the primary.

The 1987 primary seemed no testimonial to the Rainbow Coalition. Neither the Washington administration's neighborhood approach to development nor its reform agenda seemed enough to win new converts. Yet there were advancements worthy of note. Washington did not pick up much new white support, but his vote totals among the city's gays and lesbians soared. An estimated eighty percent of the gay vote went for Washington. Two northwest side precincts where Washington fared surprisingly well stumped those pundits who didn't know that that neighborhood was known as a lesbian enclave. A majority of the city's Asian Americans voted for Washington, who named the city's first Asian-American liaison and did more than simply show up at a few Chinatown Chamber of Commerce luncheons in search of endorsements.

Those resting their hopes on a black-Latino alliance couldn't have been more pleased. Washington captured fifty-nine percent of the Latino vote, four times more than the fifteen percent he won in the 1983 primary. The black precincts in Latino wards again treated progressive Latino aldermanic candidates to overwhelming majorities. The city clerk's race, pitting Gloria Chevere against Bill Walls and the machine incumbent, Walter Kozubowski, proved another significant victory. Well-known black activists such as Lu Palmer hit the stump on Walls's behalf, yet four of every five black voters sided with Chevere. Walls received a scant four percent of the black vote.

The general election brought new problems for Washington's foes Ed Vrdolyak and Tom Hynes, both Democrats running as third-party candidates swearing they were in the race through the end. Both offered righteous arguments why the other should drop out. White committeemen quickly grew weary. Some of their precinct workers were with Vrdolyak, others with Hynes. The majority of white committeemen saw Hynes as the stronger candidate, but mainly they were in favor of a resolution between the two. With only six weeks between the primary and the general elections, Hynes and Vrdolyak were busy attacking each other, wasting precious time. Don Rose likened it to a horror film: King Kong and Godzilla fighting as the castle burned.

Vrdolyak was certainly the more spirited of the two. He put together a smart campaign, casting himself as a conservative antitax populist. This was an election between "the taxpayer" and "the freeloader," he said—between the working stiffs, and the liberal elitists and "special interests." He sprinkled conservative totems into his message, like his declaration that if elected he would make drug testing mandatory for all city employees.

Hynes promised a City Hall so quiet "you won't even know I'm there," figuring that people sought a sane alternative to Council Wars. Yet what the Hynes people saw as a plus, Vrdolyak saw as Hynes's great weakness. Only Vrdolyak could generate the enthusiasm, his supporters said, that would bring into the voting booth those white ethnics who stayed home in the primary.

Yet the simple fact was that Vrdolyak couldn't win. Polls consistently ranked Vrdolyak as one of the least popular politicians in town (if not for Ed Burke, he would probably have been the least popular). One showed

Vrdolyak's disapproval rating at sixty-four percent—a percentage point *higher,* *Tribune* columnist Steve Neal noted, than Richard Nixon's disapproval rating in the final days of his presidency. A later *Tribune* poll revealed that forty-nine percent of the city's registered voters were "absolutely opposed" to Vrdolyak as mayor.

The pundits took to speculation. Maybe Vrdolyak was in the race because it had turned into something personal between him and Washington. Maybe it was only the ploy of someone seeking to make a deal—Vrdolyak was only in the race to be bought out.

Or maybe it was a deeply felt resentment against the entire Daley bloc. He was in the trenches fighting while the Daleyites, he said, "never took a draw, never took a stand." Vrdolyak chaired the 29's caucus session; he understood that Alderman Patrick Huels, the Daley clan's man in the City Council, could be counted among the caucus's hawks, though he was silent on the council floor. Daley acted as if he were above the Council Wars, but Daley, a lifelong Democrat, made no endorsement in the Democratic primary and then avoided his party's candidate in favor of Hynes. Hynes set himself up as a voice of calm and reason amid the craziness, yet he never used his considerable influence to do anything to stem the 29's obstructionism. Why should Vrdolyak step out of the race for the likes of these dilettantes?

When Vrdolyak and Hynes were not attacking each other, the general election followed pretty much the same script as the primary. Both Hynes and Vrdolyak made much of the crime issue, especially Vrdolyak. "The mayor is basically antipolice," he said. The cover of Vrdolyak's anticrime brochure proclaimed that Chicago was losing its war on crime "because Harold Washington is more interested in registering criminals to vote than in arresting them!" He included a shot of Jesse Jackson registering two inmates at the Cook County Jail. ("Jesse Jackson," Vrdolyak said during one television interview, "says he represents the locked out. Well, this mayor represents the locked up.") Like Byrne, Vrdolyak played on a 1985 dip in the crime rate to make claims of a city where crime was suddenly out of control. He also spoke of the forty-nine years (!) that Washington did not file his tax forms.

Vrdolyak didn't shy away from the subject of race; he raised it at every opportunity, primarily to say that race was not what this election was about. In his announcement speech, Vrdolyak implored Washington not to use race as a weapon. "The first time you hear me do any of that stuff, you can call me on the carpet," he said. Minutes later Vrdolyak accused Washington of making the campaign a racial one "because that's the only way he can win."

Vrdolyak blamed Washington and his followers for Chicago's reputation as the country's most racist city. Though the quote did not plague him in press accounts as, say, Jackson's "Hymie-town" remarks hounded him, it was Vrdolyak who delivered 1983's infamous it's "a racial thing" speech. (When confronted about the speech during the 1987 election, Vrdolyak denied it, despite the reporters present who claimed otherwise.) Reporters from around the world were drawn to Chicago by the hateful Epton supporters, but as Vrdolyak saw it, Washington's refusal to recognize that twenty-nine was greater than twenty-one launched the Council Wars, tarnishing Chicago's image.

"It's time to put color voting by the boards and get somebody who can run a $3 billion-a-year corporation," Vrdolyak said. If I were black, Vrdolyak hypothesized, I would have voted for Washington in 1983. But not this time around. "He doesn't have a clue about what the job is about," Vrdolyak said. "He doesn't have the faintest idea of how to run a government."

Campaign aides were frustrated with Washington when he traded charges of anti-Semitism with Vrdolyak (winning each a censure from CONDUCT) when remaining above the fray was the wiser course. Yet for the most part Washington ignored Vrdolyak's taunts, much as it pained him. After the campaign's one and only debate, which saw a dull Washington reciting statistics and accomplishments, Washington admitted privately that Vrdolyak had badly outpointed him. "My own campaign did something to me that Vrdolyak could never do," he said to his press secretary. "They cut my balls off."

Washington again broke with strategy when he assailed Tom Hynes after the *Sun-Times* tied the county assessor to a sour-smelling city deal. Hynes responded just as Washington had hoped. Outraged, he said that

Washington's history was "one of sleaze" and that he "surrounds himself with grafters and corrupters." Washington heard rumors that Hynes was considering pulling out of the race; his brief attack was just a way of making it personal for Hynes, an inducement to keep him in the running.

Forty hours before the polls were to open, Hynes did drop out. Vrdolyak thanked Hynes for "putting the best interests of the city of Chicago before any personal ambition" and then crisscrossed the city in pursuit of Hynes voters. Some of those who had endorsed Hynes, such as Rich Daley, declined to endorse either Vrdolyak or Washington, but most switched to Vrdolyak.

Washington won the election with the same fifty-four percent of the vote he won in the primary. His share of the white vote actually decreased from the primary—dropping from fourteen percent to twelve percent—and though Vrdolyak may have been strident and hard-line, he, not the Republican in the race, Don Haider, received the vast remainder. For most voters the switch from Byrne to Vrdolyak or Hynes seemed near-automatic.

The results were no different on the lakefront. There, too, Washington's share of the vote dropped from the primary—by seven percentage points. The results in Alderman Marty Oberman's Forty-third Ward seemed particularly curious. Despite his reservations about Washington, Oberman campaigned aggressively on his behalf. The upscale Forty-third Ward had long been considered a bastion of antimachine sentiments, but no longer. Washington garnered less than thirty percent of the vote there. Its voters did not opt for the more benign choice of Haider but instead gave Vrdolyak a clean majority. Perhaps that was the great irony of Chicago politics in the late 1980s. It was no longer black Chicago that was a captive of old-time machine politics but the white community, imprisoned by racial fears and biases.

After Hynes dropped out, there was optimistic talk inside Washington's campaign of a landslide of winning with over sixty percent of the vote. The campaign figured on picking up a goodly portion of Hynes's lakefront vote and maybe a smattering of white ethnic voters who couldn't tolerate Vrdolyak. Until a few days before election day, the Washington campaign's daily tracking polls showed Washington with nearly thirty percent of the white vote and a significant number of undecideds. Newspaper polls showed him receiving somewhere around sixteen percent of the vote on the southwest and northwest sides. Yet he received the same five percent he received in the primary.

"They just couldn't do it," a Washington strategist said years later. "The white voters got into the booths and saw a black face, and their hands started to shake and they just couldn't do it."

Washington was bitter. He took it personally that so many whites chose Vrdolyak over him, but he put up a good front. He spoke of the "mandate for a movement" but knew full well that his vote margin was nothing of the sort.

His supporters didn't seem to care much, though. At the victory party that night he delighted them by singing a disastrously off-key rendition of "Chicago, Chicago, That Toddlin' Town." They cheered him when he made a boast he had made so many times: he would be mayor for twenty years, he said playfully.

21

THY

KINGDOM

AT

HAND

Long after it was too late, long after the controversies, the bad press, and the grumbling even among loyal partisans, Harold Washington would admit that Renault Robinson was a poor choice to head the Chicago Housing Authority. While overseas, relaxing in the company of several aides, Washington broached the subject.

I know he's not working out, Washington confessed late at night and full of drink. He said that the problem was the inspiring role Robinson had played in his life. Washington was at least twenty years Robinson's senior, but he was impressed by this young cop who fearlessly battled the police brass, who was still walking a beat at the same time he was battling them in the courts and in the media. People were pressuring Washington to move Robinson aside, but he said it was hard to stop believing in a man like that.

Despite the promise of a new order, the state of the CHA had hardly improved with Washington's election. A resident was still as likely as in the past to carry her groceries twenty or thirty floors to her high-rise apartment because the elevators were broken; she still felt unsafe on those stairs, if walking at night, because there were always burned-out light bulbs that took forever to replace.

What press the CHA generated was invariably bad. There were reports of infighting at the top and also allegations that cast Robinson as no different from his predecessors. To top it off, the city missed the due date for an application that meant the loss, at least temporarily, of $7 million from the federal government. Robinson blamed the executive director under his charge; the executive director blamed Robinson. The snafu and subsequent fighting remained a top news story in the final months of 1986, with the 1987 election fast approaching.

In January 1987, with election day less than two months off, Washington ordered Al Miller to prepare a resignation statement for Robinson to read to the press. More than a few supporters noted that it took the pressures of an approaching election to spur Washington into action at the CHA.

The first vision of public housing in Chicago was a liberal one. For those in the fledgling public housing movement across the country, Chicago was something of a mecca. The city was home to Elizabeth Wood, Edith Abbott, and J. S. Fuerst, heroes to those agitating nationally for a federal policy that provided adequate housing for all. Their vision was of low-rise, well-integrated projects that were first and foremost to blend in with the neighborhood. There was the glory of the Ida B. Wells Homes, built in Chicago in the early 1940s, three- and four-story walk-ups and two-story row houses with grassy courtyards. They were the envy of the ghetto.

But this vision gave way in the 1950s and 1960s to huge housing projects of clustered high rises. "Canyons of despair that should never have been built," Harold Washington said of the rows of massive high rises that constituted the majority of units at the CHA. Built cheaply, they were "mindful of gigantic filing cabinets with separate cubicles for each human household," federal investigators wrote. Inside, the walls were cinder block; in the dead of winter, windows were open in housing projects around the city because otherwise the apartment dwellers felt as if they were inside the furnaces steaming out of control downstairs.

But in 1983 they became Washington's problem. There were those who advocated that they be demolished—some because they were sympathetic to the squalor and pain of those trapped in these behemoth towers, others because they saw the profit that could be made tearing down projects like Cabrini-Green on the edge of a pricey neighborhood. But with no place to house those living there, the city was stuck with these projects that were riddled with crime, drugs, and so many murders that death was as much a way of life for children growing up there as it was for the young in Lebanon and Belfast. So dangerous were the projects that children said "if they grow up" rather than "when they grow up."

Robinson seemed a strange choice to head an agency so desperately in need of a major overhaul that perhaps there existed no one who was capable of handling the task. Heading the CHA board was not unlike serving as mayor of a small impoverished city. The 145,000 people who lived in CHA housing, if a city unto themselves, would be the second largest in the state. And Robinson was certainly not the kind of manager who worked miracles. He was trained to be a cop and had earned a master's degree in urban studies. Robinson headed a relatively tiny organization in the Afro-American Police League, dirt poor with no staff outside himself. That was the extent of his management experience unless one included his brief and disastrous stint as Washington's first campaign manager in 1983. Maybe Washington should have taken that as some kind of sign. Robinson was a crusader, not a manager.

The reaction to Robinson's promotion to CHA board chairman was as predictable as it was harsh. Ed Burke said the appointment "stinks to the high heavens . . . the worst appointment in [Chicago's] history." Editorials in the *Tribune* and *Sun-Times* said all the right things about giving Robinson a chance, but their disgust came through nonetheless.

Washington himself realized he was gambling. He recognized Robinson's shortcomings as a manager, yet he also saw him as a man hungry for change. "Thank goodness for his troublemaking through the years on the CHA board," Leanita McClain, who grew up in the Ida B. Wells projects, wrote soon after Robinson's appointment, "or there would have been no voice for the tenants." What he lacked in administrative abilities he would make up for in energy and ambition—so, at least, Washington hoped. Robinson could hire gray-suited bean counters to make the necessary structural changes. "A damned-if-you-do, damned-if-you-don't" job,

Leanita McClain wrote: better Robinson should be damned for doing too much than a technocrat damned for doing too little.

In Robinson, the CHA had at its helm a man of folk hero status inside black Chicago. If nothing else, Robinson would symbolize a break with the past, no small issue among a class of people in desperate need of hope. In a sense Washington was envisioning a version of himself at the CHA. Robinson would shape the policy and surround himself with technocrats. It wasn't a bad plan if Robinson possessed a fraction of Washington's understanding of the art of politics.

Robinson never wanted the CHA. As a member of the CHA board, he made it his business to get a firsthand look at the scope of the agency's problems; that was enough to scare him off. When Washington first mentioned it, Robinson said no. But Washington had a way of wearing down people's resolves. He played to Robinson's ego; he made the job something he owed to every resident of the CHA. You're the only one, he told him.

Robinson approached his new job with a crusading zeal. Whistle-blowers inside the agency came to him with stories of featherbedding and cheating and graft. They told of contractors that would do a job worth, say, $25,000, bill the agency for $55,000, spread around $15,000 in political contributions, and keep another $15,000 for themselves. He considered the faucets the agency bought for its thirteen hundred buildings and wondered why his predecessors chose the kind that required a plumber to fix rather than ones with a washer easy to replace. He was convinced that half the budget was waste.

Initiating basic efficiencies first would seemingly please the liberals and the press. But for Robinson it meant money for an agency barely making its bills, let alone dealing with faulty elevators and its outmoded heating plants. As a symbolic gesture he cut his own salary from $72,000 to $60,000.

Robinson moved fast. He fired the agency's executive director, if for no other reason than his connection to the old order. He fired a few hundred union craftsmen and seven hundred janitors. He canceled the CHA's elevator repair contract.* He also imposed sweeping changes on the unions.

---

*The 1982 HUD study showed that the CHA's maintenance costs were more than twice that of other Rust Belt public housing authorities. New York City's housing authority, for instance, spent $4,000 per elevator in maintenance costs. Private companies managing subsidized housing in Chicago spend about the same. In contrast, the CHA spent $18,000 per elevator. The study also found that CHA elevators were broken more often—a full one-third were out of service at any given time—than in New York or other cities.

No longer would it take a $20-an-hour electrician to change a light bulb, he declared; instead, the task would fall upon the $8-an-hour janitor.

The union tradespeople were told they should expect a pay cut. They were full-time employees in a field in which hourly pay was based on a presumption of seasonal employment, yet they were paid on the high end of the wage scale. Speaking before a meeting of the CHA janitors, Robinson said that either they started working up to speed, or he'd fire every last one of them. The CHA's overtime budget was obscene, so he told the janitors that they would now be following a seven-day schedule, rotating weekends off. He fired a slew of people working in the heating plants. The unions screamed bloody murder.

Robinson spoke with Washington about all the toes he was stepping on. He warned the mayor of the confrontation with the unions. "I either take it on or I don't, and if I don't, I'm gone," he says he told Washington.

"Well, let's see how far you get, tiger."

Robinson's first months in office were replete with well-meant but ill-fated changes. The CHA was held together by string, chewing gum, and Band-Aids; firing employees at all levels of the bureaucracy meant firing those who held this Rube Goldberg–like agency together. He boldly canceled the elevator repair contract two weeks after taking over as board chairman without first lining up an alternative company. Even Robinson himself, less than two months later, was among those declaring an elevator "crisis" at the CHA. He fired the heating plant employees just prior to winter. As luck would have it, Chicago suffered through a particularly harsh season that year. Pipes froze and burst in projects around the city. At that point it wasn't the editorial writers or the unions but the residents who were screaming. The residents were no happier about the work slowdown prompted by Robinson's threats against the janitors.

Robinson could do nothing about the enmity among many of those working under his charge. They were put there by the Old Guard and were in every way hostile to this brash new man who seemed to think he had all the answers. Yet Robinson compounded his problems by making new enemies. He was chairman, not a board unto himself, but he failed to consult with his colleagues before implementing most of his decisions. He bruised the feelings of his allies and also left himself open to criticism. Hadn't Robinson accused Charles Swibel of autocratic rule?

Robinson spent $14,600 in CHA dollars on a new car for himself and $20,000 to refurbish his office. His office expenses included money for a microwave and a $102 pen set. Every department head was entitled to a city car, but one doesn't just go out and buy one and then bill the city—which is what Robinson did. The new office furniture made page one, as did news that Robinson hired his brother-in-law as his right-hand man at $27,000 a year. The brother-in-law was in the news again the next day when it was revealed that he was a gang leader in his teens and did time for armed robbery in the 1960s. Fellow board member Leon Finney only offered the obvious when he said, "Renault gave his enemies a very big target."

Stung by bad press, Robinson refused to return reporters' phone calls. He granted an interview to the man who wrote the book chronicling his battle against the Chicago police and then declared during their conversation that it would be the last one he ever granted.

"It seems there's something about public housing," Robinson said in that interview, "and something about whites that says . . . that the residents are animals who don't know how to live, that no blame should be put on the workmen who steal and cheat. I was seen as blaming the wrong group." But Robinson's bad press was due to more than a hostile media. The head of the CHA's tenant organization decried his spending precious dollars on a car and office furniture; she asked Robinson to resign. So, too, did Nate Clay, in his "Axeman" column in the *Metro News*. Robinson, Clay wrote, was a man "unschooled in the fine art of efficient management," an "embarrassment," and a "headache" that Washington did not need.

Late in 1983, at Washington's urging, the CHA board announced with much fanfare that it was limiting Robinson's control over the day-to-day operations of the agency. Washington insiders admitted that the change was merely cosmetic, aimed at taking the heat off Robinson.

Brenda Gaines took charge at the CHA after Robinson was forced to resign late in 1986. Gaines had worked as a housing official for the federal government and was among the more highly regarded technocrats inside Washington's government. She was horrified by the state of the CHA's books. Reforms that should have been a priority in 1983 were still needed four years later. The managers of the various projects had no input into the budget; they were given money and instructed how they were to spend it. But, then, HUD's stinging 1982 report had deemed "incompetent" fourteen of the city's nineteen project managers. The CHA was in desperate need of rehabilitation but, Gaines said, the city wasn't doing all it could to pursue available rehabilitation dollars from the federal government. Among the more immediate problems Gaines faced were vendors cutting off services and the threat of a HUD takeover.

"No one can convince me that things didn't improve under Washington," Gaines said long after leaving government. On the far west side, Chicago joined the cutting edge of public housing when it turned over the day-to-day affairs of the LeClaire Courts housing project to a tenant management board. Tenant leaders were granted access to City Hall. There were many other experiments aimed at involving residents in the decision making at the CHA, but Gaines also thinks Washington deserved low marks for failing to initiate a host of basic changes at the CHA.

"Extraordinary resources were needed, yet we were placed on the back burner," said Joe Gardner, a former community organizer who took a top position at the CHA after a year as Washington's top political adviser. "Our approach wasn't proactive but reactive." Gardner was particularly angry at those Washington advisers who thwarted his attempts to convince Washington to visit the projects, blaming it on what he called a "middle-class bias."

"It was like, 'We live over here and that's Beirut over there and we don't need Harold near the place.'" The taint of the CHA debacle, Washington strategists reasoned, could only hurt their man at the polls.

The early days of Washington's second term were not without its joys. There were the hardships suffered by Burke and Vrdolyak to savor. Burke was reelected to the council, but he accused his former colleagues in the 29 of selling him out.

The first big test of loyalties was the new council committee assignments. The plan Washington drew up removed Burke as Finance chair and was approved forty to nine by a majority that included Alderman Patrick Huels, Daley's man in the council. Burke was bitter. He said in the council that day, "I wish I could have heard them when they said, 'Your Honor, I really didn't want to be against you, it was Vrdolyak and Burke who made me do it.'" Burke derided his former allies who "forfeited their legislative independence and their autonomy to submit to the dictates of the mayor." This new coalition between the Old and New Guards wasn't about good government or progress but politics, plain and simple, Burke said. Washington called Burke's speech "a real tearjerker."

Burke was not a total loser, however. Not many months after losing the election to Washington, Vrdolyak surrendered the party chairmanship. No longer an alderman (his brother Victor took his place), he spoke of securing a countywide office through the Republican party. With Ed Vrdolyak no longer in the council, Burke was finally no one's number-two man. He was the undisputed leader of the nine hard-liners resolutely opposing Washington.

Vrdolyak's vision was a coalition of disaffected white Democrats and suburban Republicans. Some Republican leaders were dubious of allowing a place at the table for this big-city rapscallion, but others welcomed him with open arms. The city's Republican party, despite its resurgence in 1983, was something of a joke. Maybe Vrdolyak held the key to the future.

Alderman Richard Mell was among those immediately switching sides to Washington. While Hynes and Vrdolyak were trying to decide who was going to drop out, Mell made his move. He confessed that he didn't get the jobs he was after or any other perks he sought, but he couldn't envision another four years opposed to Washington, now the undisputed party powerhouse. In his conversations with Washington, Mell, just as Burke had figured, blamed his hard-line stance on the two Eddies.

Yet there wasn't time for basking in victory. Where the likes of Richard Mell were coming around, Washington's hardcore supporters were expressing their impatience. There were complaints in activist circles that their brothers and sisters who had put on suits and silk blouses to work at City Hall were now too busy and important to see them. Those on the outside spoke of new strategies for dealing with a mayor whom they considered sympathetic to their concerns but who had yet to come through in critical areas. The bankers and the corporate executives were meeting with Washington to win him to their positions; the activists realized that they, too, would need to pressure Washington. With Vrdolyak out of the way, they could make noise without fear of abetting the enemy.

Washington's failings at the CHA didn't cause nearly the ruckus as Byrne's. Washington and his supporters didn't mention the CHA much during the reelection campaign, as they had in 1983, and most of his supporters didn't press him to do so. Few leaders spoke out despite their disappointments, for to have criticized Washington then was to play into the hands of the Vrdolyak faction. When the *Tribune* ran a twelve-part series chronicling the myriad of problems at the CHA, there was an outcry among Washington supporters. In the past these activists working on behalf of the poor would have appreciated the newspaper's efforts to highlight a pressing problem. A similar series four years earlier, as the city prepared for its previous mayor's race, would have been applauded. In late 1986 it was declared an attack on Washington by a white-owned, white-controlled newspaper, despite its endorsement of Washington's reelection.

Washington's honeymoon ended with his reelection. His supporters didn't blast him in high-profile news conferences, but they let him know in no uncertain terms that they were growing impatient. They wanted far more from him than a Freedom of Information Act or an Affirmative Action Program aimed primarily at black businessmen.

Allowing the CHA to remain a back-burner issue was only one of their complaints. How about health care? Or the depressed economies of the city's poorer neighborhoods? What had he done in those two areas? How come this mayor had done nothing about solid-waste recycling? asked the environmentalists drawn to Washington by his progressive platform; the peace activists were pleased Washington made Chicago the single largest Nuclear Weapon–Free Zone in the country, but they were frustrated when the mayor took part in the ceremony to dedicate a nuclear submarine the USS *Chicago*. The majority of students enrolled in public schools were black, but education hadn't been much of a priority, either.

As Washington segued into his second term, it was no longer good enough to be better than his predecessors. Washington was being judged against a much tougher standard: his own promises and the high expectations of his supporters.

Almost everyone inside the administration would list the CHA as a disaster or at least a great disappointment. Another consensus failure was the health department. As was the case with Robinson, most of the blame would fall on the shoulders of Washington's choice to head that department, Lonnie Edwards.

Edwards was no one's first choice for the job. He was an administrator at Cook County Hospital, so he had experience working inside an unwieldy bureaucracy like the city's health department. He was black, and that meant something; Washington had named Dr. Quentin Young, white, president of the Board of Health and sought a black department head. But Edwards wasn't the type to lead a crusade against a department in desperate need of an overhaul. Offers were made, all were rejected. Six months into Washington's term, the city was still without a health director. "Lonnie," said one member of the search committee, "got the job by default."

By the start of the second term it seemed just about everyone was disgusted with Edwards. The city was returning precious dollars earmarked for AIDS programs, which made Edwards persona non grata inside the gay community. "Health Care Workers for Washington" gathered at rallies, their belief in Washington still strong but their distaste for Edwards equally intense. They could have drawn up nearly the exact platform for the 1987 campaign as they had in 1983.

Edwards ran his department with far more caution than Robinson ran the CHA, in part, some theorized, because of Robinson. Inside City Hall some described it as the "Renault Robinson syndrome." Edwards was slow to fire the Shakman-exempt employees or institute any sort of wholesale change. Health care workers behind Washington hoped his administration would be an active and aggressive, community-oriented department; instead, Edwards ran the department scared of controversy.

Edwards had his black critics, to be sure, yet some of Washington's more nationalistic supporters believed the attacks on him were largely based on race. To them the controversy boiled down to a group of white leftists attacking a black man. Edwards was an experienced black professional with some talents, they argued. Why get rid of him?

There was more to the health department's problems than Edwards. Quentin Young leaned on Washington for months to get him to sit down with George Dunne, president of the County Board and an ally, to work out problems between the city and the county that meant duplication and waste of precious resources, yet Washington never acted on Young's urgings.

The scope of the city's health problems—one out of five Chicagoans had no health insurance; another fifteen percent were on Medicaid—and the severe budget limitations were overwhelming obstacles. The city's high infant mortality rates were in part due to a shortage of skilled nurses. In Chicago there was one nurse for every eighteen thousand residents living below the poverty line, compared to one for every three thousand in Los Angeles. The city desperately needed more inspectors to deal with problems such as lead poisoning, and money to correct the problem once lead paint was discovered. Yet what city department wasn't in need of money?

An accounting early in the Washington administration found that the CHA needed $750 million to tend to the poor physical condition of most buildings. Yet the CHA received only $8.9 million in rehabilitation money from the federal government in 1986. Removing asbestos, which had been linked to lung disorders and cancer, would cost $53 million alone. One in three children in big cities like Chicago lives in poverty, according to the Children's Defense Fund. The financial burden of dealing with that kind of problem was impossible to calculate.

The federal government was no longer a reliable funding source. Cities bore the brunt of Reagan's domestic cuts. Chicago officials estimated that the city lost a cumulative $1 billion in federal funds during the first six years of Reagan's administration. Revenue sharing was phased out while Washington was mayor; several other programs were cut before he entered office; the city's share of community development funds dropped from $140 million to $85 million during his first term. The ratio of the federal government's housing budget to its military expenditures, *Harper's* revealed, was 1:5 in 1980 and 1:31 in 1989. Yet High Tax Harold's fiddling with the property-tax rate or any of a variety of nuisance taxes meant alienating further the white homeowners on the southwest and northwest sides.

When put on the defensive, Washington invariably blamed the city's problems on the federal government. "It may be impossible to manage a public housing authority today given the shortage of federal dollars," he said. Claiming his was a "two-front war," he stressed in his second inaugural address his fight against the machine's legacy—"corruption, mismanagement, and indifference"—and a president who had written off the Rust

Belt cities "like failed industries . . . left to sink or swim if they can." It is with the federal government that "the ultimate blame must lie."

Reporters were inclined to dismiss Washington's verbal assaults on the federal government as nothing more than an excuse. First it was Vrdolyak ("the perfect alibi," wrote one *Tribune* columnist), and now it was the feds. He was a mayor, reporters said among themselves, in need of a whipping boy to account for his shortcomings.

The opinion makers saw Washington as a mayor not particularly interested in running the city. The joke in the City Hall press room was that Washington had embraced Ronald Reagan as his management guru. Washington's promise to "play a much larger role on the national political scene" (as he told the *New York Times*) was seen as a sign that he was already looking beyond Chicago.

This sentiment was well represented in an article by the writer Eugene Kennedy about Washington ("A Good Politician—Period") that appeared in *Chicago* magazine five months into his second term. Kennedy wrote of Washington's "distracted aura," citing by way of proof Washington's comment to the *Times*. "His role as mayor is incidental to building his own power," Kennedy stated. He wrote of a Washington who approached his job with arrogance and indifference. "Under Harold Washington," Kennedy wrote, "the city is beginning to look uncared for and over-grown, like an old estate whose gardeners take the money and don't mow the lawn."

Kennedy may have stated it more strongly than others sharing this opinion, but the prevailing view among those with a regular forum in the media was that Washington was not the sort for overhauling the bureau-cracy. He would make changes here and there, they speculated, but his main focus would be the next election.

Most supporters didn't see Washington replacing one alibi with another, yet many wondered whether Washington could make headway on those issues that counted most to them: the schools, the CHA, the lack of affordable housing, and the like. Any of these issues was its own nightmare. The dropout rate in the schools was fifty percent; in one school nearly one-fourth of the female students gave birth in a single year; there were gangs, drugs, and violence, and kids trying to learn when they lived in unhappy and unhealthy homes. The number of Chicagoans living below the poverty line was estimated at anywhere between six hundred thousand and eight hundred thousand, representing at least one in every five residents. Could even the most well-meaning politician do much but tinker?*

Those who looked ahead to Washington's second term with optimism pointed to Washington's willingness to speak openly about the city's problems. That alone proved him different from his predecessors. Supporters also spoke of accomplishments during his first term. He initiated a program borrowed from Philadelphia that employed ex-gang leaders to keep the peace among warring gangs and began what he called the "Women's Apprenticeship Program," aimed at opening up to women city jobs such as bridge tender and truck driver. They couldn't deny disappointments like the CHA, but there were important, if unheralded, victories. The fight for more affordable housing was one example.

The city's new Housing Abandonment Prevention Program was generally well received by those working in the housing field. Abandoned buildings scattered through the city's poorer neighborhoods meant both a blight on the community and the loss of already scarce affordable housing. The city asked select community organizations to identify buildings dangerously on the edge of disrepair. Each group was to develop its own strategy for saving a building. One option was to help a landlord apply for available low-interest city loans; another was to use the corporation counsel's office to transfer the building's ownership to the community group itself. The program wasn't a complete success—a few community groups were not up to the task—but it was considered an experiment worth pursuing.

The administration received high marks for other ideas aimed at providing decent affordable housing. The Washington administration initiated a program whereby tax-delinquent apartment buildings still in decent shape were turned over to qualified community groups, which took on the role of landlord. The city helped underwrite the rehabilitation costs. Washington also won praise for the job his corporation counsel's office did prosecuting slum landlords in housing court. The cozy relations between

---

*The "Hollow Prize" thesis, Professor H. Paul Friesma called it in 1969: blacks taking over City Hall and other institutions once those institutions have fallen into disarray.

the landlords and the city's attorneys assigned to housing court were a thing of the past. Under Washington, more than once a judge rebuked a city lawyer for overzealousness.

Les Brown, head of the Chicago Coalition for the Homeless, said with Byrne the challenge was getting her to admit the city had a homelessness problem. "Washington was a different story entirely," Brown said. He tripled funding for homeless programs, and his staff used what powers it had to open doors on the homeless coalition's behalf. City Hall served as a gathering place to devise strategy. Where Brown was never able to meet with Byrne or her top staff, "access was never a problem to Washington and his aides."

Still, money was a big impediment to any real progress. Programs such as the Housing Abandonment-Prevention Program, though focused on poorer communities, didn't do much to help those most in need. Even the low rents charged by not-for-profit community groups were above the means of those living on public assistance. Community development funds accounted for almost every cent of the housing budget, yet CD dollars could not be used to subsidize rents even if the city was so inclined. Chicago didn't have the money in its corporate budget to absorb the yearly costs of subsidizing the rents for those who couldn't afford decent housing.

Encouraging changes early in Washington's second term heartened those who wanted to believe Washington could perform miracles. Despite protests, Washington was aggressively seeking a replacement for Edwards and others considered hostile to progressive change. The mayor assumed more of a leadership role in the U.S. Conference of Mayors to push for what he called an "urban crusade." He called his pet project the National Urban Agenda. One key plank called for a five-year, $25 billion housing superfund to fix up the nation's housing projects; another was a trust fund that would set aside $2.5 billion a year to foster public-private partnerships to build housing for low- and moderate-income families. Washington hoped he could use the Conference of Mayors as a means of pressuring the Democratic presidential hopefuls to commit to the problems of affordable housing.

There was also the Washington administration's negotiation of phase two of the Presidential Towers project. Phase one, built while Byrne was mayor, was something of a scandal. The project sat at the edge of downtown, on land formerly occupied by a string of hotels that advertised "transients welcome." Built with $159 million in low-interest, tax-free federal loans, Presidential Towers was like subsidized housing for yuppies. (There was a Bennigan's tavern in its atrium as well as a health club and a French restaurant on the premises. One-bedroom apartments rented for between $700 and $865 a month.) Federal housing loans stipulated that twenty percent of the units must be set aside for low- and moderate-income residents, but in 1980 Congressman Dan Rostenkowski slipped an exemption into an omnibus bill that relieved developers of that burden.*

The city had committed itself to phase two of the project before Washington took office. When developers approached city officials about refinancing the loan, rather than pushing for the twenty percent set aside—what would it mean but slightly cheaper rents on studio apartments?—the city wrangled about $14 million from its developers, who were only too happy to comply. The money was put in a trust fund rather than folded into the city's housing budget. A panel of those working in the affordable housing field would determine how the money was spent. Negotiations like these buoyed the hopes of housing activists.

Yet the naysayers inside Washington's coalition could marshal contrary evidence of their own. Jacky Grimshaw, a black woman who served as the city's top lobbyist after Tom Coffey was fired, derisively called "Zulus" those inside City Hall who were still acting as if they were rock throwers on the outside. She disdained Gloria Chevere's 1987 run for city clerk when she was Washington's deputy campaign manager, dismissing her boss's support as a by-product of the Latino community's "blackmail."

The dissatisfaction among Washington's Latino supporters was a case in point. There was no doubt that the black-Latino coalition had benefited Latinos politically. But whether the same was true for policy—what the Latinos were getting or not getting from the administration—was another matter entirely.

Alderman Jesus Garcia was the ranking Latino in Washington's coalition. Where Washington looked on Alderman Luis Gutierrez as full of himself in a scary kind of way, Garcia he regarded as principled and trust-

*Byrne and Rostenkowski were the project's most influential benefactors. One of the three developers was Daniel Shannon, a former business associate of Rostenkowski's and manager of the congressman's blind trust portfolio. The $159 million loan Rostenkowski won for Presidential Towers represented about sixty-two percent of all federal money made available in 1983 for subsidized developments. The city floated a $180 million bond to provide an additional low-interest loan.

worthy. Garcia had emerged as a political leader in his part of the city only because the man whose aldermanic campaign he managed in 1983 had been murdered, and then only after he tried to resist those trying to push him forward. Gutierrez was a fiery speaker, and therefore a useful ally, but Washington still held Gutierrez at a distance.

Garcia said an attitude prevailed within the city's housing department that affordable housing was a "black problem rather than one faced by the poor of all colors. Some people inside the administration have the idea that Latino progress can only come at the expense of black progress." Top aides were willing to hire mediocre black administrators, Garcia and other top Latino supporters said, yet seemed particularly fussy when choosing among seemingly qualified Latinos. Within the context of a multiracial coalition, a black-first attitude was a form of racism.

One high-ranking white official spoke of a meeting he attended where someone Latino was being considered for a job in the mayor's office. The problem was that another Latino was already similarly situated. "If you give them two, then they'll always expect two," someone said—exactly the rationalization the machine used for its tokenism, an irony that seemed to elude some top black officials.

Another source of contention among Latinos was the executive order signed by Washington that struck citizenship questions from all city applications, unless expressly required by federal law. It also prohibited the city from collaborating with federal immigration investigators unless ordered to do so by a court. The same Latino leaders who spoke highly of Washington for signing this measure were dismayed by talk of watering it down if not gutting it completely. Some saw it as an unnecessary source of tension with the federal government; others failed to understand why the administration would stand up for the rights of these illegals, given black unemployment.

Washington stuck by his executive order, but that did not leave the mayor with entirely clean hands. Washington would not have been as forgiving with a white official saying about blacks what some black appointees were saying about Latinos. Only seven or eight percent of the city's commissioners, directors, and first deputies were Latino—positions presumably filled by Washington. Washington did not handle well a meeting with about twenty Latino supporters shortly after his reelection. Pressed about his mediocre hiring record, he said finding qualified Latino managers was not easy, especially when compared to finding qualified Latino laborers. "What he meant is that it's hard to convince talented Latino professionals to come work with the city because they can make much more in the private sector than with the city," Press Secretary Al Miller said. "But it came out like he was saying that Latinos are good at being shovel carriers but not meant for management positions.

"It was as if he were Jane Byrne and the blacks were coming in to say they're being discriminated against," Miller said.

Some believed Washington was making too many accommodations. Eight of the twenty-seven new committee chairpersons were former Vrdolyak stalwarts. Washington retained Fred Roti as chairman of the Buildings Committee—the same Fred Roti he promised would go, along with Burke and Vrdolyak. The city did not need twenty-seven committees.

The party's 1988 county ticket was another sore point. In the fall of 1987 Washington spoke of a "dream slate"—a biracial slate of candidates. As a show of party unity he endorsed candidates he had long opposed as tied to the machine, but his support wasn't without its conditions. Anyone wanting it and hoping for its continuation would have to embrace certain ideals, yet there were naysayers nonetheless. Voting for the likes of Aurelia Pucinski, the daughter of one of his foes and a candidate for clerk of the circuit court, seemed too much for even Washington to ask.

Blind opposition was no longer a factor in the council, but the second term did not bring about a complete break with the recent past. There were isolated cases of the kind of racial fearmongering that marked Washington's first term. Shortly after Washington won the primary, the *Sun-Times* felt compelled to run an editorial disparaging a widespread rumor that Washington intended to purge high-ranking whites from government. The paper never saw fit to mention, however, that it was its own gossip columnist, Michael Sneed, who brought about the need for the editorial. A former Byrne press secretary married to a former Byrne chief of staff, Sneed wrote a gossip column that gave the rumor its most conspicuous pulpit if not its start.

There were also moves afoot to encroach on Washington's powers, such as HUD's attempts to take over the CHA. Closer to home there were countless takeover bids. Legislation was introduced in Springfield that would strip the city of its statutory authority over the park district, the

McCormick Place convention centers, Navy Pier, and the Port Authority. Another measure would create a regional airport authority, thereby taking control from the city of O'Hare and Midway airports. There was also new-found interest in an elected school board: suddenly a great many regular Democrats believed that a school board appointed by the mayor wasn't a good idea.

These assaults on the mayor's powers did not move his supporters quite as similar assaults had in the past. Three rallies were organized to show support for Washington in his fight with HUD, but they drew barely three hundred people in total. There was a teachers' strike in the fall of 1987, Chicago's ninth in eighteen years. Washington took a hands-off position. He wouldn't be a Daley, he said, who overstepped the bounds of his power; his job at the schools was to name a school board, not set policy.

Many supporters believed this was nothing but a well-reasoned excuse for avoiding a political quagmire. A group of parents, primarily black and Latino, stood outside City Hall calling, "We want Harold." It was the same chant voiced the night of his 1983 primary victory, but in this case they were not celebrating Washington but imploring the mayor to do something.

Grumbling gave way to public criticisms by erstwhile loyal supporters. The man Washington chose to take Quentin Young's place as president of the Board of Health, Dr. Jorge Prieto, publicly criticized the administration for failing to do enough about infant mortality. Shortly after the resolution of the school strike, a former deputy press secretary, Chris Chandler, wrote a long article ("Get Moving, Mr. Mayor") featured in the Sunday *Sun-Times* perspective pages. "Some of his strong supporters and campaign workers from the first campaign are now bitter," Chandler wrote. "They feel Mr. Washington . . . is betraying his core constituency by not even attempting improvements in the basic social areas of health, housing, and education."

The question that dominated the Washington coalition in the second half of 1987 was whether Washington was both able and willing to take the political risks to make sweeping changes. Even those convinced that Washington was genuinely committed to the progressive beliefs he espoused harbored their doubts. He was politically adept; if nothing else, his defeat of Vrdolyak had showcased his political acumen. It wasn't a mat-ter of strength, either. Washington had amassed considerable political capital by the start of his second term—he was a politician who recognized power as a precursor to change. Yet whether he could do much more than traditional mayors about the social ills plaguing any major metropolis was in doubt.

In late November, just before Thanksgiving, the writer Salim Muwakkil was a few days late finishing an article exploring this very question. The publication he was writing for, *In These Times,* had wholeheartedly supported Washington through his reelection. Muwakkil himself had written several of the articles that enthusiastically reported on Washington's triumphs. Now it was time, Muwakkil felt, that his national audience contemplate the larger questions about the hopes and limitations of this black-led progressive coalition. The piece quoted well-known figures in the black community who criticized if not Washington himself, then his administration. More than one promised to aim at Washington the kind of protests suffered by Byrne if Washington didn't get off the dime. It was one deadline that Muwakkil was relieved to have missed.

22

THE

EMPIRE

STRIKES

BACK

Harold Washington died at his desk the day before Thanksgiving. He was talking with his press secretary, Al Miller, when Miller, glancing at his notes, heard a "rattling, raspy sound"—the kind of crude noise, he would later say, that a man makes outdoors when collecting his phlegm to expel a big gob of spit. He looked up. Washington was leaning forward, his cheek pressed against the desk. Miller thought he was bending over to pick up something from the floor, but then he realized Washington wasn't moving.

Miller jumped from his chair. Washington's bodyguards and then the paramedics worked on Washington's lifeless body. Miller knew then that he was witnessing the end of an era—he knew that Washington wasn't going to make it. It was eleven in the morning on November 25, 1987. They were just getting started on the real business of government, and now it was all coming to an end.

Alderman Richard Mell immediately dashed up the stairs to the fifth floor, so anxious and worried, he explained on a radio talk show, that he didn't wait for an elevator. Mell joined a group already gathered in concern. Among them was a new alderwoman named Helen Shiller. The way Shiller tells it, Mell accosted Ernie Barefield, Washington's chief of staff. "Mell demanded to know if Washington was going to make it," Shiller said. "He kept asking, 'Is he dead? Is he dead?'"

Mell wasn't wasting time. The acting mayor, by law, is chosen from among the council's fifty aldermen. Mell returned to his office and worked the phone. The council's Latino aldermen, he understood, would be key. If he could lure the Latinos into his camp, he just might be elected mayor. Alderman Luis Gutierrez was among those he called.

It was 11:30 A.M.—Gutierrez remembers glancing at his watch when the phone rang. Later, when Gutierrez had time to think, he would realize that Mell might have been the last person on this planet he wanted to hear from at that moment. At 11:30 the doctors were working on Washington at Northwestern Memorial Hospital.

Later Mell explained that he called Gutierrez to offer condolences; the conversation just naturally drifted to politics. In Gutierrez's recollection Mell barely hesitated before making his pitch: "He said, 'Your mayor's dead. I'm calling you because I want you to keep your options open. I don't want you to rush and make hasty decisions.'"

What an asshole, Gutierrez thought to himself. An ally, a friend, an important man in his life—his political mentor, really—is hanging on for dear life, and this fool was already making a campaign speech. As if Richard Mell, who had fought the court-ordered special elections that won Gutierrez a spot in the council, would ever win his vote.

Gutierrez's first thought after hanging up was that Mell had really blown it this time. Washington will come out of this, Gutierrez told himself. Me and the mayor will have a good laugh then, he thought. Then he was "scared shitless." He wanted to cry. "What did that bastard know that I didn't?" he asked himself.

As vice-mayor, Alderman David Orr was the man of the hour. Should Washington be rendered incapacitated or die, Orr would take his place until the council met to name an acting mayor. He was out in his ward dressed in jeans and running shoes when Washington's chief of staff, Ernie Barefield, called. He went home to change before heading downtown.

Orr did not head to City Hall but to Washington's political office, one block away. That was Barefield's decision. Orr found it troubling that he was going to the coalition's political center rather than the place of government. Crass, he told himself. No one knew if Washington was dead or alive, yet they were already meeting to work out a postmortem plan.

The main purpose of the meeting was to keep Washington's coalition together. Alderman Jesus Garcia was there, representing the Latino wing of the coalition, and Larry Bloom, who along with Orr represented Washington's white lakefront support. The group was weighted with blacks new to movement politics—Wilson Frost, Eugene Sawyer, Tim Evans, and John Stroger. These former machine stalwarts worried Washington's staff. Would they hold rank?

Orr recalled a feeling of relief when he looked at one participant, Eugene Sawyer, who appeared genuinely heartbroken. During their talks Sawyer harped on the theme of unity. We must keep the coalition together, he said several times. Perhaps grief would be the glue that held them together, Orr thought to himself.

Yet everyone present recognized that achieving unity would be no easy feat. Their coalition had never been more than an uneasy one held together by special circumstances and a shrewd popular leader. Temptation hovered just outside the door.

The call came at 1:36. The mayor was dead, and Orr was needed over at the hospital. Orr made it there in minutes, yet it would be nearly an hour before the official announcement came. Tim Evans, the mayor's council floor leader, was late.

Several of Washington's top aides viewed Evans as the logical successor. Evans standing up at the podium when the announcement was made, they figured, would communicate a sense of continuity and inevitability. Those waiting in the hospital anteroom—Washington family members and assorted medical staff, among others—were doing a slow burn. Permitting Evans to appear among them was one thing; waiting the thirty-plus minutes it took him to get there another.

Long before the start of the press conference word had leaked that Washington was dead. As reporters and others milled around, news reached them of an official message of condolence from Mayor Tom Bradley.

Apparently someone at City Hall was already calling to pass the bad news. The beat reporters shook their heads. The rest of the country was better informed than those standing outside the hospital's emergency room. The delay seemed quintessential Chicago: putting the kibosh even on the mayor's death.

Mourning took many forms. After hanging up with Richard Mell, Luis Gutierrez headed for City Hall. It was the uncertainty that weighed on him. He wanted to be with other people who also felt scared and over-wrought. Jesus Garcia, too, went to City Hall, also out of a sense of wanting to be a part of *something*. Both found the scene vulgar. Several of the black machinists made little effort to hide their sense of liberation. They were, Garcia said, "almost jovial. . . . They sensed a new day had come."

You could see it in their faces and in the way they acted. "Hey, Louie, don't take it too rough," Gutierrez quoted one alderman as saying. A prayer service was held in the City Council chambers. Several aldermen took that opportunity to walk the aisles collecting home phone numbers.

Gutierrez and Garcia would have done better to walk outside to Daley Plaza, across from City Hall, where hundreds of people had gathered, first to wait for any news and then to join in a mass public cry. Or perhaps they could have walked in the black community.

There was a hush in black Chicago. It was like people were dealing privately with Washington's passing, like a death in the family. On one black radio station, the DJ said he would just play music because he didn't feel like talking. A traffic reporter started to give a report on the rush-hour commute but interrupted herself to say it didn't seem important at a time like this. A photograph in the *Tribune* showed a black cop at his guard post just outside the mayor's outer office, wiping tears from his eye. One black radio reporter managed as best she could. She would break into tears, seek refuge, and then return to her post, like a good soldier. Other reporters, including several Washington had believed to be hopelessly biased against him, found it difficult to suppress their tears.

The reaction was mixed among those whites who never thought to vote for Washington. "I don't have any grief," a man named George Sajkick told a *Tribune* reporter looking for quotes in Vrdolyak's ward. "It's phony for us to mourn a guy we hated." That night, there were many public toasts to the new day that dawned with Washington's death. Sajkick admitted that his kid brother went out and tied one on. One bar in the Beverly neighborhood was selling buttons, HAROLD'S DEAD; WE WANT ED. There were poignant moments as well, as when two contrite members of Vrdolyak's ward organization said during a television interview that they were having a hard time at the moment to figure out why they had hated Washington.

"He was a political man," Vrdolyak said in a public statement. "That was his life. He really didn't have a personal life, a family life. So all he had was politics. . . . He didn't have to separate politics from his life because he only had politics." It was Vrdolyak's tribute to Washington, but it read more like an explanation. Vrdolyak had a wife and four kids and played golf and went on vacations. Washington had nothing but politics. Was it any wonder that Washington bested him in Council Wars?

The national news treated Washington's death as a major story. The network anchors broadcast the news right after reporting on a prison riot in Louisiana. The *New York Times* placed Washington's death on its front page—one of seven pieces about Chicago politics the *Times* would run in the seven days after he died. The headline over his *Times* obituary read, LEADER WHO PERSONIFIED BLACK RISE TO URBAN POWER. The *Tribune* published a story under the headline CITIES LOST THEIR STRONGEST VOICE. The headline aptly summed up the opinion offered by mayors from around the country after Washington's death.

Time magazine saw it differently. The caption under the picture they ran of Washington read, CHICAGO'S FIRST BLACK MAYOR: "IT'S OUR TURN NOW." The newsweekly described him as a "flamboyant former ward heeler" who served a month in jail. The *Time* obituary also mentioned that several of his aldermanic allies had been indicted on federal bribery charges.

At home the tributes generally praised Washington to the skies. "For now, in the immediacy of his death," the *Sun-Times* wrote, "we see his remarkable career as a meteor that lit up the sky and shone brightly on a landscape that itself changed with the illumination, then faded all too rapidly." Reporters spoke of Washington the reformer, as if there was no doubting the appellation. They expressed a respect for his political skills and complimented the man on his steadfast fairness to people of all colors.

These glowing reports prompted anger among Washington supporters. He was mediocre while alive but a paragon when dead. If the papers were sincere in these postmortem assessments of Washington as a mayor for all Chicago, if they believed Washington did not discriminate against the city's white residents, why hadn't they reported this while he was alive? Four and one-half years of frustrations came out all at once—at the media, at the mayor's foes, at anyone and everyone who stood in his way. "They murdered him, you know," more than one supporter said aloud. "It just took him time to die."

There was anger directed at Vrdolyak and the media and the white liberals, but also at Washington himself. How could a man as smart as Washington be so stupid about his own health. At 285 pounds, he was, the county medical examiner reported, 100 pounds overweight. ("Harold's problem," Washington's good friend Bennett Johnson said, "was that he moved too slow and ate too fast.") He gained something like 60 pounds while in office. He bragged that he would be mayor through the year 2003, yet he dabbed double pats of butter on rolls and had an unconquerable weakness for sausage, ham hocks, and other foods heavy in fat and sodium. The coroner declared that his last breakfast was "gluttonous." The same man who had once won a gold medal in a citywide track meet would joke that he "couldn't run around a dime."

As with the tax forms he never bothered to file and the lawyer's disciplinary hearings he blew off, Washington approached his health with cavalier indifference. For weeks he had been complaining of a virus or congestion that wouldn't go away, yet he did nothing about it. He canceled appointments for stress tests that could have told him that his arteries were clogged. He grew tired of Quentin Young, his personal physician, berating him about his weight, his heart, and his frantic pace, so he sought another doctor. The new doctor hassled him, too, but to no avail. He was supposed to take medication for his high blood pressure, but the medication incapacitated him sexually so he just stopped taking it. "He'd rather screw than survive," one old flame said with a sentiment somewhere between bitterness and love.

Friends nagged him about his health as well. Dempsey Travis set up four appointments for Washington with his own doctor, but Washington canceled each one as the appointed day approached. For Christmas one year Travis bought Washington an exercise bicycle. Months later Travis sneaked a peek at the bike's odometer—Washington had barely used it. His personal secretary of twenty years, Delores Woods, chided him about his weight, as did his old political associate Howard Saffold, head of his security detail. No one could convince him to take the time to deal with his health.

Those around Washington responsible for his schedule would assume some of the blame. They knew Washington was overworked, and they knew he didn't allow himself time to rest. Three times that fall Washington said as much and canceled the entire day's schedule without notice. With a feeling of annoyance he could not say was altogether unfamiliar, Al Miller considered his boss's schedule the day Washington died. In the Loop by 8 A.M. for an interview with CNN (Cable News Network); on the south side for a ground-breaking ceremony; then back to the Loop for a full complement of afternoon and evening activities. But Miller confessed that he was the one who pushed the idea of the CNN interview. It was an interview with a national media outlet about the country's public housing crises—how could Washington turn that down?

There was paranoid talk about fatal injections secretly administered to Washington. Some found it suspicious that Washington died with only a white man, Al Miller, in his office. The medical examiner reported that Washington's heart had ballooned to nearly three times its normal size— normal for a massive heart attack but like the stuff of a Robert Ludlum novel to the layperson. The family refused an autopsy, which only fueled suspicion.

Yet the coroner had also declared Washington a hundred pounds over-weight, and there were also the statistics about the average life expectancy of a black man, about eight years less than a white man's. Washington died at age sixty-five. According to the *New England Journal of Medicine,* fifty-five percent of men living in Bangladesh live past age sixty-five, compared to only forty percent of men living in Harlem. The writer Alexander Cockburn offered in his typically acerbic but insightful way that perhaps the most apropos headline to announce Washington's death should have been WASHINGTON DIES ON SCHEDULE REQUIRED BY U.S. CAPITALISM.

The early line on successors to Washington had Tim Evans the favorite, but that was because the press didn't understand the council's black caucus. The winner needed twenty-six votes minimum, and Evans could count on no more than fifteen. As the mayor's floor leader, Evans was a lightning rod for the disaffection of the black machinists hostile to Washington's agenda. "Harold's hitman," one black alderman said of Evans.

Bill Henry was another of those holed up in City Hall working the phones while Washington lay lifeless on a hospital gurney. ("Zip up my pockets," Washington once joked as Henry drew near.) With Washington out of the way, Henry, William Beavers, and other black machinists saw an opportunity. They were damned if they would let Tim Evans jeopardize their chance at the spoils.

Those who considered Evans only the lesser of evils were likely to be found in Danny Davis's camp. The IVI (Independent Voters of Illinois) gave Evans a fifty-six percent rating in the last half of Byrne's term while Davis scored eighty percent.

If Evans was "moldable," then Davis was one of them. Ideologically, he was the closest thing to a Harold Washington the council had to offer. He was an able practitioner of rainbow politics and well regarded by the white liberals for his solid support of government reforms. Lu Palmer was among his prominent supporters. He, too, was among those at the fore-front of a black–Latino alliance. In the midst of a tough campaign—a campaign he ended up losing—Davis freed up a small contingent of his best volunteers to work the black precincts on behalf of a Latino ally in a nearby ward. His movement credentials in the black community were impeccable.

Yet twice he had run for Congress, losing both times to a candidate the pros believed he should have beaten. He seemed to lack the raw hunger that drives most politicians. So when he let it be known that he, too, was placing his hat in the ring as a possible successor to Washington, even those who respected the man tended not to take him too seriously. Maybe it was because Davis didn't always bother to shave for council meetings or because he wore his ties loose and was known to wear polyester. Jesus Garcia chided himself for not pushing Davis harder. "He's a visionary," Garcia said. "He's fought the good fight for years." What difference should it make that the man was sloppy?

———

Any of the old-line white aldermen could bank on twenty-four votes. The problem was that the remaining two votes would be just about impossible to pick up.

The council's twenty-eight whites wouldn't be voting as a single bloc. Orr, Bloom, and Helen Shiller were firmly on the progressive side. No one knew what to expect from Edwin Eisendrath, who had taken Marty Oberman's place in the council upon Oberman's retirement. He tied his candidacy to Bill Singer, but still it seemed unlikely that he could bear the likes of a Richard Mell or an Ed Burke as mayor.

The three white candidates were Mell, Burke, and Terry Gabinski, a quiet machine alderman whose tenure in the council dated back to 1969. Gabinski was among the small group of hard-liners who remained aligned with Burke.

Mell was the most aggressive of the white would-be's. He tried to win Eisendrath's vote by promising him the chairmanship of the Education Committee. He offered to hire Bill Singer as the city's corporation counsel. In his pitch to Jesus Garcia and Luis Gutierrez, he promised to name a Latino chief of staff and then sweetened the deal by offering to "give" them the park district. Mell promised Juan Soliz "a blank check" for his vote.

Mell also aggressively pursued Larry Bloom's vote. He phoned something like two or three times a day, Bloom said. He offered to make him corporation counsel; he offered him a high-paying job at a prestigious law firm. (Channel 9 reported that Bloom's salary, had he taken Mell up on his offer, would have been $200,000 a year.) He was, Mell said in one radio interview, "offering the world" to any two aldermen willing to put him over the top.

The smart money was on Eugene Sawyer. Sawyer was quiet and amiable, a get-along kind of politician whom the white aldermen would turn to once they gave up hope of finding another two votes. He had been a loyal machine foot soldier since the 1950s and was well schooled in the machine's you-scratch-my-back-I'll-scratch-yours philosophy.

Sawyer was also the most marketable of the black machinists. Those pushing his candidacy stressed that in 1983 he was the first black committeeman to endorse Washington. No black alderman had served in the council as long as Sawyer. He was the council's president pro tem, which meant he handled the gavel when Washington was out of the room. It was a ceremonial post, but his backers played it up nonetheless.

Sawyer's candidacy seemed to have a momentum all its own. Bill Henry was Sawyer's unofficial campaign manager, and William Beavers was Henry's right-hand man. The two lobbied hard on Sawyer's behalf even though Sawyer had only given them his halfhearted consent. In the few days after Washington's death he was still pushing the unity line. "Unity," he told reporters on Friday. "That's what we're working for." At a private meeting of the black caucus that same day, someone put the question directly to him: Do you want to be mayor? The way one alderman told it, Sawyer just mumbled an answer that no one could quite make out. "Then Beavers," the alderman continued, "came up behind him and said, 'Speak up, man.'" Henry assigned a twenty-four-hour guard to watch Sawyer—not so much out of fear for Sawyer's life but fear that someone might persuade him to drop out.

Those committed to Washington's agenda saw nothing in Sawyer that would draw them to his candidacy, yet at the same time there was nothing awful about him, either. "Sawyer was completely loyal to whatever Harold pushed for, in some ways more loyal than many of us," said Alderman Jesus Garcia, one of Washington's more progressive council allies. "He was real quiet. He almost *never* spoke, not even to say stuff like, 'Hey, let's hear the man speak.' As a matter of fact, I'm having a hard time remembering anything the man's ever said."

Garcia only wished he could say the same of Henry or Beavers. They both complained regularly that the mayor was making too many concessions to the reformers and that the Latinos were getting too much. Henry was something of a legend among City Hall insiders. He was a caricature of the prototypical machine boss, and his petty tyranny thwarted more than one project in the community. There was the Business Enterprise Center, for instance, a joint public-private project designed to bring small industries to north Lawndale, one of the city's poorest neighborhoods. Henry insisted he choose his own contractor, a man already fired for inferior work in a previous city deal. Several of the subcontractors on the project were heavy contributors to his campaign fund. Not surprisingly, a couple of months before Washington's death the entire venture closed, a complete failure.

Two days after Washington's death Sawyer met with Ed Burke, at Henry's urging. Washington insiders took this as a foreboding.

It wasn't hard to figure what Burke saw in Sawyer. He would provide a few choice committee assignments and jobs, but the more prescient white ethnic aldermen understood he offered much more. By supporting Sawyer they could do plenty of damage to the black movement. Sawyer would be mayor for only fifteen months before he would face an election. What better way to pave the way for a mayor of their own choosing than to sow divisions within the black community. By weekend's end most of the remaining Vrdolyak bloc was Sawyer's for the taking. It seemed the old machine coalition was coming back together, only this time around a black mayor.

Whatever Sawyer's initial reluctance, whatever sense of obligation and loyalty he felt, these considerations were put aside. The word in the press Monday morning, as people readied themselves for Washington's funeral, was that Sawyer had the votes but was waiting until after the funeral to make his announcement, out of respect for the departed.

Among those trying to resolve the Sawyer-Evans split was Jesse Jackson. Jackson was in the Middle East when Washington died, but he flew home the next day. A score of politicians surrounded by a phalanx of camera crews and reporters greeted him as he got off the airplane. Then the press portrayed him as a media hound.

The list of "outsiders"—nonaldermen—who sought a role in the naming of the new mayor was long. The gossips had Ed Kelly, Ed Vrdolyak, and Charles Swibel playing a role, to list only a few of the more well-known names. One journalist revealed that Swibel, Vrdolyak, and Burke met within a few hours of Washington's death. Like Jackson, George Dunne also returned from out of town to influence the selection of a new mayor. Yet it was only Jackson's involvement that made page-one news on three consecutive days; the Swibel-Vrdolyak-Burke meeting received barely a mention in the news. Jackson was about the only black leader who stood a chance of keeping the black side of the coalition together, but Mike Royko labeled him a "buttinsky."

Jackson's quest failed; the black caucus remained splintered. Jackson was only one of hundreds of people—top city officials, community activists, scores of black leaders—trying to talk sense into Sawyer, but the headline of the *Sun-Times* article announcing that Sawyer appeared to have the votes read, SETBACK FOR JESSE. It wasn't a setback for the Washington coalition; it wasn't a setback for the Washington agenda; it wasn't a setback for black Chicago or for those believing in the mayor's politics. No, it was a setback for Jesse Jackson and his presidential campaign.

Congressman Dan Rostenkowski was another influential player in the City Council drama. For a time after Daley's death Rostenkowski was Chicago's top political figure nationally. "A case study of the dangers of getting in over your head," the *Washington Monthly* wrote when ranking Rostenkowski among the country's six worst congressmen based on the views of fellow congressmen, lobbyists, staffers, reporters, and others. "Hogs get slaughtered but pigs get fat," he explained to a *New York Times* reporter. Yet the local media treated him with an affection and respect that bordered on reverential. He was always "Rusty," chairman of the powerful House Ways and Means Committee, Chicago's powerful native son who might just succeed Thomas P. "Tip" O'Neill as House Speaker.

Then Jackson ran for president, overshadowing Rostenkowski as Chicago's undisputed Big Name. Jackson didn't enjoy any such reverence. When Jackson met with Mikhail Gorbachev in Geneva in 1985, the national press portrayed the impromptu meeting as a serious discussion of peace and Soviet Jewry. The *Sun-Times* portrayed Jackson as an all-too-willing pawn for a Soviet chess master, while the *Tribune* styled him as a publicity hound.

In the wake of Harold Washington's death, the Chicago press enjoyed trying to humiliate Jackson as a powerless politician even in his own backyard. The media crowned him a would-be kingmaker, they covered him as a kingmaker, and then when he failed to play the role of kingmaker, they deemed it a "crushing blow to his presidential campaign."

On a cold steel gray day Chicago buried Harold Washington. The sun had not shined that entire week, as if ordered not to appear by a pulp writer looking for a simple symbol of grief. Jackson surrogates lobbied Washington's staff to hold the funeral at Operation PUSH. They lost that fight and also failed in their quest to have Jackson give the eulogy. Jackson would be only one of many dignitaries asked to offer a few words. The crowning moment was the CHA youth choir's rendition of the spiritual, "Keep On Moving."

Evans spoke at the funeral, but Sawyer did not. Evans worked the crowd as people assembled, smiling and waving and shaking hands as he made his way to the stage. Reverend Herbert Martin gave the eulogy. He used his pulpit to offer his own subtle endorsement of Evans, while offering an equally subtle rebuke of Jackson. "The sharks have gotten scent of our blood," Martin said. "No time for kingmaking. No time for ego trips. No time for self-serving agendas or hungry power grabs. We must walk together in unity of mind and singleness of purpose to keep the spirit of reform alive." Our sadness, Martin cautioned, "must not allow our enemies to rejoice." Along the nine-mile route from the church to the cemetery, people held aloft old political posters and also signs that called for unity.

After Washington's body was lowered into the ground, Bill Henry told reporters he had commitments from twelve black aldermen and that a vote would be held the next day. Feelings boiled over later that evening at a city-sponsored memorial, an event meant as a tribute to Washington and his political beliefs that ended up a pro-Evans rally. When the more outspoken among Washington's supporters grew uneasy with the event's nonpartisan tone, they initiated a coup. With a mayor being jammed down their throats, it was no time to be subtle. The emcee was pushed aside, and they put up their own roster of speakers. The *Sun-Times* columnist Vernon Jarrett was among those speaking extemporaneously. "Treat your black enemies the same as you do the Ku Klux Klan!" he bellowed from the rostrum. Either do something about those black aldermen consorting with Washington's enemies, he said, or "they will destroy us before the white man can get to us."

Jarrett's speech seemed symbolic of the racial split endemic to Chicago politics. Black callers to the *Sun-Times* said they were grateful for Jarrett's daring to tell it like it was; whites were flabbergasted and irate. It was a matter of decorum—this, after all, was a memorial rally—and also a matter of journalistic ethics. Ed Vrdolyak led the charge. He went to the *Sun-Times* and also to WLS-TV where Jarrett was under contract as an on-air commentator, demanding they take "immediate action." Vrdolyak appeared on television news programs calling on those sharing his outrage to call WLS and the *Sun-Times*. In the streets that afternoon a leaflet that provided telephone numbers appeared.

Jarrett may have offered the most memorable speech, but it was Conrad Worrill who set the night's tone. He called on every person there to show up at City Hall in protest. We've come too far, he said, to be sold out by these Negroes pretending to be black. Gutierrez followed Worrill to the podium. "We will surround City Hall because it is ours," he said.

The same call was repeated several more times that night and into the next day as the city prepared for the next evening's City Council meeting. It seemed, however, that it would be nothing more than one last fling for the most committed of Washington's supporters. Henry, after all, was claiming that Sawyer's twelve black votes were "signed and etched in concrete." He could count on nearly all the votes of those aldermen representing the northwest and southwest sides. If Henry was to be believed, the final vote wouldn't even be close.

In the City Council chambers aldermen who never cared for Washington while he was alive stood to gush over him now that he was dead. "I loved you like a brother," Alderman George Hagopian, a stalwart Vrdolyaker, said. Burke rose to praise Washington, as did Roman Pucinski and most of those who had been a part of the 29. Richard Mell wore a Washington button pinned to his lapel.

The aldermen also postured for the press in the council anterooms as their colleagues spoke on the council floor. Several aldermen claimed that their life had been threatened and blamed it on the previous evening's rhetoric. ("They not only threatened to kill me," one claimed, "but they threatened to defeat me for committeeman!") A white lakefront alderwoman named Kathy Osterman rebuked the likes of Vernon Jarrett and Conrad Worrill for their conduct the previous evening. "That's not what Harold Washington was all about," she fantasized. The first council meeting lasted from around ten in the morning until three in the afternoon.

The crowds started arriving at City Hall at 5 P.M. Within the hour the hallways outside the City Council chambers were packed; a sea of people spilled out across LaSalle Street. They didn't ring City Hall, but the newspapers estimated a crowd of five thousand. One writer compared it to a scene from a Frank Capra movie, "except that even Capra would never have indulged in something this corny, the people . . . coming downtown to stop an election."

The council meeting did not resume until well after nine, despite the advertised 5:30 start. Sawyer was upstairs meeting with Orr and Evans about possibly postponing the meeting. Sawyer was nervous about the crowd amassing outside City Hall—so, at least, he told Orr. Orr's security detail had fears of its own. If you think it is best that we postpone this, Sawyer told Orr at one point, it is okay with me. Sawyer agreed that Orr would call the meeting to order, find no quorum, and then adjourn.

Those behind Sawyer were furious. Let's have a vote and get this over with, they implored. Richard Mell for one couldn't believe what he was hearing. "He's got it and he won't take it," Mell said to anyone who would listen. "God, I'd do anything—anything!"

About a dozen Washington aldermen, including Sawyer, gathered in Tim Evans's office. Sawyer told the group that no job was worth the bloodletting going on in the black community. "We can work this thing out," he told them. Henry and Beavers were furious but saw little choice. Everyone agreed to resolve this within the family.

Then Ed Burke demanded that he be let in. Most were against the idea, but Sawyer insisted. Burke walked straight to Sawyer: "You made a commitment to us. You're going to keep your commitment."

Sawyer explained that he had changed his mind. "I'm not running anymore," he told Burke.

"Yes, you are. We have the votes to elect you, and we're putting your name in nomination." Luis Gutierrez recalled Burke quoting General Sherman at that point: "Something like, 'If nominated, I will not run; if elected, I will not serve.' It was like Burke was saying, 'Hey, dude, I've heard that before, and it didn't work.'

"Sawyer wasn't angry, he was just kind of docile. He tells Burke, 'I'm not gonna run. I don't want to be mayor.' I'm feeling great because we've got it, but I'm also feeling real bad. . . . I felt embarrassed for [Sawyer]. You should've seen him in the chair—you had to have compassion."

Burke convinced Sawyer that he at least owed it to his colleagues to inform them of his decision. Sawyer left with Burke. The next his former allies saw of Sawyer he was walking into the council surrounded by bodyguards, his newfound allies in tow. Sawyer's allies smiled the smile of victors.

In a hearing room just behind the council chambers, Burke and most of those behind Sawyer's constituency met to buttress Sawyer's resolve.

They held hands and were led in prayer by a black preacher. They prayed for the city in this time of pain.

Burke told Sawyer that others spent millions on a campaign to win what he was being handed like a gift. "It's now or never!" Mell threatened. Sawyer capitulated. Mell ran out of the room, screaming, "We've got a mayor! We've got a mayor!" Even Mell later confessed that that was a really "goofy" thing to do.

The crowds at City Hall were making their presence known. They waved dollar bills in the air and asked, "How much, Gene? How much?" One tossed a handful of change onto the council floor, hitting an alderman. They taunted the black aldermen behind Sawyer during the frequent breaks in the proceedings. "You dog!" "You Oreo!"

Those in the hallways and outside chanted on and off all night. "Sawyer's in a Cadillac, driving for Vrdolyak." People held signs that read, "Uncle Tom Sawyer."

Aldermen peered down from second- and third-story windows. One could hear the chants, crisp and loud. The crowds rattled the resolve of more than one black alderman; where Henry said twelve were behind Sawyer Monday night, by midnight that number dwindled to six. Even William Beavers switched to Evans. He cited the thousand phone calls his office received that day, only forty-eight of them in favor of Sawyer.

Sawyer changed his mind again. Seemingly it wasn't the crowds or their taunts but the presence of a single Washington supporter in the chambers. He left his meeting with his new allies and spotted Mary Ella Smith, Washington's companion. Reporters witnessing the scene swear that his knees literally buckled. Sawyer walked over to Smith. "I can't do this," he supposedly told her. "I can't do it. This is not what Harold would have wanted." All the while Smith patted Sawyer's hand. Resolutions were put before the council that would pave the way for a vote, yet Sawyer voted against himself on more than one procedural question. He left the council chambers, and Burke immediately called for a recess.

Burke caught up with Sawyer somewhere in the bowels of City Hall. He was flushed, his voice loud. Any of dozens of people could hear him berating Sawyer. Among those listening was Alderman Keith Caldwell, who had been a firm Sawyer supporter until that night. "You don't talk to someone like that," Caldwell told Burke. "You have no right to treat him like that." Burke didn't argue, he simply lowered his voice. Sawyer continued to listen, quietly.

Sawyer slipped into a utility closet with Reverend Claude Wyatt, his pastor, for about fifteen minutes. One alderman explained that Sawyer was with his pastor praying for strength. "You mean praying for balls," an aide to Bill Henry said within earshot of a reporter.

Meanwhile, the Burke faction scrambled for an alternative. They offered their support to Juan Soliz, but that still left Soliz a vote or two short—his three Latino colleagues refused to vote for him unless he also won some black votes. The job was Larry Bloom's for the asking, but he, too, balked at winning the post without a single black or Latino vote in a city sixty percent nonwhite.

Tempers flared all night. Richard Mell slammed an ashtray down on a tabletop, cutting his hand. He pointed to an Evans supporter and screamed, "You're dead! You're dead!" Dorothy Tillman and Bill Henry mixed it up when in the council chambers. Tillman taunted Henry, who exploded. Two aldermen grabbed the burly Henry to prevent him from striking her. I'm no Martin Luther King, Henry said: "If people slap me, I'm gonna slap them back." Alderwoman Anna Langford confronted a knot of people sitting at the back of the council. They implored her to switch her vote to Evans. We're a movement, one of them told her. Langford said, "Oh, fuck the movement. These are politicians."

Tim Evans was flushed with expectations and held court with reporters. His foe doesn't have what it takes to be mayor, he told those crowding around him, Sawyer lacked the votes and the resolve.

Sawyer was holed up in his office. The television was on, and Sawyer heard what Evans said. He jumped from his chair. This is it, he told those sitting with him, he was in to stay. This resurgence lasted only a few minutes though. The television cameras occasionally focused on Sawyer sitting in his council seat looking blue, but he didn't go anywhere for the rest of the night.

David Orr was the last hope for those behind Evans. As acting mayor he presided over the meeting; as a staunch member of the Washington bloc, everyone knew where his sympathies lay.

For a time Orr called only on Evans supporters who would introduce some nonsense motion with no purpose other than to hold off the inevitable. Richard Mell grew frustrated and stood on a table frantically waving his arms, calling on Orr to recognize him. Orr ignored him.

Anyone counting on Orr to hold the opposition back with a goal line stand didn't understand the man. He had given his word to Sawyer, Evans, and Burke that he would be fair. This man who throughout his career preached the importance of the process would not permit an all-night filibuster. Orr called on Edwin Eisendrath, who called for a vote. The time was 1:50 A.M. Endorsement speeches followed.

Those aldermen who stood to endorse Evans or Sawyer were needlessly posturing in the middle of the night. But all five local news stations carried the City Council meeting live, and the A.C. Nielsen Company estimated that, at 2 A.M., 480,000 people were still watching.

Dorothy Tillman gave the night's most rousing speech. She compared the black aldermen behind Sawyer to the slaves who, after the Emancipation Proclamation, returned to the plantation, fearful of freedom. "Don't return to plantation politics," she pleaded. "Don't be used."

The speechmaking ended just before 4 A.M. and a final vote was taken. Sawyer was named acting mayor with an ominous twenty-nine votes. The meeting was adjourned at 4:16 A.M. The city had a new mayor.

Notes

on

Sources

Up front I need to acknowledge the contradiction of a writer who criticized the press within these pages yet nonetheless relied on the city's two daily newspapers as an invaluable source. Quotes culled from articles appearing in the *Tribune* and the *Sun-Times* are sprinkled throughout the book. Quotes are also borrowed from back issues of the Chicago *Reader*, *Chicago* magazine, the *Chicago Reporter*, the *Defender*, and the *Metro News*, and from the hours of television and radio shows I taped over the years.

Several books deserve special mention, for they helped shape more than a single chapter: Professor Paul Kleppner's excellent *Chicago Divided: The Making of a Black Mayor* (Northern Illinois University Press, DeKalb, 1985); Mike Royko's classic, *Boss* (E.P. Dutton & Co., New York, 1971); Dempsey Travis's two books about Chicago politics, *An Autobiography of Black Politics* (Urban Research Press, Inc., Chicago, 1987) and *Harold: The People's Mayor* (Urban Research Press, Inc., Chicago, 1989); Alton Miller's *Harold Washington: The Mayor, The Man* (Bonus Books, Chicago, 1989), an insider account of his one thousand days as Washington's press secretary;

Barbara Reynolds's *Jesse Jackson: America's David* (JFJ Associates, Washington, D.C., 1975), which not only offers an interesting account of Jesse Jackson's Chicago years (pre-1975) but also provided an abundance of rich Chicago color; Abdul Alkalimat's and Doug Gills's writings on Chicago politics in *The New Vote, Politics and Power in Four American Cities,* edited by Rod Bush (Synthesis Publications, San Francisco, 1984); and Ben Joravsky and Eduardo Camacho's *Race and Politics in Chicago* (Community Renewal Society, Chicago, 1987). All served as excellent source material, as did a WLS-TV posthumous profile of Harold Washington hosted by Harry Porterfield.

Statistics and stray facts were culled from *Chicago: Race, Class, and the Response to Urban Decline* (Temple University Press, Philadelphia, 1987) by Larry Bennett, Kathleen McCourt, Philip Nyden, and Gregory Squires. David Fremon's *Chicago Politics Ward by Ward* (Indiana University Press, Bloomington, 1988) proved a valuable guide. As every student of Chicago politics knows, no single book offers as many insights into the Daley machine than Milton Rakove's *Don't Make No Waves, Don't Back No Losers* (Indiana University Press, Bloomington, 1975).

My thanks to several journalists for their generosity during the research phase of this book: John Conroy, who lent me his interviews with Ed Vrdolyak conducted in the mid-1970s; Larry Bennett, who let me use notes and interviews from his research on SON-SOCC; and Joe Feinglass and Rod Such, whose interviews shortly after the 1983 mayor's race were a valued resource. The friendly and helpful staff at Chicago's Municipal Reference Library were a treasure trove of information, in contrast to the image of indifferent bureaucrats. I'd also like to thank the staff at the *Metro News,* especially Nate Clay, for allowing me to sit in their offices poring over back issues of their weekly; the Chicago *Reader,* especially Dolph Tuohy, for packing up more than five years of their paper for me; the *Chicago Reporter,* especially Ann Grimes, for the back copies sent to me; Kari Moe, a top Washington staffer who allowed me to sift through the boxes and file drawers of memos and reports she had saved from her time in City Hall; and filmmaker Bill Stamets, whose tapes of old City Council meetings and whose quirky eye allowed me to re-create several scenes within the pages of this book. Thank you, too, Bill, for the boxes of clippings, press releases, and other souvenirs of Council Wars you collected over the years.

Yet the bulk of this book is based on hundreds of hours of interviews. In a sense I was at work on this project long before I understood that setting a book in Chicago during the Washington years would provide a national audience insights into racial politics in the United States and provide a glimpse of the complex world that is black politics. My journalistic relationship with many of the people listed as sources for this book dates back to 1983, when I began writing about local politics for the Chicago *Reader*. Five years spent in the City Hall press room provided me with both a bird's-eye view of the drama and a feel for how the city's beat reporters viewed the fight.

Below is a partial list of those I've interviewed about Chicago politics. It is a partial list both because a complete one would be unwieldy and because many sources asked that I do not mention their names (to them, my quiet thanks). My gratitude especially to those whom I imposed upon for several hours of interviews and then called again asking for yet another session.

Where people refused to be interviewed for this book, especially a principal player such as Ed Vrdolyak or Jesse Jackson, every effort was made to find alternative sources. While I would have much preferred to have spoken with Vrdolyak, I hasten to add that politicians are typically terrible sources for useful information. I learned far more about the inner workings of Washington's government from top aides, for instance, than I ever did from Washington himself. To compensate for my lack of access to Vrdolyak, I spent countless hours in the library reading everything I could about him, as well as talking to those who could provide insights into the man. I especially appreciate the assistance of those staff people on the Vrdolyak side of things for the hours they spent with me.

Among the better-known figures (at least within Chicago) I interviewed for this book are Richard Barnett, Hal Baron, William Beavers, Ed Bell, Bill Berry, Larry Bloom, Ed Burke, Pat Caddell, David Canter, Nate Clay, Tom Coffey, Slim Coleman, Bob Crawford, Danny Davis, Wallace Davis, Marco Domico, Kit Duffy, Edwin Eisendrath, Elinor Elam, Richard Elrod, Tim Evans, Mike Flannery, Charles Freeman, Brenda Gaines, Jesus Garcia, Joe Gardner, Harry Golden, Jr., Jacky Grimshaw, Luis Gutierrez, Bernard Hansen, Bill Henry, Paul Igasaki, Ken Jackson, Walter Jacobson, Al Johnson, Bennett Johnson, Phil Krone, Vito Marzullo, Jean Mayer, Clarence McClain, John McDermott, Paul McGrath, Richard Mell, Rob Mier, Alton Miller, Grayson Mitchell, Kari Moe, James Montgomery, Salim Muwakkil, Steve Neal, Marty Oberman, Pat O'Connor, David Orr,

Clarence Page, Lu Palmer, Sam Patch, Roman Pucinski, Al Raby, Renault Robinson, Don Rose, Bobby Rush, Miguel Santiago, Andy Shaw, Bill Singer, Juan Soliz, Marion Stamps, Bob Starks, Dorothy Tillman, Maria Torres, Juan Velazquez, Harold Washington, Laura Washington, Wayne Whalen, and Conrad Worrill.

To help the book's narrative flow I typically did not give full credit to a particular news source deserving mention, hoping the listing below would suffice:

Book One: I borrowed from many accounts when putting together chapter one. *Boss* was especially useful, as was the *Lords of the Last Machine* (Random House, New York, 1987) by Bill and Lori Granger and an entertaining essay about Chicago by Tom Geoghegan appearing in *The New Republic*. Steve Bogira's excellent *Reader* piece about the Airport Homes fight served as my main source for that part of the chapter. Many journalists wrote retrospective pieces about Martin Luther King, Jr.'s Chicago battles; I borrowed most heavily from articles written by Brent Staples and Ben Joravsky.

Salim Muwakkil's Question and Answer with Lu Palmer, which appeared in the *Reader,* provided a valuable snapshot of Palmer's thinking in the early 1980s. Another *Reader* piece, by David Jackson ("Just One Black"), provided valuable information about Palmer's 1982 plebiscite. I'm indebted in chapter three to both those who knew Washington earlier in his career and the numerous profiles of Washington that have appeared over the years, especially Dempsey Travis's two books; *Harold Washington: A Political Biography* (Chicago Review Press, Chicago, 1983), by Florence Levinsohn; and a *Tribune* magazine piece about Washington by Cheryl Devall, John Kass, and John Camper. Robert McClory's *The Man Who Beat Clout City* (Swallow Press, Chicago, 1977), chronicling Renault Robinson's battles with the police brass and the Chicago machine, was also helpful in the writing of chapter three. Much of the background material about Jane Byrne in chapter four appeared in a pair of biographies, *Brass: Jane Byrne and Pursuit of Power* (Contemporary Books, Inc., Chicago, 1983) by Kathleen Whalen Fitzgerald (the source for the Elena Martinez tale); and *Fighting Jane: Mayor Jane Byrne and the Chicago Machine* (Dial Press, New York, 1980) by Lori and Bill Granger. I also borrowed from a *Reader* article I co-wrote with my colleague Ted Cox and from another by Mike Miner, who wrote an excellent piece about the sense of betrayal several dedicated reformers felt after working on Byrne's 1979 mayoral campaign. Mike also wrote "Black and White and Red All Over" a *Reader* piece critiquing the *Tribune*'s and *Sun-Times*'s coverage of the 1983 primary.

Barbara Reynolds's *Jesse Jackson: America's David* proved invaluable to chapter five, as were the dozens of feature pieces written about Jackson back in the 1960s and 1970s. The material about Richard M. Daley in chapter six was pieced together from a variety of primary and secondary sources. Doug Cassel wrote a particularly good piece in the *Reader* examining Daley's record as a state legislator; James Tuohy wrote for the *Chicago Lawyer* in 1989 an excellent piece about Daley's tenure as state's attorney that was useful in chapter seven. Ben Joravsky and Eduardo Camacho's *Race and Politics in Chicago* was also helpful in the writing of chapter seven, as was an excellent profile of Bill Berry by *Sun-Times* reporter Tom McNamee.

Don Rose's regular "Pol Watching" column, irreverent and caustic; Dave Moberg's fine reporting; and Paul McGrath's "The Washington Strategy"—all appeared in the *Reader* and served as a wonderful source of material for chapters eight through eleven. The *Chicago Reporter*'s series about race and the 1983 primary, as well as Ralph Whitehead, Jr.'s article in the *Columbia Journalism Review,* also deserve special mention.

Vernon Jarrett's column in the *Sun-Times* alerted me to Jesse Jackson's "Background and Off-the-Record Information on the Role that Reverend Jesse L. Jackson Played in the Harold Washington Victory" memo. Florence Levinsohn's reporting allowed me to chronicle Washington's law license suspension in chapter ten; Dave Moberg deserves credit for allowing me to place Washington's tax troubles in their proper perspective in that same chapter.

A Foot in Each World (ed. Clarence Page, Northwestern University Press, Evanston, 1986), a collection of essays and articles by Leanita McClain, edited by ex-husband Clarence Page, provided a great many insights into McClain, as did several articles written after her suicide, most notably a piece by *Washington Post* reporter Kevin Klose.

Book Two: Dave Moberg's excellent 1983 *Chicago* magazine piece ("The Man Who Wants to Break the Mold") was the best source on the early days of Council Wars. Helpful, too, in the writing of chapter twelve was a fine piece by *Sun-Times* writer Rick Soll, based on a day-long interview with Vrdolyak a couple of days after his Council Wars victory; a Ralph Whitehead profile of Vrdolyak appearing in the (now defunct)

Chicagoan, in 1973; Bob Seltzner's extensive reporting about Vrdolyak in the *Daily Calumet; Chicago Lawyer* and Channel 5 for breaking the story of Seltzner's diary; and Roger Simon's excellent Vrdolyak profile appearing in *Chicago* in 1984. Also my thanks to the half dozen ex-members of Vrdolyak's ward organization who sat down for interviews with me. Thanks, too, to the Balanoff clan for their help.

Chapter thirteen benefited from Ann Grimes's account chronicling the rise of SON-SOCC in the wake of Washington's victory. Ben Joravsky was the reporter in chapter sixteen who accidentally witnessed Washington's refusal to speak directly with Vrdolyak, choosing instead to speak through intermediaries. The *Reporter* served as my source for Vrdolyak's besting Washington in the 1984 Democratic convention that appears near the end of chapter sixteen.

Former *Sun-Times* reporter Brian Kelly wrote an excellent midterm piece for *Chicago* magazine that helped in the writing of chapter seventeen; an article by Don Rose served as the source for the story I tell in that same chapter in which Bill Singer approaches Vrdolyak about pulling strings on behalf of a client.

Book Three: The city's Latino Institute was an important source for statistics used in chapter nineteen. An article by Ben Joravsky and Jorge Casuso helped me capture the flavor of the special election that gave Washington his twenty-fifth vote in the council. Andrew Hacker's work for the *New York Review of Books* was particularly helpful in the section looking at Byrne's use of crime as a campaign issue in the 1987 election.

Much of the information about Renault Robinson's early days at the CHA was from a Question and Answer between Robinson and journalist Robert McClory. Alex Kotlowitz's *There Are No Children Here* (Doubleday, New York, 1991), a moving account of two boys growing up in a west side housing project, also proved helpful in the writing of chapter twenty-one.

There was lots of good reporting in the days following Washington's death. Of particular note is an excellent piece by David Jackson that appeared in *Chicago* magazine ("The Making of Mayor What's-His-Name"). In writing chapter twenty-two I also borrowed from articles by Ted Cox and Achy Obejas, both of the *Reader;* the *Tribune's* Ann Marie Lipinski and Bruce Dold; Mike Royko's interview with Washington's personal physician; WBEZ's weekly "Inside Politics," hosted by Bruce DuMont; and an article in *Chicago Enterprise* by Tom Roeser.

Index

ABOUT THE AUTHOR

Gary Rivlin reported on city politics for the Chicago *Reader* from 1983 through 1988. His work has appeared in many publications, including *The Nation, In These Times,* and the *San Francisco Chronicle.* He is currently a staff writer for the *East Bay Express* and lives in San Francisco.